OXFORD CONSTITUTIONAL THEORY

Series Editors

Martin Loughlin, John P McCormick, and Neil Walker

Sovereignty's Promise

OXFORD CONSTITUTIONAL THEORY

Series Editors:
Martin Loughlin, John P. McCormick, and Neil Walker

One consequence of the increase in interest in constitutions and constitutional law in recent years is a growing innovative literature in constitutional theory. The aim of *Oxford Constitutional Theory* is to provide a showcase for the best of these theoretical reflections and a forum for further innovation in the field.

The new series will seek to establish itself as the primary point of reference for scholarly work in the subject by commissioning different types of study. The majority of the works published in the series will be monographs that advance new understandings of the subject. Well-conceived edited collections that bring a variety of perspectives and disciplinary approaches to bear on specific themes in constitutional thought will also be included. Further, in recognition of the fact that there is a great deal of pioneering literature originally written in languages other than English and with regard to non-anglophone constitutional traditions, the series will also seek to publish English translations of leading monographs in constitutional theory.

Sovereignty's Promise

The State as Fiduciary

Evan Fox-Decent

McGill University

OXFORD
UNIVERSITY PRESS

OXFORD
UNIVERSITY PRESS

Great Clarendon Street, Oxford OX2 6DP

Oxford University Press is a department of the University of Oxford.
It furthers the University's objective of excellence in research, scholarship,
and education by publishing worldwide in

Oxford New York

Auckland Cape Town Dar es Salaam Hong Kong Karachi
Kuala Lumpur Madrid Melbourne Mexico City Nairobi
New Delhi Shanghai Taipei Toronto

With offices in

Argentina Austria Brazil Chile Czech Republic France Greece
Guatemala Hungary Italy Japan Poland Portugal Singapore
South Korea Switzerland Thailand Turkey Ukraine Vietnam

Oxford is a registered trade mark of Oxford University Press
in the UK and in certain other countries

Published in the United States
by Oxford University Press Inc., New York

First published 2011

British Library Cataloguing in Publication Data

Data available

Library of Congress Cataloging in Publication Data

Library of Congress Control Number: 2011939971

Typeset by SPI Publisher Services, Pondicherry, India

ISBN 978–0–19–969831–8

for my parents
Wally and Joan Fox-Decent

Acknowledgements

This book began as a PhD dissertation written at the University of Toronto while I was in its joint JD/PhD (philosophy) programme. Special and heartfelt thanks go to my supervisor, David Dyzenhaus. Even while on sabbatical in New Zealand, he remained in touch and encouraged me to persevere and deal with the thickets of detail that frequently obscured the idea. He read countless drafts of earlier versions of most of the chapters produced here, providing insightful and constructive suggestions within days (sometimes within the same day) of having received the latest bit. A student could not have a more dedicated and capable supervisor. What is more, although the thesis was defended in 2003, he has since offered equally generous comments on sections of the book that have been updated to take account of more recent developments in administrative law.

I am also very grateful for the assistance I received from the readers on my committee, Arthur Ripstein and Lorne Sossin. Their comments were invaluable, and always forthcoming, especially in the final days leading up to submission, when I made numerous unreasonable calls on their time to review successive drafts and discuss ideas. They, too, have since given me generous comments on subsequent work towards this book.

I owe a similar debt to several colleagues at McGill University's Faculty of Law: Helge Dedek, Richard Janda, Robert Leckey, Rod Macdonald, Fréderic Mégrét, Victor Muñiz-Fratecelli, Lionel Smith, and Steve Smith. I would also like to thank many others for encouragement, discussion, and comments, including, Daniel Brudney, Evan Criddle, Wally Fox-Decent, Dennis Klimchuk, Matthias Mahlmann, Margaret Martin, Colleen Murphy, Sean Rehaag, Robert Shaver, Kaveh Shojania, Malcolm Thorburn, Mark Walters, and Raquel Yrigoyen Fajardo.

Various portions of the book were presented and discussed at a number of conferences: the Lon Fuller and Contemporary Legal Controversies two-part conference held at the law faculties of McGill University and the University of Toronto (2005); the Young Scholars Conference held at the Faculty of Law of McGill University (2008); the *Dunsmuir* Roundtable held at the Faculty of Law of the University of Toronto (2008); and a 2008 session of the McGill Political Theory Workshop. My thanks go to the organizers and participants.

Special thanks are also due to a teacher, Johnston Smith, from St Paul's High School in Winnipeg. While he did not did participate directly in this project, he sparked my interest in political philosophy, leading me to adopt a sceptical view of state authority.

I also owe a debt to several students who provided research assistance above and beyond the call of duty: Paul Clark, Matt Finn, Anthony Guindon, Carlos Iván Fuentes, and Nelcy López Cuéllar.

Two former students, Stefan Szpadja and Robert Whillans, merit thanks for reading through the manuscript cover-to-cover during the final revisions stage and providing innumerable helpful comments in every chapter. Robert, in fact, did this twice over, under unreasonable time constraints, and also took on the laborious task of converting the notes to a modern, uniform style.

This book would not have been possible but for the support of the Faculty of Law and the Department of Philosophy of University of Toronto while I was completing a JD and later writing my doctoral thesis. In addition to my committee, Brian Langille in Law and Joyce Wright in Philosophy were especially supportive. McGill's Faculty of Law has since become my academic home. It has been an especially fertile and collegial setting for interdisciplinary research, in large part due to the leadership of its former Dean (now Justice) Nicholas Kasirer and its present Dean Daniel Jutras. Also, I would like to thank the Social Science and Humanities Research Council of Canada for financial support throughout my doctoral and post-doctoral studies, as well as during the latter stages of the project.

During the home stretch, Gary Hill of OUP provided exceptional copy-editing. Every chapter has been improved by his work.

Some of the arguments in this book have appeared in articles written over the past few years, and while they have been extensively rewritten, I am grateful to the journals in which they were originally published for granting permission to use them in this book. Much of Chapter II appeared in 'Fashioning Legal Authority from Power: The Crown-Native Fiduciary Relationship' (2006) 4 New *Zealand Journal of Public and International Law* 91. Chapter IX is a revised version of 'Is the Rule of Law Really Indifferent to Human Rights?' (2008) 27(6) *Law and Philosophy* 533. Parts of Chapters I and IV were published in an earlier form in 'The Fiduciary Nature of State Legal Authority' (2005) 31 *Queen's Law Journal* 259.

Finally, I would like to thank Adriana Goreta, for extraordinary patience and support, and my parents, Wally and Joan Fox-Decent, who have been there for me throughout the course of the project.

Contents

'[A]s when there is a controversy in an account, the parties must by their own accord set up for right reason the reason of some arbitrator, or judge, to whose sentence they will both stand, or their controversy must either come to blows, or be undecided, for want of a right reason constituted by Nature; so is it also in all debates of what kind soever: and when men that think themselves wiser than all others clamour and demand right reason for judge, yet seek no more but that things should be determined by no other men's reason but their own, it is as intolerable in the society of men, as it is in play after trump is turned to use for trump on every occasion that suit whereof they have most in their hand.'

—Thomas Hobbes, *Leviathan*.[1]

'Beyond the trust, beyond the company, the most fundamental of fiduciary relationships in our society is that which exists between the community (the people) and the State and its agencies.... Though it had earlier stirrings, the fiduciary principle in *private* law began its uninterrupted march to prominence from the middle of the last century [the 19th century]. And as we now well appreciate, its object was to safeguard against the abuse of fiduciary power and position. Yet much more so than in the private sector, it was—and is—in the realms of government that fiduciary power is the most pervasive, the most intense, and its abuse, the most threatening to the community and to its trust in its institutions.'

—Paul Finn, 'The Forgotten "Trust": The People and the State.'[2]

[1] Thomas Hobbes, *Leviathan with Selected Variants from the Latin Edition of 1668*, ed Edwin Curley (Indianapolis: Hackett Publishing, 1994), v.iii, 23.

[2] PD Finn, 'The Forgotten "Trust": The People and the State' in Malcom Cope (ed), *Equity: Issues and Trends* (Sydney: Federation Press, 1995), pp 131–2.

Table of Cases and Legislation

Prologue: Hobbes and Legal Order

I. THE DEMANDS OF LEGALITY

In 1610 Sir Edward Coke upheld the cause of a doctor who was both judged and fined by the same Royal College of Physicians that stood to benefit from the fine, giving effect to the doctrine that no person may be judge and party of the same cause.[1] Coke declared that 'when an Act of Parliament is against common right or reason, or repugnant, or impossible to be performed, the common law will controul it and adjudge such Act to be void'.[2] For Sir Edward, the common law was the repository of legality, and legality constrained how public authority (even legislative authority) may be exercised. That is, for exercises of authority to be more than exercises of mere power, they must comply with the demands of legality. The justification and nature of the demands of legality comprise the subject matter of this book.

These demands may arise from positive law, such as constitutional documents and legislation. But sometimes the positive law is silent: there was no law on the books prohibiting the Royal College of Physicians from imposing a self-serving fine. In cases such as these, judges who follow Sir Edward give effect to legal principles despite the absence of statutory provisions on which to ground them. These statute-independent or freestanding principles are interesting from the point of view of an inquiry into the nature of law because their existence suggests that legitimate exercises of public power are constrained by moral and structural features intrinsic to legal order. Within the common law legal tradition, these moral and structural features are constitutive of the rule of law.

In the coming chapters I explore some of the ways in which the rule of law is embodied in principles of public law, and how these principles are best justified and explained. In particular, I discuss the contemporary demands of legality which crystallize in public law duties of fairness and reasonableness. The duty of fairness requires public decision-makers to act impartially and independently. Also, individuals must have the opportunity to know and reply to the case

[1] *Dr Bonham's Case* (1610), 8 Co Rep 107a, 118a, 77 ER 638 (CP). [2] Ibid, 652 (ER).

against them. The duty of reasonableness requires decision-makers to base their decisions on reasonable interpretations of their enabling statutes. As we shall see, reasonable interpretations take seriously statutory purposes and values, but they also take seriously fundamental values said to reside in the common law and exist independently of statutes, such as equality and liberty. Judges will sometimes set aside administrative decisions that infringe equality or liberty if the infringement is not expressly authorized by statute. This is the principle of legality that lies at the heart of common law constitutionalism, a constitutional theory that looks to the common law for values and principles capable of guiding statutory interpretation.

Many judges, however, are suspicious of statute-independent duties of fairness and reasonableness. They believe that courts should not foist on public bodies legal obligations that the legislature has declined to impose, for the legislature alone has authority to create legal rights and obligations. Now, commonwealth courts have long held that public officials must exercise their authority reasonably in the sense that they may not use their powers arbitrarily or capriciously. In Canada, the courts have extended this injunction against arbitrariness with the result that where important interests are at stake, the duty of fairness will generally apply regardless of whether there is an explicit basis for it in the relevant statute. Yet it is the legislature rather than the judiciary that is presumed to have authority to create legal rights and obligations through its lawmaking power. The challenge presented by freestanding duties of fairness and reasonableness, then, is to explain and justify them in the absence of legislative endorsement.

Some judges rely on a background assumption of legislative intent. In the case of fairness, the background assumption would be that the legislature always intends delegated power to be exercised fairly, and that fair exercises of power require procedural safeguards such as hearings and disclosure. But some statutory grants of authority provide no procedural safeguards and are discretionary in nature. Often the conferral of discretion is put in broad and subjective terms of simply whether 'the Minister is of the opinion . . . '.[3] In these cases it is problematic to rely on legislative intent, for the legislature seems to have supplied the Minister with as unfettered a discretionary power as ordinary language will allow.

Not surprisingly, appeals to legislative intent fail to convince judges who think that the separation of powers licenses them to enforce only those

[3] See eg *Williams v Canada (Minister of Citizenship and Immigration)* [1997] 2 FC 646 (FCA), Strayer JA: '[T]he test is not whether the permanent resident *is a danger to the public* but whether the "Minister *is of the opinion*" that he is such a danger' (emphasis in original). Strayer JA concluded, ibid, 672–3, that the principles of fundamental justice 'have never imposed a duty on [administrative] tribunals to give reasons where a statute has not specifically so provided'.

duties which are clearly grounded in positive law. These judges have a telling reply against the view that statute-independent duties can rest on an intent the legislature has failed to express: if the legislature really did intend to include certain procedures, it could have easily made those requirements explicit. So, to answer the separation-of-powers argument and vindicate the demands of legality found in freestanding duties such as fairness and reasonableness, another story needs to be told. We shall see that this story is an account of the theoretical underpinnings of common law constitutionalism.

We begin with the premise implicit in Sir Edward's decision in *Dr Bonham's Case*: a failure to comply with the demands of legality reduces exercises of public authority to exercises of mere power. The distinction is critical because the demands of legality jointly constitute the rule of law, and the rule of law, I contend, permits certain exercises of power to count as exercises of authority. For present purposes, exercises of mere power can be understood as the threat or use of force for which there is no moral justification, such as the mugger's threat 'your money or your life'. Exercises of authority, on the other hand, may be backed by threats of force or coercion, but their prescriptions are justified on moral grounds, such as the role they play in securing a regime of secure and equal freedom. People subject to authority are thought to have moral reasons for acting in accordance with it, reasons which are independent of the punishment they may face if they fail to do so.

For the remainder of this prologue I use Thomas Hobbes' venerable discussion of sovereignty to illustrate how legal order can ground authority in a way that makes sense of the power/authority distinction implicit in *Dr Bonham's Case*. Hobbes has been called 'the greatest English political philosopher',[4] and as we shall see, his conception of the state mirrors in many ways the republican conception of the state defended throughout this book: the state is a fiduciary of the people over whom it exercises power. As a fiduciary, the state owes its people a single but complex legal obligation, one which arises solely from the fiduciary character of its relationship to the people. The state must govern its people in accordance with the demands of legality, which is to say, in accordance with the rule of law.

The fiduciary conception of the state both predates and succeeds Hobbes. Citing Plato for the principle that public officials must concern themselves with the entire community rather than just a part of it, Cicero concluded that '[t]he guardianship of the state is a kind of trusteeship'.[5] Similarly, Locke asserted less than 40 years after the publication of *Leviathan* that legislative

[4] From the editors' introduction to Thomas Hobbes, *On the citizen*, trans Richard Tuck and Michael Silverthorne (Cambridge; New York: Cambridge University Press, 1998) (first published in 1641), p xxxiii.

[5] Cicero, *On Moral Obligation*, trans John Higginbotham (Berkeley: University of California Press, 1967) (first published in 44 BC), ch 25, p 69.

power is 'only a fiduciary power to act for certain ends'.[6] And Bentham too, much like Burke, would later say that '[a]ll political power is fiduciary'.[7] Nonetheless, Hobbes is of special interest because, unlike Locke, Bentham, and Burke, he uses determinate legal principles to construct a fiduciary theory of political and legal authority. Despite Hobbes' iconic standing in the liberal tradition, we shall see that his account of sovereignty has important republican features. Within this account, the constitution of legal order within a relationship of mutual trust does the heavy lifting.

I argue in Chapter IV that fiduciary relationships arise if one party (the fiduciary) has broad discretionary power of an administrative nature over the important interests of another (the beneficiary), and the beneficiary is unable, either as a matter of fact or law, to exercise the entrusted power. The common law recognizes many types of fiduciary relations, including those which exist between principal and agent, solicitor and client, directors and their corporations, and partners and their partnerships. Similarly, parents and doctors are fiduciaries of their children and patients respectively. These latter kinds of relationships may give the impression that a fiduciary conception of the state is necessarily paternalistic and unable to account for the idea that the people are (or should be) authors of the law as well as its subjects. I consider the paternalism objection in Chapter III, in the context of the Crown-Native fiduciary relationship the courts have recognized in Canada. Beginning with Hobbes, however, will help us see from the start that the fiduciary account of state authority is neither paternalistic nor authoritarian because the people (in a sense to be explained) are the authors of state authority. It is for this reason that on this book's cover the people wear the crowns.

Starting with Hobbes will also illuminate important differences between the fiduciary theory of the state and the social contract tradition. Hobbes' theory contains elements of both. I will argue that for Hobbes the origin of sovereign authority arises from the people's presumed consent amongst themselves to a social contract that institutes sovereignty. The ongoing relationship between the people and the sovereign, however, is based on authorization and trust (or, more precisely, the implications of the position of trust held by the sovereign).

Hobbes also provides us with a valuable opportunity to see that the position one takes in the contemporary debate on freestanding public duties

[6] John Locke, *Second Treatise on Civil Government*, as reproduced in *Social Contract* (Oxford: Oxford University Press, 1948) (first published in 1690), pp 125–6, ch 13, para 149.

[7] Jeremy Bentham and John Bowring, *The Works of Jeremy Bentham* (Edinburgh: Tait, 1843), ch 14 'View of a Complete Code of Laws', p 182; Edmund Burke, *On Empire, Liberty, and Reform: Speeches and Letters*, ed David Bromwich (New Haven: Yale University Press, 2000).

will be influenced by one's underlying view of law and legal order. If one holds the positivist theses that there is no necessary connection between law and morality (the separation thesis), and that all legal rights and obligations may be identified independently of their content and solely in virtue of their institutional source (the sources thesis), then statute-independent public duties will appear suspect. These duties have no clear institutional source (in principle, agencies could adopt them without judicial prompting), they can only be identified by reference to their moral content (eg fairness), and if they are intrinsic to legal order (as their freestanding status suggests), then they reveal a necessary connection between law and morality. If one denies the positivist theses, then statute-independent duties are possible, but still call for an explanation. Notwithstanding Hobbes' reputation as the father of legal positivism, he anticipates the puzzle that freestanding duties present, and supplies a rich and non-positivist explanation of them.

2. THE PEOPLE AS THE AUTHORS OF SOVEREIGNTY

An inchoate and compressed indication of Hobbes' solution to the puzzle of freestanding duties is found in his claim that 'no man is obliged by a covenant, whereof he is not author, nor consequently by a covenant made against, or beside the authority he gave' (L xvi.6, 102).[8] In the context of Hobbes' social contract, this means that no individual may be subject to an obligation that demands more of her than is consistent with the scope of authority she can be deemed to have granted to the state. An important aspect of the state's authorization, I claim, is that its institutions must exercise their powers on behalf of the legal subject and in accordance with the demands of legality, or, as Hobbes might put it, consistent with the demands of equity and the other laws of nature. This interpretation of Hobbes is controversial. I can lay out only a *prima facie* case in its defence. A more orthodox understanding of Hobbes conceives of the sovereign as a supreme authority vested with unlimited power to make and repeal laws possessing whatever form and content the sovereign wishes to give them. In this section, I first set out the role that authorization plays in Hobbes'

[8] References to *Leviathan* throughout the book are indicated by in-text parenthetical citations and are to chapter (or 'R&C' for the Review & Conclusion), paragraph and page number from the Curley edition: Thomas Hobbes, *Leviathan with Selected Variants from the Latin Edition of 1668*, ed Edwin Curley (Indianapolis: Hackett Publishing, 1994). References to the 1668 Latin edition are indicated by 'OL' (*Opera Latina*) and are from the selected variants translated by Curley. References to *De Cive* are indicated by 'DC' and are to chapter, paragraph, and page number from the Tuck and Silverthorne edition, *supra* note 4. References to *The Elements of Law* are indicated by 'EL' and are to chapter, paragraph, and page number from the Gaskin edition: Thomas Hobbes, *Human Nature and De Corpore Politico*, ed JCA Gaskin (Oxford: Oxford University Press, 1994). Unless otherwise indicated, italics are from the original.

discussion of the state, and then respond to the orthodox interpretation of Hobbes' text.

Hobbes is well known for his claim that individuals may be taken to consent to state authority because each would always prefer the state to the state of nature, a condition in which life for the individual is 'solitary, poor, nasty, brutish and short' (L xiii.9, 76). Were the subject to experience this lawless condition of each against all, she would contract with others to establish sovereignty because each person can expect to do better with a sovereign than without. In this sense, each person is presumed to consent to sovereignty, and so the legal obligations that flow from sovereignty are consistent with Hobbes' view that there can be 'no obligation on any man which ariseth not from some act of his own' (L xxi.10, 141).[9]

The presumed contract formed in contemplation of the state of nature, however, is not between the sovereign and the subject, but between the subjects themselves. Although the original covenant gives rise to sovereignty, the relationship between sovereign and subject is one of authorization rather than contract. As a consequence, 'there can happen no breach of the covenant on the part of the sovereign' (L xviii.4, 111). Nonetheless, while it is trivially true that the sovereign cannot breach the original covenant, his officers and the institutions of sovereignty may violate the terms of the authorization contained within it. Such violations, I later suggest, would undermine the legitimacy of legal order.

As for the sovereign's subjects, they owe obedience 'as long, and no longer, than the power lasteth by which he is able to protect them' (L xxi.21, 144).[10] Hobbes envisions a reciprocal relationship between protection and obedience, affirming in the conclusion of *Leviathan* that his overarching purpose has been 'to set before men's eyes the mutual relation between protection and obedience' (L R&C.17, 497). Hobbes' 'mutual relation' is articulated through an account of authorization which supplies the framework for both the sovereign's powers and the subject's obligations.

The conceptual problem that Hobbes sought to answer was how the state, as an abstract and artificial construct, may be conceived of as a person that represents and acts on behalf of just those persons subject to its powers. Put another way, Hobbes wished to explain how the state could stand in a relation to its subjects that would let them distinguish valid claims to sovereign authority from those without merit.

[9] For present purposes we need not detain ourselves on whether the presumption of consent means hypothetical or tacit consent. I discuss both in Chapter V.

[10] For ease of exposition, I will refer to the sovereign throughout as Hobbes does, ie in the masculine as 'he' or 'his'.

Hobbes conceives of the state as an artificial rather than a natural person, and as such it can represent only the multitude who 'confer all their power and strength upon one man, or upon one assembly of men, that may reduce all their wills, by plurality of voices, unto one will' (L xvii.13, 109). The person who represents the state is the sovereign, who is either a single natural person or an assembly of natural persons, but in his public capacity he is an artificial person in that he represents and acts in the name of each person subject to his authority. But while the sovereign is the actor who exercises public power, he is not the author of his actions.

The authorship of sovereignty rests with the subject, an authorship Hobbes summarizes in his formal definition of the state (L xvii.13, 109):

> one person, of whose acts a great multitude, by mutual covenants one with another, have made themselves every one the author, to the end he may use the strength and means of them all, as he shall think expedient, for their peace and common defence.

Elsewhere, Hobbes claims that a multitude establish a sovereign when each can be deemed to affirm that 'I authorise and give up my right of governing myself to this man, or to this assembly of men, on this condition, that thou give up thy right to him, and authorize all his actions in like manner' (L xvii. 13, 109). He reiterates that 'the consent of a subject to sovereign power is contained in these words *I authorize, or take upon me, all his actions'* (L xxi.14, 142).

Hobbes compares authority to ownership. Whereas ownership gives one a right to exclusive use and possession of a thing, authority denotes a right to act on one's own behalf or on behalf of another (L xvi.4, 101–2):

> And as the right of possession is called dominion, so the right of doing any action is called AUTHORITY. So that by authority is always understood a right of doing any act; and *done by authority*, done by commission or licence from him whose right it is.

Connecting the subject's consent and authorship to the sovereign's actions permits Hobbes to say that those actions are in fact the actions of the subject because the subject is their author. And, says Hobbes, since it is impossible to injure oneself, the sovereign cannot by his actions injure the subject (L xxi.19, 143–4). Similarly, the subject cannot accuse the sovereign of wrongdoing because 'seeing every subject is author of the actions of his sovereign, he punisheth another for the actions committed by himself' (L xviii.7, 113). Hobbes does concede that 'they that have sovereign power may commit iniquity', but they may not commit 'injustice, or injury in the proper signification' (L xviii.6, 112–13). By identifying the subject with the sovereign's actions, Hobbes eliminates the possibility of complaints of injustice against the sovereign, since all such complaints would be against the very person who made them (eg L xxiv.7, 162).

Authorization gives Hobbes the necessary criterion to resolve the conceptual problem mentioned earlier of distinguishing legitimate claims of representation and sovereign authority from counterfeits, since the actions of the sovereign are attributable to the subject if, and only if, the subject has authorized the sovereign to act on her behalf. Conversely, if a pretend representative has not been authorized, and if the pretender attempts to assert authority through some exercise of power, that action cannot be attributed to the subject because the subject is not the author of the action. It follows that the pretend sovereign can make no claim to the subject's obedience because he acts without her authorization. Such would be the predicament of a foreign power that proclaimed sovereignty over an unconquered people who had their own sovereign. Without the 'mutual relation of protection and obedience' that authorization makes possible, there is no basis for legal obligation.

Hobbes' discussion of slaves held in prison or bonds underscores the point. Unlike conquered persons who become subjects following defeat on the battlefield, captive slaves are not trusted with their corporal liberty, and as a result 'have no obligation at all' (L xx.10, 131). The subject, on the other hand, 'hath corporal liberty allowed him, and upon promise not to run away, nor do violence to his master, is trusted by him' (ibid). By making liberty a condition of obligation, Hobbes is able to connect sovereignty by acquisition (or conquest) to the social contract story of sovereignty by institution: because conquered subjects are trusted with life and liberty, they can be presumed to have covenanted with others to authorize and obey their new sovereign.[11] They now enjoy the conquering sovereign's protection, and 'every man is supposed [presumed] to promise obedience to him in whose power it is to save or destroy him' (L xx.5, 130). While the sovereign has a like power over captive slaves who may beg for their lives and even profess their submission, they cannot be understood to authorize the sovereign because they do not enjoy the benefits of protection, ie security of life *and* liberty. In other words, security of life and liberty are necessary conditions of authorization, while authorization is the necessary and sufficient condition of obligation. But how, exactly, is authorization supposed to take place?

Quentin Skinner has developed a sophisticated account of authorization in defence of an orthodox interpretation of Hobbes' theory of the state. Skinner rightly affirms that 'public acts of a sovereign will count as valid acts

[11] Admittedly, the more natural reading of the text in chapter 20 is that the vanquished covenant directly with the sovereign. The proposed interpretation, however, coheres better with his more general account of authorization, as well as with the reality of Hobbes' day, acknowledged in the Review and Conclusion, in which many subjects enjoyed protection without expressly submitting to a conquering sovereign (L R&C.7, 491).

of the state if and only if the sovereign has been authorised to perform them by each and every member of the multitude'.[12] Critical to Skinner's view of Hobbes—and where we part ways—are the mechanics of authorization he attributes to Hobbes, ie the structure and content of the interaction between subject and sovereign which results in the sovereign's authority and the subject's obligation to obey the law.

Recall that Hobbes says that an act 'done by authority' is done 'by commission or licence from him whose right it is'. Skinner infers from this that the subject's grant of authority to the sovereign must take the form of a voluntary transfer of right. And when the transfer occurs, Skinner says, the authorizing subject gives up the right to perform the action himself.[13] The transfer of a right to act thus implies a renunciation of the right, Skinner claims, as well as a duty not to interfere in the transferee's exercise of the right once it has been transferred.

The right that is allegedly transferred to the sovereign is the 'right of nature'. For Hobbes, this is a liberty-right possessed by individuals in the state of nature. It entitles them to do whatever they think is appropriate to ensure their self-preservation (L xiv.1, 79). It is a 'right to all things' (L xiv.5, 80). In the state of nature, Hobbes says, '[t]o *lay down* a mans *right* to anything is to *divest* himself of the *liberty* of hindering another of the benefit of his own right to the same' (L xiv.6, 81). To give up one's right in the state of nature, then, means giving up the right of preventing others from exercising their 'right to all things'. This renunciation confers no additional right on others, as Hobbes is quick to point out: 'For he that renounceth or passeth away his right giveth not to any other man a right which he had not before (because there is nothing to which every man had not right by nature), but only standeth out of his way' (L xiv.6, 81).

In short, because people in the state of nature already have a right to do anything they wish in pursuit of self-preservation, the renunciation of that right by one person cannot have the effect of providing a further right (or an enlargement of a right) to someone else. Therefore, Hobbes' view of renunciation of right in the state of nature, including the idea of '*divesting* himself of the *liberty* of hindering another', does not show that a transfer of right to another takes place. Because a simple laying down of right in the state of nature does not effect a transfer of right, it cannot support Skinner's claim that an authorized party gains its authorization from a transfer of right alleged to occur pursuant to a renunciation.

[12] Quentin Skinner, *Visions of Politics* (New York: Cambridge University Press, 2002), p 202.

[13] Ibid, pp 185–6.

Hobbes does at one point affirm a duty not to interfere once a right has been renounced or transferred to another person (xiv.7, 81):

> And when a man hath in either manner [renunciation or transfer] abandoned or granted away his right, then is he said to be OBLIGED, or BOUND, not to hinder those, to whom such right is granted or abandoned from the benefit of it; and [it is said] that he *ought*, and it is his DUTY, not to make void that voluntary act of his own, and that such hindrance is INJUSTICE, and INJURY, as being *sine jure* [without right], the right being before renounced, or transferred.

Skinner concludes from this passage that '[o]nce you have covenanted, you must leave it to your representative, who is now in possession of your right of action, to exercise it at his discretion'.[14] This is again too quick, and mischaracterizes the point of Hobbes' remarks.

In the text from Hobbes quoted immediately above, Hobbes is not speaking to authorization, but rather is laying the groundwork for his analysis of contract. In this context, one aimed at specifying the features of contract, Hobbes says that a transfer of right occurs when the transferor 'intendeth the benefit thereof [of the right] to some certain person or persons' (xiv.7, 81). That is, the transferred right is to benefit the person to whom it is transferred.[15] Cases of authorization are fundamentally different, even if they arise from a contract.

An agent under contract does not acquire the principal's right in the thing she is contracted to administer. On the contrary, she acquires the principal's consent for the sole purpose of representing him and managing the affairs she is entrusted to manage. If she has been contracted to administer an estate, for example, she may be entrusted with the authority to possess and administer the estate's assets, but she does not acquire legal and beneficial title to them. Her office requires that she faithfully respect her principal's rights in the things administered such that the principal, and not the agent, receives the full benefit of them. Transferring the principal's underlying rights to the agent such that she became their legal and beneficial owner would defeat from the outset the very point of the agency. Hobbes, I argue momentarily, was fully aware of this elementary analysis of authorization.

Skinner, however, interprets Hobbes as saying that 'we are led by reason to recognise that the best means of attaining peace and the other contentments of life will be to transfer our rights [of nature] to a sovereign who will exercise them on our behalf'.[16] It follows from the transfer of this right,

[14] Ibid, p 186.

[15] This is so notwithstanding that because a transfer of right is a voluntary act, 'it is either in consideration of some right reciprocally transferred to himself or for some other good he hopeth for thereby' (L xiv.8, 82).

[16] Skinner, *supra* note 12, p 203.

Skinner says, that the sovereign enjoys a limitless right of action. And this shows that the original covenant 'is not a means of limiting the powers of the crown; properly understood, it shows that the powers of the crown have no limits at all'.[17] Skinner's argument coheres well with the orthodox view which insists that Hobbes makes the sovereign all powerful to prevent a slide towards the state of nature. But Skinner's construal of authorization is deficient for several reasons, and its deficiency reveals that the sovereign's authority does not amount to an unscripted carte blanche.

As suggested above in the discussion of contract and authorization, Skinner conflates the right of action which an authorized agent must possess to act from authority with the primary rights or interests of the principal that the agent is authorized to administer. There is no reason to presume that a commission or licence to act in respect of certain rights means that those rights are transferred to the agent. The presumption in cases of authorization is just the opposite. Hobbes says that acts done by authority are done by commission or licence from 'him whose right it *is*'. If the right had transferred to the agent, one would expect Hobbes to acknowledge the transfer with a change of tense. So even if we concede for the moment that some transfer of right is necessary for a relationship of authorization to take hold, and if we follow Skinner further to assume that the subject transfers his right of governing himself to the sovereign, those premises do not imply that what is transferred for the purpose of establishing sovereignty is an unfettered right of action as broad as the subject has in the state of nature. All that needs to be transferred is a limited right of action sufficient to grant to the sovereign the power and authority necessary to establish legal order in accordance with the terms of the authorizing original covenant.

There are other problems with Skinner's account of authorization worth noting, and these difficulties reveal tensions in the orthodox understanding of Hobbes. The right of nature that is supposed to be transferred to the sovereign and do the authorizing work is not a claim-right that, by itself, can generate or underlie legal obligations owed by others to the right-holder. The right of nature is a free-standing liberty-right rather than a claim-right with legal implications. Whereas a claim-right denotes that someone else owes the right-holder a correlative duty, a liberty-right does not entail correlative duties. The liberty-right-holder is simply free to act as she pleases within the scope of the right.[18] People may exercise a liberty-right to acquire obligations, such as when they enter into covenants, but the mere fact of liberty in one person does not—in the absence of a legal relationship—give

[17] Ibid, p 208.

[18] See generally W Hohfeld, *Fundamental Legal Conceptions*, ed W Cook (New Haven: Yale University Press, 1919).

rise to a legal obligation on the part of another. So it is unclear how giving up this liberty by transferring it to the sovereign—but not through a covenant with him—is supposed to make the subject the author of the sovereign's action and thereby generate the subject's obligation to obey.

Just as troubling for Skinner's account are the things that the subject cannot be obligated to do as a matter of law. Because covenants are voluntary acts they are presumed to further the good of the person making the covenant. For example, an individual cannot surrender the right to preserve her life, since she could not be deemed to pursue her good through such a surrender (xiv.8, 82; xxi.12, 142). As a consequence, the subject has no obligation to surrender her life if called on by the sovereign to do so.

Skinner refers to this absence of obligation in a quizzical footnote in an article on liberty,[19] but there is no mention of the limits of obligation in his discussion of authorization. This is a stark omission, for Skinner is keenly aware of the importance to Hobbes of the 'mutual relation between protection and obedience'. A possible explanation for the omission is that if one limits the basis of both sovereign authority and legal obligation to a transfer from subject to sovereign of the unlimited right of nature, then the significance of the original covenant to legal obligation disappears. That is, the covenant no longer limits the scope of obligation to that which the subject can be taken to have consented because the covenant no longer plays a role in setting the terms of public authority and legal obligation.

Moreover, Hobbes' theory of punishment explicitly rejects the idea that the sovereign's authority to punish arises from a transfer of right from subject to sovereign. In setting out this theory, Hobbes first reminds the reader that the subject cannot give 'any right to another to lay violent hands upon his person' (L xxviii.2, 203). In making a commonwealth, the subject 'giveth away the right of defending another, but not of defending himself' and he also 'obligeth himself to assist him that hath the sovereignty in the punishing of another, but of himself not' (L xxviii.2, 204). This presents a puzzle. Individuals are expected to lay down their right of nature only to the extent that others are so willing. On entering civil society, 'no man' is 'to reserve to himself any right which he is not content should be reserved to every one of the rest' (L xv.22, 97). But no one can covenant away their right to defend themselves, so no one can require others to do so (even if it were possible). It follows that individuals in the state of nature could transfer to the sovereign only a right of punishment that would come with an

[19] Quentin Skinner, 'The Proper Signification of Liberty', *Visions of Politics: Hobbes and Civil Science* (Cambridge: Cambridge University Press, 2002), p 209, n 87, citing *Leviathan*, *supra* note 8 for 'the remarkably extensive range of things that a subject, "though commanded by the Soveraign", may "without Injustice refuse to do"'.

eviscerating proviso: the right (such as it is) cannot be exercised against any subject. Because everyone must make an exception for themselves, on the transfer theory everyone would benefit from the same exception and so all would be immune from punishment.

Hobbes has another reason, too, for resisting the transfer theory. He points out that 'to covenant to assist the sovereign in doing hurt to another, unless he that so covenanteth have a right to do it himself, is not to give him a right to punish' (L xxviii.2, 204). Since punishment proceeds from public authority only, and there is no public authority in the state of nature, it 'is manifest, therefore, that the right which the commonwealth (that is, he or they that represent it) hath to punish is not grounded on any concession or gift of the subjects' (L xxviii.2, 204).

Hobbes' solution is to ground the right of punishment on the sovereign's own pre-commonwealth right of nature (ibid):

> [T]his is the foundation of that right of punishing which is exercised in every commonwealth. For the subjects did not give the sovereign that right, but only (in laying down theirs) strengthened him to use his own as he should think fit, for the preservation of them all; so that it was not given, but left to him, and to him only, and (excepting the limits set him by natural law) as entire as in the condition of mere nature, and of war of every one against his neighbour.

Hobbes at last, in chapter 28, cashes in the distinction drawn earlier in chapter 14 between renunciation and transfer. To summarize: the sovereign's authority to punish is not transferred to him by his subjects because they have no such right to transfer. Nor does it arise from a transfer of his subjects' right of nature. Instead, the sovereign's right to punish is grounded on the subject's 'laying down' their right of nature and strengthening his. Just as noteworthy, the right to punish is to be used 'for the preservation of them all' and subject to 'the limits set him by natural law'. These qualifications allow Hobbes in the remainder of 28 to distinguish acts of punishment from acts of hostility. More generally, as we shall see presently, they play a constitutive role in his conception of public authority. Skinner's discussion of authorization neglects altogether Hobbes' theory of punishment.

3. THE CONSTITUTION OF LEGAL ORDER

Hobbes thinks that legal order has a fairly determinate constitution, and that it is part and parcel of sovereignty. Political order may take a variety of forms—democracy, aristocracy, and monarchy—but certain constitutive parts of legal order are constant throughout. These constants are embodied in Hobbes' laws of nature, and include a number of principles of legality:

impartiality in adjudication (equity), equal or proportionate distribution of things (or by lot if common use or division is not possible), submission of disputes to an impartial arbiter, the idea that no person may be judge of her own cause, and recognition of witness testimony in disputes over facts.[20] I argue now that the laws of nature are partially constitutive of the authority the sovereign enjoys to announce and enforce law, and so a breach of them undermines his authority and the claim he has to his subjects' obedience. I will refer to this account as the constitutional interpretation of the laws of nature.[21]

For Hobbes, a law of nature is 'a precept, or general rule, found out by reason, by which a man is forbidden to do, that, which is destructive of his life or taketh away the means of preserving the same' (L xiv.3, 79; also DC ii.1, 33). Hobbes defines the 'fundamental law of nature' as a 'precept, or general rule of reason, *that every man ought to endeavour peace, as far as he has hope of attaining it.* . . . ' (L xiv.4, 80; also DC ii.2, 34; EL xv.1, 82). And all the laws of nature are 'immutable and eternal' (L xv.38, 99). In sum, the laws of nature are immutable and prescriptive rules we can know through reason.

Their importance to Hobbes is suggested by their location in *Leviathan*. Immediately after discussing the state of nature in chapter 13, he sets out these laws in chapters 14 and 15 as the constitutional programme required both to supplant the state of nature and to minimize the tendencies to slip back into it once civil society is established. That is, he articulates the laws of nature prior to his discussion of authorization in chapter 16, prior to his analysis of the state in chapter 17, and prior to his description of the types of sovereignty in chapters 18 and 19. If the laws of nature were optional in the sense that the sovereign could adopt them into the civil law or not at his sole discretion, one would expect them to be tagged on only after he had worked out the central concepts of authorization, the state, and sovereignty. Hobbes' does not turn his attention to the civil law—the kind of law the sovereign can enact and repeal at his discretion—until chapter 26. Arguably, Hobbes identification of the laws of nature with reason explains their absence from the argument that the sovereign can make and repeal civil law as he pleases: the sovereign can neither make nor repeal the laws of nature because their authority depends on reason as well as the sovereign's will.

However, the view that the laws of nature represent constraints on the sovereign is in tension with other important passages in *Leviathan*. Hobbes seems to deny flatly that the laws of nature are laws that create legal

[20] See L xv.23–33, 97–8; also EL xvi.12–13, 92; xvii.3–7, 94–6; DC iii.15–24, 50–2.

[21] David Dyzenhaus offers a similar account: David Dyzenhaus, 'Hobbes and the Legitimacy of Law' (2001) 20 Law & Phil 461.

obligations, for only the sovereign has the authority to create those obligations (L xv.41, 100):

> These dictates of reason men use to call by the name of lawes, but improperly; for they are but conclusions or theorems concerning what conduceth to the conservation and defence of themselves, whereas law, properly, is the word of him that by right hath command over others.

His discussion of the laws of nature and the civil law in chapter 26 of *Leviathan* (the 'mutual containment thesis') elaborates the point: (L xxvi.8, 174):

> The law of nature, and the civil law contain each other, and are of equal extent. For the laws of nature, which consist in equity, justice, gratitude, and other moral virtues on these depending, in the condition of mere nature . . . are not properly laws, but qualities that dispose men to peace and to obedience. When a commonwealth is once settled, then are they actually laws, and not before, as being then the commands of the commonwealth, and therefore also civil laws; for it is the sovereign power that obliges men to obey them.

More specifically, Hobbes claims that law—civil and natural—must have certain institutional properties to create legal obligations that bind on action (L xxvi.8–23, 174–81). First, the law must have a known author who is recognized to have law-making authority and effective power. Second, a law must have an authentic interpretation, ie an interpretation that is authentic because it is rendered by a judge appointed by the sovereign. Finally, the civil law must be published, since for it to succeed as a command it must be made known to those subject to it. These properties—a known author with sovereign power, publicity, and an authentic interpretation—require the legal institutions of civil society.

It may seem that Hobbes is committed to positivism given his incorporation of the laws of nature within civil law and the emphasis he places on institutionalization. In the remainder of this section I will attempt to reconcile Hobbes' apparent commitment to positivism with the constitutional interpretation of the laws of nature. We can begin this reconciliation using a distinction Hobbes draws with respect to different types of obligation. Hobbes requires institutions to be in place in order for full-blooded legal obligations to arise and bind on action *in foro externo* (in the external forum). At the same time, Hobbes thinks that the laws of nature bind *in foro interno*—on conscience, 'to a desire they should take place'—in the state of nature as well as in civil society (L xv.36, 99). He says that '[t]he Laws of Nature oblige in Conscience always, but in effect then *only where there is Security*' (L xv.36, 99, emphasis added). If the security condition also applied to the *in foro interno* application of the laws of nature, then the laws of nature would apply *in foro interno* only in civil society, where the sovereign is present to provide security. But then Hobbes would have no reason to base the *interno/externo* distinction on the presence of security. For security to play a role in making the distinction, it must be the case that the laws of nature bind on conscience (*in foro interno*) even when there is no security, as is the case in the state of nature.[22]

This suggests that, for Hobbes, at least some part of the *normative* authority of the laws of nature—their normative capacity to sustain legal obligations—can be specified independently of the institutional formalities and sovereign power that make those laws obligatory *in foro externo*. Even though the laws of nature are 'not written, nor otherwise published', they create legal obligations once civil society is in place (ibid). Hobbes is explicit in this regard: because the laws of nature can be known 'not upon other men's words, but every one from his own reason', those laws 'therefore, need not any publishing, nor proclamation' (ibid). This feature of the laws of nature is difficult to reconcile with the positivist view that all legal obligations arise *solely* from the sovereign's will, since the normative dimension of the laws of nature is apparent through reason alone and explicable independently of his will.

An objector might point out that it is still the sovereign who has ultimate interpretive authority over the laws of nature. Hence they place no real limitations on the sovereign, who can declare them to be more or less whatever he wants. Hobbes' argument for sovereignty, however, seems to presuppose that the subject can judge if the sovereign complies with at least some of the laws of nature, ie the laws that govern the institutions of legal order (eg equity, equal use of things in common, impartiality in adjudication, etc). His justification of these laws is always cast in terms of how their breach leads to conflict, yet the sovereign alone is entitled to set up the institutions that make their breach possible. It follows that the sovereign, and only the sovereign, can breach them. As with the other laws of nature, Hobbes calls them 'articles of peace, upon which men may be drawn to agreement', and so they participate in the justification of sovereignty (L xiii.14, 78). They are 'the precepts by which men are guided' to avoid 'the condition of war' (L xxxi.1, 233–4). Plausibly, the laws of nature are 'articles' of the original covenant that people are presumed to agree upon. But for them to play a meaningful role in the justification of sovereignty, they must be reasonably determinate and intelligible *independently* of sovereignty, which is why Hobbes says they are knowable both through reason and in the state of nature.

While the sovereign retains final interpretive authority, the contribution of the laws of nature to the argument for sovereignty would be undermined if, on entering civil society, the sovereign could interpret them in any way he

[22] For the contrary view, see Michael Oakeshott, *Rationalism in Politics and Other Essays*, new and expanded edn (Indianapolis: Liberty Press, 1991).

pleased. After all, why would people be 'drawn to agreement' on them if, in practice, they are meaningless? And if the argument for sovereignty is weakened, then so too is the sovereign's authority. Hobbes insists that because sovereignty, in the long run, 'cannot be maintained by any civil law or terror of legal punishment', the argument for it must be 'diligently and truly taught' to the people (L xxx.4, 220). Assuming, then, that the basic content of the institutional laws of nature is not lost once people enter civil society, an interpretation that flagrantly violated them would subvert the sovereign's authority in two ways. First, as I will argue below, it would weaken the subject's obligation to obey. Second, the infringing interpretation would undermine legal institutions and move civil society towards the state of nature by promoting conflict.

One might think that these consequences could perhaps serve as useful advice to the sovereign but that they are not really constraints. The point of my argument, however, is not to show that the sovereign's powers to interpret are limited in the sense that they are subject to review by another authority (on Hobbes' account, this reviewing authority would be the sovereign). Nor do I mean to imply that an abuse of interpretive powers would justify rebellion, as Locke might claim.[23] Rather, the point is much weaker and conditional: if the sovereign wishes to issue interpretations of the laws of nature that are not destructive of his authority and the subject's obligation to obey, then he must do so in a way that does not flagrantly violate them, especially when their meaning is relatively plain and determinate.

Under this constitutional account of the laws of nature, they constitute the fundamental (if embryonic) normative framework within which sovereign authority must operate so as to achieve the ends of sovereignty (peace and security) while making a claim to the subject's obedience. Several passages from *Leviathan* support this reading. Hobbes asserts that violation of the laws of nature 'can never be made lawful. For it can never be that war shall preserve life, and peace destroy it' (L xv.38, 100). Elsewhere he flatly states that 'sovereigns are all subject to the laws of nature, because such laws be divine, and cannot by any man or commonwealth be abrogated' (L xxix.9, 213). At yet another place, Hobbes says that 'whatsoever is not against the law of nature may be made law in the name of them that have the sovereign power' (L xxvi.41, 188). This suggests that if a sovereign were to issue a decree that violated the laws of nature, then in some sense the decree would fail to constitute law. Hobbes alerts us to the sense he has in mind in the same paragraph: 'in all things not contrary to the moral law (that is to say, to the law of nature) all subjects are bound to obey that for divine law

[23] For Locke, because sovereignty belongs to the people and is held in trust by government, the people are entitled to rebel and overthrow abusive rulers. See Locke, *supra* note 6.

which is declared to be so by the laws of the commonwealth' (ibid). The suggestion here is that the subject is not bound to obey commands 'contrary to the moral law'. And in his chapter that segues from the secular argument for the commonwealth to an extended scriptural argument, Hobbes says plainly that 'subjects owe to sovereigns simple obedience in all things wherein their obedience is not repugnant to the laws of God' (L xxxi.1, 234).

In *The Elements of Law* he is explicit: 'the civil law cannot make that to be done *jure*, which is against the law divine, or of nature' (EL xxix.5, 179). So too in *De Cive*: 'Reason itself however changes neither its end, which is *peace and self-defence*, nor its means, namely those virtues of character which we have laid out above, and which can never be repealed by either custom or civil law' (DC iii.29, 54–5). In the Latin version of *Leviathan* Hobbes confirms that 'the laws of nature are not changed or restricted by the civil law, but only natural right is' (OL xxvi.8, 175). A plausible explanation of Hobbes' commitment to the laws of nature is that he thinks they provide immutable building blocks of legal order, and thus they are partially constitutive of the sovereign's authority and the subject's obedience.

The laws of nature also provide the legal framework within which judges are to interpret and apply civil law. In setting out the 'things that make a good judge (or a good interpreter of the laws)', Hobbes first points to '*a right understanding* of that principal law of nature called *equity*' (L xxvi.28, 184).[24] In interpreting the law, a proper understanding of equity is important because 'the intention of the legislator is always supposed to be equity; for it were a great contumely for a judge to think otherwise of the sovereign' (L xxvi.26, 183). Thus, 'if the word of the law' does not 'authorize a reasonable sentence', the judge ought to 'supply it with the law of nature' (ibid). By way of illustration, Hobbes gives the case of a man who leaves his house empty and upon return is kept out by force. The written law says only that if someone is put out of their house by force they shall be restored by force. Hobbes claims that although in his hypothetical case 'there is no special law ordained' that expressly governs the dispute, its resolution nonetheless 'is contained in the same [written] law; for else there is no remedy for him at all, which is to be supposed against the intention of the legislator' (ibid).

Hobbes offers the case to make a Dworkinian point, to show how the laws of nature can 'supply' a 'reasonable sentence' when the written law alone cannot do so. The judge must rely on the idea that the 'intention of the legislator is always supposed to be equity', and this reliance on equity

[24] For discussion of Hobbes' complex view of equity, see Dennis Klimchuk, 'Hobbes on Equity' in D Dyzenhaus and T Poole (eds), *Hobbes and the Law* (Cambridge: Cambridge University Press, forthcoming 2012).

implies that the judge must adopt one of just two permissible approaches to the case. The first is that equity on its own requires the 'reasonable sentence' in light of the indeterminacy of the written law. The second is that equity points to the general purpose underlying the written law—provision of a remedy to wrongfully dispossessed home owners—which in turn justifies a wide interpretation of the law conducive to a 'reasonable sentence'. The judge is not entitled, as Hart might suggest, to observe that the written law is indeterminate and then use her discretion to decide the case one way or the other. While perhaps not Dworkin's idealized judge Hercules, there is in Hobbes' judge the glimmer of a proto-Dworkinian.

Similarly, if a judge has no positive law to go on, the laws of nature will fill in the gaps and provide the required legal principles, for in those circumstances the judge's sentence 'ought to be according to the reason of his sovereign (which being always understood to be equity, he is bound to it by the law of nature)' (L xxvi.14, 177–8). The laws of nature also play this gap-filling role whenever the sovereign's administrative officials lack statutory instructions. They as much as judges are 'obliged to take for instructions the dictates of reason . . . which being always understood to be equity, [they are] bound to it by the law of nature' (ibid). Hobbes concludes that these 'instructions of natural reason may be comprehended under one name of *fidelity*, which is a branch of natural justice' (ibid). In other words, when public officers carry out their public obligations, they owe a specific duty of loyalty (*fidelity*) to the sovereign, and the content of the duty is supplied by the interchangeable principles of 'natural justice', the 'dictates of reason', and the laws of nature. While the duty of loyalty is owed to the sovereign, the sovereign's offices are designed to secure peace and security for his subjects. There is a good sense, then, in which the duty of loyalty to the sovereign is ultimately a duty owed to the people.

To sum up: in each branch of the state—the administration, the judiciary, and the legislature—public actors are to be guided by equity and the other laws of nature. These laws structure and fill the recesses of legal order. Notwithstanding the sovereign's wide interpretive power, Hobbes believed that a failure to abide by the laws of nature would subvert the sovereign's authority and the subject's duty to obey.

4. TRUST AS THE BASIS OF THE STATE-SUBJECT RELATIONSHIP

Bearing in mind these implications and the constitutional role Hobbes assigns to the laws of nature, consider now how they may be incorporated into his conception of authorization. Against the background threat of the state of nature, the subject is deemed to have covenanted with others to authorize a sovereign to establish legal order because it is in everybody's interest to do so. When individuals renounce their right of nature, they do not transfer it to the sovereign so as to become his slaves.[25] Rather, they are deemed to have consented amongst themselves to establish a sovereign licensed to exercise public power solely for the sake of establishing legal order consistent with the laws of nature.

Now, on the orthodox understanding of Hobbes, the subject's relationship to the sovereign rests on consent in the sense that sovereignty flows from the original covenant. And once civil society is established, the subject's actual relationship to the sovereign is not mediated by consent or anything else. The sovereign is taken to possess the right of liberty that the subject has transferred to him, and so, as Skinner put it, 'the powers of the crown have no limits at all'. But the orthodox view overlooks the moral precept that Hobbes thought actually connected the sovereign to the people: trust.

Once we are in civil society, the subject's ongoing relationship to the sovereign is mediated and based on trust. Trust is what we are left with once we have consented to an original covenant that authorizes irrevocable power that the sovereign has unilateral authority to exercise. And trust is the moral medium that connects public authority to the people. The presence of trust implies that sovereign power has been authorized subject to the condition that it will be used exclusively for the purpose for which it has been conferred, ie the procurement of legal order consistent with the laws of nature. A breach of trust on the part of the sovereign would not justify a Lockean rebellion, but it would undercut the subject's obligation to obey.

In support of this position, I briefly canvas some of ways in which Hobbes assigns a role to trust in his discussion of authority and the sovereign's offices. When Hobbes posits equity as a law of nature, he describes the judge as one who is 'trusted to judge between man and man' (L xv.23, 97). Similarly, Hobbes says that the arbitrator who distributes 'to every man his own' is someone who can be said to 'perform his trust' (L xv.15, 95). Trust also plays a pivotal role in Hobbes' justification of the principle of impartial dispute resolution. If the judge would gain from one side's victory in the dispute, 'no man can be obliged to trust him' (L xv.32, 98). Hobbes seems to suggest here, consistent with the argument made earlier, that a person subject to judicial authority cannot be obligated to take the judge's decision as binding if the judge has taken a bribe. The consequence of corruption, Hobbes warns, is that 'the condition of war remaineth, contrary to the law of nature' (ibid).

[25] Compare Jean Hampton, *Hobbes and the Social Contract Tradition* (Cambridge: Cambridge University Press, 1988), pp 114–28 (arguing that Hobbes' argument for absolute sovereignty implies a master/slave relationship between sovereign and subject).

Hobbes is just as explicit in his discussions of the relationship between the sovereign and the people, and the sovereign's duties which are said to flow from the trust reposed in him. He describes the office of the sovereign as one arising from the people's trust: 'The office of the sovereign . . . consisteth in the end for which he was trusted with the sovereign power, namely, the procuration of *the safety of the people*' (L xxx.1, 219). In the same vein, he says that a monarch with authority to appoint a successor 'is obliged by the law of nature to provide, by establishing his successor, to keep those that had trusted him with the government from relapsing into the miserable condition of civil war' (L xix.11, 123). Hobbes elsewhere acknowledges that 'a sovereign monarch, or the greater part of a sovereign assembly, may ordain the doing of many things in pursuit of their passions, contrary to their own consciences', and qualifies such action as 'a breach of trust, and of the law of nature' (L xxiv.7, 162). One cannot commit a 'breach of trust' unless one is under a duty to abide by the requirements of an office held in trust.

Given Hobbes' explicit reliance on consent and his celebrated account of authorization, it is suggestive that he uses 'trusted' or 'entrusted' in places where, if consent were the sole desiderata, he could have simply said 'authorized'. Hobbes may have preferred the language of trust because it indicates a moral relationship capable of sustaining the commonwealth on an ongoing basis. That is, Hobbes uses consent to explain the *origins* of sovereignty, but its justification over time—and so its *nature*—is explicated in the language of a 'mutual relation' based on trust.[26] The sovereign is entrusted with the commonwealth's peace and security, while the subject is entrusted with life and liberty. So long as the sovereign fulfils the obligations that arise from this trust by ruling in accordance with the principles of legal order, the subject has an obligation to obey the law. Together, the laws of nature and the moral relationship of reciprocal trust supply the constitutional framework of legal order.

***

I have tried to show that the orthodox reading of Hobbes fails to account for his understanding of the laws of nature, and that the subject's surrender of her right of nature does not involve a transfer to the sovereign of an unfettered discretionary power. Instead, the concept that animates Hobbes' discussion of authorization is entrusted or *fiduciary* power. As noted above fiduciary power arises when one party, the fiduciary, is entrusted with a unilateral right of

[26] The interpretation I am urging here helps explain the infamous 'rebel's catechism' in *Leviathan*, where Hobbes says that if 'our refusal to obey frustrates the end for which the sovereignty was ordained, then there is no liberty to refuse; otherwise there is' (L xxi.15, 142). Skinner's account of authorization makes no attempt to explain this and similar passages.

action over the interests of another, the beneficiary, where the beneficiary is in principle or in practice unable to exercise this power. In these circumstances, the duty of the fiduciary is to act with due regard for the best interests of the beneficiary. In the case of the fiduciary state and its officials, public authorities have a right of action over the people's interest in living within a legal order rather than a state of nature. But the right of action is expressly limited to the terms of its authorization. A failure to abide by those terms would subvert the state's authority and the moral claim it could otherwise make to its subjects' obedience.

In the remaining chapters I argue that seeing the state as a fiduciary explains its authority to legislate, administer, adjudicate, and otherwise provide for legal order. The state-subject fiduciary relationship also explains the default limits of public authority, limits that constitute the rule of law and emerge as freestanding public duties that constrain exercises of authority. Those duties help to guarantee what Hobbes sought from the original covenant, that exercises of public power necessarily take place within an institutional and stable legal framework. As we shall see, the legitimacy of the framework is supplied by a fiduciary principle of legality. This principle transmits authorization to the state on behalf of the subject, and thereby permits the state to act authoritatively on the subject's behalf, but always subject to fiduciary constraints.

I

Introduction: The State as Fiduciary and the Rule of Law

1.1 INTRODUCTION: *RONCARELLI* AND THE FACT OF SOVEREIGNTY

To this day, *Roncarelli v Duplessis*[1] ranks among the most important cases in Canadian jurisprudence on the rule of law. Justice Rand wrote in the majority, while Justice Cartwright (as he then was) dissented. Their judgments reveal two fundamentally distinct approaches to judicial review and the rule of law. On Cartwright J's side is a roughly positivist conception that subjects administrative bodies to legal duties of fairness and reasonableness only if such duties are anchored in statute. Freestanding or common law duties are suspect from this point of view because they cannot be identified by reference to a legislative source. On Rand J's side is a non-positivist and common law constitutionalist approach. Under this conception, administrative bodies are subject to public law duties without the prompt of statute. Common law constitutionalists such as Rand J see these duties as intrinsic to legal order, and integral to both the rule of law and the legitimacy of the administrative state. The argument for the rule of law defended here takes its inspiration from Rand J's common law constitutionalism, and justifies itself against the approach taken by Cartwright J. So *Roncarelli* sets the stage nicely for the argument to come.

In 1946, Premier Maurice Duplessis engaged in a self-described 'war without mercy' against the Jehovah's Witnesses. The Witnesses were distributing pamphlets to proselytize their creed. Hundreds were arrested under local by-laws that required a licence for peddling goods of any kind. Frank Roncarelli, a well-known proprietor of an upscale restaurant and a Witness himself (but not a distributor of Witness materials), gave security for the bail of some 380 arrested Witnesses.

[1] *Roncarelli v Duplessis* [1959] SCR 121 (*Roncarelli*).

Duplessis discovered that Roncarelli was behind the bail security. He told the Chairman of the Quebec Liquor Commission to cancel Roncarelli's liquor licence. Duplessis let it be known that the cancellation of the licence was not temporary, but permanent, that Roncarelli was to be barred from obtaining a licence 'forever'.[2] The cancellation had a predictably catastrophic effect on Roncarelli's business, forcing him into bankruptcy. Roncarelli sued Duplessis for damages, alleging that the Premier had abused the authority of his office.

In his defence, Duplessis relied on Article 35 of the Act Respecting Alcoholic Liquor,[3] which read: 'The Commission may cancel any permit at its discretion'.[4] The statutory discretion was not expressly qualified or limited in any way. Duplessis argued that it was wholly a matter for the Commission to decide whether to cancel the licence. Cartwright J agreed, saying that the Commission enjoyed an 'unfettered discretion' to grant or revoke licences.[5] He adopted the argument of Duplessis' counsel, one which captures the attitude many judges have expressed over the years towards discretionary decision-making:[6]

> Under the Statute, no one has a pre-existing right to obtain a permit, and the permit being granted under the condition that it may be cancelled at any time, and no cause of cancellation being mentioned and no form of procedure being indicated, the cancellation is a discretionary decision of a purely administrative character.

In other words, because there is no pre-existing right to obtain a permit, nor conditions placed on when it may be cancelled, holding a permit is a privilege which may be revoked at any time, for any reason, and without the benefit of a hearing or the giving of reasons to the affected licensee. Cartwright J held that whereas judges deal in pre-existing 'legal rights and liabilities' established by statute or 'long-settled principles' of the common law, administrative tribunals base their decisions on 'policy and expediency', unconstrained by legal norms and standards.[7] On this view, an administrative tribunal, 'within its province, is a law unto itself'.[8] The majority in *Roncarelli* took a very different approach.

Rand J held that 'there is no such thing as absolute and untrammelled "discretion," that is that action can be taken on any ground or for any reason that can be suggested to the mind of the administrator'.[9] Discretion, Rand J said, 'implies good faith in discharging public duty; there is always a

[2] *Roncarelli, supra* note 1, p 133. [3] *Act Respecting Alcoholic Liquor*, RSQ 1941, c 255.

[4] *Roncarelli, supra* note 1, p 139. [5] Ibid, p 167. [6] Ibid.

[7] Ibid, p 167, citing *re Ashby et al* [1934] OR 421, p 428; 3 DLR 565; 62 CCC 132 *per* Masten JA.

[8] *Roncarelli, supra* note 1, p 167, citing *re Ashby et al, supra* note 7, p 428.

[9] *Roncarelli, supra* note 1, p 140.

perspective within which a statute is intended to operate; and any clear departure from its lines or objects is just as objectionable as fraud or corruption'.[10] He concluded that to permit without recourse the suspension of a licence critical to one's livelihood, 'according to the arbitrary likes, dislikes and purposes of public officials acting beyond their public duty', would signal 'the beginning of disintegration of the rule of law as a fundamental postulate of our constitutional scheme'.[11]

In ascribing an unwritten constitutional status to the rule of law, Rand J went much further than saying that in this particular case discretionary power had been used for an improper or unauthorized purpose. He insisted that '*no* legislative Act can, without express language, be taken to contemplate an unlimited arbitrary power exercisable for a purpose, however capricious or irrelevant, regardless of the nature or purpose of the statute'.[12] As David Mullan suggests, and as we shall explore further in later chapters, this aspect of Rand J's judgment points to 'a common law (or common sense) perspective of what would be impermissible under *any* Act'.[13] This perspective is sometimes referred to as common law constitutionalism because it treats the common law as a repository of principles that constitute the rule of law and control statutory interpretation, all in the service of the people affected by an exercise of public power.[14]

For Rand J, the absence of a statutory requirement limiting permit revocations to specific causes was inconsequential because, for him, the grant of any legal power carries with it an obligation to exercise the power non-arbitrarily, ie fairly and reasonably. This is the first premise of a larger argument that will unfold over the course of this book, one which speaks to the *manner* in which public power must be exercised. The basic idea is that exercises of public power that fail to respect the demands of fairness and reasonableness are unlawful and subversive of the state's legal authority. A further premise (one that I assume without argument) relates to the *source* of public powers: every public power must be authorized by a publicly recognized legal source, such as a constitution or legislation. Yet another necessary and constitutive condition of lawful authority concerns the *form* of law: legislation must generally conform to certain formal requirements, eg it must be public and clear. More controversially, the rule of law, properly

[10] Ibid. [11] Ibid, p 142. [12] Ibid, p 140 (emphasis added).

[13] David J Mullan, 'Judging the Judgment of Judges: *CUPE v. Ontario (Minister of Labour)*' (2003) 10 *Canadian Labour and Employment Law Journal* 431 (emphasis in original).

[14] See eg, TRS Allan, *Constitutional Justice: A Liberal Theory of the Rule of Law* (Oxford: Oxford University Press, 2003); David Dyzenhaus, *The Constitution of Law: Legality in a Time of Emergency* (Cambridge: Cambridge University Press, 2006); Mary Liston, 'Governments in Miniature: The Rule of Law in the Administrative State' in Lorne Mitchell Sossin and Colleen M Flood (eds), *Administrative Law in Context* (Toronto: Emond Montgomery Publications, 2008).

understood, points to a further necessary condition of legality: the *content* of law must respect human rights, where 'respect' includes cases of rights restrictions that are publicly justifiable. As we shall see in subsequent chapters, these four rule-of-law conditions are independently necessary and jointly sufficient to distinguish lawful authority and legal order from mere coercive power.

As in Rand J's judgment, commentators on the rule of law generally characterize it as a bulwark against the potential arbitrariness of public officials. While controversy surrounds what the rule of law entails and does not entail, there is broad consensus that the rule of law is a necessary feature of any properly functioning and just legal order. The common intuition is that without the rule of law we are left with the mere rule of the rulers, unfettered by the constraints of legality. State power without the rule of law threatens us with an insecurity in which *Roncarelli*-like abuses loom as ever-present storm clouds on the horizon, regardless of whether the rulers actually exercise their powers capriciously or not.[15] In other words, state power without the rule of law places public officials in a relationship of domination *vis-à-vis* their people, since those officials could abuse their powers with imunity.

For republicans, domination is an evil independently of whether the power holder actually mistreats the people subject to her power. Domination denotes dependence, which is living at the whim or mercy of another. It explains why slavery is wrongful even if the slave-master allows the slave to live a life similar in all respects to the life she would live were she free. The point is that the victim in a relationship of domination never knows where she stands or when the whip will be cracked. As Philip Pettit argues, the rule of law supplies a republican antidote to domination by ensuring that individuals are subject to general laws rather than the arbitrary power of their rulers.[16]

The aim of this book is to defend a common law constitutionalist and republican account of the rule of law. A major focus of the argument is the justification and explanation of freestanding duties of fairness and reasonableness commonly associated with the rule of law. These duties reflect Rand J's hostility to arbitrariness, and to apprehend them properly we will spend some time discussing cases in which they arise. As the minority

[15] Hobbes saw that the deep viciousness posed by lawlessness is not actual, ceaseless violence, but the possibility that violence might wantonly and arbitrarily visit itself on anyone at anytime: 'For as the nature of foul weather lieth not in a shower or two of rain, but in an inclination thereto of many days together, so the nature of war, consisteth not in actual fighting, but in the known disposition thereto, during all the time there is no assurance to the contrary' (L xiii.8, 76).

[16] Phillip Pettit, *Republicanism: A Theory of Freedom and Government* (New York: Oxford University Press, 1997), esp pp 174–7. Pettit adopts the orthodox view of Hobbes discussed in the Prologue, and uses Hobbes as an 'authoritarian' foil to help illuminate his idea of freedom as non-domination. See eg, ibid, pp 37–9, 41–5. Like Skinner, Pettit overlooks the role the laws of nature play in Hobbes' account of public authority.

judgment in *Roncarelli* attests, however, Rand J's findings and the considerations that support them are insufficient to convince those who favour the dissent. There are perhaps many reasons for Cartwright J's unreceptiveness to Rand J's arguments, including a patent hostility to the idea of legal standards operating within the administrative state. Nonetheless, as we shall now see, the deeper problem is that Rand J's arguments do not engage directly the more principled concerns that motivate the dissent.

As Cartwright J observed, the authorities had some basis in statute for revoking Roncarelli's licence, since on its face the Act Respecting Alcoholic Liquor gave the Commission unqualified discretion to cancel permits. While Rand J attempts to defend his view in part on the basis of statutory interpretation, the statute itself is unclear with respect to the breadth of the discretion conferred. So Rand J must resort to statute-independent arguments related to good faith in the discharge of public duty and the common law perspective within which legislation is presumed to operate.

Neither of these arguments is likely to persuade someone sympathetic to Cartwright J's position. The idea of good faith presupposes that there is some standard against which the aims and purposes of a discretionary decision may be assessed. For Cartwright J, however, the statutory power is itself sufficient warrant for the decision, regardless of the reasons for which it was taken. It follows that the aims and purposes of the decision-maker are irrelevant and therefore immune to judicial scrutiny. Moreover, as we have seen, for the Cartwright camp the permit falls on the privileges side of a rights/privileges distinction they support. Courts protect rights while administrative bodies extend privileges. Courts, therefore, have no business interfering with political and discretionary decisions concerning privileges because privileges lack underlying legal entitlements.

Because Rand J found that Duplessis and the Commission had revoked Roncarelli's permit for an improper purpose tantamount to fraud or corruption, he did not need to consider other grounds for attacking the decision. One such ground could have been a lack of procedural fairness, since Roncarelli was given no opportunity to present his case to the Commission. If a reviewing court determines that a decision-making body's procedures lack fairness—eg if the affected individual is not given an opportunity to know and respond to the case against her—the decision may be overturned regardless of the substantive reasons for which it was made. This is the basic process/substance distinction that animates judicial review of fairness. It is the cornerstone of extensive jurisprudence on the rule of law because it serves the dual roles of engaging fairness and permitting judges to distinguish review of legality from review of the merits along a process/substance divide.

The contemporary debate over the duty of procedural fairness mirrors Cartwright and Rand J's disagreement.[17] Cartwright J's Canadian successors, such as Martland and Sopinka JJ, insist that legal rights and obligations, including the duty of fairness, must have some basis in statute.[18] Meanwhile, judges who follow the path laid down by Rand J, such as Laskin CJ and L'Heureux-Dubé J, similarly fail to engage the arguments of Cartwright J and his successors.

L'Heureux-Dubé J, for example, includes the duty of fairness among the principles of fundamental justice found in s 7 of the Canadian Charter of Rights and Freedoms.[19] In addition, she gives a public policy argument in support of the public's interest in the 'proper use' of delegated statutory powers.[20] But even if we agree with her arguments, it does not follow that, in the absence of a statutory entitlement, frontline decision-makers owe a legally binding duty of fairness to every person subject to their authority. The most L'Heureux-Dubé J's arguments show is that fairness is in *some* moral sense an important value or principle. Yet that which is morally required is not, without more, legally required. Her arguments do not establish that decision-makers owe a legal, rather than simply moral, duty of fairness to the individual before them. Nor do they explain judges' authority to impose such duties when the legislature has not established them. Hence, Cartwright J and his successors can concede the premises taken to support fairness, and admit that fairness is a morally laudable goal of public administration, but still insist that the kind of fairness at issue is simply whatever can be won through politics and implemented by the legislature.

The difficulty is that proponents of fairness have yet to articulate a sufficiently general but structured legal relationship in which to situate it. The lack of such a relationship presents a gap between, on the one hand, fairness as a free-floating moral principle, and on the other, the imposition of a legal duty of fairness on particular officials in particular cases.

I attempt to bridge the gap by showing that an overarching fiduciary relationship exists between the state and each person subject to its authority. Because the fiduciary relationship is legal in nature, it generates legal duties,

[17] *Nicholson v Haldimand-Norfolk Regional Board of Commissioners of Police* [1979] 1 SCR 62 (*Nicholson*); *Board of Education of the Indian Head School Division No 19 of Saskatchewan v Knight* [1990] 1 SCR 653 (*Knight*); and *Dunsmuir v New Brunswick*, 2008 SCC 9; [2008] 1 SCR 190 are the leading Canadian cases on fairness, discussed in Chapter VII.

[18] Martland J wrote for the dissent in *Nicholson*, *supra* note 17. Sopinka J wrote the minority judgment in *Knight*, *supra* note 17.

[19] *Knight*, *supra* note 17, p 683. *Canadian Charter of Rights and Freedoms*, Part I of the Constitution Act, 1982, being Sch B to the Canada Act 1982 (UK), 1982 c 11 (Charter).

[20] *Knight*, *supra* note 17, p 675.

including, I will argue, L'Heureux-Dubé J's duty of fairness and Rand J's duty of reasonableness. Here, I indicate briefly the shape the argument will take.

This overarching fiduciary relationship arises from what we may think of as the fact of sovereignty. The fact of sovereignty consists in the sovereign powers the state claims and exercises, most notably, powers of legislation, administration, and adjudication. Through legislation, the state determines the form and content of each person's rights and obligations. Through administration, officials implement public law regimes to give effect to legislation. Through adjudication, the judiciary interprets legislation and settles disputes over rights and duties. To ensure that legal order prevails, the state assumes a monopoly on the use of coercive force. These general attributes of the state point to a non-consensual relationship of proclaimed authority between state and subject, notwithstanding democratic channels (in democratic states) through which the people's voice may be heard.

I illustrate the implications of the fiduciary model using mainly jurisprudence from Canada and other commonwealth jurisdictions. The underlying fact of sovereignty, however, is true of all states. In later chapters, I canvass case law and scholarship from two non-commonwealth jurisdictions, the United States and Israel, which acknowledge the consequences to public law of the fiduciary position of the state's institutions. The fiduciary model can help explain public law in these various jurisdictions, notwithstanding historical and institutional differences, because the fact of sovereignty obtains in all.

As we shall see in greater detail, the relationship between the administration and the people possesses the constitutive features of fiduciary relationships: trust, authorization, discretionary and unilateral power, and vulnerability. Legislatures authorize and entrust administrative bodies to carry out their mandates exclusively for the common good. Boards typically have broad discretionary powers they can exercise unilaterally, making the individuals subject to them especially vulnerable to their power. These latter features—discretionary and unilateral power, and vulnerability—figure prominently in the 'rough and ready' guide to fiduciary relations proposed by Wilson J in a leading Canadian case on fiduciary relationships, *Frame v Smith*[21]:

(1) the fiduciary has scope for the exercise of some discretion or power;
(2) the fiduciary can unilaterally exercise that power or discretion so as to affect the beneficiary's legal or practical interests; and

[21] *Frame v Smith* [1987] 2 SCR 99, para 60 (*Frame*). Wilson J's 'rough and ready' guide has since been reaffirmed, with some qualifications, in a number of important fiduciary cases. See eg, *Lac Minerals Ltd v International Corona Resources Ltd* [1989] 2 SCR 574; *Canson Enterprises Ltd v Boughton & Co* [1991] 3 SCR 534; *Hodgkinson v Simms* [1994] 3 SCR 377 (*Hodgkinson*); *Galambos v Perez* 2009 SCC 48; [2009] 3 SCR 247. In *Hodgkinson*, the majority noted that Wilson J's guidelines are more descriptive than analytic in that they 'constitute *indicia* that help recognize a fiduciary relationship rather than the ingredients that define it', *Hodgkinson*, p 409.

(3) the beneficiary is peculiarly vulnerable to or at the mercy of the fiduciary holding the discretion or power.

These indicia, properly elaborated, reflect the circumstances that give rise to both the fiduciary's authority and duty to act on the beneficiary's behalf. A fiduciary relationship arises, I argue, if, and only if, one party holds discretionary power of an administrative nature over the important interests of another, and this latter party (the beneficiary) is unable, either as a matter of fact or law, to control or exercise the power held by the fiduciary. Discretionary power of an administrative nature is always other-regarding, purposive, and institutional in nature.

Before examining further the main features of the fiduciary state, however, it is important to see that the fiduciary concept is not a modern and lawyerly (and so marginal) contrivance, but rather an idea born of a rich and complex legal history animated by a concern to protect the integrity of relations of trust.

I.2 A BRIEF HISTORY OF THE FIDUCIARY CONCEPT

We saw in the Prologue that the fiduciary status of public bodies was recognized long ago by Cicero. Similarly, the legal fiduciary concept traces back to Roman times. The term 'fiduciary' comes from the Latin *fiduciarius*, and refers to 'one who holds anything in trust'.[22] The Roman law concepts of *fideicommissum* and *fiducia* allowed fiduciaries to hold property on behalf of and for the benefit of another, foreshadowing the separation of legal from beneficial title that would structure the medieval 'use' and later the trust.[23] The *fiducia* permitted a debtor to transfer ownership of property to a creditor until the debt was repaid, during which time the property could not be sold.[24] The *fideicommissio* or trust allowed a testator to use an intermediary to leave property to someone legally incapable of inheriting property, such as an unmarried adult. The testator would leave the

[22] Online Oxford English Dictionary, 2nd edn, *sub verbo* 'fiduciary', online: <http://www.oed.com>.

[23] Fiduciary concepts in fact predate Roman law, appearing in the laws of Hammurabi of Ancient Mesopotamia. They are also present in other legal systems, including Islamic Law, Germanic (Salic) law, and the Jewish law of agency. See Avisheh Avini, 'The Origins of the Modern English Trust Revisited' (1996) 70 Tul L Rev 1139; Tamar Frankel, *Fiduciary Law: Analysis, Definitions, Relationships, Duties, Remedies Over History and Cultures* (Anchorage, AK: Fathom Pub Co, 2008), pp 7–14.

[24] See M Szto, 'Limited Liability Company Morality: Fiduciary Duties in Historical Context' (2004) 23 Quinnipiac L Rev 61, pp 89–90; Ernest Vinter, *A Treatise on the History and Law of Fiduciary Relationship and Resulting Trusts, Together with a Selection of Selected Cases*, 3rd edn (Cambridge: Heffer, 1955), pp 2–9 (affirming the Roman influence on the development of modern fiduciary law). According to Vinter, Roman praetors imposed fiduciary-like duties on guardians *vis-à-vis* wards, physicians *vis-à-vis* patients, husbands *vis-à-vis* wives, tutors *vis-à-vis* pupils, and even magistratus provincials *vis-à-vis* the people within the provinces where they were garrisoned.

inheritance to a legally qualified heir, who then had an obligation to pass it or certain other objects on to the intended beneficiary.

The Roman Catholic Church of the Middle Ages adapted these Roman concepts under the doctrine of *utilitas ecclesia* ('for the advantage of the church'). *Utilitas ecclesia* gave clerics the beneficial use of property while others held legal title, thus allowing clerics to use property without violating secular and religious prohibitions that barred them from legally owning it.[25] This ecclesiastical doctrine preceded the development of the use following the Norman Conquest,[26] a form of land trust which 'entailed the transfer of legal title (*enfeoffment*) to a person who was to hold the property (the *feoffee to uses*) for the benefit of another (the *cestui que use*)'.[27] Uses were popular because they permitted the beneficial owner to avoid liabilities that attached to legal ownership under the feudal system, such as 'relief' payments that were tantamount to inheritance taxes owed to the lord when land passed to an adult heir.[28] The popularity of the use led to the Statute of Uses of 1535 that converted equitable estates into legal estates, thereby rendering them subject to legal liabilities. Many uses, however, were structured so as to escape conversion, and these became trusts enforceable in courts of equity.[29]

Courts of law and equity came into existence as a result of the English King's prerogative to interfere with the ordinary legal processes of communal courts through the issuance of writs.[30] Writs were remedies tailored to address specific kinds of cases. The Chancellor (the King's secretary), through the Chancery (the secretariat of the state), standardized writs that responded to similar circumstances. By the latter half of the 12th century, these writs had displaced customary law and became the basis of common law forms of actions. From the 12th through 14th centuries, there were no separate courts of law and equity; the king's judges administered forms of

[25] See Avini, *supra* note 23, p 1149; Szto, *supra* note 24, p 92, relying on Frederick Pollock and Frederic William Maitland, *The History of English Law Before the Time of Edward I*, 2nd edn (London: CUP, 1968) (first published in 1895).

[26] George G Bogert and George T Bogert, *Law of Trusts*, 5th edn (St Paul, Minn: West Pub Co, 1973), p 6.

[27] Avini, *supra* note 23, p 1143 (citations omitted).

[28] Ibid, p 1144.

[29] See ibid, p 1147, citing Bogert and Bogert, *supra* note 26, pp 12–13. Avini writes the following: 'The enactment of the Statute, however, did not result in its intended effect. Certain equitable interests escaped conversion by virtue of both the Statute's plain language and its construction as interpreted by the common-law courts. [. . .] Furthermore, the Statute was interpreted to void only general trusts and to be inapplicable to special, or active, trusts. Thus, modern English and American trusts are the result of the Court of Chancery's interpretation of the uses as "trust," thereby surviving the Statutes of Uses'.

[30] The history recounted here is taken from detailed accounts provided by Timothy S Haskett, 'The Medieval English Court of Chancery' (1996) 14(2) LHR 245; Thomas O Main and Timothy Haskett, 'Traditional Equity and Contemporary Procedure' (2003) 78 Wash L Rev 429.

action that would later fall under both jurisdictions.[31] At the urging of barons wary of the king's power to make new law through the issuance of writs, the common law became a relatively autonomous legal system that operated independently of the king. Its writs were fixed, narrowly construed, and rigidly applied, with highly technical rules governing pleadings, procedure, and rules of evidence.

The king, however, retained his prerogative to decide cases. Individuals whose circumstances did not fit within the narrow scope of established writs, or who were prejudiced by the common law's technical formalities, could petition the king for relief. Suppose, for example, a debtor paid off his debt but did not ensure that his sealed bond was cancelled when the debt was paid down. At common law, the debtor would have no remedy against a creditor who sought to collect the 'debt' a second time. Actual payment was no defence because the law regarded a sealed bond as incontrovertible evidence of the debt, and so the debtor would have to make a second payment. The king referred petitions arising from such cases to the Lord Chancellor, the 'keeper of the king's conscience', and a person familiar with Ecclesiastical and Roman law.[32] The Chancellor's jurisdiction came to be known as equity, and in the 14th and 15th centuries the Court of Chancery emerged as a distinct court.

The Court of Chancery required the specific performance of contracts when justice so required, reformed or rescinded contracts tainted by fraud or mistake, and enjoined some of the more common torts such as trespass and nuisance before they were committed.[33] Courts of equity, unlike courts of common law, were entitled to order discovery of documents needed to enforce legal rights, order bonds cancelled where they served unjust ends, and order oral contracts to be performed.[34] Equity supplemented the common law, permitting 'complete justice' to be done, by attuning the requirements of justice underlying the common law to the factual circumstances neglected by the rigid forms and procedures the common law had come to assume.[35] Equity emerged as a distinctive body of law guided by overlapping principles of natural justice, conscience, a concern that

[31] Haskett, *supra* note 30, n 23, citing GB Adams, *Council and Courts in Anglo-Norman England* (London and New Haven: Yale University Press, 1926), pp 185–205. Other authors have made similar albeit less comprehensive arguments. While recognizing an early equity / common law overlap, they doubt that the King's judges dealt with equity to the same extent as common law. And they resist the idea that it is possible to reduce the history of equity to its formal establishment as a discrete body of law handled by a court with a separate jurisdiction. See Main and Haskett *supra* note 30, p 441, and Haskett, *supra* note 30, p 250.

[32] Main and Haskett, *supra* note 30, n 74, citing Garrard Glenn and Kenneth Redden, 'Equity: A Visit to the Founding Fathers' (1945) 31(4) Va L Rev 753 pp 760–1.

[33] Main and Haskett, *supra* note 30, p 443.

[34] Haskett, *supra* note 30, p 252.

[35] *Harnett v Yielding* (1805) 2 Sch & Lef 549, *per* Lord Redesdale.

substantive considerations triumph over formal constraints, and flexibility in the making of equitable orders.[36]

Courts of equity supervised relationships of trust. These included property trusts which borrowed their form of divided ownership (legal and beneficial title) from uses. But prior to the 19th century, trusts also covered a much wider field of confidential relations, and arose whenever someone undertook 'to exercise a power, to conduct a sale, to supervise an estate or business, or in some other way to become [another's] employee or agent'.[37] It was not until the early 19th century that the term 'trust' was restricted to property trusts, while other trust-like relationships were referred to as 'quasi-trusts', and eventually simply as fiduciary relationships.[38] Under any name, however, and from its earliest days, the trustee or fiduciary was expected to administer an estate, manage a business, or exercise a power *loyally*, on behalf of the beneficiary and without regard to the fiduciary's interest.[39]

In 1854 the English Parliament passed the Common Law Procedure Act that partially merged the procedures of law and equity. In the following two decades, a single court, the High Court of Justice, administered equity in one of its divisions. The English Court of Chancery was thus abolished.[40] Despite the procedural fusion, the Judicature Acts of 1873 and 1875 preserved the substantive difference between law and equity, with the latter prevailing in case of conflict.[41]

[36] See DR Klinck, 'Doing "Complete Justice": Equity in the Ontario Court of Chancery' (2006) 32 Queen's LJ 45.

[37] LS Sealy, 'Fiduciary Relationships' (1962) 20(1) Cambridge LJ 69, pp 69–70.

[38] Ibid, p 71.

[39] See eg, *Keech v Sandford* (1726) 25 ER 223, Sel Cas Ch 61 Ch (Eng); *Walley v Walley* (1687) 23 ER 609, Vern 484 Ch (Eng).

[40] See Main and Haskett, *supra* note 30, p 476. Canada followed suit. In 1881 Ontario passed the Ontario Judicature Act to consolidate the Court of Queen's Bench and the Court of Common Pleas (the common law courts) with the Court of Chancery, all within the High Court of Justice.

[41] Ibid. Throughout this book I will at times refer to 'common law fiduciary relationships'. I do not mean to deny the equitable origins of fiduciary law. The point is to signal that fiduciary relationships can arise independently of statute, and that their justification lies in constitutive aspects of the fiduciary-beneficiary relationship rather than positive law. Furthermore, as an anonymous reviewer pointed out to me, there is arguably a good sense in which equity, broadly construed, has always inhered in the common law, as suggested by *Dr Bonham's Case*, and as depicted in the writings of Christopher St Germain and Sir John Dodderidge (see TFT Plucknett and JL Barton (eds), *St German's Doctor and Student* (London: Selden Society, vol 91, 1974; Sir John Dodderidge, *The English Lawyer. Describing A Method for the Managing of the Lawes of this Land* (London: printed by the Assignes of I More, 1631)). Roughly speaking, these authors assign to equity within the common law much the same role that Hobbes assigns to equity within legal order, as discussed in the Prologue. The reviewer's helpful suggestion, that I cannot pursue here, is that 'but for the peculiar way that the court system developed in England, the fiduciary concept would likely have arisen as part of the common law itself, and so, in essence, the collapsing of common law and equity within one court system after the 1870s is, in a way, a return to an earlier idea, that the common law of England embraced the ancient idea of equity derived from sources like Aristotle'.

Over time, courts have extended the fiduciary concept from trusts to scores of private relations and professional relationships.[42] I will examine several of these fiduciary relationships and others that, taken together, pave the way to affirming a state-subject fiduciary relationship: ie parents *vis-à-vis* children (the normative basis of the fiduciary obligation); directors *vis-à-vis* corporations (fiduciary duties can arise in the absence of pre-existent legal interests); shipmaster agents of necessity *vis-à-vis* cargo owners (fiduciaries can bind their beneficiaries without prior consent); pension fund directors *vis-à-vis* fund beneficiaries (fiduciary duties can be owed to multiple beneficiaries with competing claims, a crucial point discussed immediately below); arbitrators *vis-à-vis* the parties before them (fiduciaries can sometimes hold powers their beneficiaries are not entitled to exercise); and the Crown *vis-à-vis* Aboriginal peoples (a general, public fiduciary relationship is possible).

I.3 TOWARDS FIDUCIARY DUTIES IN PUBLIC SETTINGS

In later chapters I argue that public law duties of fairness and reasonableness may be justified and understood as public fiduciary obligations which supply content to the rule of law. This idea may seem especially implausible to private lawyers accustomed to viewing the fiduciary duty as exclusively a duty of loyalty to a particular beneficiary, so I pause now to sketch a conceptual argument in support of it.

The prevailing view in Canada is that the fiduciary principle can have no general application to public law because such an application is inconsistent with the content of the duty of loyalty.[43] There is an obvious tension between imposing rigorous and sometimes costly procedural safeguards, on the one hand, and concerns of administrative efficiency on the other. In some cases the affected individual's interest is bound to conflict with the interest of the general public. From the standpoint of fiduciary doctrine, it is not immediately apparent that the state can be a loyal fiduciary of both the individual and the general public, because the duties owed to each may conflict.

As we shall see now, however, the discrete fiduciary duty of loyalty is necessarily transformed into duties of fairness and reasonableness in private law cases with multiple beneficiaries whose interests conflict.[44] The plasticity

[42] See Jerry W Markham, 'Fiduciary Duties Under the Commodity Exchange Act' (1992) 68 Notre Dame L Rev 199, p 214 (setting out the expansion of the fiduciary concept).

[43] See eg, *Harris v Canada* 2001 FCR 1408; [2002] 2 FC 484 (FCTD) (*Harris*). I discuss *Harris* and the prevailing view in Chapter VI.

[44] See generally, PD Finn, *Fiduciary Obligations* (Sydney: Law Book Co, 1977), ch 13.

of the duty in the private sphere suggests that the hallmark duty of loyalty is not so immutable as to foreclose application of the fiduciary principle to public settings. While I later aim to show that public law duties of fairness and reasonableness are public fiduciary duties, the present argument seeks simply to lend a measure of initial plausibility to the prior idea that it is possible for administrative agencies to owe fiduciary duties of fairness and reasonableness to multiple beneficiaries.

In some multiple beneficiary cases the common law has developed sophisticated rules to guide the fiduciary's exercise of discretion. The rules in *Howe v Lord Dartmouth*,[45] for example, are intended to guide trustees who must convert assets from a will and then apportion income or deemed income among distinct beneficiaries who have conflicting interests. More generally, in such contexts the duty of loyalty has to manifest itself as fairness and reasonableness because the fiduciary principle can authorize the use of fiduciary power only to the extent that such use respects each person's co-equal status as a beneficiary of the fiduciary principle's authorization of fiduciary power. Put another way, the fiduciary principle, as a legal principle, must treat similarly situated beneficiaries as equals who possess a moral worth or dignity capable of triggering the principle's application. Call this the 'equal dignity constraint'. But for that constraint, the fiduciary principle could set arbitrarily the terms of the fiduciary's mandate to the prejudice of others who are similarly situated.[46]

We can now see that the duty of fairness arises from two features of the law's ability to authorize fiduciary power. First, we must presume that the law *can* authorize *some* fiduciary power where there are multiple classes of beneficiaries, as in fact it does.[47] Second, the law is *incapable* of authorizing *any* kind of fiduciary power that can be exercised arbitrarily between legal persons. The duty of fairness, then, arises as a default principle, because fair exercises of fiduciary power—exercises which conform with the constraint of equal dignity and an absence of arbitrary discriminations—are all that the law is capable of authorizing as a matter of principle.

[45] *Howe v Lord Dartmouth* (1802) 7 Ves 137 and *Re Earl of Chesterfield's Trusts* (1883) 24 Ch D 643.

[46] There may be some cases in which a fiduciary has a reason to treat distinct classes of beneficiaries differentially (eg a trustee may be required by the terms of the trust to protect the interests of an infant beneficiary above all others). But these are not problem cases because the presence of a reason implies that the differential treatment is not arbitrary.

[47] As Finn puts it: 'It is uncontroversial fiduciary law that where a fiduciary serves classes of beneficiaries possessing different rights, though obliged to act in the interests of the beneficiaries as a whole, the fiduciary is nonetheless required to act fairly as between different classes of beneficiary in taking decisions which affect the rights and interests of the classes *inter se*', PD Finn, 'The Forgotten "Trust": The People and the State' in Malcom Cope (ed), *Equity: Issues and Trends* (Sydney: Federation Press, 1995), p 138.

A similar argument can be made with respect to the fiduciary's duty of reasonableness. Whereas fairness sets a limit on how the fiduciary may exercise power as between distinct classes of beneficiaries, reasonableness establishes a floor applicable to the interests of them all. A fiduciary could not claim to fulfil her duty by disregarding wantonly but even-handedly the interests of each beneficiary. As the Supreme Court of Canada held in *Wewaykum Indian Band v Canada*,[48] when the Crown has a fiduciary duty to parties whose interests conflict, that duty requires it to act 'with loyalty, good faith, full disclosure appropriate to the subject matter and with "ordinary" diligence in what it reasonably regarded as the best interests of the beneficiaries'.[49] The law cannot authorize the fiduciary to exercise discretionary control over the beneficiary's interests without requiring the fiduciary to act in what she reasonably regards as the beneficiary's best interests.[50]

Indeed, the nature of the duty of loyalty suggests that loyalty *must* take the form of fairness and reasonableness where beneficiaries have competing claims against the same fiduciary. If a fiduciary were to favour one party arbitrarily at the expense of another to whom she owed the same duty of loyalty, she would necessarily violate her duty to the party suffering the relative disadvantage. Fairness coupled with reasonableness permit a public fiduciary to universalize her duty of loyalty in such a way as to fulfil her legal obligation to act in the interest of each.[51] In other words, these duties supply the legal framework necessary for the fiduciary to exercise discretionary

[48] *Wewaykum Indian Band v Canada* 2002 SCC 79; [2002] 4 SCR 245.

[49] Ibid, para 97.

[50] There is much debate in fiduciary scholarship over the question of whether fiduciary duties encompass duties of care. While the fiduciary duty to act in what one reasonably regards as the best interests of the beneficiary may resemble a tort duty of care, it is nonetheless distinct. Tort duties are negative duties of non-interference in the sense that they can be satisfied by not doing anything that interferes with another person's bodily integrity or property. The fiduciary duty to act with due regard for the best interests of the beneficiary usually requires more than non-interference; it requires sensitivity and action commensurate with the degree of discretionary control the fiduciary possesses over the beneficiary's entrusted interests. A fiduciary may act negligently in what she reasonably regards as the best interests of the beneficiary. For instance, a company officer may order her company to purchase certain assets in compliance with her fiduciary duty, but she may make the order without doing routine due diligence, in breach of her tort duty. For argument in favour of the so-called fiduciary duty of care, see Steven Elliot, 'Fiduciary Liability for Client Mortgage Fraud' (1999) 13 Trust Law Int'l 74. For the contrary view, see *Bristol and West Building Society v Mothew* [1998] Ch 1 CA (Eng) *per* Millet LJ. For an approach that seeks a middle ground (though one much closer to Millet LJ's opinion), see Peter Birks, 'The Content of the Fiduciary Obligation' (2000) 1 Isr LR 3.

[51] There is a parallel here to democratic theory, which generally asserts that representatives must act on behalf of everyone and not only on behalf of those who voted them into office. Whereas democratic theory explains this feature in terms of the political legitimacy of the democratic process (which usually involves elections), the fiduciary view of legal authority explains impartiality in Kantian terms of what a fiduciary must do to attend loyally and attentively to the interests of a wide constituency.

authority in a way that permits her to act as loyally as possible on behalf of each person subject to her authority. It is in this sense that, in a public setting with multiple classes of beneficiaries, we can say that loyalty amounts to fairness and reasonableness.

Thus, the argument in favour of conceptualizing public authority in fiduciary terms is not based simply on an analogy to private fiduciary relations (an analogy I do attempt to establish in later chapters). Perhaps what matters most in conceptualizing public authority in fiduciary terms is the underlying idea that power cannot be exercised by a public body without a concomitant assumption of duties of fairness and reasonableness. These duties embody a commitment to loyalty, and therefore help to justify the fiduciary's legal authority to exercise power on behalf of each person subject to it. On this account, the most fundamental and general fiduciary duty is not loyalty to an individual or a discrete class of beneficiaries, but fidelity to the other-regarding purposes for which fiduciary power is held. Such fidelity includes loyalty (or fairness and reasonableness as variants of it), but reflects better the nature of the fiduciary principle as one capable of application, in the prescribed circumstances, to any number of classes of beneficiaries.

The remainder of this introduction elaborates further on some of the general features of the rule of law that flow from the fiduciary view of the state.

1.4 A LEGAL CONCEPTION

The fiduciary conception of the rule of law is based on a kind of relationship and normativity that is legal in nature. The argument is also political. It is an argument for a legal order congenial to liberal democracy because it ensures that delegated powers are used equitably in the furtherance of public goals.[52] Thus the fiduciary conception of the rule of law has political implications in that it conditions the exercise of public power. Nevertheless, there is no commitment to a particular substantive or distributive theory of justice, nor reliance on the kinds of arguments and justifications that attend full-blown theories of justice.

The methodology common to most contemporary political philosophy considers an array of possible outcomes or a process of acquisition in which units of value (eg happiness, resources, primary goods) are distributed across a set of persons. The justice of the outcomes or the process is then

[52] As the discussion of Hobbes in the Prologue suggests, the idea of the state as fiduciary is consistent with a wide range of political orders and programmes. The reference to liberal democracy in the text should not be read to imply the exclusion of other political orders. That said, in Chapter IX I discuss in general terms the kinds of regimes and legislation that would strain the idea of legality defended here.

considered in light of our intuitions regarding values such as substantive fairness,[53] happiness,[54] equality,[55] or the sanctity of property rights and free exchange.[56] The methodology adopted here to evaluate the idea of the state as fiduciary is far more circumscribed in that it is limited to consideration of the demands of legality. Specifically, I consider the relevance of a particular legal doctrine—fiduciary doctrine—to the state's authority to secure legal order. And, while the view endorsed has ineliminable liberal elements, such as the freedom and equality of persons, it is republican as well as liberal in that the conception of freedom it seeks to uphold includes freedom as non-domination. There is also at least one sense in which the theory's scope is wider and more inclusive than liberalism.

The defining hallmark of liberalism is that the ultimate unit of moral value is the individual. For law, however, the unit to which rights and duties attach is the legal person.[57] The two are not the same. An individual has legal personality, but so do a wide variety of groups, such as unions, corporations, communities, Indigenous peoples, and municipalities.The rule of law applies to legal persons, and not just to individuals. The rule of law is therefore consistent with any political theory, liberal or otherwise, which does not violate the fiduciary constraints of the state-subject fiduciary relationship.

Defending the rule of law and a conception of the state from a legal perspective may seem either overly restrictive or premised on a hopelessly romantic (and false) vision of law's autonomous emancipatory potential. Many theorists from disparate points of view claim that law is or should be an instrument in the service of a broader agenda. For utilitarian reformers such as Bentham and Mill, law was simply the tool through which progressive social and economic policies were to be implemented. The same is true of contemporary positivists, such as HLA Hart and Joseph Raz. For those who subscribe to Law and Economics, the instrumental value of law lies in its ability to maximize market efficiencies by lowering transaction costs or

[53] See eg, John Rawls, *A Theory of Justice* (Cambridge, Mass: Belknap Press of Harvard University Press, 1971), and especially his discussion of the world we would choose to live in if we had to choose from behind a veil of ignorance that deprived us of knowledge of our actual position in the world.

[54] See eg, John Harsanyi, 'Cardinal Utility in Welfare Economics and in the Theory of Risk-taking' (1953) 61(5) *Journal of Political Economy* 434. Harsanyi first developed the veil of ignorance thought experiment that Rawls would later use, but Harsanyi thought it supported an argument for utilitarianism.

[55] See eg, RJ Arneson, 'Liberal Egalitarianism and World Resource Distribution: Two Views' (1989) 23(3) *Journal of Value Inquiry* 171 and G Cohen, 'Self-Ownership, World-Ownership, and Equality' in Frank S Lucash and Judith N Shklar (eds), *Justice and Equality Here and Now* (Ithaca: Cornell University Press, 1986).

[56] See eg, Robert Nozick, *Anarchy, State, and Utopia* (New York: Basic Books, 1974).

[57] For positivists the idea of legal personality may not denote moral value *per se*, but the legal person is nonetheless the basic unit in any legal order to which rights and obligations attach.

otherwise enabling resources to be acquired by their highest valued user. For Critical Legal Studies scholars, law is chiefly an instrument of oppression, ossifying unjustifiable distributions of resources through the legalized privilege that property affords.

There are advantages, however, to adopting a conception of the rule of law that treats legal norms and standards as intrinsically valuable in their own right, independent of the particular social goals or policies they may (or may not) help to secure. If legal norms can be shown to have intrinsic value, then their authority requires no further *prima facie* justification in terms of some greater good or political ideal. On this view, legal norms are independently valuable, and within that value we find the moral basis of the state's legal authority, as well as the subject's duty to obey the law.

In addition, if the rule of law can be articulated as an intrinsically valuable principle of legality, it offers some insulation from the vicissitudes of politics. The executive may always choose to exercise power in contravention of the rule of law, but it may be forced to pay a political price because, whatever the reasons for its actions, it will be vulnerable to criticism that such actions offend morality precisely because they offend legality.

On a more positive note, the state-subject fiduciary relationship may be shown to constitute and justify legal authority to the same extent and on the same basis as it constrains exercises of public power. As a consequence, and as I argue later, a state that lives up to its fiduciary mandate gives its subjects a reason to obey its laws. One of the basic functions of the state is to secure a regime that protects the legal rights of those within it. As a final resort, it deploys the courts and legal institutions to guarantee those rights. But more important than enforcement mechanisms is the fidelity to law the state can demand in virtue of the legitimacy of its legal authority. Because the state as fiduciary owes an impartial duty of loyalty to abide by the rule of law to those within its jurisdiction, it has a moral argument on which to base its claim to legal authority, and in return (other things being equal) can expect allegiance to its laws. When the state violates its fiduciary duty and the rule of law, its legitimacy comes into question, and so too does the obedience it can reasonably expect from its people.

Finally, and most significantly, we shall see that the fiduciary theory of the state gives us reason to think that legal order does have intrinsic moral value, and so any adequate elaboration of the rule of law must take this non-instrumental moral value into account. I argue that there is a necessary, conceptual connection between law and morality, one that is ultimately grounded on the moral worth of human agency within the state-subject fiduciary relationship.

I.5 A RELATIONAL CONCEPTION

To say that a conception of the rule of law is relational means that there is some relationship on which it is based. This relational aspect does not confer any normative laurels on the conception, for slaves and masters too are in a certain kind of relationship. Yet the relational dimension has consequences for the structure of the model under consideration. A relational conception of the rule of law cannot be grounded solely on the characteristics of a single party to the relationship, for example on the dignity of the person subject to the law. Nor, conversely, can the conception be based entirely on an abstract notion of public duty ascribed to state authorities in the absence of any reference to the persons to whom the duty is owed. A relational conception of the rule of law implicates at least two distinct parties, and seeks to derive the implications of the rule of law from the relationship between them.

In this case, the fiduciary relationship, at its most abstract level, is between the state and each person subject to its power and authority. The civil or political status of the person subject to state authority does not matter because the relational view looks to the characteristics of the relationship alone to establish legal standards and obligations. For this reason, I refer to the person subject to state authority as a subject, agent, individual, or party rather than a citizen. The fiduciary and relational conception explains why anyone subject to legal authority, regardless of status, is an equal co-beneficiary of the rule of law.

Another feature of the relational account is that it goes beyond philosophizing over first principles. Consider once again the common law duty of procedural fairness that constrains discretionary decision-making. Judges who support such a duty often trace it to a principle of fairness said to inhere in the basic tenets of the common law. This principle in turn relies on the intuition that arbitrary exercises of legal powers are intrinsically unlawful. But an appeal to non-arbitrariness is insufficient to advance the debate. It fails to convince Cartwright J and his successors because, in their view, discretionary decisions *can* be rendered for virtually any reason whatsoever.

Instead, what is required to undermine Cartwright J's position is a conception of the rule of law that succeeds in positing a relationship between the decision-maker and the individuals. The Cartwright camp assumes that the decision-maker and the individual do not stand in a legal relationship to one another. So, if the legislation is silent, administrative agencies constitute 'a law unto themselves'. Without a legal relationship on which to rest the duty of fairness, it will always be open for a judge of Cartwright J's ilk to say that procedural safeguards are required as a matter of law only if there is a basis for them in the relevant statute. The fiduciary view provides such a relationship.

1.6 A KANTIAN, INTERACTIONAL CONCEPTION

Closely related to the relational and legal nature of the fiduciary view is its capacity to recognize the right-bearing capacity of practical interests subject to public authority, such as Roncarelli's interest in a liquor permit. This view contrasts with the orthodox approaches to both administrative law and the law of fiduciary obligations. Legal standards in administrative law are not usually justified and characterized in the first instance as individual rights. The orthodox view is that public law is more about remedying public wrongs than affirming individual rights.[58] Its language reflects this perspective: legal norms are described primarily as duties (eg the duty of fairness, the duty to give reasons) rather than rights. Justifications of public law duties tend to refer to public values such as the need for a bulwark against executive arbitrariness and the public's interest in the proper use of statutory authority.

The mainstream approach to fiduciary doctrine parallels the orthodox approach to public law; in both cases, inquiry focuses on the content of the relevant legal duties and the conditions under which they arise. The approach I advocate pays equal attention to the beneficiary's right and the fiduciary's duty, and conceives of them as correlative to each other. The presence of one entails the presence of the other because, in the event of breach, the reason for vindicating the beneficiary's right must also be a reason to hold the fiduciary liable.[59]

The fiduciary conception of the rule of law is driven by a concern for rights which flow exclusively from a particular kind of interaction and legal relationship. The interactional genesis of such rights makes them intrinsic to law because they arise solely from the factual circumstances that trigger the fiduciary principle, circumstances in which vulnerable interests are entrusted to the discretionary authority of others. The intrinsic-to-law view is brought into sharp relief by comparing it to the instrumental understanding of fiduciary doctrine at times suggested by Leonard Rotman, Canada's leading scholar on the fiduciary relationship recognized to exist between the Crown and Canada's First Nations.[60]

[58] See eg, The Right Honourable Lord Woolf of Barnes, 'Droit Public-English Style' (1994) PL 57, pp 61–5. With the advent of the Charter, there has been a shift in emphasis in Canadian public law towards the recognition and vindication of rights. However, if Charter rights are not at stake, public law norms such as fairness and reasonableness are still characterized primarily as obligations rather than rights, and to that extent reflect the orthodox view of public law.

[59] See Ernest Joseph Weinrib, *The Idea of Private Law* (Cambridge: Harvard University Press, 1995), ch 3. The approach I adopt to the law of fiduciaries is indebted to the analysis of private law Weinrib elucidates in *The Idea of Private Law* and elsewhere. See esp Ernest Joseph Weinrib, 'The Juridical Classification of Obligations' in Peter Birks (ed), *The Classification of Obligations* (Oxford: Clarendon Press, 1997). While Weinrib's focus is tort law, he suggests that it applies with equal force to fiduciary cases.

[60] See Leonard Ian Rotman, *Parallel Paths: Fiduciary Doctrine and the Crown-Native Relationship in Canada* (Toronto: University of Toronto Press, 1996).

In general, Rotman defends a context-sensitive approach to fiduciary law, one that takes seriously a relationship's particular features in light of general legal principles that underlie fiduciary doctrine. Nevertheless, he also attributes a broader public policy goal to the fiduciary principle: 'The policy underlying the law of fiduciaries is focused on a desire to preserve and protect the integrity of socially valuable or necessary relationships which arise from human interdependency'.[61] Public policy rationales such as this are instrumental because they see the law as an instrument in the service of some good that is external to the parties' relationship. The fiduciary's duty is not justified on the basis of legal characteristics found within the relationship, such as those outlined by Wilson J in *Frame*. Rather, the duty is justified instrumentally in terms of a further purpose (socially valuable relationships), and in abstraction from the relationship in which it operates. The relational and intrinsic-to-law view, on the other hand, conceptualizes fiduciary law as a matter of rights and duties which are justified exclusively on the basis of the interaction between the fiduciary and the beneficiary.

There are at least three ways in which the justification of the fiduciary's obligation is connected to the beneficiary's correlative right. First, the justification for imposing a fiduciary duty relies on the beneficiary having a right to the duty in the circumstances of its application. Second, the content of the obligation (the duty to act within the other-regarding purpose for which fiduciary power is held) cannot be justified without reference to the underlying right. Finally, the beneficiary's right supplies a moral argument for the justice of imposing a fiduciary duty and its remedial consequences on someone who assumes fiduciary powers. But to see how the beneficiary's right participates in the justification of the fiduciary's obligation in any of these ways, we need to examine the moral basis of the right.

Kant sets out the requisite moral basis in an argument concerning the duties parents owe their children, duties that arise as a consequence of a particular unilateral undertaking on the part of the parents[62]:

[61] Ibid, p 152. This rationale surfaces frequently in the fiduciary literature. See eg, Tamara Frankel, 'Fiduciary Law: The Judicial Process and the Duty of Care', *The 1993 Isaac Pitblado Lectures: Fiduciary Duties/Conflicts of Interest* (Winnipeg: Law Society of Manitoba, 1993), p 145.

[62] Immanuel Kant, *The Metaphysics of Morals*, trans by Mary Gregor (New York: Cambridge University Press, 1991) (first published in 1797), pp 98–9 (6:281) (emphasis in original, footnote omitted). Kant divides his discussion of morals into doctrines of right and virtue. Right goes to norms that can be enforced with state power (laws); virtue goes to norms that state power cannot be called on to enforce (ethics). I limit my discussion to certain aspects of Kant's theory of right. It is settled law in Canada that parents owe their children fiduciary duties: *M(K) v M(H)* [1992] 3 SCR 6. For an argument that US family law should follow suit, see Elizabeth S Scott and Robert E Scott, 'Parents as Fiduciaries' (1995) 81 Va L Rev 2401.

> [C]hildren, as persons, have by their procreation an original innate (not acquired) right to the care of their parents until they are able to look after themselves, and they have this right directly on the basis of principle (*lege*), that is, without any special act being required to establish this right.
>
> For the offspring is a *person*, and it is impossible to form a concept of the production of a being endowed with freedom through a physical operation. So from a *practical* point of view it is a quite correct and even necessary Idea to regard the act of procreation as one by which we have brought a person into the world without his consent and on our own initiative, for which deed the parents incur an obligation to make the child content with his condition so far as they can. They cannot destroy their child as if he were something they had *made* (since a being endowed with freedom cannot be a product of this kind) or as if he were their property, nor can they even just abandon him to chance, since they have brought not merely a worldly being but a citizen of the world into a condition which cannot now be indifferent to them even just according to concepts of Right.

To understand Kant's argument, we need to review briefly some of the central features of his theory of right, which includes a very specific conception of the idea of innate right on which his argument rests. For Kant, rights embody our moral capacity for putting others under legal obligations.[63] If I take first possession of a thing, I acquire a property right to it such that others are now under an obligation to let me possess, use, and alienate it as I see fit.[64] If I enter into a contract, I acquire a contractual right to the other party's performance, and thereby place that party under an obligation to perform.[65] Kant refers to property and contractual entitlements as acquired rights, because some act is required on the part of the right-holder for her to acquire them. An innate right, on the other hand, 'is that which belongs to everyone by nature, independently of any act that would establish a right'.[66] All rights at private law, for Kant, are either innate or acquired. Moreover, persons have one, and only one, innate right, which each possesses equally by virtue of their shared humanity: that is, the right to as much freedom as can coexist with the freedom of everyone else.

Freedom, Kant explains, is 'independence from being constrained by another's choice'.[67] It follows that in a world where interaction with others is unavoidable, law must enshrine rights within a regime of equal freedom in which no party can unilaterally impose terms of interaction on another. Individuals must treat each other as ends and never as mere means; they must not instrumentalize one another. Just as importantly, however,

[63] Kant, *supra* note 62, p 63 (6:237).

[64] Ibid, p 84 (6:263). For Kant's discussion of property rights, see ibid, pp 82–90 (6:261–70).

[65] For Kant's discussion of contract, see ibid, pp 90–5 (6:271–6).

[66] Ibid, p 63 (6:237). [67] Ibid, p 63 (6:238).

individuals are entitled to independence in the sense that one person cannot be left to depend on the mercy of another; individuals must not stand in a relationship of domination to one another. Kant thought that the state had duty to provide support to the poor precisely because the poor would otherwise be left dependent on others.[68] The normative constitution of equal freedom, then, consists in principles of non-instrumentalization and non-domination. These principles set the limits of rightful action by illuminating what it means to enjoy independence from another's choice.

With these precepts in mind, consider Kant's claim that children have an innate right to their parents' care. It is easy to see that the child's right cannot be an acquired right, since the child does nothing to acquire it. She is simply born. The part that needs further explication is how the child's innate right to equal freedom—a right to equal independence from the wills of others, including her parents—can place the parents under an obligation to care for the child. Although strangers have the same innate right to equal freedom as the child, parents owe them none of the special duties they owe their children.

To establish the necessary connection between parent and child, Kant points to the act of procreation, an act that brings a helpless and vulnerable child into the world without the child's consent. Procreation is the interactional trigger that gives rise to the parents' obligation. But the obligation is not perpetual; it lasts only until the child reaches majority and can act on her own behalf.

Putting together these features of the parent-child relationship with Kant's theory of right, we can now explain how the child's innate right of humanity gives rise to her parents' obligation. The child's innate right is a moral capacity to place her parents under obligation without any action being required of the child. This much shows that the obligation is possible, not that it is actual. What makes it actual, and necessary from the point of view of Kant's theory, is the presence of the parent-child relationship to which the child cannot consent. Specifically, the child cannot consent to either the creation of the relationship or the ongoing exercise of parental powers within it. Because the parents' legal powers over the child cannot be justified on the basis of mutual consent, those powers can meet the demands of legality only if the law places the parents under an obligation to exercise them in what they reasonably regard as the child's best interests.

It follows that the child's inability to consent, not the child's inability to care for herself, is the critical factor that combines with the parents' act of procreation to trigger the obligation. The child's lack of capacity to care for

[68] Ibid, pp 135–6 (6:325–6).

herself informs the content of the obligation; the parents must act in what they reasonably regard as the child's best interests. Nonetheless, a mere inability to care for oneself is not sufficient to give rise to a parental obligation, even in the presence of a legal relationship. We can enter into contracts with consenting parties who have little ability to care for themselves (perhaps due to sickness or disability) without incurring parent-like obligations towards them. These considerations suggest that the child's inability to consent matters to parental obligation in a way that her inability to care for herself does not.

For Kant, the parents' obligation takes hold because no party can unilaterally impose terms of interaction on another. When the parents unilaterally create a person who cannot survive without their support, the child's innate moral capacity to place the parents under obligation is triggered to ensure the child's security. The parents' freedom to procreate can thus coexist with the child's right to security from the perils of a condition to which she never consented.[69] Put another way, the parents have brought into being a 'citizen of the world', and one implication of citizenship in Kant's world of secure and equal freedom is recognition and affirmation of the child-citizen's innate moral capacity to put her parents under obligation.

The child is thereby treated as a person worthy of respect in her own right, as an end, and not as a mere thing the parents can destroy or abandon.[70] The child has dignity by virtue of her moral personhood, and dignity proscribes regarding her as if she were a mere thing. By the same

[69] Kidnappers of children present a puzzle. I will argue in Chapter IV that fiduciary relations must take the form of legal institutions which can respect the requirements of secure and equal freedom. The family is one such institution. Thus, adoptive as well as biological parents are fiduciaries because both bring a child into their custody within a legal institution, ie the family. But kidnapping is not a legal institution because kidnapping is intrinsically wrongful. It would seem to follow that kidnappers are not in a fiduciary relationship with their child victims. Yet suppose a kidnapper (perhaps a non-custodial parent) seizes an infant, absconds to a foreign jurisdiction, and raises the child. If the kidnapper deprives the child of an education, sexually abuses him, or hires him out and keeps the proceeds of his labour, the kidnapper commits a series of additional wrongs that the initial (and persisting) wrong of kidnapping cannot fully explain. The kidnapper appears to breach parent-like fiduciary obligations owed to the child as a consequence of the kidnapper's custody of the child. We can account for these fiduciary or parent-like obligations if we assume that kidnapping makes the kidnapper the child's *guardian*. The kidnapper *qua* kidnapper owes no fiduciary duties, but the kidnapper *qua* guardian does, because the guardian-ward relationship is a legal institution susceptible to fiduciary duties. In the case of kidnapped *adults*, however, kidnappers do not owe fiduciary duties to their victims because adults cannot relate to each other as guardian and ward. Adults cannot relate to each other this way because (comatose patients aside, and unlike children) both are capable of consenting (or not) to the relationship. We will see in Chapter IV that kidnappers owe adult hostages tort but not fiduciary duties (even though some of these duties look fiduciary-like, such as the kidnapper's duty to feed the hostage).

[70] Because persons are self-determining and free beings capable of being held responsible for their actions, Kant can define a person as 'a subject whose actions can be *imputed* to him', Kant, *supra* note 63, p 50 (6:223). A thing, on the other hand, is '[a]ny object of free choice which itself lacks freedom', and thus a thing 'is that to which nothing can be imputed', ibid (emphasis in original).

token, legal personality and the idea of dignity intrinsic to it supply the moral basis of the beneficiary's right to the fiduciary obligation. A relationship in which the fiduciary has unilateral power over the beneficiary's interests can be understood as a relationship mediated by law only if the fiduciary (like the parent) is precluded from exploiting her position to set unilaterally the terms of her relationship with the beneficiary. The fiduciary principle renders the beneficiary's entrusted interests immune to the fiduciary's appropriation because those interests, in the context of fiduciary relations, are treated as inviolate embodiments of the beneficiary's dignity as a person. In short, the fiduciary principle authorizes the fiduciary to exercise power on the beneficiary's behalf, but subject to strict limitations arising from the beneficiary's worth as a person and vulnerability to fiduciary power.

Because the fiduciary's authority to exercise power is explicable in terms of the bounds set by the beneficiary's personality, the fiduciary duty may be characterized as a duty to exercise power exclusively for the sake of the other-regarding purposes for which it is held. Moreover, the presence of the beneficiary's personality in the fiduciary relationship explains why lawful exercises of fiduciary power must be other-regarding: the beneficiary is a separate legal person and worthy of respect in her own right.

The idea of personality also explains why the fiduciary duty can be characterized independently of any particular purpose. Personality denotes a capacity for purposive action, but it does not denote any particular purpose or action *per se*. Thus, rightful exercises of fiduciary power, in principle, may attempt to satisfy any lawful purpose so long as the purpose is other-regarding in the sense that it respects the limits established by the beneficiary's personality within a regime of equal freedom. In most cases, of course, the fiduciary's power will be constrained explicitly; for example, by the terms of a trust, a company's objectives, a governing statute, or a court order. But the nature of the other-regarding obligation that attends an exercise of fiduciary power, as in the parent-child case, remains explicable in terms of the beneficiary's innate moral capacity to place the fiduciary under obligation.

I argue in a later chapter that a moral idea of trust premised on a Kantian conception of right helps explain both the authority and obligation under which a fiduciary exercises power. As with our innate right of humanity, trust can place others under obligation without the right-holder doing anything to acquire the right to the obligation. It is sufficient for the law, through the fiduciary principle, to entrust the fiduciary with administrative power over others. To say that the fiduciary does and must exercise power on the basis of the beneficiary's trust is just to say the following: the beneficiary is a person innately capable of subjecting the fiduciary to a legal obligation to respect the beneficiary's entrusted interests as legally protected interests properly belonging to the beneficiary alone. Acting on the basis of trust, then, is acting with due regard for the fact that the beneficiary is a person who must be treated as an end in herself, as a being whose interests in the context of a fiduciary relationship are not subject to the fiduciary's appropriation. It is in this sense that, in the parent-child case, the law requires the parent to act on the basis of the child's trust precisely because the child cannot consent to the parent-child relationship. As we shall see in greater detail, the Kantian justification of the fiduciary obligation helps to explicate the sense in which fiduciary relationships are trust-like.

1.7 A CHALLENGE TO LIBERTARIANISM

While the fiduciary theory of the state commended here does not presuppose a full-blown theory of justice, it does promise a fresh reply to libertarianism. Libertarians such as Robert Nozick and Richard Epstein claim that the only valid legal norms are the norms of private law, and so the rule of law should be limited to the state enforcing private legal obligations and criminal law (the minimal state).[71] The administrative state, for them, is suspect because it interferes with private order. The fiduciary conception of the state suggests a three-step argument against libertarianism. The first is to grant the authority of private law. The second is to show that the state and subject face one another in circumstances legally equivalent to those which give rise to a particular kind of private law relationship, namely, a fiduciary relationship. The third step is to argue that this relationship has anti-libertarian consequences, such as affirmation of an administrative state that interferes with private order, and recognition that a commitment to the rule of law entails a commitment to human rights. If this argument succeeds, it will fall to the libertarian to explain why private legal norms are authoritative when they structure relations between private parties, but lack authority when the state participates in a fact situation characteristic of one to which private legal norms would otherwise apply.

The libertarian will face a steep climb because the normative basis of the fiduciary obligation (or the beneficiary's right) is drawn exclusively from Kant's austere theory of right. As we have seen, for Kant, rights at private law are grounded on freedom rather than welfare. Private law is regarded as an autonomous mode of justice that is indifferent to welfare and egalitarian concerns. Issues of need, happiness, preference satisfaction, or desire

[71] See Nozick, *supra* note 56; RA Epstein, 'No New Property' (1990) 56 Brook L Rev 747.

fulfilment are irrelevant. So too is distributive justice and any calls it might make to address inequalities by redistributing resources. Relying on Kant's theory of private law therefore permits the fiduciary view of the state to engage the libertarian on what are arguably her own best terms.

I.8 BEYOND THE STATE

Before turning to a summary outline of the argument, a brief comment is in order on the scope of the fiduciary theory of public authority and the state-centric focus of this book. Sovereign states are not the only entities that exercise state or state-like powers. In many areas of the world, non-state actors exercise powers of unilateral public administration comparable to the sovereign powers of conventional states. Examples include such varied institutions as the UN Interim Administration for East Timor, the Palestinian Authority, and the legal institutions of Aboriginal peoples. That the international community does not recognize these entities as full-fledged sovereign states does not render the fiduciary principle inapplicable to them, for as we shall see, it is an entity's assumption of state or state-like administrative powers, not *de jure* statehood *per se*, that triggers the fiduciary principle. If the general argument in favour of a fiduciary theory of public authority is persuasive, then quite plausibly any entity that assumes quasi-sovereign administrative power over individuals will be subject to fiduciary constraints. I will also suggest later that the fiduciary view of authority is fractal in the sense that it retains the same structure on any scale. This fractal property allows the fiduciary theory to explain (non-consensual) authority on any scale, from parent-child relations through to the state-subject relationship. But the centre of attention of this work remains the state-subject fiduciary relationship.

I.9 SUMMARY OF THE ARGUMENT

In Chapter II, I discuss the fiduciary relationship the Supreme Court of Canada has recognized between the Crown and Aboriginal peoples. The First Nations case is significant because it demonstrates that public and far-reaching fiduciary obligations are possible. The Court, I argue, has turned to fiduciary doctrine in an attempt to legitimize the Crown's claim to sovereignty over Canada's Indigenous peoples. While the result is an improvement over prior Aboriginal subjection to unfettered Crown discretion, we shall see that the legitimacy of Crown sovereignty in relation to Aboriginal peoples remains starkly limited by the reluctance of the Crown to recognize Aboriginal sovereignty.

In Chapter III, I reply to arguments that allege that the public fiduciary model no has wider application than the Crown-Native relationship. The *sui generis* nature of Aboriginal rights and the Crown-Native relationship supports a conclusion that some fiduciary duties owed to Aboriginal peoples will have distinctive content. But non-Aboriginals, too, confront a state with irresistible sovereign powers that trigger an overarching fiduciary obligation.

Chapter IV develops a distinction to be introduced in Chapter II between legal and political authority. Legal authority is the authority to make, interpret, administer, and enforce law. This authority to establish legal order arises from the state-subject fiduciary relationship. Political authority presupposes legal authority, but has other elements as well, such as the authority to determine the content of ordinary law through legislation. Political authority also encompasses issues of political representation; states are more or less democratic depending on how these issues are resolved. In Chapter IV, I also set out the necessary and sufficient conditions that give rise to fiduciary relations, and explain how the state-subject relationship satisfies them. I conclude that legal authority rests on the state-subject fiduciary relationship and a presumption that the state must exercise power on the basis of public trust, whereas democratic political authority rests (in part) on consent.

In Chapter V, I test the fiduciary theory of legal authority by asking whether it can support a defeasible duty to obey the law. The currently popular view is that there is no such duty, even if the law (or legal regime) in question is reasonably just. I argue in favour of a duty to obey on grounds that the state is a *public agent of necessity* whose mandate is to establish legal order on behalf of everyone subject to its powers. As an *agent*, the state is entitled to bind its principals by announcing law, always subject to fiduciary constraints. The state is an agent of *necessity* because its legal authority arises directly from law, from the fiduciary principle, rather than from the consent of the people. The state is a *public* agent of necessity because it possesses and exercises public powers that private parties are not entitled to exercise.

Chapter VI seeks to explain why Canadian courts have recognized so few public fiduciary duties outside the Crown-Native context, and why the connection has yet to be drawn between public law duties of fairness and reasonableness, on the one hand, and public fiduciary obligations, on the other. Courts have insisted that the claimants show a pre-existent right to the subject matter of the alleged fiduciary obligation, much as Cartwright J insisted on a pre-existing statutory limitation to control discretion. They have also clung fast to a formal private / public distinction according to which fiduciary duties belong almost exclusively to private law. The reasons that explain the dearth of fiduciary doctrine in public law, however, do not justify its absence. In developing this argument I will rely on the pioneering work of the scholar cited in the epigraph to this book, Paul Finn (now Justice Finn of the Federal Court of Australia), and in particular, on his careful explanation of how the idea of the state as fiduciary came to be neglected in commonwealth public law.

In Chapter VII, I argue that the duty of procedural fairness is best explained and justified as a public fiduciary duty. The fiduciary theory offers a novel reply to the most familiar objection raised against the idea of a common law duty of fairness. The objection is that judges illegitimately 'make law' and violate the separation of powers when they impose procedural safeguards that lack a basis in statute. On the fiduciary theory, the freestanding duty of fairness arises from the actual fiduciary conditions of public administration. Thus, judges who impose the duty no more infringe the separation of powers than judges who vindicate rights at private law: in both cases, the relevant rights and obligations arise from the circumstances of the parties' interaction.

In Chapter VIII, I claim that the fiduciary model answers a difficult question that arises in hard cases of administrative law in which an individual is subject to a drastic exercise of public power: if the individual has no pre-existing right to the vulnerable interest at stake (such as an interest in continued residence in a state in which she is not a citizen), why should the vulnerable interest figure at all in the balance when a decision-maker is called on to interpret and apply a statutory power? Under the fiduciary theory, the vulnerable interest must figure in the balance because fiduciaries owe solicitude to the people subject to their power. The chapter works out some of the details of this conception of administrative law, and relates them to evolving public law doctrines of judicial deference, review of agency interpretations of law, and review of discretion.

While Chapters VI through VIII consider the rule of law's regulation of the exercise of delegated public power, Chapter IX considers the lessons to be drawn from the fiduciary model concerning the form and content of legislation. Most contemporary scholarship on the rule of law follows Lon L Fuller in presuming that legislation respectful of the rule of law must generally conform to formal requirements such as publicity and clarity. Yet there is no consensus on the justification of these requirements. Against the instrumental view of positivists such as Joseph Raz, I argue that the rule of law has intrinsic moral value. This intrinsic value arises from the state-subject fiduciary relationship, and is ultimately grounded in human agency and dignity. I further contend that once we situate this non-positivist understanding of the rule of law within a fiduciary conception of the state, we can see that the rule of law, properly understood, places limits on the content of legislation: the legislature cannot pass laws which grossly violate human rights without at the same time running afoul of the rule of law.

To sum up: Chapters II and III show that it is possible for the state to stand in a public fiduciary relationship to its people. Chapters IV and V set out the theoretical underpinnings of the fiduciary theory of the state. Chapters VI through VIII explore the legal consequences of the administration's fiduciary position *vis-à-vis* the people. Chapter IX situates the fiduciary view of the state within a broader philosophical discussion of the rule of law, and shows how fiduciary constraints limit the form and content of legislation.

PART I

THE CROWN-NATIVE FIDUCIARY RELATIONSHIP

II

Seeking Sovereignty

2.1 INTRODUCTION

At the centre of the argument in this book is Hobbes' claim that a state's legal authority over its subjects requires special justification. The basic elements of the justification are revealed by two ways in which the state can fail to secure legal order. One way is through institutional weakness. Any properly functioning state needs legal and public institutions that can interpret and enforce the law as it is declared. If a state's institutions are ineffectual, they cannot guarantee the rights of persons subject to its authority. This is a failure of *de facto* sovereignty, as it is a failure in the state's actual ability to assert its statehood.

The second way in which the state can fail to secure legal order is by not living up to the moral demands of sovereignty, demands which crystallize in the rule of law. Consider a conquering state that enslaves the people of a defeated nation. The conquerors put in place a system of rules to regulate the master-slave relationship. The slaves know in advance, for instance, the punishment they will face if they resist their masters or attempt escape. Slaves are permitted to own a limited class of private property that can ground claims in tort and contract, but only as against other slaves. The slaves' rights are null as against their masters and the state itself. If one thinks that a state's assertion of sovereignty carries with it no obligations towards the state's people, this example does not show a failure on the part of the state to secure legal order. It shows only that the order established is wicked. I discuss slavery in Chapter IX, and suggest that while a slave regime may have elements one can find in a legal order properly so-called, at base it is just order backed by force. This is a failure in legality, or a failure of *de jure* sovereignty, as it is a failure to live up to the requirements of the rule of law rather than an inability to enforce the law.

Settler societies such as Canada potentially face an analogous failure in legality *vis-à-vis* Aboriginal peoples. Many First Nations have long rejected the settler state's claim of authority over them. In this chapter I argue that because there is no compelling account of how First Nations lost sovereignty over themselves and their lands to the Crown, the Supreme Court of Canada has recognized the existence of a Crown-Native fiduciary relationship in a bid to legitimize Crown sovereignty and resist a failure in legality. In other words, the Court has recognized the fiduciary relationship as a consequence of the Crown's unilateral assertion of sovereignty over Aboriginal peoples. Because many First Nations never consented to become subjects of the Crown and continue to resist its authority today, only the presumption of a fiduciary relationship has the potential to save the Crown's authority over First Nations from suffering a wholesale failure in legality.

Even short of this wholesale failure, there are reasons to think that the Court's use of fiduciary doctrine cannot save the all-things-considered legitimacy of Crown assertions of sovereignty. The fiduciary principle simply provides the most a court can offer to articulate a legal standard in the place of unfettered discretion. Despite having this legal standard in place, it remains far from clear that the Crown's claim to sovereignty over First Nations is more legitimate than their own claims of self-determination. Indeed, as we shall see, the fiduciary conception of public authority supports the idea that the people of every nation have a collective right of self-determination which entitles them to construct and maintain for themselves the legal institutions under which they live. I argue that unless a Crown-Native fiduciary relationship is assumed, the Crown's assertion of sovereignty amounts to an ongoing conquest which, if relatively bloodless, is nonetheless sustained by the threat of force and unmitigated by even minimal compliance with the demands of legality.

The distinction made here between partial compliance with the demands of legality and all-things-considered legitimacy is not novel. International law provides an instructive analogy. If one state invades another without provocation, but nonetheless subscribes faithfully to the Geneva Conventions, the invader conforms to at least some of what legality demands. The aggressor's conformity does not legitimize the invasion, it simply renders the invasion less corrosive of legality and less unjust than it would be otherwise. At its weakest, then, the fiduciary principle constrains exercises of state power, irrespective of its origins, with the aspiration that, in circumstances such as these, some legality is better than none.[1]

In what follows I discuss the leading cases on the Crown-Native fiduciary relationship, beginning with *Guerin v The Queen*[2] and *R v Sparrow*.[3] As a consequence of the Crown's assertion of sovereignty and the ensuing fiduciary relationship, the Crown must overcome an onerous justificatory burden if its

[1] Arguably, some legality is not always better than none. Statutes can establish kangaroo courts or show trials, for example. These help authoritarian power-holders appear to respect the demands of legality, when in fact legal forms are being used to subvert legality. For discussion, see David Dyzenhaus, *The Constitution of Law: Legality in a Time of Emergency* (Cambridge: Cambridge University Press, 2006).

[2] *Guerin v The Queen* [1982] 2 SCR 335 (*Guerin*).

[3] *R v Sparrow* [1990] 1 SCR 1075 (*Sparrow*).

legislative or administrative actions infringe Indigenous rights. Crown legal authority over First Nations and their lands, therefore, is both constituted and constrained by the framework supplied by the fiduciary relationship. While the judiciary's recognition of the relationship is explained as an attempt to legitimize Crown sovereignty, the best justification for viewing the Crown as a fiduciary relies on the vulnerability of Aboriginal peoples to the Crown's irresistible sovereign powers, the 'fact of sovereignty' introduced in the last chapter.

2.2 *GUERIN*, *SPARROW*, AND THE RESISTANCE OF ABORIGINAL TREATY RIGHTS TO DUALISM

One of the striking features of *Guerin* and *Sparrow* is that they are both unanimous decisions. The unanimity is striking in *Guerin* because the Court broke away entirely from past decisions that characterized Crown-Native relations in terms of legally unenforceable 'political trusts',[4] as well as from others that saw the formal requirements of trust law as an impenetrable barrier to the imposition of trust-like obligations on the Crown.[5] In *Sparrow* the unanimity is surprising given the extent to which the Court broadened the scope and elevated the status of the Crown's fiduciary obligations.

In *Guerin*, a Musqueam band surrendered reserve land to the Crown for the purpose of leasing it to a golf club. The Crown agent acquired the surrendered land on the assurance of specific, promised terms. The Crown then proceeded to lease the land on undisclosed terms that were less valuable to the band. The Crown agent concealed that other parties were interested in the lands, and that another Crown official seriously doubted the merits of the deal. The agent in fact urged and bullied the band into a lease he knew to be of sub-market value. The Crown refused to show the lease to the band, and it was not until 1970 (13 years after the surrender) that Chief Delbert Guerin was able to obtain a copy by going himself into the dusty basement of a local office of the Department of Indian Affairs and searching through boxes of government documents.[6]

[4] The leading British cases on political trusts are *Kinloch v Secretary of State for India* (1882) 7 AC 619 HL (Eng) and *Tito and Waddell (No 2)* [1977] 3 All ER 129 Ch (Eng). The leading Canadian case was *St Ann's Island Shooting and Fishing Club Ltd v The King* [1950] SCR 211 (*St Ann's*).

[5] See eg *Pawis v R* [1980] 2 FC 18 (FCTD). Laskin CJ died before the Court rendered judgment in *Guerin*. Three judges—Beetz, Chouinard, and Lamer JJ—concurred with Dickson J (as he then was). Wilson J found an express trust present on the facts, while Estey J held that the Crown was the band's agent. In the result, all judges found that a fiduciary relationship of one kind or another existed.

[6] For a comprehensive account of the case, the history that led to it, and the development of First Nation fiduciary law since, see James I Reynolds, *A Breach of Duty: Fiduciary Obligations and Aboriginal Peoples* (Saskatoon: Purich Publishing, 2005). Reynolds was one of the lawyers who represented the Musqueam in *Guerin*.

The Court found that a fiduciary obligation arose from the Musqueam's interest in the reserve land and the Indian Act's surrender requirements.[7] Dickson J noted that First Nations are prohibited from directly transferring their lands to third parties, and that any sale or lease can only be carried out after a surrender to the Crown has taken place, with the Crown then acting on the band's behalf.[8] The Crown thus had a general fiduciary obligation to act exclusively on behalf of the band, and a specific duty to seek fresh authorization from the band once it became apparent that the Crown could not secure the terms on which the band had surrendered its land.

The Court's reasoning was based entirely on common law fiduciary doctrine, with Dickson J (as he then was) finding that the Crown owed a fiduciary duty because it fell within the ambit of the following test: 'where by statute, agreement, or perhaps by unilateral undertaking, one party has an obligation to act for the benefit of another, and that obligation carries with it a discretionary power, the party thus empowered becomes a fiduciary'.[9] The Constitution Act 1982 was not yet in effect and did not figure in the decision. Because Dickson J tied the Crown's fiduciary duty to the surrender process, it was not clear following *Guerin* whether the fiduciary doctrine had wider application. Six years later, *Sparrow* established that it did.

Sparrow was charged with fishing with a drift-net longer than was permitted by his band's food fishing licence. The issue was whether s 35(1) of the Constitution Act 1982 limits Parliament's power to regulate Aboriginal fishing. The Court had yet to interpret s 35(1), which states that '[t]he existing aboriginal and treaty rights of the aboriginal peoples of Canada are hereby recognized and affirmed'.[10] Dickson CJ and La Forest J, writing for the Court, looked to the common law for interpretative guidance, noting that '[t]here is no explicit language in [s 35(1)] that authorizes [the courts] to assess the legitimacy of any government legislation that restricts aboriginal rights'.[11]

The judges cited two streams of jurisprudence on Aboriginal rights in support of an overarching Crown-Native fiduciary relationship. The first stream concerns treaty interpretation. The Court referred to *Nowegijick v The Queen*[12] for the principle that 'treaties and statutes relating to Indians should be liberally construed and doubtful expressions resolved in favour of the Indians'.[13] But the deeper principle on which the Court relied came from *R v Taylor and Williams*,[14] a pre-Constitution Act 1982 case on treaty interpretation

[7] Indian Act RSC 1952, c 149, s 18(1).

[8] *Guerin*, *supra* note 2, p 376.

[9] Ibid, p 384.

[10] Constitution Act 1982, being Sch B to the Canada Act 1982 (UK), 1982, c 11, s 35(1).

[11] *Sparrow*, *supra* note 3, p 1109.

[12] *Nowegijick v The Queen* [1983] 1 SCR 29.

[13] *Sparrow*, *supra* note 3, p 1107.

[14] *R v Taylor and Williams* (1981) 34 OR (2d) 322 (Ont CA) (*Taylor and Williams*).

that established a 'general guiding principle' for the interpretation of s 35(1): '[i]n approaching the terms of a treaty...the honour of the Crown is always involved and no appearance of "sharp dealing" should be sanctioned'.[15] The honour of the Crown is the subject of the second stream. This doctrine speaks to 'the responsibility of Government to protect the rights of Indians arising from the special trust relationship created by history, treaties and legislation'.[16]

Putting the pieces together, the common law principle that informs the proper interpretation of s 35(1) was set out in the following terms[17]:

> [T]he Government has the responsibility to act in a fiduciary capacity with respect to aboriginal peoples. The relationship between the Government and aboriginals is trust-like, rather than adversarial, and contemporary recognition and affirmation of aboriginal rights must be defined in light of this historic relationship.

While federal legislative powers over First Nations remain intact, exercise of those powers is subject to a justification requirement: 'federal power must be reconciled with federal duty and the best way to achieve that reconciliation is to demand the justification of any government regulation that infringes upon or denies aboriginal rights'.[18] Infringing legislation that lacks the proper justification is therefore unconstitutional.

The Crown's justification must be framed in terms that are consistent with the Crown-Native fiduciary relationship and must show that the Crown has acted in accordance with 'a high standard of honourable dealing'.[19] The honour of the Crown plays an illuminating role in this context. It underscores that the Crown's very legal authority to govern Indigenous peoples is at issue. Dickson CJ and La Forest J insisted that '[t]he way in which a legislative objective is to be attained must uphold the honour of the Crown', and that '[t]he special trust relationship and the responsibility of the government *vis-à-vis* aboriginals must be the first consideration in determining whether the legislation or action in question can be justified'.[20]

The honour of the Crown provides a useful jurisprudential platform from which to build on the fiduciary doctrine of *Guerin*. In *Guerin* the honour of the Crown is implicated in the manner in which the Crown performed a specific administrative function. In *Sparrow*, on the other hand, the honour of the Crown is at stake when it enacts legislation that affects the rights of Aboriginal peoples. In both cases, administration and legislation, the honour of the Crown supplies a fiduciary standard and framework of legality from which discrete fiduciary duties emerge.

[15] *Sparrow, supra* note 3, p 1107, citing *Taylor and Williams, supra* note 14.

[16] *Sparrow, supra* note 3, p 1107.

[17] Ibid.

[18] Ibid, p 1077.

[19] Ibid, p 1107.

[20] Ibid, pp 1110, 1114.

The Court in *Sparrow* devised a proportionality test to determine whether legislation alleged to infringe s 35(1) is constitutionally valid. If an Aboriginal individual or band is determined to have been acting pursuant to an Aboriginal right that was not extinguished prior to the Constitution Act 1982, inquiry turns to whether the legislation has the effect of interfering with an Aboriginal right. The onus is on the Aboriginal party to show that the limitation is unreasonable, that the regulation imposes undue hardship, or that the regulation denies the right-holder her preferred means of exercising her right.

If the right-holder can show a *prima facie* infringement, the onus shifts to the government to justify it. The government must first show that the legislative objective behind the regulation is 'valid' or 'compelling and substantial'[21] (eg conservation and resource management). Then, the court scrutinizes the requirements of the Crown's fiduciary obligation.

In the case of fishing rights, the Crown's fiduciary duty is to give priority to Aboriginals who depend on fishing for food over non-Native fishers, but the Crown can still limit the total catch for the sake of conservation. More generally, the Crown owes a duty of minimal impairment, as well as a duty to consult. The Crown cannot simply barrel ahead with conservation plans without consulting affected Aboriginal parties and seeking to minimize the effect of the infringement. If the infringement involves an expropriation, then compensation will usually be due. In all cases the content of the fiduciary duty is to be determined on a case-by-case basis that is sensitive to the underlying rights it is meant to protect.

R v Badger[22] extended the conceptual framework from *Sparrow* to Aboriginal treaty rights. Infringements of such rights, therefore, must be justified in light of the Crown's fiduciary duty to preserve and protect them.

The Crown and First Nations have entered into roughly 500 treaties over the course of the last four centuries.[23] The courts have developed a 'liberal and generous' approach to treaty interpretation which pre-dates the Constitution Act 1982.[24] According to this approach, one based explicitly on the

[21] Subsequent courts have adopted 'compelling and substantial' as the standard. See eg *Delgamuukw v BC* [1997] 3 SCR 1010, p 1108 (*Delgamuukw*).

[22] *R v Badger* [1996] 1 SCR 771.

[23] Donald J Purich, *Our Land: Native Rights in Canada* (Toronto: J Lorimer, 1986), p 95, as cited in Patrick Macklem, *Indigenous Difference and the Constitution of Canada* (Toronto: University of Toronto Press, 2001), p 133.

[24] The first in this line of cases is *R v White and Bob* (1964) 50 DLR (2d) 613; 52 WWR 193 (BCCA); *aff'd* (1965) 52 DLR (2d) 481n (SCC) (*White and Bob*), though the honour of the Crown first appears in relation to Aboriginal treaties in *Province of Ontario v Dominion of Canada and Province of Quebec; In re Indian Claims* (1895) 25 SCR 434. Prior to *White and Bob*, the courts had held that First Nations could make only limited claims on the basis of treaty rights either because the treaty obligations amounted to only a 'personal obligation' undertaken by the Crown's representative, or because First Nations were not deemed to have the requisite status to enter into treaties. See *A-G of ON v A-G of Canada: Re Indian Claims* [1897] AC 199, p 213 (PC) and *R v Syliboy* [1929] 1 DLR 307 (NS Co Ct).

honour of the Crown, literal interpretations are to be avoided, ambiguities are to be resolved in favour of the Aboriginal party, First Nations' understandings of the treaties are to be taken into consideration, and extrinsic evidence may be relied on as part of the interpretive exercise.[25] The goal of treaty interpretation is 'to choose from among the various possible interpretations of common intention the one which best reconciles the interests of both parties at the time the treaty was signed'.[26]

The liberal and generous approach to First Nation treaty interpretation proceeds from two assumptions that run counter to the common law's ordinary understanding of treaty law. The first is that Crown agents without formal treaty-making powers, such as local military commanders[27] or Governors,[28] are capable of binding the Crown. The second is that the obligations arising from treaties, though not implemented by statute, are enforceable against the Crown. In other words, Canada's dualism with respect to international treaties (the doctrine that requires legislative implementation of ratified treaties for them to have direct domestic effect) does not apply to First Nation treaties. Indeed, the presumption concerning the legal effect of First Nation treaties runs in the opposite direction. Prior to their constitutionalization in 1982, First Nation treaty rights imposed (or are now deemed to have imposed) common law duties on the Crown, and as such they could be extinguished or restricted by nothing less than an explicit Act of Parliament. Pre-1982 legislative and regulatory schemes of general application that limit access to game and fisheries, for example, do not exhibit the degree of explicitness required to extinguish Aboriginal and treaty rights to hunt and fish.[29]

[25] See eg *Simon v The Queen* [1985] 2 SCR 387 (*Simon*); *R v Sioui* [1990] 1 SCR 1025 (*Sioui*); *Badger, supra* note 22; *R v Marshall* [1999] 3 SCR 456 (*Marshall*); Leonard Ian Rotman, 'Taking Aim at the Canons of Treaty Interpretation in Canadian Aboriginal Rights Jurisprudence' (1997) 46 UNBLJ 11.

[26] *Marshall, supra* note 25, p 511, citing *Sioui, supra* note 25, pp 1068–9.

[27] See eg *Sioui, supra* note 25.

[28] See eg *White and Bob, supra* note 24; *Simon, supra* note 25; *Marshall, supra* note 25.

[29] See eg *Sioui, supra* note 25; *Sparrow, supra* note 3. Many commentators have argued that the Court's approach to Aboriginal treaties is fundamentally flawed because Parliament, prior to 1982, is understood to have had unilateral authority to extinguish treaty rights just so long as its legislation uses clear and explicit words, and because post-1982 Parliament can unilaterally infringe treaty rights if such infringements conform to the test laid out in *Sparrow* and *Badger*. See eg G Christie, 'Justifying Principles of Treaty Interpretation' (2000) 26 Queen's LJ 143; James Youngblood Henderson, 'Empowering Treaty Federalism' (1994) 58 Sask L Rev 241; Macklem, *supra* note 23. Roughly, these writers say that to understand Parliament to have unilateral authority to extinguish treaty rights implies that the Aboriginal parties must be taken to have surrendered their own sovereignty through the treaty process, and thereby to have become subjects of the Crown. Because no such surrender in fact occurred, this underlying and critical premise is false, and therefore treaties ought to be viewed as constitutional accords from which no derogation is possible absent mutual and informed consent. As will become clear, I agree that Aboriginal peoples did not enter treaties with the Crown to surrender their sovereignty and become the Crown's subjects. Indeed, this claim is critical to the larger argument

I do not mean to suggest that the liberal and generous approach to Aboriginal treaties is problematic on account of the fact that it runs counter to dualism; I have argued elsewhere that dualism itself is problematic.[30] Still, while the Court insists that Aboriginal treaties are *sui generis* accords rather than international agreements,[31] the separation-of-powers rationale that underwrites dualism with respect to international agreements applies with equal force to Aboriginal treaties: in both cases the executive may be alleged to usurp the legislature's law-making power if the treaties it has ratified (Aboriginal and international alike) are given legal effect in the absence of implementing legislation. And, generally speaking, Aboriginal treaties were concluded by the executive but were not implemented through legislation.[32] Below I argue that the Crown-Native fiduciary relationship justifies the Court's refusal to let dualism subvert the idea that Aboriginal treaties gave rise to legal rights and obligations prior to their constitutional entrenchment. At the same time, seeing judicial recognition of the fiduciary relationship as a response to Crown assertions of sovereignty brings into focus the nature of the deficit in legitimacy that the Court attempts to mend through the imposition of fiduciary obligations.

In summary, judicial recognition of fiduciary and treaty obligations owed to First Nations is based on common law understandings of fiduciary doctrine and Aboriginal treaty interpretation, matters on which s 35(1) is entirely silent. Section 35(1) merely elevates the status of existing Aboriginal and treaty rights from the common law to the constitutional level.

2.3 THE BASIS OF THE CROWN-NATIVE FIDUCIARY RELATIONSHIP

We have seen in *Guerin* that Dickson J traced the fiduciary obligation to the Crown's position as intermediary in land surrenders. Once the Court extended the Crown-Native fiduciary relationship to comprehend Aboriginal and treaty

that the judiciary has turned to fiduciary law to compensate for the Crown's unilateral assertions of sovereignty over First Nations.

30 Armand De Mestral and Evan Fox-Decent, 'Implementation and Reception: The Congeniality of Canada's Legal Order to International Law' in Oonagh E Fitzgerald and Elisabeth Eid (eds), *The Globalized Rule of Law: Relationships between International and Domestic Law* (Toronto: Irwin Law, 2006), p 31; David Dyzenhaus and Evan Fox-Decent, 'Rethinking the Process/Substance Distinction: Baker v. Canada' (2001) 51 *Univeristy of Toronto Law Journal* 193.

31 See eg *Simon*, *supra* note 25, p 404: '[a]n Indian treaty is unique; it is an agreement *sui generis* which is neither created nor terminated according to the rules of international law'.

32 Of course, some treaties have been implemented by legislation. Most modern land claims settlements, for example, enjoy implementation. But implementation does not arise in the major Aboriginal treaty cases (eg *Marshall*, *Simon*, and *Sioui*, *supra* note 25).

rights, however, the Crown's position as intermediary can no longer serve as an adequate explanation of the Crown's fiduciary obligations. Many of these contemporary obligations apply to contexts where land surrenders are not in issue, such as cases involving treaty rights to fish and trade.[33] A more general explanation is needed, one that pays close attention to the constitutional framework within which judges take themselves to be working.

A central feature of this framework is an assumption that the Crown has exclusive and plenary sovereign authority over First Nations and their ancestral lands. In *Sparrow*, Dickson CJ and La Forest J held that 'while British policy towards the native population was based on respect for their right to occupy their traditional lands . . . there was from the outset never any doubt that sovereignty and legislative power, and indeed the underlying title, to such lands vested in the Crown'.[34] From *Sparrow* on, the Supreme Court has held that the purpose of s 35(1) is to reconcile Aboriginal rights which pre-date contact with Crown assertions of sovereignty.[35] As Lamer CJ put it in *Van der Peet*, 'the doctrine of aboriginal rights exists, and is recognized and affirmed by s 35(1), because of one simple fact: when Europeans arrived in North America, aboriginal peoples *were already here*, living in communities on the land, and participating in distinctive cultures, as they had done for centuries'.[36] Along with Aboriginal prior occupation, the Court often recognizes that First Nations lived with 'their own practices, traditions and cultures'.[37] But until *Haida Nation v British Columbia (Minister of Forests)*[38] in 2004, discussed below, conspicuously absent from the Court's reconciliation thesis was explicit recognition that prior to and well after contact, Aboriginal peoples also lived with their own sovereign powers, in both the *de jure* and *de facto* senses. While the Court has developed elaborate tests to determine the existence and nature of Aboriginal rights, Crown sovereignty is taken as an immutable fact against which Canadian law relating to Aboriginal peoples must fashion itself.

Of course, it is not surprising that Canadian courts presume Crown sovereignty. Commonwealth judges understand themselves to be charged with interpreting and applying the law of the land. They do not see their mission as one involving an inquiry into the justice of historical and contemporary assertions of Crown sovereignty. Indeed, Canadian courts have declined to use even the Act of State doctrine to justify their unwillingness to review the Crown's claims to sovereignty over Aboriginal peoples.

[33] See eg *Marshall, supra* note 25.

[34] *Sparrow, supra* note 3, p 1103.

[35] See the *Van der Peet* trilogy: *R v Van der Peet* [1996] 2 SCR 507 (*Van der Peet*); *R v Gladstone* [1996] 2 SCR 723; *R v NTC Smokehouse Ltd* [1996] 2 SCR 672.

[36] *Van der Peet, supra* note 35, para 30 (emphasis in original).

[37] Ibid, para 31.

[38] [2004] 3 SCR 511 (*Haida*). See also *Taku River Tlingit First Nation v British Columbia (Project Assessment Director)* [2004] 3 SCR 550.

According to this doctrine, municipal courts have no jurisdiction to review the manner in which a state acquires new territory.[39] The idea that 'there was never any doubt from the outset that sovereignty... vested in the Crown' suggests that the reason for the absence of the doctrine in Canadian jurisprudence is that to deploy this doctrine or any other in defence of Crown sovereignty would imply that some defence of it is needed. Because Crown sovereignty is taken as a given, no defence of it is required, not even an Act of State justification that lets judges wash their hands of the matter.

Now, the mere fact of Crown sovereignty does not imply an absence of Aboriginal sovereignty. Several writers suggest that the way ahead lies in recognizing and promoting legal pluralism so that Canada distributes sovereign powers across three jurisdictions: federal, provincial, and Aboriginal.[40] I recommend the same approach below and in the next chapter. Nonetheless, the courts have not drawn this conclusion, taking Crown sovereignty to imply an extinguishment of Aboriginal sovereignty. This is why, until *Haida*, the reconciliation thesis has been cast in terms of reconciling Crown sovereignty with prior Aboriginal *rights*, meaning rights that reflect prior occupation of land and pre-contact traditions and customs, rather than in terms of reconciling prior Aboriginal *sovereignty* with assumed Crown sovereignty.

In treaty cases, however, the courts are compelled to grapple with the fact of pre-existing Aboriginal sovereignty. States do not usually enter into treaties with people over whom they are sovereign; they simply legislate.[41] And, it is far from clear that Native peoples ever intended to surrender their sovereignty or underlying title in the lands they occupied. While land surrender treaties became part of British colonial policy in the 19th century, from the Aboriginal perspective there is no reason to suppose that, as a rule, those treaties were intended to permit colonizers to put land to a use that was inconsistent with Aboriginal uses.[42] If the liberal and generous approach to treaty interpretation is taken seriously so that doubts and ambiguities are resolved in favour of First Nations, there is scant basis to suppose that First Nations intended to give up

[39] Hall J (dissenting, but not on this point) discusses the doctrine in *Calder v A-G of British Columbia* [1973] SCR 313, but not for the purposes of immunizing Crown sovereignty from judicial scrutiny.

[40] See eg Macklem, *supra* note 23; James Tully, 'A Just Relationship between Aboriginal Peoples and Canadians' in Curtis Cook and Juan David Lindau (eds), *Aboriginal Rights and Self-government: The Canadian and Mexican Experience in North American Perspective* (Montreal: McGill-Queen's University Press, 2000), pp 39–71.

[41] Imperial states may enter into treaties with peoples who are their subjects, but Canada has never claimed to be an imperial state.

[42] This is exactly the opposite of the assumption made in *Sioui*, *supra* note 25, pp 1071–2: 'The Hurons were only asking to be permitted to continue to carry on their customs on the lands frequented to the extent that those customs did not interfere with enjoyment of the lands by their [British] occupier'.

sovereignty by entreating with the Crown. The better view is that First Nations were open to sharing their lands with the French and British (and later Canada) on mutually agreeable terms, but that they intended their relations with non-Aboriginals to proceed on the parallel paths vividly depicted by the Two-Row Wampum belt used to consecrate many treaties. The Two-Row Wampum consists in two parallel rows of purple shells against a background of white shells. Three white beads—symbolizing peace, friendship, and respect—separate and connect the two purple rows. As Rotman observes, '[t]he three rows [of white beads] were the link between the nations, but just as their paths never cross on the wampum belt, neither was to attempt to steer the other's vessel'.[43]

Some commentators and courts have taken a very different view of Canada's history, and see the Crown's general fiduciary obligation arising from an agreed upon trade-off of Aboriginal sovereignty for Crown protection. The Supreme Court recently quoted with approval the italicized portion of the following instructive passage from Professor Slattery[44]:

> The Crown has a general fiduciary duty towards native peoples to protect them in the enjoyment of their aboriginal rights and in particular in the possession and use of their lands. This general fiduciary duty has its origins in the Crown's historical commitment to protect native peoples from the inroads of British settlers, in return for a native undertaking to renounce the use of force to defend themselves, and to accept instead the protection of the Crown as its subjects. . . . *The sources of the general fiduciary duty do not lie, then, in a paternalistic concern to protect a 'weaker' or 'primitive' people, as has sometimes been suggested, but rather in the necessity of persuading native peoples, at a time when they still had considerable military capacities, that their rights would be better protected by reliance on the Crown than by self-help* (emphasis added).

Putting aside for one moment the issue of whether or not Aboriginal peoples generally understood themselves to be giving up sovereignty for protection, it is worth noting that acceptance of British protection did not require the surrender of Aboriginal sovereignty. Nations commonly enter into treaties with one another for the sake of protection; there is no presumption that the weaker party loses its sovereignty to the stronger.[45]

[43] Leonard Ian Rotman, *Parallel Paths: Fiduciary Doctrine and the Crown-Native Relationship in Canada* (Toronto: University of Toronto Press, 1996), p 32.

[44] Brian Slattery, 'Understanding Aboriginal Rights' (1987) 66 Can Bar Rev 727, p 753, quoted in *Wewaykum Indian Band v Canada* 2002 SCC 79; [2002] 4 SCR 245 (*Wewaykum*), para 79. Slattery does not defend the merits of the position he describes, he simply states that this is the current state of Canadian law. This is also the argument of King J in *Logan v Styres* (1959) 20 DLR (2d) 416; [1959] OWN 361 (Ont HC) (*Logan*).

[45] John Borrows claims that no attempt was made to persuade Aboriginals to give up their sovereignty during negotiations of the important Treaty of Niagara (1764), the treaty in which some 24 Aboriginal nations agreed to accept the promise of British protection contained in the Royal Proclamation of 1763. See John Borrows, 'Wampum at Niagara: The Royal Proclamation, Canadian Legal

Britain could have provided the protection it promised in the Royal Proclamation of 1763 and elsewhere by exercising its jurisdiction over British subjects, whether or not those subjects were on British soil. The British did not need to have sovereignty over Aboriginal lands in order to retain jurisdiction over British subjects who chose to invade those lands.

Moreover, even if Aboriginal peoples did agree, in some sense, to surrender sovereignty and become British subjects for the sake of protection, arguably the deal is unconscionable and void from the beginning because it rests on an interaction analogous to hostage-taking. Imagine that a Mafia Don discovers that his foot soldiers have kidnapped a child without his authorization and are demanding a ransom from the parents. The Don advises the parents that if they pay the ransom he can assure the safe return of their child. The parents ask if he will simply order his men to return their child, but he declines their request. The parents pay the ransom, the child is returned safely, and the Don shares in the spoils. But the Don has no defensible entitlement to these spoils. The only reason the parents pay is to nullify the kidnappers' illegitimate threat, a threat the Don could have nullified of his own accord. In relying on the Don for protection rather than self-help, the parents do not forfeit their right to make a claim against him for the money he takes from the ransom.

By the same token, there is no reason to think that First Nations irrevocably gave up their sovereignty to Britain on the basis of the Crown's promise to police its own settlers, because the only basis of the surrender was the illegitimate threat of a settler invasion. The Crown is not entitled to exploit the threat for the sake of enlarging its territory (and sovereignty) at the expense of Aboriginal peoples. What the sovereignty-for-protection argument misses is the manner in which the Crown profits from a threat of wrongdoing made by its own subjects. If the honour of the Crown is to mean anything, it must mean that the Crown cannot profit from illegitimate threats of violence it had jurisdiction to control.

So, there is little basis to ground the Crown's fiduciary obligation in a trade-off between Aboriginal sovereignty and Crown protection. Rotman suggests instead that the Crown-Native fiduciary relationship arises from the nation-to-nation relationship once enjoyed between First Nations and European powers. He claims that prior to the removal of France as a major colonial power in North America in 1760–61, Crown-Native relations were based on treaties that reflected mutual need, respect, and trust. The Crown's subsequent fiduciary obligations, he claims, are 'founded on the mutually recognized and respected sovereign status of the Crown and the aboriginal

History and Self-Government' in Michael Asch (ed), *Aboriginal and Treaty Rights in Canada: Essays on Law, Equity, and Respect for Difference* (Vancouver: UBC Press, 1997), p 155.

peoples'.[46] Looking to treaty relationships to find a basis for the Crown's fiduciary obligations, however, is problematic for conceptual reasons having to do with the nature of fiduciary duties.

A fiduciary must exercise entrusted power exclusively for the sake of the purposes for which it is conferred. In private law the hallmark fiduciary obligation is the duty of loyalty. As with contracts, there is nothing inherent to treaties to suggest that the parties owe one another the selfless duty of loyalty required of fiduciaries; all that is required is performance of the treaty's obligations. The underlying assumption is that self-interested parties have come to mutually agreeable terms that further the interests of each. Canada, the United States, and Mexico do not owe one another fiduciary duties in virtue of entering into NAFTA.[47] The mere fact that the Crown assumed treaty obligations to protect Aboriginal peoples and their land does not show, without more, that those obligations are fiduciary in nature. Historically, a much closer analogue to a trust arises from the Treaty of Paris (1763) in which France (the putative settlor) and Britain (the putative trustee) negotiated religious and cultural guarantees for French Canadians (the putative beneficiaries). The courts have never said that Britain's treaty obligations to France, in favour of French Canadians, gave rise to fiduciary duties. An important difference between the Treaty of Paris (1763) and the Treaty of Niagara (1764) is that the former but not the latter clearly extinguished a prior sovereignty and established British sovereignty in its place.

Notwithstanding the Supreme Court's recent recital of the sovereignty-for-protection argument, the better explanation of judicial recognition of the fiduciary relationship lies in the Court's aspiration to legitimize Crown sovereignty in the absence of a compelling narrative of how First Nations lost theirs. This explanation accounts for the Court taking Crown sovereignty to be an incontestable given, as well as for the Court's systematic failure to apply the liberal and generous approach to the single most important issue of Aboriginal treaty interpretation, ie whether or not First Nations knowingly and willingly surrendered their sovereignty to the Crown through the treaty process. Furthermore, this understanding of the fiduciary relationship illustrates how the Crown's broader fiduciary duties today arise as justifiable complements to its more limited duties to protect Aboriginal lands. All such duties arise as a consequence of the sovereign powers and authority the Crown has assumed over Aboriginal peoples and their lands, with or without their consent.

[46] Rotman, *supra* note 43, p 13.

[47] North American Free Trade Agreement Between the Government of Canada, the Government of Mexico and the Government of the United States, 17 December 1992, Can TS 1994 No 2, 32 ILM (entered into force 1 January 1994).

McLachlin CJ squarely affirms this explanation of the rise of fiduciary doctrine in *Mitchell v MNR*,[48] a case in which the Court upheld an Aboriginal right to bring goods across the Canada-US border free of customs duties. The Chief Justice's summary of the historical evolution of Crown-Native legal relations is especially revealing[49]:

> English law, which ultimately came to govern aboriginal rights, accepted that the aboriginal peoples possessed pre-existing laws and interests, and recognized their continuance in the absence of extinguishment, by cession, conquest, or legislation. At the same time, however, the Crown asserted that sovereignty over the land, and ownership of its underlying title, vested in the Crown. With this assertion arose an obligation to treat aboriginal peoples fairly and honourably, and to protect them from exploitation, a duty characterized as 'fiduciary' in *Guerin v. The Queen*, [1984] 2 S.C.R. 335.

In other words, the assertion of Crown sovereignty gave rise to a general fiduciary obligation to treat First Nations 'fairly and honourably, and to protect them from exploitation'. McLachlin CJ does not try to justify the Crown's historical assertion of sovereignty, and the passage presupposes that the Crown's assertion extinguished Aboriginal *de jure* sovereignty. Her use of the fiduciary principle in this context, however, is clearly motivated by a desire to take some of the sting and imperiousness out of the Crown's assertion of sovereignty. Whereas Aboriginal peoples once had their own 'pre-existing laws', they now can (and must) rely on fiduciary law to ensure that the Crown respects their rights and protects their interests.

This view of the basis of the Crown's fiduciary duties also better respects the normative structure of the fiduciary principle. Whereas parties to a contract or a treaty agree amongst themselves to the terms of their interaction, the beneficiary in a fiduciary relationship is vulnerable to the fiduciary's power and is often unable to negotiate the terms of the relationship. Since the law does not permit one party to set unilaterally the terms of its interaction with another, the fiduciary principle intercedes when one party unilaterally assumes discretionary power over another to ensure that the power holder has due regard for the best interests of the beneficiary. The fiduciary's authority to exercise power is thus justified in the eyes of the law because all such exercises of power must be in the service of the beneficiary's interests. In this sense, as suggested in the last chapter and as we shall see further in Chapter IV, the fiduciary may be said to act with entrusted authority regardless of whether or not the beneficiary has actually done anything in particular to entrust her interests to the fiduciary's care. By saying that the Crown's relationship with First Nations is 'trust-like, rather

48 *Mitchell v MNR* 2001 SCC 33; [2001] 1 SCR 911 (*Mitchell*).

49 Ibid, para 9 (references omitted).

than adversarial', the Court is able to side-step the issue of whether the relationship is based on treaties and consent, while imposing on the Crown fiduciary obligations that arise from the relationship's trust-like nature.

2.4 THE LIMITS OF THE CROWN'S LEGITIMACY

By positing the Crown as fiduciary, the Court precludes the Crown from setting unilaterally the terms of its interaction with First Nations, and supplies to Crown-Native relations a measure of legitimacy that would be lacking were the Crown able to set the terms of those relations at its sole discretion. How much legitimacy the fiduciary principle can afford to Crown-Native relations is highly debatable. While First Nations are beneficiaries who the Crown must consult and attempt to accommodate, they cannot command the Crown to legislate in accordance with their wishes, nor can they veto legislation that infringes their rights but passes the justificatory test laid out in *Sparrow*. Furthermore, non-Aboriginal judges of the Supreme Court of Canada are the ultimate arbiters of whether the *Sparrow* test has been satisfied in any given case. For Aboriginal peoples who reject Crown sovereignty and insist on their own, it is far from clear that the fiduciary principle, as understood and applied today, can fully legitimize the Crown's claim to authority over them.

However, the Australian experience, where courts have not recognized a Crown-Native fiduciary relationship, suggests that Aboriginal peoples are better off with its recognition than without it. Australian Professor Larissa Behrendt laments that in the absence of a judicially-recognized Crown-Native fiduciary relationship, 'Aboriginal title holders [in Australia], are captive to the whim of the legislature', and that '[d]espite the many flaws and the impotence of the fiduciary doctrine in Canada, Australia offers sober reflection on what can happen if there is no recognition of the doctrine'.[50]

This sober reflection reveals that while the fiduciary principle may not save the Crown's claim to political authority, compliance with fiduciary standards confers a measure of legitimacy that is intrinsic to and constitutive of the Crown's *legal* authority. Whereas political authority comprehends matters of political representation as well as the Crown's capacity to determine the substantive content of legislation, legal authority reflects the extent to which exercises of Crown power conform to the demands of legality, such as the demands imposed by fiduciary law. To the extent that exercises of Crown power respect the relevant fiduciary constraints, those exercises

[50] Larissa Behrendt, 'Lacking Good Faith: Australia, Fiduciary Duties and the Lonely Place of Indigenous Rights' in Law Commission of Canada (ed), *In Whom We Trust: A Forum on Fiduciary Relationships* (Toronto: Irwin Law, 2002), pp 264–5, as cited in Reynolds, *supra* note 6, p 226.

of power enjoy a measure of legal authority. This modest achievement of legal authority differentiates Canada from Australia but should not be overstated.

The measure of legal authority attained by subscription to the fiduciary principle is truly modest in the case of Aboriginal peoples who are denied the ability to govern themselves. Self-determination is a collective human right of the people of every nation. As we shall see in the next chapter, the fiduciary view of public authority requires respect for Aboriginal self-determination. And, if the argument in Chapter IX succeeds in showing that the rule of law proscribes violations of human rights, then the Crown's refusal to respect this human right subverts its claim to legal authority over First Nations.

It is worth pausing to consider what the implications might be if the courts accepted that Aboriginal peoples, for the most part, never surrendered their *de jure* sovereignty, notwithstanding the Crown's present *de facto* sovereignty over them.[51] One possible consequence would be that the Crown could not infringe Aboriginal and treaty rights without the consent of the relevant First Nation. Requiring the Crown to secure Aboriginal consent in such cases would give effect to Aboriginal sovereignty. First Nations would have the power to veto legislation that infringes their rights. While this may seem utopian in Canada, there is now a precedent for it in international law.

The Inter-American Court of Human Rights imposed a duty to obtain consent on the government of Suriname in the *Case of the Saramaka People v Suriname*.[52] This duty applies to large-scale projects that would have a major impact within Saramaka territory. The ruling thusly gives the Saramaka people a measure of effective sovereignty over their lands and resources. Despite a few *obiter dicta*,[53] the Supreme Court of Canada has yet to require the Crown to obtain First Nation consent in an Aboriginal rights or treaty case. All that has been required is consultation, accommodation, and justification.

Arguably, the Court supposes that to require the Crown to obtain Aboriginal consent in all but exceptional circumstances would, in effect, give Aboriginal peoples co-legislative authority with the Crown. Section 91(24) of the Constitution Act 1867 exhaustively grants such authority to the federal

[51] See eg Macklem, *supra* note 23; Christie, *supra* note 29; J. Borrows, *Recovering Canada: The Resurgence of Indigenous Law* (Toronto: University of Toronto Press, 2002); Mark Walters, 'The Morality of Aboriginal Law' (2006) 31 Queen's LJ 470. Walters in fact suggests that the Supreme Court has already moved in this direction in the *Haida* decision: *Haida*, *supra* note 40, pp 513–14.

[52] Preliminary Objections, Merits, Reparations, and Costs. Judgment of 28 November 2007. Series C No 172.

[53] See eg *Delgamuukw*, *supra* note 21, para 168, Lamer CJ: 'Some cases may even require the full consent of an aboriginal nation, particularly when provinces enact hunting and fishing regulations in relation to aboriginal lands'.

Crown.[54] In *R v Pamajewon*,[55] the leading case on Aboriginal self-government, Carr J held at trial, and the Supreme Court later accepted, that the Royal Proclamation of 1763, the Robinson Huron Treaty of 1850, and s 91(24) established that 'any right of self-government which was once held by the Shawanaga First Nation had been extinguished by the clear and plain intention of the Crown'.[56]

Turning to fiduciary doctrine, then, permits the Court to take a middle position between uncontrolled Crown discretion, on the one hand, and requiring the Crown to obtain Aboriginal consent, on the other. The middle position lets the Court hold the Crown to certain legal obligations that lend a measure of legitimacy to Crown sovereignty, but within a constitutional arrangement in which Aboriginal sovereignty, if recognized at all, is subordinated to Crown sovereignty.

The *Haida* decision on the duty to consult is especially important because, for the first time, the Supreme Court unequivocally recognized pre-existing Aboriginal sovereignty. The Court in *Haida* had to consider the legality of the Crown's issuance of a Tree Farm Licence to a forestry firm over objections of the Haida people. The Haida alleged that the Crown had not provided adequate consultation as required by *Sparrow* and subsequent case law. They have claimed Aboriginal title to the relevant lands for the past 100 years, but their title has yet to be legally recognized. The Crown argued that the duty to consult flows exclusively from its fiduciary duty to protect established Aboriginal rights. Rejecting this argument, the Court held that where a *prima facie* case in favour of an Aboriginal right and the potential for irreparable harm posed by the Crown's intended action is made out, the Crown has a duty to consult and accommodate (though not a duty to gain consent). The Court's rationale was that the honour of the Crown is always at stake in dealings with First Nations, even in the absence of a legally recognized Aboriginal right. Where such rights are established, the Crown is under a fiduciary duty to consult and accommodate.

Haida is part of a trend in recent jurisprudence that appears to prefer using the honour of the Crown rather than fiduciary duty as the fundamental basis for Crown liability. In *Haida*, the Court reiterated its recent holding in *Wewaykum*:

[54] Section 91(24) grants jurisdiction to the federal Crown over 'Indians, and Lands reserved for the Indians'. This jurisdiction is granted to the exclusion of provincial Crowns, but, as the subsequent text suggests, courts have interpreted it to mean that the federal Crown has exclusive jurisdiction in this domain.

[55] *R v Pamajewon* [1996] 2 SCR 821 (*Pamajewon*).

[56] Paraphrased in *Pamajewon*, ibid, p 829. The Supreme Court had drawn the same conclusion in *Calder*, *supra* note 39, relying on the authority of s 91(24).

> '[F]iduciary duty' as a source of plenary Crown liability covering all aspects of the Crown-Indian band relationship... overshoots the mark. The fiduciary duty imposed on the Crown does not exist at large but in relation to specific Indian interests.[57]

Notice, however, that the honour of the Crown gives rise to the same *kind* of duty of consultation and accommodation that would arise if a fiduciary duty were owed. The difference is that the Crown may not have to consult and accommodate to the same *degree*. The similarity in kind is not surprising, since the Court in *Guerin* and *Sparrow* relied heavily on the honour of the Crown to explain how the circumstances in those cases gave rise to fiduciary obligations.

The Court's understanding of the interplay between the honour of the Crown and fiduciary law in the First Nations case is as follows. There is a general fiduciary relationship between the Crown and First Nations that yields duties 'in relation to specific Indian interests'. Yet not all duties in a fiduciary relationship are fiduciary duties. While the honour of the Crown is the normative bedrock of its fiduciary duties to First Nations, for such duties to crystallize there must be a 'specific' interest to which they attach (eg a *Guerin*-like interest in land, or an Aboriginal or treaty right). In the absence of such an interest, fiduciary-like duties may still be owed if Crown action threatens otherwise unprotected Aboriginal interests, since the honour of the Crown is always at stake. The honour of the Crown penetrates every facet of the Crown-Native relationship. But the fundamental relationship is still trust-like or fiduciary in character, even if the Court insists, for doctrinal reasons, that some of the Crown's fiduciary-like obligations to First Nations are not, strictly speaking, fiduciary duties. And so the honour of the Crown participates in the same quest for legitimacy that motivates the Court's imposition of fiduciary duties.

Haida's great significance for our purposes lies in its affirmation that Aboriginal peoples did not simply occupy Canada with distinctive customs and traditions prior to colonization, but rather were sovereign over themselves. Writing for the Court, McLachlin CJ held that[58]:

> Treaties serve to reconcile pre-existing Aboriginal sovereignty with assumed Crown sovereignty, and to define Aboriginal rights guaranteed by s 35 of the *Constitution Act, 1982*. Section 35 represents a promise of rights recognition, and [it] is always assumed that the Crown intends to fulfil its promises. This promise is realized and sovereignty claims reconciled through the process of honourable negotiation (references omitted).

[57] *Haida*, *supra* note 38, para 18, citing *Wewaykum*, *supra* note 44, para 81.

[58] *Haida*, *supra* note 38, para 20, citing *Badger*, *supra* note 22, para 41.

This is the first time that the Court explicitly mentions and acknowledges 'pre-existing Aboriginal sovereignty'. Of equal interest, Crown sovereignty is characterized as 'assumed' rather than as a legal fact about which 'there was never any doubt from the outset'.[59]

The point of treaties is to reconcile these sovereignties and to define the content of the treaty rights enshrined in s 35(1), rights the Crown would have a fiduciary obligation to protect. Pre-existing Aboriginal sovereignty gives First Nations the authority to negotiate treaties, and the honour of the Crown 'requires negotiations leading to a just settlement of Aboriginal claims'.[60] The requirement of negotiation is part and parcel of an enlarged understanding of consultation and accommodation. The duty to negotiate in good faith also expands the idea of reconciliation, one which 'flows from the Crown's duty of honourable dealing toward Aboriginal peoples, which arises in turn from the Crown's assertion of sovereignty over an Aboriginal people and *de facto* control of land and resources that were formerly in the control of that people'.[61] In short, the Court recognizes that both the honour of the Crown and the Crown's fiduciary obligations arise from Crown assertions of sovereignty over peoples who once enjoyed effective sovereignty over themselves.

We can now see why dualism is wholly absent from modern Canadian jurisprudence on Aboriginal treaty interpretation. For the Crown to have any *de jure* sovereignty over First Nations at all, it must respect the treaty terms on which such authority has been assumed and asserted, regardless of whether those terms were ever subsequently incorporated into domestic legislation. Dualism is a shield invoked to insulate Parliament's law-making power from alleged executive incursion. But dualism must retreat when adherence to it would subvert the honour of the Crown because that honour is the very basis of Parliament's legal authority to legislate over First Nations.

Moreover, once we see the fiduciary relationship as an effort to sustain the legitimacy of Crown sovereignty, we can see that the ousting of Aboriginal sovereignty implicit in the Court's conception of Crown sovereignty is the source of the legitimacy deficit that the fiduciary relationship attempts to correct. Hence, as Aboriginal peoples negotiate modern treaties through which they gain recognition of their *de jure* sovereign powers and the *de facto* ability to exercise them (eg the 1998 Nisga'a Agreement), the Crown's fiduciary obligations will gradually begin to recede because the basis for

59 *Sparrow*, *supra* note 3, p 1103.

60 *Haida*, *supra* note 40, para 20.

61 Ibid, para 32. McLachlin CJ at this point cited her previous holding in *Mitchell*, *supra* note 48, para 9, that '*[w]ith this assertion* [of sovereignty] arose an obligation to treat aboriginal peoples fairly and honourably, and to protect them from exploitation' (emphasis added in *Haida*).

them—legitimization of Crown power in the absence of effective Aboriginal sovereignty—will itself begin to disappear.

Now, there are powerful objections to the fiduciary approach to Crown-Native relations. One is based on the notion that the Crown-Native fiduciary relationship is intractably paternalistic. Another is that fiduciary doctrine is dangerous in this context because it seeks to legitimize colonialism. Yet another is that the fiduciary principle is ill-suited to Crown-Native relations because it is unhelpful in cases involving competing Aboriginal parties: how can the Crown be a loyal fiduciary to both? And, even if the objections can be met, one might doubt the relevance of the Crown-Native case to the broader state-subject case, since the Crown-Native relationship is often said to be *sui generis*. The next chapter addresses each of these concerns.

III

Some Objections

3.1 INTRODUCTION

In the previous chapter, I argued that the Crown-Native fiduciary relationship lends the Crown a limited measure of legitimacy *vis-à-vis* Canada's First Nations, ie more legitimacy than the Crown would have were the executive free to set the terms of its relations to Aboriginal peoples at its sole discretion. Even this deliberately modest claim may seem too strong. One might think that the fiduciary principle is suitable for the parent-child case, but that to extend it to Crown-Native relations is to treat First Nations as wards of the state, and ultimately, to seek a justification of the unjustifiable: colonialism. As we shall see, the idea of the state as fiduciary, properly understood, can answer this objection.

A further objection relates not to the desirability of deploying the fiduciary principle in this context, but to the question of whether the Crown can act as a loyal fiduciary of First Nations at all, since in some cases the interests of distinct First Nations are bound to conflict (to say nothing of First Nations' interests *vis-à-vis* the interests of non-Aboriginals). In Chapter I we saw that the duty of loyalty can be recast as a duty of fairness and reasonableness in private law contexts with multiple beneficiaries. We test this argument now in a public law setting in which two Aboriginal groups make competing claims against the Crown.

Finally, I consider whether the Crown-Native relationship has *sui generis* attributes which suggest that it cannot support an application of the fiduciary principle to the Crown's relations with non-Aboriginals. The First Nations case, I argue, is analogous to Ronald Dworkin's 'hard cases' in that both bring to the surface what is present but less visible in ordinary cases. The justification of Crown sovereignty over First Nations just makes explicit the fiduciary requirements of the ordinary justification of sovereign authority.

3.2 PATERNALISM, COLONIALISM, AND LEGAL PLURALISM

One might object that the Supreme Court's use of fiduciary doctrine in the Crown-Native case is paternalistic because it treats First Nations as helpless children rather than agents. The paternalism objection takes as its starting point the alleged inferiority or incapacity of one party *vis-à-vis* another. Fiduciary doctrine, the objection might go, presupposes that Aboriginal beneficiaries are incapable of managing their own interests. Just as fiduciary law compels parents to care for children who can not take care of themselves, so too it requires the Crown to administer Native affairs on the assumption that First Nations are incapable of doing so.

Evidence of this assumption is found in the Indian Act provisions on the inalienability of Aboriginal lands and the land surrender process. The initial stated purpose of the restriction on alienation, following similar restrictions found in the Royal Proclamation of 1763, was to force settlers to go through the Crown to acquire land in order to avoid fraudulent or unconscionable direct purchases from First Nations. Today the courts view inalienability as a desirable feature of Aboriginal title, one that protects First Nations' 'special bond' with their land.[1] If First Nations decide that the bond is no longer so special, they can surrender their land, but only to the Crown. Non-Aboriginals face no analogous restrictions on their land holdings. On its face the restriction is paternalistic in that it is imposed unilaterally by one party for the alleged benefit of another. Viewed in this light, the Crown's fiduciary obligations from *Guerin v The Queen*[2] that purport to protect First Nations in cases of land surrender may be thought to arise solely as a consequence of the Indian Act's paternalism.

The fiduciary principle, however, does not condone the Indian Act's paternalism, nor does it imply that Aboriginal peoples need the Crown to administer their affairs because they lack capacity. Fiduciary doctrine is indifferent to the merits of the restriction on alienation and the land surrender process. It is concerned solely with the legal obligations that arise when the Crown acts in accordance with its statutory authority to stand as an intermediary in land surrenders. In other words, the fiduciary obligation controls the legality, not the merits, of exercises of sovereign power. As an equitable precept, the fiduciary obligation cannot undo the Indian Act's paternalism, only substantive legislative reforms can achieve this. The most that can be expected of the common law fiduciary principle is that it can impose a legal standard where discretion would otherwise prevail.

[1] *Delgamuukw v BC* [1997] 3 SCR 1010, para 128.

[2] *Guerin v The Queen* [1982] 2 SCR 335 (*Guerin*). See Chapter II for discussion.

In Canada, where a fiduciary framework informs the judiciary's interpretation of s 35 of the Constitution Act 1982, the legal standard set by the fiduciary principle in relation to Aboriginal and treaty rights assumes a constitutional dimension to which legislation must conform. The Crown's fiduciary obligation in the case of s 35 rights is not based on a *Guerin*-like entitlement derived from a statutory scheme. Rather, as we saw in the previous chapter, the obligation to consult, accommodate, and justify is based on reconciliation of Crown legislative authority with pre-existing Aboriginal rights and sovereignty. In this context, one might think that paternalism shrouds the judiciary's assumption (at least pre-*Haida*) that Crown legislative authority over First Nations extinguishes Aboriginal sovereignty. There is merit to this concern, but it is really an objection that goes to the underlying legitimacy of Crown sovereignty over First Nations.

We also saw in the previous chapter that when the Crown is confronted with Aboriginal peoples who wish to govern themselves, the legitimacy that flows from the Crown's adherence to fiduciary constraints is especially limited. There is greater legitimacy than there would be if the Crown denied Aboriginal self-determination *and* failed to perform its fiduciary obligations. Plausibly, however, the optimal state of affairs would be one in which the Crown recognized Aboriginal peoples' right of self-determination while complying with whatever residual fiduciary duties remain to protect Aboriginal and treaty rights. As we shall see now, the fiduciary model of public authority requires respect for self-determination. So, rather than offer an apology for unwanted and sometimes paternalistic assertions of Crown sovereignty, the fiduciary view helps explain the severe damage that such assertions do to the legitimacy of public authority.

On the fiduciary model, sovereignty ultimately resides in the people of every nation. (More on this idea of popular sovereignty in Chapters IV through VI.) The people have plenary authority to decide under which political and legal institutions they wish to live, the roles of those institutions, and the means of staffing them. Once those institutions are established, they have and retain legal authority to the extent that they faithfully execute the public functions entrusted to them. This is how the collective agency of a people comes to be expressed through self-determination. To deny self-determination through force of law is to engage in an ongoing bloodless conquest in which the conquered are not the agents or subjects of law, but rather its victims. They are its victims because the law to which they are subject is not theirs, and so in a good sense they are not even subject to law; they are subject to force. They stand in a position akin to Hobbes' captive slaves: subjugated against their will, the state lacks authority to govern them. This is as true in a multinational state in which Aboriginal peoples are denied self-determination as it is when one state invades and occupies another.

The broader view of the state as fiduciary looks to legal pluralism as an option that falls between the status quo and the balkanization that would occur if First Nations seceded in order to assert sovereign power. The pluralist route affirms the legitimacy of First Nations' legal institutions on the basis of their capacity to establish their own legal orders. On this approach, the state's sovereign authority is not monopolized by the state's formal legal institutions, but rather is shared and vested in all institutions in which legal standards operate. The Crown's present fiduciary obligations in no way preclude First Nations from seeking greater autonomy and recognition of their own legal institutions. Properly understood, the Crown's fiduciary obligations include a pluralist duty to accommodate Aboriginal self-determination through recognition of the legitimacy of Aboriginal legal institutions. Hence, the Crown-Native fiduciary relationship does not entail either paternalism or colonialism; on the contrary, it calls for emancipation.

3.3 RECONCILING COMPETING CLAIMS

In *R v Sparrow*[3] the Court found that the Crown's fiduciary duty requires giving constitutionally entrenched Aboriginal rights priority over non-Aboriginal interests. The principle of constitutional supremacy thus prioritizes Aboriginal subsistence fishing over non-Aboriginal sport and commercial fishing.[4] As a matter of law, it is relatively easy to see how the Crown can act as a loyal fiduciary of Aboriginal peoples when confronted by non-Aboriginals with competing, but not constitutional, claims: the Constitution is the supreme law of the land, the rights enshrined within it take priority over other rights, so the Crown must regard those constitutional rights preferentially.

Suppose, however, that two Aboriginal parties make competing claims of equivalent status against the Crown. Can the Crown be a loyal fiduciary of both? And what if the claims relate to statutory or common law entitlements rather than constitutional rights? The Supreme Court had to consider these issues in *Wewaykum Indian Band v Canada*,[5] a case involving two neighbouring bands from the Laich-kwil-tach First Nation of British Columbia.

The bands each made claims against reserve lands possessed by the other. The two reserves have been in the possession of the respective bands since the end of the 19th century. Both bands alleged that, but for the Crown's breach of various fiduciary obligations, its people would be in rightful

[3] *R v Sparrow* [1990] 1 SCR 1075 (*Sparrow*).

[4] Ibid, p 1116. This issue came to the fore in *R v Marshall* [1999] 3 SCR 456, a case in which the Supreme Court gave the treaty claims of Aboriginal fishers priority over federal fishing regulations, and, as a consequence, priority over non-Aboriginals' ability to fish.

[5] *Wewaykum Indian Band v Canada* 2002 SCC 79; [2002] 4 SCR 245 (*Wewaykum*).

possession of both reserves. The claims arose from a number of clerical errors made by the Department of Indian Affairs during the process of reserve creation, with some records indicating that all the lands in dispute belonged to one band, while other records indicated that all the lands belonged to the other.

Writing for the Court, Binnie J held that the Crown owed the bands fiduciary duties both during the process of reserve creation and after the reserves were established. Once a reserve is established, the duty of the Crown is the duty from *Guerin* to preserve and protect the band's legal interest in the land on the reserve. In *Wewaykum*, however, the Court had to consider the implications of the fiduciary principle in the context of a reserve creation process in which two bands as well as non-Aboriginal parties had a stake in the outcome.

In these circumstances, Binnie J found that '[t]he Crown can be no ordinary fiduciary; it wears many hats and represents many interests, some of which cannot help but be conflicting'.[6] Binnie J spent considerable time in *Wewaykum* cautioning against overuse of fiduciary doctrine, and reminding his readers that not every obligation in a fiduciary relationship is necessarily a fiduciary obligation. In the process of reserve creation, he said, the Crown mainly 'exercises a public law function under the Indian Act—which is subject to supervision by the courts exercising public law remedies'.[7] Still, he held that a fiduciary relationship arose on the facts of the case because the Crown intervened as an intermediary to deal with others (including the province) on behalf of the bands.

The Crown's fiduciary duty to the bands, Binnie J said, is to act 'with loyalty, good faith, full disclosure appropriate to the subject matter and with "ordinary" diligence in what it reasonably regarded as the best interest of the beneficiaries'.[8] Given the conflicting demands of the bands, the Crown's duty was 'to be even-handed towards and among the various beneficiaries'.[9] In other words, when the Crown is a fiduciary of multiple beneficiaries, its duty is to treat them fairly. Interestingly, Binnie J said that the Crown owes non-Aboriginals caught up in the reserve creation process the same public fiduciary duty of fairness, since the Crown's relationship with them shares the same fiduciary features as the Crown's relationship with the bands[10]:

> In resolving the dispute between Campbell River Band members and the non-Indian settlers named Nunns, for example, the Crown was not solely concerned with the band interest, nor should it have been. The Indians were 'vulnerable' to the adverse exercise of the government's discretion,

[6] Ibid, para 96. [7] Ibid, para 93. [8] Ibid, para 97.
[9] Ibid. [10] Ibid, para 96.

> but so too were the settlers, and each looked to the Crown for a fair resolution of their dispute.

In the result, Binnie J dismissed the bands' appeals, finding that the Crown had provided adequate consultation and had treated them fairly in the reserve creation process.

The point to be taken from *Wewaykum* is that the question for Canadian jurists now is not *whether* public fiduciary duties can be owed to multiple beneficiaries (they can), but rather *how* we are best able to explain and justify them. Before turning in the next chapter to this question and the theoretical underpinnings of the state-subject fiduciary relationship, however, we need to consider the extent to which the Crown-Native fiduciary relationship is *sui generis*. If the relationship is entirely *sui generis* it will have limited relevance to the wider idea of the state as fiduciary.

3.4 THE *SUI GENERIS* ARGUMENT

The Crown-Native fiduciary relationship, like Aboriginal and treaty rights, is commonly referred to as unique or *sui generis*.[11] Some scholars and judges conclude that because the fiduciary relationship is *sui generis*, it provides no basis for supposing that the Crown is in a fiduciary relationship with non-Aboriginals.[12] Let us call this the *sui generis* thesis, and consider its merits.

There is no question that the Crown-Native relationship reflects a distinct history. Patrick Macklem argues convincingly that this history reveals several important differences between the relationship of the Canadian state to Aboriginal and non-Aboriginal Canadians respectively, and that these differences merit constitutional protection.[13] The differences consist in prior Aboriginal occupation of Canada, distinctive Indigenous cultures under threat by non-Aboriginal institutions and ways of life, pre-existing Aboriginal sovereignty, and First Nation participation in treaty processes with the Crown. These differences are indeed important, but as Macklem suggests,

[11] See eg ibid, paras 72, 76, 78, and 80; *Guerin*, *supra* note 2, p 385.

[12] See eg *Hogan v Newfoundland (Attorney General)* 2000 NFCA 12; 183 DLR (4th) 225; leave to appeal to the SCC dismissed [2000] SCCA No 191. The claimant alleged that the Crown had breached a fiduciary duty when it changed the relationship between Newfoundland's education system and religious authorities. Cameron JA rejected the claims, finding that the 'relationship [between the Crown and Aboriginal peoples] is an unparalleled one.... The submission of the appellants that a fiduciary duty similar to that owed by the Crown to aboriginal peoples is owed to the class represented by the appellants cannot succeed', ibid, p 67. See also *Callie v Canada* [1991] 2 FC 379 (FCTD) (the Crown's fiduciary obligations to First Nations arise solely as a result of the *sui generis* nature of the Aboriginal interest in the land). But see *Authorson v Canada (Attorney General)* (2002) 58 OR (3d) 417 (Ont CA); *rev'd* 2003 SCC 39 (the Crown can be a fiduciary of non-Aboriginals).

[13] Patrick Macklem, *Indigenous Difference and the Constitution of Canada* (Toronto: University of Toronto Press, 2001).

they can be respected through generous recognition of Aboriginal and treaty rights to which non-Aboriginals can make no claim. Put slightly differently, the Crown owes special public fiduciary duties to First Nations that it does not owe to non-Aboriginals. Yet, as we shall see, the special *content* of those duties does not undermine the broader idea that the state is a fiduciary of every person subject to its power.

The fundamental question is whether the distinct historical and contemporary features of the Crown-Native relationship are each necessary and jointly sufficient to ground the Crown's fiduciary duty. If they are, then the *sui generis* thesis stands vindicated. The Supreme Court's reconciliation thesis may appear to support the *sui generis* thesis. The Court makes much of Aboriginal prior occupation of land, and of Aboriginal peoples' pre-existing cultures, traditions, rights, and (with *Haida*) sovereignty. I argue that prior occupation and pre-existence are incidental rather than necessary to the fiduciary relationship. What really does the work for the Court is the unilateral manner in which the Crown has asserted sovereignty over First Nations. I then consider other reasons for thinking that the pre-existent and inherent nature of Aboriginal rights does not support the *sui generis* thesis.

Consider what the Court's position would have been if the Crown's assertion of sovereignty over First Nations was based on their consent. Suppose that, around the time of the Royal Proclamation of 1763, First Nations entered into a treaty with the Crown in which they expressly and unequivocally consented to be ruled by the Crown. Assume also that there are no complicating issues of duress, coercion, or exploitation. Part of the hypothesized treaty includes guarantees that Indigenous persons shall be accorded the same rights and opportunities enjoyed by non-Aboriginals. Let us suppose that the treaty also includes provisions to allocate disproportionate resources to First Nations to ensure the survival of their distinct cultures. Also, the treaty recognizes inherent Aboriginal rights, the jurisdiction of Aboriginal legal institutions, and limited rights of self-determination, while at the same time guaranteeing First Nations a representative presence in the political and legal institutions of the wider Canadian state. Finally, let us assume that the treaty is incorporated into law as the Constitution Act 1763, and functions as a control on legislation and administration, much as the Canadian Charter of Rights and Freedoms[14] now operates.

Were such a treaty to have become entrenched as a Constitution Act, and respected as the Charter is respected today, it is far from clear that the courts would have found that the Crown is in a fiduciary relationship with First Nations. As noted in the previous chapter, the courts have declined to find that

[14] Canadian Charter of Rights and Freedoms, Part I of the Constitution Act 1982, being Sch B to the Canada Act 1982 (UK), 1982, c 11 (Charter).

the Crown is in a fiduciary relationship with French Canadians, notwithstanding that France rather than French Canadians surrendered to the British, and then entrusted Britain to protect French language and culture in Canada. This comparative argument suggests that, for the Supreme Court, the mere pre-existence of inherent Aboriginal rights and the entrenchment of Crown sovereignty are not jointly *sufficient* conditions for imposing a general fiduciary duty on the Crown. If mere pre-existence of Aboriginal rights and Crown sovereignty alone were sufficient, then the manner in which sovereignty over First Nations was acquired—whether through a treaty of mutual and informed consent or through proclamation and fiat—would make no difference.

But it seems that the manner in which sovereignty was acquired and asserted does make a difference. If it did not, then the Crown would have to be viewed as capable of dictating unilaterally to First Nations the fundamental terms of the Crown-Native relationship. To avoid this consequence and maintain the honour of the Crown, the Court uses the fiduciary principle to set the default terms of the Crown's relationship with Aboriginal peoples.

Now, one may still think that, whatever the importance of the manner in which the Crown has asserted sovereignty over First Nations, the pre-existence of Aboriginal sovereignty and rights (including rights to land arising from prior occupation) plays an indispensable role in the justification of viewing the Crown as a fiduciary of Canada's First Nations, and from this indispensable role the *sui generis* thesis follows. Pre-existence is important, but to reiterate, the pre-existence of inherent Aboriginal rights informs the content of the Crown's public fiduciary obligations rather than the threshold question of whether public fiduciary obligations extend to non-Aboriginals. The following four arguments tell against the significance of pre-existence *per se* to Aboriginal rights, and thereby undermine pre-existence as a *necessary* condition of the rights the Crown's overarching fiduciary obligation is intended to protect. The final, fifth argument considers the relevance of pre-existing Aboriginal sovereignty to the *sui generis* thesis.

3.4.1 Aboriginal rights: inherent but dependent

The first argument is based on the Court's understanding of 'inherent' in the context of inherent Aboriginal rights. The case of Aboriginal title shows the sense in which the Court takes these rights to be inherent, but nonetheless dependent on a presumption of Crown sovereignty.

Aboriginal title in land derives from First Nations' historic occupation and use of their lands, and not from treaty, executive order, or legislative enactment.[15] In this sense, Aboriginal title is not contingent on any particular act of

[15] See eg *Mitchell v MNR* 2001 SCC 33; [2001] 1 SCR 911, para 146 (*Mitchell*).

government. In *Sparrow*, however, the Court reaffirmed its view that from at least the Royal Proclamation of 1763 onward, there was 'never any doubt that sovereignty and legislative power, and indeed the underlying title, to lands vested in the Crown'.[16] Therefore, while Aboriginal title derives from occupation and use of land that predates Crown sovereignty, its recognition by the Court is inexorably tied to an announcement of that sovereignty. The Court never suggests that Aboriginal title may ground a claim against Crown sovereignty or underlying title. Rather, it is a burden on that title.

While pre-existence plays a role in establishing Aboriginal rights to lands historically occupied by First Nations, those rights impose obligations on the Crown only once the Crown is deemed to hold the underlying title to the lands on which Aboriginal rights place a burden. That is, the moment Aboriginal title imposes legal obligations on the Crown is precisely the moment the assertion of Crown sovereignty obliterates Aboriginal peoples' pre-existent right to land (ie the right they enjoyed under Aboriginal rather than Crown law). The actual right that grounds present Crown obligations is not one that predates Crown sovereignty, but rather is one that, for the Court, is necessarily coextensive with Crown sovereignty. It follows that the pre-existent right does not impose legal obligations on the Crown while the post-Crown-sovereignty right does. This is just the effacing effect on pre-existent rights that the Court's blunt presumption of Crown sovereignty entails.

The analysis presented here is consistent with the doctrine of continuity which holds that 'the Crown, upon discovering and occupying a "new" territory, recognized the law and custom of the aboriginal societies it found and the rights in the lands they traditionally occupied that these supported'.[17] As we have seen, however, the Crown's recognition of the 'rights in the lands' of Aboriginal peoples is premised on an assumption of Crown sovereignty rather than on respect for Aboriginal rights as they existed prior to Crown sovereignty, as rights subject to and structured by Aboriginal rather than Crown law.

Because pre-existent Aboriginal rights do not underlie the Crown's present duties to Aboriginal peoples, they cannot distinguish the Crown's duties to First Nations from the Crown's duties to non-Aboriginals, and so they cannot support the *sui generis* thesis. Prior occupation of land supplies the content of Aboriginal rights, but the right of Aboriginal title to which the Crown's fiduciary obligation attaches is a burden-right which presupposes Crown sovereignty and underlying title to land.

[16] *Sparrow*, *supra* note 4, p 1103.

[17] *R v Van der Peet* [1996] 2 SCR 507, para 268.

3.4.2 The normative insignificance of pre-existence to Aboriginal rights

The second argument against an alleged pre-existence requirement is based on the sense in which pre-existence is an incidental and normatively insignificant feature of inherent Aboriginal rights. While it is of course the case that the activities which give rise to these rights predate Crown sovereignty, it is not the pre-existence *per se* of those activities that makes them worthy of the legal protection. What makes those activities the proper subject of rights, in principle and according to the Court, is their contribution to the flourishing of distinct Aboriginal cultures. It is this flourishing rationale, not pre-existence, that is central to the Court's recognition of Aboriginal rights. The flourishing rationale explains the Court's view that Aboriginal rights are not 'frozen' in time, but may evolve to protect specific activities that did not exist prior to Crown sovereignty, such as fishing with drift nets. Pre-existence attends the rights story, but plays no normative role within it.

3.4.3 The incapacity of mere rights

The third argument arises from the incapacity of inherent Aboriginal rights—or any kind of inherent rights—to generate by themselves a fiduciary obligation. It is the particular features of the Crown's interaction with First Nations—an interaction which begins with an assertion of sovereignty and culminates with exercises of administrative power—that give rise to a fiduciary duty. This sort of interactional requirement holds for all fiduciary duties, not just those present in the Crown-Native case.

A fiduciary duty is triggered only if a fiduciary relationship can be established. As we shall see in the next chapter, a mere right or legal interest—unless it is the right or interest of a party already recognized as the beneficiary of a fiduciary obligation—is never enough to ground a fiduciary obligation. In the absence of a fiduciary relationship, rights to hunt or fish or occupy certain lands cannot by themselves justify a fiduciary duty. Such pre-contact activities inform the content of Aboriginal rights, but they do not, without more, show those rights to be the subject matter of a fiduciary obligation.

3.4.4 The scope of the Crown's fiduciary duties

A further consideration against limiting the Crown's public fiduciary duties to First Nations on the basis of pre-existence is that the scope of the duties already touches rights other than those which pre-existed European settlement. The Crown's fiduciary obligations extend broadly to the Crown's 'dealings with Aboriginal peoples',[18] and those dealings may arise as a result of entitlements found in treaties, as well as in the administration of the Indian Act or other public law regimes. Statutory and treaty entitlements generally are not based on inherent and pre-existent Aboriginal rights, yet the Court takes them to be sufficient to establish a legal interest which can underlie a fiduciary obligation. Pre-existence, then, is neither a necessary nor sufficient condition of imposing a public fiduciary duty on the Crown, and thus cannot support the *sui generis* thesis.

3.4.5 Pre-existing Aboriginal sovereignty

One might think that the Crown is in a general fiduciary relationship with Aboriginal peoples alone because the Crown unilaterally asserted sovereignty over First Nations who once exercised *de facto* and *de jure* sovereignty over themselves. As we saw in Chapter II, the Supreme Court has held the Crown to be a fiduciary of First Nations in order to legitimize Crown sovereignty over First Nations, a sovereignty that is simply assumed.

Sovereignty, however, is always assumed. All states claim and assume authority over their people, and they exercise the same kinds of legislative, adjudicative, and administrative powers over them that the Crown exercises over First Nations in Canada, notwithstanding fiduciary duties that constrain these powers. This is the fact of sovereignty discussed in Chapter I. The Crown's invidious denial of Aboriginal sovereignty and the unilateral assertion of its own explains judicial recognition of the fiduciary relationship in the Crown-Native case, as well as the judiciary's reluctance to view the Crown as a public fiduciary elsewhere. The ultimate moral and legal justification of the Crown-Native relationship, however, remains tied to its fiduciary characteristics, ie to the Crown's possession and exercise of irresistible power over First Nations. Because the Crown exercises the same kinds of powers over all its subjects, the Crown-Native case supplies a rich precedent from which to extend the idea of the state as fiduciary to every person subject to state power. As in the First Nations case, the Crown's relationship with the public at large is best viewed as 'trust-like, rather than adversarial',[19] for the honour of the Crown is just as much at stake in its dealings with non-Aboriginals.[20]

[18] *Sparrow, supra* note 4, p 1114.

[19] Ibid, p 1107, Dickson CJ and La Forest J, characterizing the nature of Crown-Native relationship.

[20] In pioneering work on the state as fiduciary canvassed further in Chapter VI, Paul Finn notes that although the position of Aboriginal peoples 'in our public trust must be a distinctive one', they are 'beneficiaries of the *same* fiduciary (or trust) relationship' which exists between the state and the people (emphasis in original). PD Finn, 'A Sovereign People, A Public Trust' in PD Finn (ed), *Essays on Law and Government, Vol 1: Principles and Values* (Sydney: Law Book Company, 1995), p 18.

As Hobbes observed, whether sovereignty arises from acquisition or institution, the duties of the sovereign remain the same. Today we make the same point when we affirm that all states, regardless of their origins, are expected to govern in accordance with the rule of law. From the standpoint of the requirements of the rule of law, it makes no difference whether the present government (or form of government) came to power through democratic elections, constitutional reform, conquest, a *coup d'état*, secession, revolution, or any other means. As a principle of ongoing good governance, the rule of law is indifferent to the manner in which sovereignty is acquired because the target of its prescriptions is the current wielder of public power. Those prescriptions remain in force even if the government of the day systematically violates them, as arguably occurs when a settler state denies an Aboriginal people the right of self-determination. The fiduciary view of the state shares the rule of law's indifference to the origins of state power, and focuses instead on its present nature and consequences.

In summary: the *sui generis* features of the Crown-Native relationship—prior occupation of Canada; pre-existent Aboriginal customs, traditions, activities, rights, and sovereignty; and participation in a treaty process—show that the Crown owes distinct fiduciary obligations to Aboriginal peoples not owed to non-Aboriginals. The *sui generis* features do not show that the Crown-Native fiduciary relationship itself is entirely *sui generis* because the best justification of the relationship flows from the fact of sovereignty to which everyone in a state is subject. It follows that the *sui generis* thesis is false.

In the next chapter we consider in greater detail the general characteristics of the circumstances that give rise to a fiduciary relationship, and the argument that the state and subject are in such a relationship.

PART II

THE FIDUCIARY THEORY OF THE STATE

IV

Fiduciary Relationships and the Presumption of Trust

4.1 INTRODUCTION

We consider now the general argument for an overarching state-subject fiduciary relationship. I begin by distinguishing *de facto* and *de jure* sovereignty, and then explain how these dimensions of sovereignty relate to the distinction discussed in Chapter II between a state's legal and political authority. Legal authority flows from the rule of law and goes to the authority of the state to announce and enforce law, to establish legal order rather than some other kind of order. I argue in later chapters that a commitment to legal order, properly understood, entails a commitment to principles of fairness (Chapter VII), reasonableness (Chapter VIII), and human rights (Chapter IX). Political authority relates to the state's authority to determine the substantive content of law within the constitutional framework of principle supplied by the state's legal authority. As we shall see, consent is a plausible ground of political but not legal authority. Trust and the fiduciary principle's authorization of state power best justify legal authority. Together, legal authority and democratic political authority express the ideal of popular sovereignty, the notion that all public power ultimately derives from the people.

This chapter is primarily concerned with the circumstances that give rise to fiduciary relationships. The fact situation is much as Wilson J described it in *Frame v Smith*[1]: the candidate fiduciary must have unilateral discretionary power to affect the legal or practical interests of a peculiarly vulnerable party. The power at issue, however, must be of a certain kind: it must be administrative in nature in that it must be other-regarding, purposive, and institutional in character. And the beneficiary's vulnerability must arise from an incapacity on the part of the beneficiary to exercise or control the power entrusted to the fiduciary. The conjunction of these circumstances—the

[1] *Frame v Smith* [1987] 2 SCR 99.

fiduciary's possession of administrative power that the beneficiary is unable to exercise or control—explains the fiduciary's discretionary and unilateral authority, and reveals the fiduciary's position as one of trust. The argument concludes by connecting the foregoing analysis of fiduciary relationships to the position of the state's legal institutions *vis-à-vis* the people subject to them.

A further burden of this chapter is to explain the role of trust in fiduciary relations, including the state-subject fiduciary relationship. As we saw in *R v Sparrow*,[2] fiduciary relations are often said to be 'trust-like', or to involve trust in some sense. Specifying the role of trust, however, is complicated by the fact that many fiduciary relationships are nonconsensual (eg parent-child, trustee-beneficiary, state-subject). To make matters worse, the beneficiary might intensely distrust the fiduciary. If the beneficiary himself does not actually entrust his interests to the fiduciary's care, in what sense are fiduciary relationships trust-like? I argue that the position or office of the fiduciary is one of trust precisely because the beneficiary is unable, either as a matter of fact or law, to control the fiduciary's power. In fiduciary relations, it is the law rather than the beneficiary that entrusts the fiduciary with legal powers.

4.2 THE NATURE OF SOVEREIGNTY

State sovereignty denotes the effective authority of a state to rule and represent a permanent population within a given territory.[3] The possible forms sovereignty may assume (democracy, aristocracy, monarchy) are implicit in the idea, as are the kinds of claims that may be made in virtue of it, such as claims against other states and claims of obedience against those subject to the sovereign.

In Chapter II, I suggested that we can distinguish *de facto* and *de jure* sovereignty. *De facto* sovereignty refers to a brute ability to govern through effective institutions, whereas *de jure* sovereignty refers to the state's authority to do so. A rule-of-law abiding state governed by its own legal institutions enjoys *de facto* and *de jure* sovereignty. An illegal occupier may have *de facto* sovereignty but lacks permanent *de jure* sovereignty. While arguably the illegal occupier would have to possess the authority necessary to maintain legal order,

[2] *R v Sparrow* [1990] 1 SCR 1075, p 1107. See Chapter II (2.2) for discussion.

[3] See eg Patrick Macklem, 'What is International Human Rights Law? Three Applications of a distributive Account' (2007) 52 McGill LJ 575, p 586; RESTATEMENT (THIRD) OF FOREIGN RELATIONS OF THE UNITED STATES § 201 (1987) ('Under international law, a state is an entity that has a defined territory and a permanent population, under the control of its own government, and that engages in, or has the capacity to engage in, formal relations with other such entities').

the occupation is unlawful and so the occupier remains under a duty to cease the occupation. The international community gives the belligerent occupier a temporary and emergency warrant to maintain legal order because the occupier, during the occupation, is the only entity capable of doing so.[4] But the warrant is understood to be good only until such time as the public authority with legitimate *de jure* sovereignty is restored.

We can distinguish two further elements implicit in the idea of *de jure* sovereignty: the *legal* and the *political* bases of sovereignty. On the fiduciary theory, the legal basis of *de jure* sovereignty rests on a fiduciary relationship between the state and its subjects, and the state's compliance with its terms. The legal basis of sovereignty grounds the claims states can make against other states as an agent of its people, as well as claims against its subjects who have a (defeasible) duty to obey the law. In the next chapter we will see that the subject's duty to obey stands in a reciprocal relation to the state's fiduciary duty to the subject: the state must be under an obligation to announce and enforce law on the subject's behalf for the subject to have a duty to obey.

The political basis of *de jure* sovereignty refers to the authority of the state to determine the substantive content of its laws. The legislative branch of the state is the primary locus of this authority, but to the extent that the judiciary and the executive participate in law-making through adjudication and administration, they too share in the state's political authority. In a democracy, in the ordinary case, the state's institutions enjoy political authority inasmuch as they succeed in channelling the deliberative will or consent of the people into substantive policies. Democracy is a plausible political implication of the fiduciary model since democracy alone permits the people to hold public office holders electorally accountable.

In a democratic state, the distinction set out above between political and legal authority can be seen by comparing the way in which consent supplies a ready moral basis for the former but not the latter. In a representative democracy, periodic elections allow the people to choose their political leaders. Elected representatives thereby enjoy a popular mandate to design and implement substantive legislation which reflects the people's will, and they are subject to removal if they fail to do so. Democratically elected legislators and the policies they endorse thus embody the political authority that issues from democratic politics. Political authority is based, at least in part, on the expressed consent of the people, even if what the people are actually consenting to is the democratic process rather than its particular

[4] Belligerent occupation has much the same structure as child kidnapping. See Chapter 1, note 69. I am indebted to Evan Criddle for the idea of a temporary and emergency warrant in the case of belligerent occupation.

outcomes.[5] What is not at stake in an election, however, is the principle of government in accordance with the rule of law. Electors do not choose between some leaders who will rule through law and others who will not. An electorate does not vote on whether the winner of a fair and open election will have the authority to announce and enforce law. Whoever is elected will govern under law and the legal institutions through which law filters.[6]

Yet another rough way to cast the distinction between legal and political authority is in terms of form and substance. Generally speaking (within limits explored in Chapter IX), legal authority goes to the form of governance through law, whereas political authority speaks to the substance of particular laws.[7] But as the parent-child case shows, form can influence and constrain substance. The fiduciary form of the parent-child relationship requires the parent to care for her child, and as we shall see, the fiduciary form of the state-subject relationship requires the state to establish legal order through the rule of law.

The authority to establish legal order—legal authority—is a precondition of political authority. Its role as a precondition suggests several related senses in which legal authority helps constitute democratic political order. First, legal authority is constitutional in the narrow sense in that it is not ordinarily subject to electoral review. It is also constitutional in that it provides an enabling framework for the exercise of political authority. And, as Hobbes was anxious to show, legal authority permits the state to exercise authority rather than mere power. In this sense, legal authority constitutes a moral as well as factual precondition of political authority.

Yet even on a robust understanding of legal authority that requires the state to comply with the rule of law, all that follows is a hypothetical

[5] It would be an overstatement to say that democratic political authority is based *entirely* on consent. As Ethan Leib and David Ponet suggest, political theory must still confront Rousseau's claim that people are only really free on Election Day. During the periods between election days, a delegation or trustee model of representation must fill the gap. Leib and Ponet show that both models have ineliminable fiduciary aspects on which their legitimacy depends. We shall see that there is an important sense in which democratic political authority trades on consent in a way that legal authority cannot. For ease of exposition I will at times say that democratic political authority rests on consent, but I do not mean to imply that this is all there is to such authority. See: EJ Leib and DL Ponet, 'Fiduciary Representation and Deliberative Engagement with Children' (2011) *Journal of Political Philosophy* (in press) doi: 10.1111/j.1467-9760.2011.00398.x.

[6] This assumption resembles Hobbes's view, discussed in the Prologue, that principles of legality operate regardless of whether sovereign power takes the form of a monarchy, an aristocracy, or a democracy. While there is debate over whether Hobbes understood those principles to act as constraints on the sovereign, he plainly thought that in some form they must be present in any properly functioning civil society.

[7] Fuller's distinction between the internal morality of law and the law's substantive aims, discussed in Chapter IX, is premised on this same idea. Lon L Fuller, *The Morality of Law*, revised edn (New Haven: Yale University Press, 1969), p 153.

obligation of the form '*if* the state wishes to possess legal authority, then it must comply with the rule of law'. The fiduciary theory explains why the requirement to respect the rule of law is also a categorical and legal obligation owed by the state to its people: the state must respect the rule of law because it is a fiduciary of its people. This obligation is itself constitutional because the rule of law both constitutes and constrains exercises of legal and (therefore) political authority.[8] The constitutional dimensions of legal authority hint that something other than periodic expressions of popular will must underlie them. That something is a presumption that legal institutions must exercise public powers on the basis of the public's trust.

4.3 FIDUCIARY RELATIONSHIPS AND THE PRESUMPTION OF TRUST

Understanding the nature of the fact situation to which the fiduciary principle responds will help us to appreciate the sense in which fiduciary relationships—including the state-subject relationship—rest on a presumption of trust rather than consent. In the next chapter we shall see that accounts of legal obligation based on tacit and hypothetical consent run into difficulty since these accounts assume that subjects can have full-blooded legal obligations without explicitly consenting to state authority. It is instructive to consider whether trust faces a similar problem, since the duty to obey the law remains whether or not we do something explicit to repose trust in the state's legal institutions.

As we shall see, an explicit declaration of trust by the subject is unnecessary. Because some fiduciary relationships can arise from unilateral action taken by the fiduciary (such as procreation in the parent-child case), and even from the mere presence of irresistible administrative power, it is not necessary that the beneficiary actually does anything in order to trigger a fiduciary obligation. The fundamental conditions which give rise to a fiduciary relationship are the following: (i) the fiduciary has administrative power over the beneficiary or certain of her interests; (ii) the beneficiary is incapable of controlling the fiduciary's exercise of power, or is incapable in principle of exercising the kind of power held by the fiduciary; and (iii) the relevant interests of the beneficiary are capable of forming the subject

[8] David Dyzenhaus and other common law constitutionalists reach a similar conclusion through analysis of common law principles that judges have at their disposal on judicial review. See eg David Dyzenhaus, *The Constitution of Law: Legality in a Time of Emergency* (Cambridge: Cambridge University Press, 2006). As we shall see in Chapters VII and VIII, the fiduciary theory provides a conceptual framework that vindicates common law principles such as fairness and reasonableness, and, most importantly, explains the legal significance of vulnerable interests to exercises of public power.

matter of a fiduciary obligation. I argue that these conditions are necessary and, importantly, sufficient to justify the fiduciary's obligation as well as her discretionary authority. Trust, as we shall see, helps explain why this is so, especially in the critical case where the beneficiary has no pre-existing right to the subject matter of the fiduciary's duty.

4.4 RELATIONSHIPS ARISING BY OPERATION OF LAW

Before turning to how the law may deem a fiduciary relationship to take hold, it is important to have a clear idea from the outset of what it means for a relationship to be deemed by law, or alternatively, to arise by operation of law. One example of such a relationship is involuntary bailment. A bailee has possession of the property of another party, but has neither legal title to it nor a beneficial interest in it.[9] The bailee has a common law duty to take reasonable care of the goods possessed by her, so she is liable if her negligence causes the goods to be lost or damaged while in her care. *Voluntary* bailees, such as carriers and shippers, acquire their duties from a voluntary interaction (eg a shipping agreement) with the owner.

An *involuntary* bailee is someone who gratuitously takes possession of property that is not hers. The involuntary bailee has no obligation to pick up and take possession of the property she happens to find, but once she does, the law deems her to hold it on behalf of its owner. She cannot treat it as if it were hers, and the law imposes on her the same kinds of duties as if she had entered into a voluntary and explicit bailment relationship with the owner.[10] She cannot sell or simply abandon the owner's property. She must retain possession, and safeguard it with reasonable care. A bailment relationship of this sort is involuntary in the sense that, once the bailee takes possession of the owner's goods, the law deems the relationship to have materialized independently of anything the bailee may do or say to deny it.

In cases of involuntary bailment, however, the duty-imposing work is done by the owner's pre-existing property right in the thing the bailee finds and possesses. As discussed below, no such pre-existing right is necessary for the state to act as fiduciary of those subjects to its authority. Compare now the circumstances in which the law deems fiduciary obligations to arise.

[9] See *Coggs v Bernard* (1703) 92 ER 107 KB (Eng) (*Coggs*).

[10] Since *Coggs*, the law has moved towards applying a general negligence test of reasonable care to all cases of bailment. See *Davis v Pearce Parking Station Pty Ltd* (1954) 91 CLR 642; *Houghland v RR Low (Luxury Coaches) Ltd* [1962] 1 QB 694; *Thomas National Transport (Melbourne) Proprietary Ltd v May & Baker Proprietary Ltd* [1966] 115 CLR 353; *Pitt Son & Badgery Ltd v Proulefco SA* (1984) 153 CLR 644.

4.5 DO FIDUCIARY OBLIGATIONS RELY ON VOLUNTARY UNDERTAKINGS?

As noted above, fiduciary doctrine does not require the beneficiary to make an explicit or public declaration of her trust in the fiduciary. Where a fiduciary relationship exists, the law intervenes to protect the beneficiary's interests over which the fiduciary has administrative power. Nor is an agreement between the fiduciary and the beneficiary necessary. As Paul Finn puts it, typically 'the duties imposed on, and the powers exercised by [the fiduciary], each have a source *other than* in an agreement between him and the person(s) for whose benefit he is required to act—with the receiver, for example, they stem from the order of the court; with the executor, from the will, legislation and general law'.[11]

One might think that a fiduciary relationship could arise solely through a voluntary undertaking on the part of the fiduciary, such as the assumption of the office of trustee.[12] Fiduciary obligations entail personal liability, so justice would seem to require that a fiduciary's liability be limited to breaches of a duty she assumes as a consequence of a voluntary undertaking. Suppose that someone becomes the innocent (unknowing) recipient of trust money, and then proceeds to give the money away. Under certain circumstances a person who knowingly receives and disposes of trust property may be held liable as a constructive trustee.[13] But it would be unduly harsh to hold an innocent recipient personally liable for breach of a fiduciary duty (or any equitable duty) of which she had no knowledge.

The case of an innocent recipient reflects one of the foundational principles on which equity is based: the conscience of the defendant must be affected for equity to intervene.[14] The innocent recipient of trust property is deemed an 'innocent volunteer', and will not be held liable for breach of a fiduciary obligation if she disposes of the property without knowledge of its

[11] PD Finn, *Fiduciary Obligations* (Sydney: Law Book Co, 1977), p 9.

[12] *Hospital Products Ltd v United States Surgical Corporation* (1984) 156 CLR 41, pp 96–7, Mason J: 'The critical feature of these relationships is that the fiduciary undertakes or agrees to act for or on behalf of or in the interests of another person in the exercise of a power or discretion which will affect the interests of that other person in a legal or practical sense'. See also *Galambos v Perez* 2009 SCC 48; [2009] 3 SCR 247 (*Galambos*); Austin W Scott, 'The Fiduciary Principle' (1949) 37(4) Cal L Rev 539, p 540.

[13] John McGhee and Edmund Henry Turner Snell, *Snell's Equity*, 30th edn (London: Sweet & Maxwell, 2000), pp 222–4 (McGhee, *Snell's*). For example, if the recipient knows of the property's trust character and knows as well that the transfer to him was in breach of trust, his disposal of it in a manner inconsistent with the terms of the trust may trigger liability in equity on the basis of dishonest assistance in the breach of a trust or, alternatively, on the basis of knowing receipt.

[14] For a recent affirmation of this principle, see the speech of Lord Brown-Wilkinson in *Westdeutsche Landesbank v Islington London Borough Council* [1996] 2 WLR 802.

trust character.[15] But we do not need to invoke the innocent recipient's lack of consent to undertake a fiduciary office (or to assume any sort of equitable obligation) to reach this conclusion; her lack of knowledge is enough. So, if knowing receipt can trigger a fiduciary obligation, it follows that it is not the putative fiduciary's consent to the obligation that necessarily gives rise to it (though consent would suffice), but rather knowing that one is in a position to which a fiduciary obligation may attach. Hence, a party may be held liable for breach of a fiduciary duty if she knows that she is in a fiduciary position but did not voluntarily assume it.[16]

This conclusion bears directly on the argument concerning the fiduciary position of the state. The application of the fiduciary principle in this context has nothing to do with whether states possess and exercise sovereign power through voluntary undertakings. If in some meaningful sense they do, this augurs well for the claim that the state is a fiduciary, since voluntary undertakings certainly can give rise to fiduciary obligations. The point of the preceding analysis is simply to show that a voluntary undertaking on the part of the fiduciary is not necessary to establish the existence of a fiduciary obligation.[17]

4.6 FIDUCIARY POWER AS ADMINISTRATIVE POWER

The fundamental interaction that triggers a fiduciary obligation is the fiduciary's exercise of a certain kind of discretionary power over the interests of another party, interests that are vulnerable by virtue of that power. But not all instances of discretionary *power* denote the presence of discretionary *authority* and a fiduciary relationship.

When a motorist approaches a pedestrian on a crosswalk, she has discretionary power to affect unilaterally and radically the interests of someone who is at her mercy and vulnerable to her power.[18] Superficially, this interaction seems to satisfy Wilson J's 'rough and ready' guide from *Frame*, but it is odd to think that the motorist and the pedestrian are in a

[15] McGhee, *Snell's*, *supra* note 13, pp 223–4. If she possesses the property, however, and is not a *bona fide* purchaser for value, she will be liable to restore it to its beneficial owner.

[16] See *M(K) v M(H)* [1992] 3 SCR 6, La Forest J, p 63: '[F]iduciary obligations are imposed in some situations even in the absence of any unilateral undertaking by the fiduciary'.

[17] I do not mean to imply that the state or its agents must have knowledge of their fiduciary position for an obligation to attach. Knowledge is necessary in the private law context due to the injustice of holding a private party personally liable for breach of an obligation that would apply but for the fact that the party neither knowingly nor willingly assumed a fiduciary position. In public law, where public actors typically are not held personally liable for the decisions they make, this consideration does not apply as a bar to finding that a public fiduciary obligation is due.

[18] I am indebted to Lionel Smith for the example, who in turn credits Morris Litman.

fiduciary relationship. Missing from Wilson J's guide is an adequate account of the nature of a fiduciary's discretionary power.

The challenge is to explain the kind of discretionary powers that do give rise to fiduciary relationships in a way that lets us distinguish exercises of sheer power with no fiduciary implications, such as the power of the motorist. This analytic exercise has to take place at the level of facts, or somewhere between facts and the ultimate legal norms thought to arise from the relevant fact pattern, since the purpose of the exercise is to give us a better sense of the nature of the circumstances to which the fiduciary principle applies. It will not do, for example, to say simply that the fiduciary principle responds to situations where one party has authority to act on behalf of another party, because part of what we are trying to explain (along with the fiduciary's obligation) is the fiduciary's authority to act on behalf of the beneficiary.

Sometimes vulnerability is taken to be the fundamental dimension of the fiduciary relationship,[19] so it may seem curious that I focus here on discretionary power. In fact, power and vulnerability are intimately related. The kind of vulnerability at issue arises on account of the fiduciary's unilateral power to affect the beneficiary's interests. While many beneficiaries, such as clients of solicitors, retain residual control over the fiduciary, these relationships are fiduciary as well as contractual because the fiduciary has some discretion to exercise her power unilaterally, without specific guidance from the beneficiary.

In the next section I argue that a necessary condition of fiduciary relations is that the beneficiary must be incapable of providing specific guidance to the power holder in at least some situations, or incapable in principle of exercising the kind of power held by the fiduciary. In this sense, the beneficiary is vulnerable to the fiduciary's discretionary power. Saying that the beneficiary is vulnerable, however, does not help to distinguish the beneficiary from the imperilled pedestrian. What is needed is an explanation of why the beneficiary's vulnerability helps to generate a fiduciary relationship rather than simply a claim in tort in the event of injury. This explanation requires further specification of the kind of discretionary power that places the beneficiary in a vulnerable position.

Sometimes the fiduciary's ability to change the legal position of the beneficiary *vis-à-vis* third parties is cited as the *sine qua non* of a fiduciary's

[19] In *Lac Minerals Ltd v International Corona Resources Ltd* [1989] 2 SCR 574, the majority held (p 599) that '[t]he one feature, however, which is considered to be indispensable to the existence of the relationship, and which is most relevant in this case, is that of dependency or vulnerability'. In *Hodgkinson v Simms* [1994] 3 SCR 377, however, the majority found that vulnerability was just one of several factors that had to be taken into account to determine whether a fiduciary relationship exists on the facts, ibid, p 409.

power.[20] However, we cannot stipulate that it is the fiduciary's legal authority to deal with third parties that picks out the factual circumstances to which the fiduciary principle applies, since this *de jure* authority is part of the fiduciary principle we are trying to explain. And as we shall now see, a mere *de facto* capacity to affect a principal's interests *vis-à-vis* third-parties does not necessarily give rise to a fiduciary relationship.

A thief who steals and converts a chattel demonstrates a *de facto* capacity to affect his victim's interests *vis-à-vis* third-parties, but we need not presume that a fiduciary relationship exists between thief and victim to explain the thief's liability. While the thief would face civil as well as criminal liability, the basis of the thief's liability is the victim's property interest in the thing stolen, just as the liability of a wrong-doing involuntary bailee would rest on the owner's pre-existing property right in the thing the bailee finds. Technically, the thief cannot be a trustee because the thief does not have legal title (trustees hold bare legal title, while beneficiaries hold the equitable or beneficial interest in the estate). And as we shall see in greater detail below, to say that the thief is an entrusted fiduciary would extend fiduciary doctrine into a domain that property law appears fully capable of handling. Thus, a *de facto* capacity to affect another's interests *vis-à-vis* third parties (such as the thief's capacity to sell stolen goods) does not necessarily trigger the fiduciary principle.

Nonetheless, the capacity to deal with third parties points us in a useful direction, since part of a fiduciary's discretionary power typically includes such a capacity. Generally, the kind of power a fiduciary exercises is more than a simple possessory or dispositive control over another party's interests. This power is complex, involving incidents that are best captured and thematically unified by the idea of administration.

Administration implies a capacity to exercise discretion on behalf of a principal with respect to certain interests, and *vis-à-vis* third parties. But administration is not random, nor is it created by the chance encounters occasioned by theft and motor vehicle accidents. Administration is *structurally* different from discrete exercises of mere power in a number of ways. Administration, in the relevant sense, implies the use of discretion for some purpose, and that purpose involves the benefit of someone other than the person conducting the administration. Where a person is conducting administration for her sole benefit, there is no possibility of a fiduciary relationship, because one cannot be in a legal relationship with oneself. Whatever the source of

[20] Macdonald JA put the point as follows: 'The reason such persons [directors] are subjected to the fiduciary relationship apparently is because they have a leeway for the exercise of discretion in dealing with third parties which can affect the legal position of their principals', *HL Misener & Son Ltd v Misener* (1977) 77 DLR (3d) 428 (NSCA), p 440.

administrative power, it always comes with a particular and other-regarding mandate, often but not always the result of an express delegation of decision-making authority. Administration, therefore, is purposeful rather than accidental in the sense that the reason for which administrative power is exercised must be consistent with the other-regarding purpose for which it is held.[21]

Administration is also necessarily institutional in nature if it is to give rise to fiduciary duties. Administration takes place within a particular institution that can persist *de jure* over time, and which is animated by its own substantive values and internal practices. The relevant values and practices will reflect the underlying purpose of the institution. In the case of a corporation, for example, the primary value is profitmaking, and internal practices include delegation of management duties to managing officers, supervisory board meetings, and periodic audits.

For the institutional aspect of administration to contribute to a general account of fiduciary relations, however, it must be construed in a more conceptual sense than one may glean from the case of the corporation. Fiduciary administrative power is institutional in this conceptual sense in that it necessarily takes place within a relationship that takes the form of a legally permissible institution, such as the family, the trust, the doctor-patient relationship, partnerships, and so on. This is not to say that every (fiduciary) relationship must fit within a pre-existing category; the Crown-Native relationship demonstrates that the fiduciary principle can apply to new contexts. Courts now habitually distinguish between *per se* and *ad hoc* fiduciary relationships.[22] Rather, the point is that for purposive and other-regarding administration to give rise to a fiduciary relationship, it must be institutional in the sense that it must be amenable to a lawful institutional framework, one that is intelligible as a legal structure capable of regulating the ongoing rightful conduct of an administrator *vis-à-vis* the beneficiary.

To satisfy this condition of legality, the relationship cannot be one that is intrinsically unlawful. Just as the law does not recognize an otherwise valid contract if the service contracted for is the commission of a crime, an intrinsically unlawful relationship cannot ground or constitute a legal institution. Kidnapping, for example, places a vulnerable hostage under the

[21] The 'other-regarding' characteristic of administrative power is intended to be read narrowly, as merely a description that distinguishes the kind of administrative power that may give rise to a fiduciary relationship from a kind that cannot. It is not intended to moralize administration, but to distinguish self-regarding from other-regarding administration. The other-regarding character of administrative power does not in itself imply that the power-holder is under an obligation to exercise her power in a certain way. This characteristic is merely a structural feature of the factual circumstances that must be present to trigger the fiduciary principle.

[22] See eg *Galambos*, *supra* note 12, para 12.

discretionary control of the kidnapper, but kidnapping is intrinsically unlawful, and therefore cannot constitute a legal institution.[23] Instead, the law seeks the immediate dissolution of such relations.

The hostage has claims against the kidnapper, such as wrongful confinement and personal injury, but these are claims under tort rather than fiduciary law. Consider the obligation of a kidnapper to feed her hostage. This may appear fiduciary-like because it involves a positive duty arising from the kidnapper's control over the hostage. But the duty is really a tort duty, and in one sense analogous to the duty of care a rescuer owes to a rescuee:[24] both must take positive actions arising from a tort duty of care because both rescuing and hostage-taking impose risks. So the tort duty arises only as a consequence of the prior *and enduring* wrong. It is not just that the origin of the relationship is wrongful, it is that the wrong of kidnapping persists until the relationship ends. In a sense, feeding the hostage is just a way for the kidnapper to mitigate the liability that would arise on grounds of personal injury if the kidnapper starved rather than fed the hostage. And so the kidnapper's civil liability and the hostage's rights to recover can be explained through tort law, without recourse to fiduciary doctrine.

Of course, legal institutions can be put to wicked ends and nonetheless remain legal institutions. Corporate fraud and intentional medical malpractice reveal a failure on the part of participants to respect the legal limits of their respective institutions. The institutions remain legal institutions, however, because it is always possible for the participants within them to interact with each other rightfully, on terms of secure and equal freedom. Not so in the cases of kidnapping and theft. Because kidnapping and theft are premised on and structured by the instrumentalization of one party by another, there is nothing the wrong-doers can do to make these wrongs rightful. Kidnapping and theft necessarily interfere wrongfully with the freedom or property of others. As intrinsically unlawful practices, kidnapping and theft cannot assume the form of legal institutions, and so they cannot give rise to fiduciary relationships.

[23] The kidnapping of children presents complications, discussed in Chapter I, because the kidnapper assumes the office of *de facto* guardian. The kidnapper *qua* kidnapper owes no fiduciary duties to a kidnapped infant whom she raises, but the kidnapper *qua* guardian does. This complication does not arise in the case of kidnapped adults because adults (comatose patients and like cases aside) are not each other's guardians. In the text I assume the kidnappee is a competent adult.

[24] *Glanzer v Shephard* 135 NE 275, p 276 (NY 1922). Cardozo J: '[O]ne who assumes to act, even though gratuitously, may thereby become subject to the duty of acting carefully'. Arguably, a gratuitous rescuer of a comatose person or child could become that person's guardian and subject to fiduciary duties, notwithstanding that at common law there is no duty to rescue. For discussion of the lack of a duty to rescue at private law, see Arthur Ripstein, 'Three Duties to Rescue: Moral, Civil, and Criminal' (2000) 19 (6) Law & Phil 751.

In conclusion, instances of discretionary power that reside outside of the institutional, purpose-laden, and other-regarding framework that administration makes possible (eg the power to mow down a pedestrian, steal or kidnap) are not the sorts of discretionary power to which the fiduciary principle responds. While the other-regarding and purposeful aspects of administrative power are factual, the institutional element has both a factual and a thin normative dimension. The normative dimension is thin because it does not explain how legal institutions can give rise to fiduciary obligations, but rather disqualifies intrinsically wrongful relationships from doing so. A much thicker normative argument is required to explain how administrative power can trigger fiduciary duties. We glimpsed this argument in Chapter I with the parent-child case, and will develop it momentarily, once we have in clearer view the second necessary condition of fiduciary relationships: the beneficiary's inability to exercise or control the power held by the fiduciary.

4.7 VULNERABILITY AS INCAPACITY

Beneficiaries are vulnerable in that they are exposed to abuses of fiduciary power. But as we saw above, mere exposure to power and abuse does not explain why the law lends some instances of vulnerability its fiduciary aegis and not others. From the fiduciary's side of the relationship, administrative power is the necessary and constitutive form of fiduciary power. We now consider vulnerability from the beneficiary's side, and attempt to specify the requisite form of the beneficiary's vulnerability in fiduciary relationships.

In many fiduciary relations (eg lawyer-client, doctor-patient, agent-principal), the fiduciary is a person to whom the beneficiary has turned for professional services or advice. The fiduciary is empowered to act on the beneficiary's behalf, and the things she is empowered to do for the beneficiary (defend a suit, tend an injury, sign a contract) are things that the beneficiary is legally entitled to do for herself. Sometimes the beneficiary retains a measure of residual control in that she can provide specific guidance to the fiduciary, such as instructions that an agent is not to sign a contract unless it contains certain terms. Nonetheless, the fiduciary will usually have a margin of discretionary authority to decide how best to further her beneficiary's interests, an authority the fiduciary can exercise without going back to the beneficiary to obtain fresh consent. For example, unless the client has given instructions to the contrary, a lawyer may negotiate and conclude a compromise settlement to a suit without seeking her client's consent.[25]

[25] See eg *Waugh v HB Clifford & Sons Ltd* [1982] 1 All ER 1095, CA (Eng).

More generally still, the fiduciary's power over the beneficiary's interests generally gives her the *de facto* ability to exercise loyally or not the entrusted power she possesses. An agent can sign or not a contract on behalf of her principal from which she will gain a secret profit. A lawyer can accept or not a bribe from the other side in exchange for settling a suit on unfavourable terms. Because the beneficiary and the fiduciary are separate persons who can act independently, the beneficiary is *de facto* incapable of exercising the power the fiduciary possesses. To this extent at least, the beneficiary is vulnerable to the fiduciary's discretion.

The beneficiary may also be barred *de jure* from controlling the fiduciary's power. In many trustee-beneficiary relationships, settlors establish trusts that deliberately restrict the ability of the beneficiary to control the trustee. For instance, parents may establish an educational trust fund that limits expenditures from the fund to educational purposes. As a rule, the trustee must respect those limits even if the child-beneficiary reaches majority and insists that she has no interest in pursuing higher education. Nevertheless, the administrative power the trustee possesses is still of a kind that, under other circumstances, could be exercised by the beneficiary: rather than establish a trust, the parents could give the investment portfolio of the would-be trust fund directly to the child. In Table I below, I call the *de facto* and *de jure* incapacity of these sorts of cases—cases in which the beneficiary could in principle exercise the kind of power held by the fiduciary—'contextual incapacity', since the scope and nature of the beneficiary's incapacity varies with contextual considerations that determine the

Table I: Types of incapacity

Type of incapacity	Type of beneficiary
Contextual incapacity: The beneficiary *can* in principle exercise the kind of power entrusted to the fiduciary, but the beneficiary is *de facto* or *de jure* unable to control or exercise the fiduciary's power.	• beneficiaries of trusts • clients of solicitors or financial advisers • patients • principals of agents
Juridical incapacity: The beneficiary *cannot* in principle exercise the kind of power entrusted to the fiduciary, either because the beneficiary lacks legal capacity, is an artificial person, or is a private party in a multi-beneficiary or public context.	• children, wards, comatose patients, persons with a cognitive disability • corporations, partnerships, joint ventures • pension fund beneficiaries, parties to an arbitration, private parties *vis-à-vis* public authority

breadth and basis of the fiduciary's discretion. We can distinguish contextual incapacity from another kind: 'juridical incapacity'.

Juridical incapacity differs from contextual incapacity in that juridically incapable beneficiaries cannot *in principle* exercise the kind of power the fiduciary exercises. We can further divide these kinds of beneficiaries into three classes, where each class is defined by the underlying explanation of its members' incapacity. First, there are persons who lack legal capacity to act as autonomous adults, such as children, wards of guardians, comatose patients, and persons with a cognitive disability. Second, there are artificial persons that cannot act except through their agents or representatives, such as corporations, partnerships, and joint ventures. Third, and most interesting for present purposes, there are beneficiaries subject to a fiduciary power to which other beneficiaries are also subject.

In the private sphere, pension funds supply an interesting example of this third class: the funds' directors must exercise their powers fairly and reasonably, taking into account the interests of each of the funds' beneficiaries.[26] Similar principles are at play in the public sphere. In Chapter II we have seen already that the Crown must act as an impartial fiduciary of First Nations with competing claims.[27] And in the Prologue we saw that one of Hobbes' most important principles of legality, a principle reaffirmed in the common law, is that no one may be judge and party to the same cause. Towards the end of this chapter, and in the next, I argue that this juridical incapacity extends to the relationship between private parties and public authority generally: private parties as such are not entitled to exercise public powers of legislation, adjudication, administration, or law enforcement.[28] As a consequence, legal subjects are especially vulnerable to state power, and in a way that resembles the vulnerability of children, artificial persons, pension fund beneficiaries, and competing First Nations: all are juridically incapable of exercising the fiduciary power that governs their interests. As we shall see in the next chapter, the legal subject's juridical incapacity plays a central role in the justification of state authority and the subject's duty to obey the law. The state's sheer power may be irresistible as a matter of fact, but its authority is also morally irresistible because private parties are not entitled to exercise it and yet they are entitled to the legal order that public power can establish on their behalf.

[26] See eg *Equitable Life Assurance Society v Hyman* [2000] 2 All ER 331, CA (Eng), *aff'd* [2000] UKHL 39; [2002] 1 AC 408; [2000] 3 All ER 961, HL (Eng). I discuss some pension fund cases in Chapter VI.

[27] *Wewaykum Indian Band v Canada* 2002 SCC 79; [2002] 4 SCR 245.

[28] Hobbes is again instructive: 'by public is always meant either the person of the commonwealth itself or something that is so the commonwealth's as no private person can claim any propriety therein' (L xxxv.15, 277).

A question arises: does incapacity really refer to a necessary condition of fiduciary relations that is logically independent of the fiduciary's administrative power? It may appear that at least *de facto* contextual incapacity is implicit within the concept of administrative power, since the very idea of administrative power seems to announce a domain in which unilateral exercises of power are empirically possible. The short answer is that, from the point of view of specifying the conditions that give rise to a fiduciary relationship, it makes no difference whether incapacity is a logically independent condition or derivable from administrative power. What matters is whether incapacity is conceptually significant in the sense that we must refer to it to explain best the conditions that trigger application of the fiduciary principle. We shall see that incapacity does enjoy this conceptual significance within fiduciary relations.

While the fiduciary's possession of administrative power gives rise to *de facto* incapacity in lawyer-client or agent-principal type relations, it neither causes nor explains juridical incapacity. In the parent-child and artificial person cases, juridical incapacity arises from the beneficiary's inability to act as an autonomous legal person, an inability that is explicable without reference to the fiduciary's power. In the public office and multi-beneficiary cases, incapacity flows from the prohibition on private parties exercising public (or public-like) powers. This prohibition is also fully intelligible without reference to administrative power. What unites these cases is a lack of capacity to control or exercise an administrative power to which the beneficiary is subject. In parent-child relations this lack of capacity implies that the child is unable to consent to the parent-child relationship, and so the fiduciary principle must set the terms of the relationship for it to be rightful. Similarly, in cases of *de facto* incapacity in which the beneficiary can consent to the relationship but cannot exercise the entrusted power simply because the fiduciary possesses it, the fiduciary principle intercedes to control the power on behalf of the beneficiary. Thus, *de facto* as well as juridical incapacity is conceptually significant because it too helps explain (independently of administrative power) why the fiduciary principle is triggered in certain circumstances.

Summing up: the fiduciary principle is triggered if (i) a person or certain of her interests are subject to administrative power that is other-regarding, purposeful, and institutional, and (ii) she is *de facto* or *de jure* incapable of controlling or exercising the power (but in other circumstances she could exercise this kind of power herself), or she is in principle incapable of exercising the kind of power the fiduciary exercises on her behalf. Administrative power is the requisite form of the fiduciary's power, while incapacity is the requisite form of the beneficiary's vulnerability. Combined, the two conditions depict administrative power that is irresistible because the beneficiary is either factually or legally incapable of exercising it. A final condition, discussed below, is that the beneficiary's entrusted interests must be capable of forming the subject matter of a fiduciary obligation.

4.8 TRUST AS THE BASIS OF THE FIDUCIARY'S AUTHORITY AND DUTY

The above characterizations of administrative power and incapacity intentionally avoid reliance on (thick) normative premises related to the fiduciary's authority and duty *vis-à-vis* the beneficiary; the point was to identify the necessary general conditions that can plausibly give rise to fiduciary relationships. We still need to set out a moral basis that can explain why the exercise of irresistible administrative power triggers a fiduciary obligation. The relevant moral basis, I argued in Chapter I, lies in Kant's conception of the person as a being who possesses an innate moral capacity to place others under obligation. This capacity operates of its own accord—without the beneficiary being required to do anything—so that when a fiduciary unilaterally exercises administrative power over a vulnerable beneficiary, she is subject to a fiduciary obligation.

In this section, I suggest that a complementary and perhaps more accessible way to understand the Kantian moral basis of the fiduciary principle is that it is premised on a presumption of trust. Specifically, when a fiduciary exercises irresistible administrative power, she does so on the basis of the beneficiary's trust. This presumption explains the fiduciary's obligation and authorization to act on the beneficiary's behalf. As we shall see, the presumption of trust illuminates the Kantian analysis of fiduciary relations in a more familiar moral light, and in a way that explains why these relationships are commonly understood to be relations of trust rather than consent. Even in the absence of pre-existing rights and prior consent, a presumption of trust and its attendant obligations can authorize the fiduciary to act on behalf of the beneficiary. On this construal, trust operates as an expressly normative concept that triggers the fiduciary principle regardless of whether or not the beneficiary has actually done something to repose trust in the fiduciary. An important consequence of the presumption of trust is that it renders the fiduciary's exercise of power justifiable to the beneficiary, for it is on the beneficiary's trust that the fiduciary's authority depends.

This characterization of the role of trust may appear curious, since we tend to think that someone has my trust only if I do something to give it to her. In the growing philosophical literature on trust, there is general agreement that trust involves a three-part relationship in which one party entrusts another with discretionary power to act on behalf of the trusting party; that is, A trusts B to do C on behalf of A.[29] Nonetheless, the conventional understanding of the three-part trust relationship can be interpreted to include the following formulation: the *law* entrusts an actor, B, to do C on behalf of A. In the critical case of this study, the fiduciary principle entrusts the state to establish legal order on behalf of the people. The state in turn exercises power on the basis of the people's trust (the public trust) precisely because the fiduciary principle has entrusted the state with public powers on their behalf. Thus, trust plays a central role in the state-subject fiduciary relationship even if the subject rejects the state's claim of authority over her and distrusts the state. As we shall see now, the idea of a presumption of trust on which I am relying reflects the way trust operates within fiduciary relationships at private law.

As Peter Birks put it, '[a] fiduciary is someone whom one can trust and rely on, as a beneficiary can trust and rely on a trustee'.[30] From a legal point of view, to say that a beneficiary can trust and rely on a fiduciary means that the law requires the fiduciary to exercise power on the basis of the beneficiary's trust. Because the fiduciary is legally required to act in conformity with obligations that flow from the trust-like nature of the relationship, the beneficiary is assured that the law protects his entrusted interests. Thus, the beneficiary has a legal basis to trust and rely on the fiduciary, whether or not he in fact trusts her. But for this legal basis, the beneficiary could not rely on the fiduciary to fulfil her obligations as a matter of law, since she would be legally free to do as she pleases. In sum, the fiduciary obligations assumed with every exercise of fiduciary power give the beneficiary reason to trust and rely on the fiduciary, since those obligations make the fiduciary liable to the beneficiary should the fiduciary breach them.

Now, it may be possible to construe trust as a kind of open-ended and hypothetical consent to discretionary power that is to be used exclusively for the trusting party's benefit. This is close to the position taken by Law and Economics scholars who claim that the default rights and duties of fiduciary law should be seen as proxies for the terms that the relevant parties would negotiate if the transaction costs of negotiation were sufficiently low.[31] On this understanding of fiduciary obligation, the beneficiary's trust cashes out

[29] See eg Annette Baier, 'Trust and Antitrust' (1986) 96(2) *Ethics* 231: 'A trusts B with valued thing C'. For just a few reaffirmations of the three-part conception, see Richard Holton, 'Deciding to Trust, Coming to Believe' (1994) 72(1) *Australasian Journal of Philosophy* 63, p 66; Russell Hardin, 'The Street-Level Epistemology of Trust' (1993) 21 *Politics and Society* 505, p 506.

[30] Peter Birks, 'The Content of the Fiduciary Obligation' (2000) 1 Isr LR 3, p 8.

[31] See eg Michael Klausner, 'Corporations, Corporate Law, and Networks of Contracts' (1995) 81(3) Va L Rev 757, p 768, where he describes the Law and Economics view according to which the content of default terms 'should be governed by a judgment regarding the terms that firms would select in the absence of transaction costs'.

as hypothetical consent to the fiduciary's authority in the following terms: 'If you assume administrative and discretionary power over any of my interests, I authorise you to use such power only so long as you use it exclusively for my benefit'.

Twisting trust into hypothetical consent in this fashion, however, may let us explain the *source* of the fiduciary obligation, but it fails to explain the *nature* of the obligation as one of loyalty. This is so notwithstanding even specific consent to a grant of authority that may be exercised solely for the benefit of the consenting party. In these circumstances, the moral authority of consent does not imply that the duty is one of loyalty. Rather, the duty flows from the specific thing to which consent was given, ie discretionary power bridled with a duty of loyalty. Consent permits us to stipulate fiduciary obligations, but there is nothing intrinsic to consent to suggest that fiduciary duties would ever arise in the absence of an express stipulation mandating such duties.

The law makes this clearer still. While contractual relations do not necessarily preclude fiduciary relations, the presence of a contract will usually weigh against the recognition of fiduciary duties, especially with respect to contracts negotiated by arm's length parties.[32] The point to a contract is to let the parties pursue their own interests on mutually agreeable terms. There is never a presumption that one party owes the other a duty of loyalty. All that is presumed is a duty of performance. The moral authority implicit in trust, on the other hand, does explain the duty of loyalty, because loyalty is necessary to sustain the purpose of the grant of authority inherent in any fiduciary relationship. In the context of fiduciary relations, entrusted authority just means authority that will be used exclusively on behalf of the beneficiary or for the purposes for which the authority is held. In short, the fiduciary principle's capacity to impose obligations of trust on the fiduciary reveals the sense in which trust is to fiduciary relations what consent is to contractual relations: both supply a non-instrumental and moral basis to legal obligations appropriate to the kind of relationship they each control.

Notice as well that there is a significant difference in the conditions under which the law can point to consent, on the one hand, and trust, on the other, to authorize us to act on behalf of others. The law can authorize us to act for another party on the basis of the other party's consent, but *only if* the other party has in fact given her consent. Sometimes, however, the law alone can authorize us to act on behalf of another party, and a plausible interpretation of this authorization is that it flows from the other party's trust. Like parents

[32] See eg *Jirna Ltd v Mister Donut of Canada Ltd* (1971) 22 DLR (3d) 639 (Ont CA); *aff'd* [1975] 1 SCR 2.

vis-à-vis children, we can find ourselves in circumstances in which the other party has not consented or done anything to entrust us with authority, and yet we may be thought to be acting on the basis of the other party's trust. The doctor in an emergency room who treats an unconscious patient may be thought to be acting on the basis of the patient's trust, and therefore the doctor must treat the patient with due regard for his best interests. While doctors in these circumstances are sometimes said to act with the patient's 'implied consent', the best explanation of this variety of notional consent is that the doctor is under a prior obligation to the patient, an obligation that flows from the trust-like nature of her office. Consent in this case (such as it is) must be 'implied' because it is not actually given.

Interestingly, Annette Baier considers infant trust of parents to display most vigorously the difference between moral relations premised on trust rather than consent[33]:

> Whereas it strains the concept of agreement to speak of unconscious agreements and unchosen agreements, and overstrains the concept of contract to speak of unconscious or unchosen contracts, there is no strain whatever in the concept of automatic and unconscious trust, and of unchosen but mutual trust. Trust between infant and parent, at its best, exhibits such primitive and basic trust.

If Baier is right, and if 'automatic and unconscious' trust can attend relationships marked by irresistible power, this may capture the sense of trust that people have in the state that exercises such power over them, even if they have never done anything explicit to repose trust in the state. The idea of automatic trust fits congenially with Kant's idea that persons have an innate right of humanity that can place others under obligation without any act being required of the right-holder.

Moreover, the possibility of automatic trust suggests that we do not strain the basic concept by supposing that the fiduciary must exercise power on the basis of the beneficiary's trust, since, according to Baier, trust can exist between two parties without either one making a show of it. In the public sphere this conception of trust is especially apt. We assume that public authorities must exercise power on the basis of a public trust, even if our officials have become very unpopular and in fact are untrustworthy. Thus we can say that corrupt officials breach the public trust even if we do not actually trust them; they violate the public trust because they are always under an obligation to act on the basis of this trust.

These arguments all tend to the following conclusion: we can act on the basis of another party's consent only if that party has actually given her

[33] Baier, *supra* note 29, pp 244–5.

consent, but we can act on the basis of another party's trust even if that party has done nothing to repose trust in us. It follows that a fiduciary can act on the basis of a beneficiary's trust even if the beneficiary has done nothing to repose trust in the fiduciary.

Puzzles appear when we consider cases in which the state exercises power over strangers who do not belong to the state and who have no previous connection to it (eg decisions on who is to be allowed to become a citizen and decisions to go to war). In these circumstances, it seems to strain even the concept of automatic trust to say that the people affected have a sense of trust in the relevant state, since by hypothesis there is no prior relationship on which to ground such trust. Nonetheless, the distinction drawn above between acting on the basis of consent and acting on the basis of trust implies that it is possible for the fiduciary state to act on the basis of the stranger's trust. The state's power remains irresistible and administrative in nature, and strangers too have an innate right of humanity capable of placing the state under obligation. It is not too far a stretch to think that the state is under an obligation to exercise power over strangers on the same basis as it exercises power over its own subjects, which is to say, on the basis of their trust. Naturally, we would expect the duties owed to extra-territorial strangers to be thinner than the duties owed to subjects, since the state is responsible to its subjects alone for the provision of domestic legal order. Working out the details of the duties states may owe foreign nationals is well beyond the scope of this work. Nonetheless, the fiduciary model points to a helpful relational theory in which to situate and justify those duties.

Arguably, our innate right of humanity alone requires the state to act subject to fiduciary constraints regardless of whether we are citizens or strangers. Trust provides an argument for state authority in addition to this Kantian account because, as the case of public trust suggests, the state is required to act on the basis of our trust (and so within fiduciary limits) even if we happen to distrust the state intensely, and even if we have never consented to the authority the state claims over us. The two arguments, however, are best read as one: they both speak to the idea that human beings possess a dignity capable of placing the state under obligation as a consequence of the irresistible administrative power the state exercises over them.

Before turning to the argument that the state is a fiduciary, one more aspect of the fiduciary conceptual framework must be developed. We need to show how the state can be a fiduciary without assuming that the subject has a pre-existing legal right to be a member of a legal order (if such a right existed, the fiduciary theory would not be necessary, and assuming it from the outset begs the question). The fiduciary theory can accommodate this demand because fiduciary obligations can protect practical interests to which the beneficiary has no pre-existing legal claim. I call these obligations pure fiduciary duties.

4.9 PURE FIDUCIARY DUTIES AND THEIR RELIANCE ON TRUST

A pure fiduciary duty is one in relation to an interest in which the beneficiary has a claim against the fiduciary alone, based solely on the trust-like nature of the relationship between fiduciary and beneficiary. For example, business opportunities commonly form the subject matter of pure fiduciary obligations, since the rest of the world is free to exploit them.[34] In contrast, a full-blooded property right cannot generate a pure fiduciary obligation because it is a right that grounds claims against the entire world, such as claims to exclusive use and possession. While fiduciary obligations may apply where the beneficiary has pre-existent rights, as is typically the case in an express trust, pure fiduciary duties most clearly bring to the surface the nature of the fiduciary obligation, since there are no pre-existing entitlements to muddy the waters.

Wilson J spent considerable time in *Frame* making the case that fiduciary duties may apply to 'substantial' and 'vital non-legal or "practical" interests'; that is, to interests in which the beneficiary has no pre-existent legal claims. Interests of this kind underlie pure fiduciary duties.[35] In *Frame*, Wilson J found that a divorced and custodial parent owed a fiduciary duty to the non-custodial parent to grant access and visitation to their children.

The characteristics of the pure fiduciary obligation also explain why the beneficiary's interest by itself cannot account for the fiduciary's obligation. Generally, a business opportunity, such as an opportunity to bid on a contract, is not a legally protected interest. Tenders usually go out with the expectation that several parties will bid on them. The fiduciary relationship between corporate officers and their company, however, precludes the officers from acting on the tender except in their capacity as fiduciaries of their company. It is the company's trust, assumed by the officers, that authorizes them to act on the company's behalf in order to take advantage of the opportunity. This same trust transforms an unprotected interest in a business opportunity into a legal interest. The law protects this interest through the imposition of a fiduciary obligation on those (and only those) who are entrusted to act on the beneficiary's behalf. In this sense, a presumption of trust justifies pure fiduciary obligations—obligations that

[34] The leading Canadian case is *Canaero Aero Services v O'Malley* [1974] SCR 592. The Supreme Court found corporate officers in breach for bidding on and winning a contract sought by their former company, even though the officers had resigned from the company before tendering their bid.

[35] *Frame*, *supra* note 1, p 136. L'Heureux-Dubé and McLachlin JJ (as she then was) have since affirmed and extended Wilson J's view that fiduciary law may protect 'a vital and "practical" interest' (in the case before them, an interest in medical care free from sexual exploitation) that had not previously come under the fiduciary aegis: *Norberg v Wynrib* [1992] 2 SCR 226, p 276.

would not exist but for the fiduciary relationship—and also constitutes the basis of the fiduciary's authority.

The warrant that trust provides also explains why the primary fiduciary duty at private law is a duty of loyalty rather than a tort duty of care. Loyalty sets the parameters within which a fiduciary's care may be exercised. A duty of care may be sufficient to mediate the relations of parties who are strangers to one another and who pursue their interests separately, but more than simple care is required in circumstances where one party is entrusted to act on behalf of another. A duty of care may generally be satisfied by refraining from causing damage or injury that violates another person's rights. The duty of loyalty is more onerous, for it seeks to ensure that the substantive purpose of the relationship between the parties is not frustrated. The duty of loyalty, in other words, supplies legal order to relations in which one party acts on behalf of another. This imposition of legality affirms the autonomy of the principal by placing the fiduciary under a duty to treat an otherwise unprotected interest as one subject to the weighty obligations that arise from trust.

4.10 THE STATE AS FIDUCIARY—THE SUBJECT'S TRUST IN THE STATE

As we have seen already, in many fiduciary relationships the fiduciary is entrusted to make judgments and exercise discretionary power that the beneficiary is not entitled to exercise. Arguably, the paradigm case of this kind of fiduciary relationship is arbitration of adjudication, where two parties either authorize an arbitrator to settle a dispute or are involuntarily subject to an adjudicative proceeding. Neither party could fulfil the arbitral role because neither can be judge and party in the same cause.

More generally, this is exactly the circumstance presented by the fact of sovereignty, under which legal subjects must entrust the specification, administration, adjudication, and vindication of their rights to the state. Private parties have no authority to make the judgments or exercise the powers necessary to determine such matters; they do not get to make laws that apply to others, nor decide legal disputes. Private parties, in other words, are juridically incapable of exercising public authority. As a result, legal subjects are in a position of *de facto* and *de jure* dependence on the state for the provision of legal order. This dependence reflects the juridical incapacity of private parties and their vulnerability to state power, which itself arises from the state's assumption and exercise of the powers necessary to govern through law and legal institutions. It is this confluence of public administrative power and juridical incapacity to which the fiduciary principle responds.

The state's fiduciary obligations may have a private law character in the sense that they may be based on a concrete interest under public administration, such as surrendered Aboriginal lands.[36] But the idea is much broader and does not depend on the identification of particular legal interests that are independent of the overarching state-subject fiduciary relationship.

As with business opportunities, a subject's interest in being the subject of a legal order is not one in which typical property rights lie. For the interest in legal order to enjoy the protection of the fiduciary principle, such an interest must embody a substantial or vital interest that is entrusted to a party who has administrative power over it. I assume that while there may be sharp disagreement regarding the appropriate contents of legal order, individuals nonetheless have a substantial interest in living in a world that is neither a Hobbesian state of nature nor one left to the caprice of an arbitrary ruler.[37] And with respect to the legislative, executive, and judicial powers entailed by sovereignty, they each in their own familiar ways are institutional, purpose-laden, and other-regarding. They each assume institutional forms and purposes so as to facilitate the ongoing construction of a legal order intended to protect rights, resolve coordination problems, and otherwise serve the people subject to their authority. Sovereign powers, in other words, are paradigmatically administrative in nature. It follows that when the state exercises these powers over legal subjects who are juridically incapable of exercising them, a pure fiduciary obligation arises. Because the obligation arises to protect the subject's interest in being a member of legal order rather than a purely coercive order (or no order), the content of the obligation is to govern in accordance with the rule of law. We shall explore some of the rule of law's features in the coming chapters.

In the next chapter we test the adequacy of the fiduciary account of state legal authority by considering whether it can support a duty on the part of the subject to obey the law. I argue that it can, and that ultimately the best characterization of the fiduciary state is that it is a public agent of necessity.

[36] *Guerin v The Queen* [1982] 2 SCR 335, discussed in Chapter II (2.2).

[37] An apt example is Fuller's hapless monarch, Rex. Fuller begins his elaboration of the internal morality of law with an exposition of what a society might look like with a benevolent sovereign too inept to understand the elementary forms that law-giving must assume to produce laws worthy of our allegiance (ie there must be some general rules, the rules should strive to be public, clear, prospective, relatively constant over time, and so on). Fuller, *supra* note 7, pp 33–41. See Chapter IX for discussion.

V

The Duty to Obey the Law

5.1 INTRODUCTION

In this chapter, I defend a fiduciary theory of the duty to obey the law, one that relies on the fiduciary conception of the state set out in the previous chapter. The argument is pitched mainly against various consent theories of the state. There are telling objections to theories that rely on either hypothetical or tacit consent. Lockean views of the state based on express consent, such as political voluntarism, avoid many of these objections, but at a price. If express consent to state authority is lacking, the state is illegitimate, and so we are led to reject the state's claim to authority over us. Ultimately, we are led to philosophical anarchism.

The aims of the fiduciary theory are twofold. The first is to harness the intuitive appeal of consent-based theories by tying the duty to obey the law to a normative order premised on human agency. The second is to avoid the problematic assumptions associated with hypothetical and tacit social contracts, as well as the anarchist implication that follows from the absence of express consent to state authority. In short, I argue that the state's legal authority and the duty to obey issue from an actual fiduciary relationship rather than from a pretend, tacit, or express contractual relationship.

Under both fiduciary and contract theories, state authority is not *sui generis* but rather is a species of a general class of authority relations. Both theories are also fractal: they retain the same fundamental normative structure on any scale. And both are about practical authority which bears on action rather than theoretical authority which bears on epistemic reasons for belief (eg the authority of experts). But, as we shall see, only the fiduciary theory can explain the authority of the state by pointing to actual morally relevant features of the state-subject relationship.

Recall the case for the fiduciary theory to this point. There are three conditions, identified and defined in Chapter IV, which are independently necessary and jointly sufficient to justify practical authority under the fiduciary theory. An exercise of the relevant power under these conditions constitutes an exercise of authority, and persons subject to such authority have a defeasible obligation to obey its directives. First, the putative authority must hold administrative power capable of affecting the interests of others. Second, persons subject to administrative power must be incapable of exercising or controlling that power because of their circumstances (contextual incapacity) or the because of the nature of the power (juridical incapacity). Finally, a fiduciary relationship must arise as a result of the first two conditions, obligating the power-holder to exercise her power in accordance with its other-regarding purpose.

As we saw in the previous chapter, the first two conditions are factual conditions with limiting moral properties or side-constraints: administrative power must be located within a legally cognizable institution (an institution wherein the relations between the parties are not intrinsically wrongful from a legal point of view), and juridical incapacity relies on a moral distinction between public and private parties, a distinction that disqualifies the latter from exercising the powers of the former. By contrast, the third condition is an overtly and substantive moral assumption. It is necessary to bridge the fact/value gap that would otherwise separate the first two conditions from fiduciary obligation, and which also, we shall see, supplies the basis of fiduciary authority.

The main focus of this chapter is juridical incapacity from the second condition. This condition was foreshadowed by Hobbes in his discussion of the arbitrator extracted in the epigraph to this book, and is central to the fiduciary theory of the state and the duty to obey the law. First, however, we need to have in view some of the general features of the debate, and then see why the most obvious basis of state authority—consent—fails to explain the duty to obey.

5.2 THE TERMS OF THE DEBATE

The duty to obey the law is commonly understood to be correlative to the state's legal authority, that is, its authority to impose legal duties on its subjects and enforce them coercively.[1] On this view, an individual has a duty to obey her state's laws if, and only if, her state has legitimate legal authority over her. It follows from this correlativity thesis that a theory of legal authority (or legitimacy) implies a theory of legal obligation, and vice versa. The correlativity thesis helps explain why so much discussion of authority over the past 30 years has focused on the problem of legal obligation.[2]

[1] See eg John Finnis, *Natural Law and Natural Rights* (Oxford: Oxford University Press, 1980), pp 231–4; Joseph Raz, *The Morality of Freedom* (Oxford: Oxford University Press, 1986), pp 23–8; A John Simmons, *Justification and Legitimacy* (New York: Cambridge University Press, 2001), pp 106–7, 130–1.

[2] For a review of the debate, see William A Edmunson, 'State of the Art: The Duty to Obey the Law' (2004) 10 *Legal Theory* 215; A John Simmons, 'The Duty to Obey and Our Natural Moral Duties' in A John

A growing minority dispute the correlativity thesis, arguing that the state's authority is merely a liberty right to coerce independent of the subject's obligation to obey.[3] Few (if any) theorists, however, would deny that if there is a general obligation to obey the law, then the state must have authority to announce and enforce law. As we shall see momentarily, the duty to obey, as normally conceived, is just a duty to do what the state requires *because the state requires it*. It is a duty to obey the law *qua* law. It is hard to imagine how such a general duty could exist if the state (or law) had no authority to demand it. If this is right, then the fiduciary account of legal obligation, if successful, will imply an account of state legitimacy.

The conception of legitimacy I defend below entails the power to create morally binding legal rules. Because the legal rules are morally as well as legally binding, subjects have a general moral duty to obey. The duty enjoys a moral status roughly analogous to the status of the duty to perform a contract: the duty is both legal *and* moral. Someone who breaches a contract breaks a promise, and so, other things being equal, is morally blameworthy as well as legally liable. But there is also an important sense in which the legal wrong itself constitutes a moral wrong: the breaching party has failed to give the other side her due, ie what she is owed as a matter of justice. I contend below that the anarchist who refuses to recognize the authority of the state also fails to give others their due by claiming an authority to determine questions of justice that private parties as such are not entitled to hold or exercise.

Along with the correlativity thesis, the conventional view of legal obligation takes the contested duty to obey to have a number of features. The duty is said to be defeasible (other considerations can override it), comprehensively applicable (it attaches to all the mandatory laws of a state), universally borne (it applies to everyone in a given state), and content-independent (the duty does not depend on the merits of particular laws).[4] I argue in the remaining chapters that the rule of law places formal and substantive constraints on putative legal rules and decisions. Those arguments entail that the duty to obey the declared rules and decisions of the state is not

Simmons and Christopher Wellman (eds), *Is There a Duty to Obey the Law?* (New York: Cambridge University Press, 2005). A good number of theories of the state and the duty to obey are *not* discussed in this chapter, including theories based on associative or communal bonds (see eg Ronald Dworkin, *Law's Empire* (Cambridge: Harvard University Press, 1986), pp 195–215) and others built on the duty of fair play (see eg George Klosko, *The Principle of Fairness and Political Obligations* (Lanham, Maryland: Rowman & Littlefield, 1992)). For persuasive critique of these theories, see Simmons, *supra* note 1, chs 2, 4.

[3] See eg R Ladenson, 'In Defense of a Hobbesian Conception of Law' in Joseph Raz (ed), *Authority* (New York: New York University Press, 1990); Christopher Wellman, 'Toward a Liberal Theory of Political Obligation' (2001) 111 *Ethics* 735, pp 741–2. See also Kent Greenawalt, *Conflicts of Law and Morality* (New York: Oxford University Press, 1989), ch 4.

[4] Matthew Kramer, 'Moral and Legal Obligation' in Martin P Goldberg and William A Edmundson (eds), *Blackwell Guide to the Philosophy of Law and Legal Theory* (Malden, USA: Blackwell Publishing, 2004), p 179.

necessarily comprehensively applicable, content-independent, universally borne, or even applicable as a defeasible duty, since decisions and legislation which fail to conform to the rule of law lack authority and therefore do not impose legal obligations. This consequence may appear to deny the duty to obey, but it does not. We can distinguish *rules and decisions* from *law.* I argue in Chapter IX that rules and decisions which fail to live up to the rule of law are not law, properly so-called. So, the inability of such rules and decisions to give rise to legal obligations is not an inability that afflicts the general duty to obey the law. This view of law is at odds with both legal positivism and the actual claim to authority that states assert. I nonetheless defend it here and in subsequent chapters.

A final clarification: I use two sets of terms in ways that are perhaps different from the ways other moral and political philosophers use them. First, for convenience, I treat 'duty' and 'obligation' as synonyms, though others may understand the scope of the former to exceed that of the latter. Second, I use 'political authority' in this study to denote the state's authority to determine the substantive content of law within the constitutional framework of principle established by the state's legal authority. So defined, a democratic state's political authority rests (in part) on consent, whereas its legal authority, I have argued, rests on a presumption of trust and the state-subject fiduciary relationship.

That said, the duty to obey the law is highly controversial because states rule their people through non-consensual coercion. People who do not wish to pay taxes are forced to pay them. People who wish to engage consensually in the sex and recreational drug trades may be prohibited from doing so. Non-consensual coercion is endemic to the state. It is not surprising, then, that many theorists have tried to undo the apparent wrongfulness of non-consensual coercion by postulating that the people, in some sense, consent to state authority, thereby making non-consensual coercion consensual. We canvass some of those efforts now.

5.3 THE LIMITS OF CONSENT

Consent is a compelling wellspring of legal obligation because it denotes a familiar moral medium through which we can relate to each other as equally autonomous agents. Because informed and voluntary consent expresses our capacity for self-determination and presupposes freedom from subjection, it lets us place ourselves under obligation autonomously. Consent flows through promises, voluntary undertakings and contract so as to allow us to change our normative position (including our legal position) by acquiring obligations we would not otherwise have.

Consent theories of legal obligation affirm that individuals *may* have a general duty to obey their state's laws, but they have this duty *only if* they have in some way consented to the state's authority to announce and enforce law. An individual may agree to membership in the state, and thereby assume the duties of membership. Or, an individual may *willingly* accept the benefits that flow from residing in the state, such as non-excludable public goods (clean air, water and drainage systems, roads, etc). For consent theorists, an individual who willingly accepts these benefits may be held to a duty to obey (or at least to a duty to contribute to the institutions that supply the benefits), whereas a mere conferral of benefits on the unwilling cannot support such a duty.

The fundamental problem consent theories face is that few individuals have ever explicitly consented to anything like the vast authority states claim. Worse still, some individuals and groups, such as rugged individualists and occupied peoples, reject outright the state's claims to authority over them. None of this seems to make any difference to the state's assertion of sovereignty over its territory and the people within it. Therefore, to defend the legitimacy of even reasonably just liberal democratic states, an account of consent must be given that does not depend on people explicitly giving it.[5] There are two routes. One supposes that the requisite consent is hypothetical, whereas the other takes the consent in question to be actual but tacit.

A familiar objection to hypothetical consent is that possible consent to some possible state does not entail actual consent to any particular state. As Dworkin puts it, a 'hypothetical contract is . . . no contract at all'.[6] Even if I would have agreed to pay you to paint my house, and you do in fact paint it, unless I have actually agreed to pay you for the work, you have no contractual claim against me. Similarly, even if I would consent to the authority of any state under conditions similar to those of the actual state in which I live, it does not follow that I owe the state a duty to obey its laws. Moreover, it is not clear why I would owe any obligations to *this* state rather than to some other state that better complies with the conditions to which I would consent. And finally, if inquiry relates to the conditions that would require me to consent to the state's authority, it is not my consent *per se* that does any of the work to justify my duty to obey the law. Rather, substantive political principles, such as Rawls' theory of justice or the utilitarian's welfare-maximizing principle, provide both the basis for my putative

[5] Of course, one may take the view that only political voluntarism (explicit consent) can render the state legitimate. This is the view of Simmons, discussed below. See eg A John Simmons, *Moral Principles and Political Obligations* (Princeton, NJ: Princeton University Press, 1979); Simmons, *supra* notes 1, 2. See also Leslie Green, *The Authority of the State* (Oxford: Oxford University Press, 1988).

[6] Ronald Dworkin, *Taking Rights Seriously* (Cambridge, MA: Harvard University Press, 1977), p 151.

consent and the justification of state authority. But a basis for consent (even a well-justified basis) and actual consent are not the same thing.

In effect, the hypothetical consent argument collapses into an argument about whether one has a duty to obey the law on the basis of the state's moral or prudential value.[7] However, we do not usually think that deliberately conferred but unsolicited moral or prudential benefits supply a sufficient basis for legal obligation. It may be rational and even morally required for me to buy an inexpensive home security system that protects my family, but this would not give a home security company the authority to force me to buy the system from it. Only actual consent to buy the system can give rise to a corresponding legal obligation.

Tacit consent avoids the pitfalls of hypothetical consent because tacit consent, although not explicit, is at least actual. There is no gap between consenting to be governed by some state under some conditions and the obligation to obey the laws of one's actual state, since it is assumed that consent has been granted tacitly to the actual state in which one lives.

Harry Beran has developed the most comprehensive contemporary account of tacit consent as the basis of political and legal obligation.[8] He claims that consent is to be inferred from our living within the state and not doing anything to deny that we consent to be governed by its institutions. He identifies three ways of denying the tacit consent on which our obligations are based: migration, secession, and public declaration. Yet it is doubtful that a failure to dissent in any of these ways justifies an inference of consent.

As Hume famously argued,[9] migration may not be practical for someone who lacks the resources to migrate. The same may be said of a group that would secede but for a lack of resources, or perhaps because of security concerns. In these cases, tacit consent to the state, if it exists at all, is given

[7] This collapse reflects why hypothetical consent accounts of obligation are really 'natural duty' accounts. See Edmunson, *supra* note 2, p 236; Cynthia Stark, 'Hypothetical Consent and Justification' (2000) 97(6) Journal of Philosophy 313. Natural duties are duties I owe independently of any obligations I have voluntarily assumed, such as the Rawlsian duty to support just institutions. The same 'particularity' objection mentioned above cuts against natural duty accounts of legal obligation. Even if I have a natural duty to support just institutions, it is not clear why that duty is owed to my state rather than to some other where my contribution to justice might be greater. For a reply to the particularity objection, see Jeremy Waldron, 'Special Ties and Natural Duties' (1993) 22 *Philosophy and Public Affairs* 3. For a reply to Waldron, some of which I discuss and respond to in the text below, see Simmons, *supra* note 2, pp 170–9.

[8] Harry Beran, 'In Defense of the Consent Theory of Political Obligation and Authority' (1977) 87 *Ethics* 260; Harry Beran, *The Consent Theory of Political Obligation* (New York: Croom Helm, 1987).

[9] David Hume, 'Of the Original Contract' in *Social Contract* (London: Oxford University Press, 1987), p 156: 'Can we seriously say, that a poor peasant or artisan has a free choice to leave his country, when he knows no foreign language or manners, and lives, from day to day, by the small wages which he acquires? We may as well assert that a man, by remaining in a vessel, freely consents to the dominion of the master; though he was carried on board while asleep, and must leap into the ocean and perish, the moment he leaves her'. Although Hume's understanding of liberty is wider than Hobbes', Hume nonetheless points to salient conceptual problems with modern-day understandings of consent theory.

under conditions of duress that vitiate consent: the subject needs to live somewhere, but given her lack of resources or security concerns, her only feasible option is to remain in the state. So failure to emigrate or secede, without more, does not show consent to the present state of affairs.

Public declaration may appear a more promising way to withhold consent, since making such a declaration against the state's authority does not require significant resources. But if we presume that such a declaration would entail a break from the state where one would lose the benefits as well as the unwanted obligations, the resource-based objection may have force here as well. And, of course, an individual's public declaration of dissent would have no effect on the authority actual states claim, revealing that at most the tacit consent model expresses an ideal and not an account of anything like actual state authority.

These apparently mundane and practical objections reveal a significant incongruity between consent theory and our intuitions regarding state authority. Notwithstanding the state's reliance on non-consensual coercion, few would think, at least pre-theoretically, that legal subjects can individually and unilaterally revoke a state's authority over some or all of its territory through a public declaration. Arguably, the right of self-determination is a collective right in part because we do not think that individuals as such have a right to secede or otherwise reside within the state's territory unencumbered by legal obligations.

Considerations such as these, however, will not answer the challenge posed by philosophical anarchists such as John Simmons. A Lockean and political voluntarist, Simmons believes that only explicit consent and a relationship much like an actual social contract can legitimize state power. Philosophical anarchism—the view that all states today are illegitimate—follows from the combination of political voluntarism and the plausible claim that most people have not actually consented to the authority their states claim over them.

The Simmons-led denial of the duty to obey the law is now regarded by some philosophers as the dominant view.[10] Although public law commentators on the rule of law have largely disregarded the dispute over obligation in political philosophy,[11] any theory of the rule of law that seeks to derive

[10] See eg Philip Soper, 'Legal Theory and the Claims of Authority' (1989) 18 *Philosophy and Public Affairs* 209; Leslie Green, 'Who Believes in Political Obligation?' in John T Sanders and Jan Narveson (eds), *For and Against the State* (Lanham, MD: Rowman & Littlefield, 1996), p 28. See also Joseph Raz, *The Authority of Law* (Oxford: Oxford University Press, 1979), ch 12; Green, *supra* note 5, ch 8. Simmons' *Moral Principles and Political Obligation, supra* note 7, is described by Wellman as 'the most significant contribution to the liberal discussion of political obligation since Socrates's *Crito*', while Edmundson ventures that 'it is no exaggeration to say that the [duty-to-obey] literature of the intervening quarter-century (since *Moral Principles and Political Obligation*) has largely consisted of efforts to overcome or deflect Simmons's objections'. Wellman, *supra* note, 3 p 750; Edmundson, *supra* note 2, p 228.

[11] For example, Trevor Allan's book on the rule of law, TRS Allan, *Constitutional Justice: A Liberal Theory of the Rule of Law* (Oxford: Oxford University Press, 2003), has been called 'the most important work on this

some measure of state legitimacy from it must eventually confront Simmons' arguments.

Simmons distinguishes sharply between the justification of the state and its legitimacy. Justification goes to the merits of particular institutions, policies, and practices. A justified state is one that resolves coordination problems, protects people's rights, safeguards the environment, and so on. Roughly speaking, a justified state is to some extent benevolent rather than wicked. Legitimacy, on the other hand, concerns the actual relationship between state and subject. The state's authority and the subject's duty to obey depend exclusively on the existence of an appropriate moral *relationship* between state and subject, and not on the moral or prudential *benefits* which may flow to the individual as a result of fair and just state policies. For the unwilling, these benefits are the fruits of a forced sale, and they therefore cannot ground a duty to obey. On Simmons' view, then, the moral evaluation of any state falls into one of four categories: (i) justified and legitimate (the Lockean ideal); (ii) unjustified and legitimate (a critical case discussed below at 5.5 below); (iii) justified and illegitimate (eg the 'benevolent dictator'); and (iv) unjustified and illegitimate (eg wicked dictators).

Simmons is a philosophical rather than a political anarchist. He is happy to admit that people living in a reasonably just state should do much of what the law requires, but this is strictly because we have independent moral reasons to aid the helplessly needy and to forbear from committing murder, assault, fraud, and so on. That these moral duties are also legal duties does not give us a further or separate reason for action. Thus, when the state calls on us to do things for which there is doubtful moral justification (eg submit to conscription in support of an imperial military), we are under no obligation to obey unless we have explicitly consented to the state's authority to direct and coerce us. Nonetheless, just as consent can make assault and battery into consensual touching, consent can likewise transform illegitimate states legitimate.

While Simmons thinks that ultimately express consent alone can legitimize state legal authority, he is always careful to rest consent on the wider and more fundamental idea that legitimacy must flow from an actual and moral relationship between state and subject. The connection Simmons observes between legitimacy and an actual state-subject moral relationship is well-founded. His mistake, I claim, is in what he considers to be the exclusive basis of the moral relationship. The foundational principle on which Simmons draws is this: in any putative relationship of authority

topic since A.V. Dicey' (David Dyzenhaus, *The Constitution of Law: Legality in a Time of Emergency* (Cambridge: Cambridge University Press, 2006), p iv). Although Allan discusses legal obligation, he does not lock horns with Simmons and others who rigorously deny the duty to obey.

(including the state-subject relationship) consent alone can authorize one party to change the normative position of the other because no party can impose obligations on another without the other's prior consent. But, as we shall see now, consensual relationships are not the only kinds of relationships in which one party may come to have authority over another, and as a consequence, may impose obligations on them.

5.4 PARENTAL AUTHORITY

While a state's adult subjects ought never to be treated like children, there is an important sense in which the state-subject relationship resembles parent-child relations: in both cases there is involuntary subjection to proclaimed authority. It is this common feature which explains why so many writers on state authority compare it to parental authority.[12] As GEM Anscombe puts it, with both parental and governmental authority, '[y]ou find yourself the subject of these whether you like it or not'.[13]

Simmons considers the possibility that 'special, but not necessarily voluntary relationships (for instance, parent-child or benefactor-beneficiary relationships)' might ground obligations analogous to the duty to obey the law.[14] He says that ordinarily children do not owe reciprocal obligations of support to their parents. I agree. However, it is not so clear that parents lack authority to direct maturing children to do things likely to contribute to their children's well-being. Naturally, the child has an independent interest in doing certain things, and inchoate moral duties that set independent limits on the child's permissible conduct when she plays with others. Yet we commonly assume that the child has reason to obey her parents, and that the child does not have a similar reason to obey the commands of strangers.

Under Raz's influential view of authority, the 'normal justification thesis,' the child has reason to obey her parents because obedience is more likely to lead the child to act on reasons which apply to her than if she acted in accordance with her own judgment.[15] But if the parents were especially wicked and attempted to sell the child into bondage, the child would not have reason to go along with their attempt. Raz might say that the parents have committed a jurisdictional error, forfeiting their usual claim to authority.[16] The problem of

[12] See eg GEM Anscombe, 'On the Source of the Authority of the State' in Joseph Raz (ed), *Authority* (New York: New York University Press, 1990), p 148; Greenawalt, *supra* note 3, pp 52–3; Hobbes, L xx.4–9, 128–30; Raz, *supra* note 1, pp 54, 57, 86, 87.

[13] Anscombe, *supra* note 12, p 148.

[14] Simmons, *supra* note 1, p 45.

[15] Raz, *supra* note 1, p 53.

[16] Ibid, p 62. Raz admits that his view of authority depends on an ability to distinguish jurisdictional from non-jurisdictional errors (only the former strip an authority of authority). As we shall see in Chapter VIII, this is a slippery and controversial distinction that permeates public law.

wicked parents reveals that simply being the parent of a child does not explain parental authority. Parental authority depends on the further assumption that the parent is under an obligation to act on behalf of the child and in the child's best interests, an obligation strangers do not have. It is this obligation that explains the existence and scope of a parent's authority to direct her child. If the parent fails to live up to her obligation, she loses authority over her child. Does the maturing child have a corresponding (quasi-) obligation to obey?

Simmons denies that children owe any obligations of obedience to their parents: 'to the extent that children have moral obligations at all, their obligations are to do those things that are obligatory for adults of similar capacities, not to do what they are told to do by their parents'.[17] Children may have embryonic moral duties to respect property and avoid harming others, but Simmons thinks we can explain these duties without referring at all to the parents' commands. He is prepared to acknowledge that parents have exclusive rights of parenthood that allow parents to make certain demands of their children, but argues that 'children are not morally obligated to fulfil any of these demands simply on the grounds that their parents have made them'.[18]

Simmons' conclusion, however, is too quick, and trades on a misleading conception of the appropriate relationship between parent, child, and morality. His basic claim is that children do not owe 'obligations of obedience to their parents'.[19] Framing the issue this way tempts us to think that the parent rather than the child is in some sense the beneficiary of the child's obligation, as is generally the case when one adult owes a moral obligation to another adult.

Suppose Smith and Jones are both adults, and Smith promises to help Jones shovel the snow from his driveway. Other things being equal, Smith has a moral obligation to help Jones, and Jones can expect to benefit from Smith's performance. When adults are involved, the performance of a moral obligation by one party will typically benefit (or at least not harm) the other.[20] But, as I will argue now, the child's moral obligation of obedience is not at all grounded on an obligation to benefit or even show respect to her parents,[21] as one is tempted to infer from the characterization of the obligation of obedience as an obligation owed *to* the parents. Once we have the basis of the child's obligation of obedience in view, we will be able

[17] Simmons, *supra* note 1, pp 51–2. [18] Ibid, p 52. [19] Ibid, p 51.

[20] A failure to perform would constitute a wrong but need not occasion harm. Consider 'harmless' invasions of privacy or trespasses. See Chapter IX for further discussion of the harm/wrong distinction.

[21] Compare: Philip Soper, *The Ethics of Deference: Learning from Law's Morals* (Cambridge: Cambridge University Press, 2002), pp 171–2 (a teenager has reason to keep a promise to his parents, even though he will not be found out, because doing so shows respect for what they would want if they were present). I discuss Soper's theory at 5.8 below.

to see both that it has a moral character and that parents are entitled to impose such obligations on their children.

The moral basis of the child's duty to obey is the child's long-term well-being, a well-being that involves the child's future self. Although the obligation is moral, it is somewhat misleading to say that the obligation is 'owed' to the parents (as opposed to simply possessed by the child), since it is not an obligation to respect a *self-regarding* claim of right that parents have against their children (I have assumed already that parents have no such claims). Rather, it is better to say that children have this obligation because their parents have an *other-regarding* claim of right against them, where the 'other' is the child, a person assumed to be incapable of fully acting on her own behalf. When dutiful parents command their children, they are acting on behalf of the moral agents their children are becoming.[22] In a sense, the presently obedient child is really subject to an obligation that has her future as much as her present self as its target.[23] The space that childhood immaturity supplies to justifiable paternalism is the space in which children can have obligations to obey parents who are acting on behalf of their present and future selves. These obligations are moral because the long-term well-being of children is a moral concern.

Consider again Raz's view of authority as applied to parents. It is unpersuasive because it fails to explain why children have an obligation to obey their parents or others who occupy parental roles, but have no obligation to obey strangers who may issue parent-like commands. Raz cannot explain the child's obligation to obey her parents because he neglects the obligation under which the parents themselves must govern their children. Suppose that a (non-custodial) stranger happens to issue the same commands to a child as the child's parent would issue in similar circumstances. On Raz's view, the stranger would be just as much an authority for the child as the parent, since by hypothesis the commands are the same, and so the child is just as likely to be better guided by them. Yet we would be reluctant to say that the stranger has authority over the child.

Our reluctance arises from the fact that strangers are not under an obligation to have due regard for the child's best interests when they issue their commands. Their directives are contingent; they simply happen to mimic what the parent would have directed the child to do. Such commands float free from the parental role and corresponding fiduciary obligation that readily explains the existence and scope of parental authority: parents (but

[22] Of course many parental commands, such as commands to share with others and respect property, do direct the child in a way that engages the interests and moral claims of third-parties.

[23] For rich treatment of the relationship between personal identity (or identities) over time and morality, see Derek Parfit, *Reasons and Persons* (Oxford: Oxford University Press, 1984).

not strangers) can act on behalf of their children in their children's best interests precisely because all such action must pursue (or least be consistent with) their children's best interests. This obligation, in turn, distinguishes parental authority from *de facto* power over children.

The fiduciary theory also explains parental authority to discipline children. Parents may discipline a child who disobeys them, but only to the extent that discipline is consistent with the parent's duty to act in the child's best interests. Teachers possess a similar though more limited disciplinary authority, with a like limitation. Strangers, on the other hand, have no authority to discipline a child who refuses to do what they say. This remains true even if discipline from the stranger would lead the child to obey the stranger's directives and following those commands would be better for the child than following the parent's commands. Once again, strangers arguably lack such authority because they are not in a relationship with the child which places them under an obligation to act in the child's best interests. In sum, by distinguishing parents from strangers who issue parent-like commands, and by explicating the moral basis of the child's duty to obey, the fiduciary theory explains why parental authority is a species of moral authority intrinsic to the actual relations between dutiful parents and their children.

One might conclude from the foregoing argument that the parent-child case shows that fiduciary authority to change the legal position of the beneficiary, if not based on consent, must be based on the beneficiary suffering from a childlike inability to act autonomously. We can distinguish the state from the parent, however, on the basis of the much narrower scope of the state's authority. Whereas the parent must (sometimes intrusively) manage and develop the child, the state's authority is limited to establishing a regime of secure and equal freedom, or legal order, rather than some other kind of order. Put slightly differently, parental authority aims at the moral development *of* the child, while state authority concerns relations *between* individuals and *between* individuals and the state. But as we saw in the Crown-Native case, and as we shall see in the chapters to come, for the state to stand in a relationship of authority to its people, the state must be under an obligation to exercise its legal powers on their behalf. In the Crown-Native case, the exercise of legislative powers must be accompanied with (at least) a duty to consult and accommodate. In the ordinary state-subject case, legislative powers are not so encumbered, but as we shall see in Chapters VII and VIII, the exercise of administrative powers gives rise to public law duties of fairness and reasonableness. Respecting these and other rule-of-law obligations lends the state a measure of legitimacy, and this legitimacy supports a duty to obey the law.

Before turning to this argument, however, it is important to see that the legitimacy flowing from the rule of law is more modest than the consent-driven and all-things-considered legitimacy of Simmons' theory, and that rule-of-law legitimacy coheres better with our considered intuitions regarding the duty to obey the law.

5.5 THE LEGITIMACY OF LEGALITY

The fiduciary conception of the state implicates solely the legitimizing effects of the rule of law, and as a consequence it explains the conventional view that the duty to obey is merely a *prima facie* or defeasible duty. Because the duty to obey depends on the state living up to the demands of legality, it is susceptible to defeating objections based on the state's exercise of political power (eg prosecution of an imperial war). While I will argue that legality, properly understood, is a necessary and sufficient condition of the duty to obey, the obligation is defeasible and relatively weak because legality is a necessary but not sufficient condition of all-things-considered legitimacy.

States can comply in widely varying degrees with the requirements of the rule of law. Thus, states can be more or less legitimate to widely varying degrees. Their legitimacy is best assessed by comparing the extent to which they actually comply with the rule of law against the extent to which they ideally should comply with it. And I assume that strict and dogmatic conformity with every conceivable rule-of-law requirement may not be desirable given countervailing considerations.[24] But if a state infringes many and complies with few rule-of-law obligations, its legitimacy will come under great strain, as will the subject's duty to obey.

For Simmons, on the other hand, legitimacy is an all-or-nothing proposition, because for him legitimacy refers exclusively to the presence or absence of an individual's consent to state authority. Either an individual consents or she does not; there is no halfway. Simmons sometimes appears to say that we can determine the degree to which a state is legitimate (or illegitimate) by comparing the number of consenters to the number of non-consenters: '[s]tates become more legitimate as they more closely approach the ideal of voluntary association, but no existing states are legitimate with respect to even a majority of its subjects'.[25] However, it is misleading for Simmons to speak in terms of the state as such becoming 'more legitimate' as more members consent, since the question of legitimacy, on his theory, is always an agent-relative question that goes to whether a particular

[24] For discussion of such considerations, see Andrei Marmor, 'The Rule of Law and Its Limits' (2004) 24 Law & Phil 1.

[25] Simmons, *supra* note 1, p 156.

individual has consented. For the unwilling, the presence of many consenters does not make the state 'more legitimate', at least not in any sense that could place the non-consenters under a duty to obey the law. Thus, on Simmons' account, states themselves are not, nor can be, more or less legitimate *per se*; states are legitimate *with respect to a given individual*, or they are illegitimate *with respect to a given individual*. As I will argue shortly, this understanding of state legitimacy is at sharp odds with our considered intuitions on the matter, and ought to be resisted.

Now, an objector might take issue with the all-or-nothing characterization of legitimacy I am ascribing to Simmons' theory by insisting that individuals may consent (or not) to particular state actions rather than to the full gamut of state legal authority. States which execute consent-based policies are legitimate; others are not. But the objection fails because the kind of consent that is needed in this context *is* consent to a general (though not necessarily absolute) authority to announce and enforce law, including at least some laws to which the consenter may object. A consent theory that requires merely consent to particular laws is not a theory of state authority at all; it is a rejection of state authority. The legitimacy of exercises of state power would depend on the consent of every individual affected by it, and so every affected individual would have a veto over the legitimacy of particular decisions and policies. Legitimate exercises of state power would be limited to cases of unanimity. Simmons himself appears to agree with this characterization: consent to state authority, he claims, limits one's entitlement to refuse to obey laws of dubious merit.[26]

For Simmons, then, the state's legitimacy *vis-à-vis* the individual really is all-or-nothing: state authority for which there is consent is legitimate; state authority which lacks consent is not. While the state's 'justification' (in Simmons' sense) can admit of degrees in relation to particular individuals, its legitimacy cannot. So long as the subject has consented to state authority and that consent remains intact, there is literally nothing the state can do to forfeit or even weaken its legitimacy. Foolish, discriminatory, and rule-of-law-infringing policies may lead individuals to withhold their consent, but those policies have no direct bearing on the state's legitimacy once consent has been given. Patently oppressive policies do not undermine the state's *prima facie* authority to announce and enforce law over consenters.

These consequences may not trouble Simmons. The possibility of wicked but legitimate states follows necessarily from the conceptual distinction he draws between a state's justification and its legitimacy. What if, however, a majority consents to a state that oppresses a non-consenting minority?

[26] Ibid, p 156, n 68.

Clearly, for the oppressed minority, the state is both unjustified (wicked) and illegitimate. For the consenting majority, on the other hand, the state may be wicked, but it is also legitimate. From this it follows, on Simmons' view, that the consenting majority has a *prima facie* duty to obey the state, even if the state demands that they contribute actively to the oppression of the minority. Of course, the state's wickedness may give rise to a duty to resist that overrides the majority's duty to obey, but the idea that consent to a wicked state can sustain even a defeasible duty to advance oppression is deeply problematic.[27]

The problem arises from the fact that consent to state authority, without more, admits of no *ex ante* restrictions; in principle, individuals can consent to any kind of state, including wicked states. The fundamental defect of political voluntarism is that it transforms legitimacy into a wholly private matter, effacing entirely the universal dimension of legitimacy, with the result that consenters have a *prima facie* duty to obey laws that contribute to oppression. Under the fiduciary view of state legitimacy, on the other hand, discriminatory persecution is illegitimate *per se* because such action is inconsistent with the state's overarching fiduciary and universal obligation (within its jurisdiction) to govern in accordance with the rule of law. The state's obligation is universal in the sense that it is owed to every person subject to state power. Thus, on the fiduciary view, the consent of some members to a state that persecutes a minority is irrelevant to the question of whether the state has authority to demand support from the consenters—it does not because the state does not have authority to pass and implement such laws.[28] The point to underline here is that the fiduciary view of legitimacy confirms that an individual's consent to the state's persecution of others cannot ground a duty on the part of the consenter to abet oppression. Consent to a state that engages in persecution makes no moral difference to the illegitimacy of state efforts to conscript willing persecutors. It follows that in some cases consent is irrelevant to questions of legitimacy and the duty to obey the law.

To sum up: the fiduciary conception of legitimacy compares favourably with political voluntarism because the former but not the latter explains why state legitimacy is neither all-or-nothing nor exclusively agent-relative. On the fiduciary view, state legitimacy is measured through a comprehensive evaluation of the degree to which the state succeeds in establishing legal order for the benefit of all. Moreover, the fiduciary theory helps us see that in some cases—cases in which some members of the state consent to the persecution of others—consent is irrelevant to legitimacy and the duty to

[27] Raz doubts that consent could ever legitimize state authority. He begins his argument with the claim that '[t]hose who consent to perform atrocities are not bound by their consent'. Joseph Raz, *Ethics in the Public Domain* (Oxford: Clarendon Press, 1994), pp 360–4.

[28] I argue in Chapter IX that these kinds of laws lie beyond the state's authority.

obey. We consider now the justification of the duty to obey that flows from the fiduciary theory of state legal authority.

5.6 A FIDUCIARY THEORY OF THE DUTY TO OBEY THE LAW

At 5.4 above, I argued that maturing children have an obligation to obey the directives of their dutiful parents, and that the moral basis of this duty is that the parents themselves are under a fiduciary obligation to act with due regard for their children's best interests. The basis of the parent's obligation, we saw in Chapter I, is the child's innate right of humanity. The child's innate right of humanity places the parents under obligation so that parent-child relations can be rightful despite the fact that they are non-consensual. *Mutatis mutandis*, a parallel argument can be made with respect to the state-subject relationship and the subject's duty to obey the law.

I have argued that the state is in a fiduciary relationship with its people, and that the state's overarching fiduciary obligation to its people is to secure legal order, to govern through the rule of law on behalf of the people. The challenge now is to show that the subject's duty to obey the law of a rule-of-law abiding state is relevantly similar to the child's obligation to obey the directives of her dutiful parents, and to do so without turning the state into a parent or the subject into a child.

We can avoid paternalism while at the same time strengthening the analogy by pointing to a common feature of both parental and state authority, but one which arises from distinct normative concerns in each case. The common feature is that in both cases neither the child nor the legal subject is entitled to make the judgments and exercise the power entrusted by law to the parent and the state respectively. In the child's case, a lack of capacity explains the child's lack of authority to make parental judgments. In the case of the legal subject, the lack of authority flows from subject's status as a private party. As private parties, legal subjects cannot announce or enforce law, nor adjudicate their own disputes. A law-making public authority is required to specify the limits of permissible action. An administrative public authority is required to enforce the law. A law-interpreting public authority is required to judge alleged transgressions. The fiduciary principle entrusts the state to play these law-giving roles on behalf of the people, but at the same time encumbers the state with rule-of-law obligations to ensure that the state's agents govern impartially, as public authorities rather than as private parties. So long as the state generally complies with the rule of law, the subject has a (defeasible) duty to obey because the fiduciary principle entrusts and authorizes the state to announce and enforce law on behalf of everyone and over everyone within its jurisdiction.

An objector might contend that the argument above trades on a fallacy. Strictly speaking, the *de jure* inability of private parties to announce and enforce law does not show that the state has authority to do so. Of course, the gap between the inability of private parties and the authority of the state is intended to be filled by the fiduciary principle and its authorization of the state's legal authority. Yet we might still wonder whether the fiduciary principle can successfully justify the imposition of legal obligations over non-consenting individuals who reject the state's authority.[29] While I have argued that parental authority gives rise to a duty to obey on the part of maturing children, the duty turns in part on the child's incapacity to govern herself. I have also argued that a fiduciary's special obligations arise from her possession of administrative power over the beneficiary rather than from the beneficiary's consent, and that these obligations justify the fiduciary's authority to subject the beneficiary to new obligations. Nonetheless, there may remain a nagging sense that, where competent adults are concerned, the beneficiary must give prior consent to the fiduciary's exercise of obligation-conferring authority. After all, new obligations impose new liabilities on the beneficiary, and many fiduciary relationships typically do arise from consent.

The agent-principal fiduciary relationship is perhaps the paradigm case of one party (the agent) possessing authority to change the legal position of another (the principal) *vis-à-vis* third parties. An agent can change her principal's legal position either by entering into a contract on behalf of the principal or by disposing of the principal's property by transferring its title to a third-party. In many agency relationships, agents such as brokers, managers and auctioneers typically gain their authority to change the legal relations of their principals through contract or the consent of the principal. Interestingly, however, several of the leading commentators on agency argue that consent *per se* is not the basis of the agent's power to affect the legal position of the principal.

Fridman points out that reliance on consent 'seems to exclude from the scope of agency situations in which the parties have not truly consented to any such relationship, yet such a relationship arises'.[30] These situations

[29] I assume that at least some groups (eg 'peoples' or 'nations' in international law) have a right of self-determination that may permit them to secede from their present state to form a new one. Secession, however, reaffirms rather than denies state authority, and so is not a problem-case from the point of view of the duty to obey the law. The problem-case, and the focus of the text, is the individual non-consenter who rejects the state's claim to authority over her and thereby denies that there is a duty to obey.

[30] GHL Fridman, *The Law of Agency*, 7th edn (Toronto: Butterworths, 1996), p 15. Markesinis and Munday share Fridman's view that consent is not the key to understanding agency: BS Markesinis and RJC Munday, *An Outline of the Law of Agency*, 2nd edn (London: Butterworths, 1986). But see FMB Reynolds, *Bowstead and Reynolds on Agency*, 18th edn (London: Sweet & Maxwell, 2006); WA Seavey, 'The Rationale of Agency' (1920) 29 Yale LJ 859.

include certain types of agency which arise by operation of law, discussed below, as well as particular factual circumstances in which the courts will deem a person to be an agent notwithstanding a lack of consent from the principal.[31] Moreover, as Fridman observes, many duties attach to the parties of an agency relationship independently of any agreement between them, notwithstanding that such an agreement can limit or modify the parties' duties. For example, even agents who act gratuitously must exercise care in the management of their principals' affairs (much like involuntary bailees, discussed in the previous chapter), and they are subject to the familiar fiduciary obligations that prohibit secret profits and conflicts of interest and duty.

Yet another reason to doubt that consent can adequately explain agency is that consent between the principal and agent is irrelevant to the legal effects of agency on third-parties once the agency relationship is established. In cases of agency by estoppel, for instance, the agent does not have the principal's consent, but she can bind the principal if the principal has held the agent out as a person who, in light of all the circumstances, could reasonably be thought to possess the principal's authorization. Typically these situations arise when the principal allows the agent to handle publicly certain aspects of her business, and the agent's position in those circumstances is one in which the relevant agency ordinarily vests.[32] Agents in these cases are said to have 'apparent' or 'ostensible' authority rather than actual authority, and they can bind the principal to good faith third-parties *even if* such agents use their apparent authority for their own benefit rather than for the benefit of the principal.[33]

These various features of agency have led Fridman and others to conclude that although most agency relationships may arise initially from consent, they are ultimately established as a matter of law, as a consequence of 'the way in which the *law* regards the relationship that has been created'.[34] On this theory, relationships of agency are best understood as a nexus of legal power and liability. This power-liability nexus connects the principal

[31] Fridman cites the House of Lords decision in *Boardman v Phipps* [1966] 3 All ER 721; [1967] 2 AC 46 as a leading case in which the 'parties to whose acting as agents no consent had ever been given were treated as "self-appointed agents"'. Fridman, *supra* note 30, p 15. Boardman, a solicitor to a trust, was deemed to be an agent of the trustees when he acquired extra shares for himself in a company in which the trust already owned a considerable number of shares, ultimately benefiting both the trust and himself. As an agent subject to a fiduciary obligation, Boardman had to account to the trust for the profit he made on the shares.

[32] See eg *Lloyd v Grace, Smith & Co* [1912] AC 716.

[33] *Lloyds Bank Ltd v Charter Bank of India, Australia and China* [1929] 1 KB 40, Scrutton LJ, p 56. The law of agency in this respect resembles the contract doctrine under which a good faith purchaser for value gains title to a chattel purchased from a rogue who lacked title.

[34] Fridman, *supra* note 30, p 13 (emphasis in original).

to third-parties through the legal power of the agent, and thus 'the essence of agency is [the agent's legal] power to affect the principal's legal relations with the outside world'.[35] The power-liability theory of agency shares with the theory of fiduciary relations defended here the conviction that consent can sometimes explain the source or origin of the relationship, but not its nature. This shared conviction reflects a deeper, structural similarity.

The power-liability theory and the idea of the state as fiduciary both affirm a type of relationship which invariably has a tripartite structure: agent/state—principal/legal subject—third-parties. The major structural difference between private agency relations and the public idea of the state as fiduciary, of course, is that in the latter case the 'third-parties' are simultaneously legal subjects towards whom the state also stands in a fiduciary relation. Under this structure, the state, acting on my behalf, imposes legal obligations on everyone else so that their interactions with me are regulated by law. By the same token, the state imposes legal obligations on me, on behalf of everyone else, to ensure that my interactions with them are regulated by law. We turn to the implications of the fiduciary model's tripartite structure momentarily.

Recall that we looked to agency to test further the claim that some fiduciaries can change the legal position of their beneficiaries without the beneficiary's consent. This is a heady proposition that may appear to stand in tension with a fundamental axiom of Kant's theory of right, ie that no party can impose unilaterally the terms of interaction on another. As we shall see now, however, some forms of agency arise not from consent or even estoppel-generating conduct on the part of the principal, but by operation of law. These forms of agency are consistent with the Kantian axiom cited above because, as with fiduciary relationships generally, the terms of interaction are set by the law rather than the agent.

There are two well-recognized types of agency that arise by operation of law: agency from cohabitation and agency of necessity.[36] Agency from cohabitation does not provide a fruitful basis for inferring that under a broader range of circumstances one person may act as agent for another without the other's prior consent, because cohabiting spouses are anything but arm's length parties to one another. However, agency of necessity is

[35] Ibid, p 21. Markesinis and Munday make almost the identical point; Markesinis and Munday, *supra* note 30, p 9.

[36] For discussion, see Fridman, *supra* note 30, pp 133–51; Markesinis and Munday, *supra* note 30, pp 40–8; Richard Stone, *Law of Agency* (London: Cavendish Publishing, 1996), pp 33–9. A third type of agency arising by operation of law is agency imposed by statute, such as receivers who act as agents under insolvency legislation. As the point of the argument in the text is to analogize from simpler, common law instances of agency to the state-subject relationship, I do not pursue agency imposed by statute.

instructive for our discussion because it does involve arm's length parties and clearly arises without the principal's consent.[37]

The clearest case of agency of necessity involves shipmasters who find themselves in an emergency situation that places the cargo they are carrying in imminent peril (eg cases in which the ship has run aground and is floundering). Shipmasters normally have no contract with the owners of the cargo. Nonetheless, courts have held that the shipmaster may act without prior authority as an agent of the cargo's owner in order to protect the goods or their value, usually by selling them to a third-party[38] or contracting services to safeguard them.[39] In the event of salvage, the cargo's owner would be liable to the salvors for the contracted price of the salvage operation. As in other cases of agency, the shipmaster-agent must adhere to fiduciary constraints by acting in good faith, in the interests of the principal, and with reasonable care. Moreover, communication with the cargo's owner must be practically or commercially impossible; the shipmaster must have made whatever reasonable efforts she could to communicate with the owner in order to receive instructions. If this last condition is satisfied, Lord Simon in *The Winston* held that '[the agent] is bound to take without authority such action in relation to the goods as [the principal], as a prudent owner, would himself have taken in the circumstances'.[40]

An obvious economic rationale of this form of agency is that cargo owners would always prefer to obtain some value for their property rather than none. If salvors and other third-parties could not rely on the shipmaster's capacity as agent to bind the owner, any agreement they entered into with the shipmaster on behalf of the owner would lack legal security. Third-parties would be left with purchased goods to which they have no title, or a contract for services rendered on which they could not sue. Under

[37] For discussion, see Fridman, *supra* note 30, pp 133–51; Markesinis and Munday, *supra* note 30, pp 40–8; Stone, *supra* note 36, pp 33–9.

[38] See eg *The Gratitudine* (1801) 3 CH Rob 240; *Australasian SN Co v Morse* (1872) LR 4 PC 222.

[39] See eg *China-Pacific SA v Food Corporation of India: The Winston* [1981] 3 All ER 688; 1982 AC 939, p 693, Lord Diplock (*The Winston*). Reynolds claims that because the shipowner is a bailee of the cargo, the shipowner's bailment relationship to the cargo owner can give rise to powers of agency. Reynolds, *supra* note 30, p 141. The common law does not go through these gyrations, and even if it did, the argument in the text that follows (or something much like it) would be needed to explain how agency powers can arise from bailment.

[40] *The Winston*, p 697. Agency of necessity has also been applied to land carriers and other contexts. In *Great Northern Railway Co v Swaffield* (1874) LR 9 Ex 132, the court found that a railway company could act as an agent of necessity for the owner of a horse it was carrying by sending the horse to a livery stable when the owner was not at the station to receive the horse, making the owner liable to the stable. In *Hastings v Semans (Village)* [1946] 4 DLR 695; [1946] 3 WWR 449 (Sask CA), a village's doctor was held to be the village's agent of necessity when he brought an indigent patient to a private hospital for emergency treatment, and thus the village was liable for the patient's medical expenses.

these conditions, third-parties would be less willing to purchase or rescue imperilled cargo, leaving it to waste.

This rationale is unconvincing because it fails to explain the impossibility-of-communication requirement, and its explanation of the shipmaster's agency is weak at best. If the wishes of owners can always be inferred, why must shipmasters attempt to communicate with them? And, given the possibility that owners can insure their cargo, why does the law not make the default position that the shipmaster must let the cargo go down with the ship, absent instructions to the contrary? No doubt some fully insured owners would rather the shipmaster abandon the cargo than sell it at a discount or pay costly salvage and storage fees.

A better explanation of the necessity doctrine is that, in the absence of communication with the owner, the law requires the shipmaster to treat the property of others as something of value in which the owner alone has a legal interest. As such, the goods cannot be treated with indifference and abandoned if an act of agency can save them or a measure of their value. As in the case of involuntary bailment discussed in the previous chapter, the critical work is performed by the status the goods enjoy as property of another party, and the idea that custody of another's property can give rise to obligations on the part of the non-owning possessor. Thus, when the shipmaster contracts with a salvor as an agent of necessity, she does so on the basis of a duty to respect the cargo owner's property and its value to her, a duty that enables and requires the shipmaster to act as an agent given her possession of another's property.

Before contracting with a third-party, however, the shipmaster is required to make reasonable efforts to communicate with the owner. Subjecting the shipmaster to this requirement is the most the law can do to ensure that the goods are treated as property of the owner, as hers and no one else's, prior to its authorization of the shipmaster's agency of necessity. Once the shipmaster becomes an agent of necessity, she is subject to fiduciary obligations for the same reason that she had to attempt to communicate with the owner: to respect the owner's right to have her property treated as hers.

We have seen already in the parent-child case that the child lacks authority to exercise the administrative power possessed by the parent; the child is *juridically* incapable of exercising parental authority. In the shipmaster case, on the other hand, the owner does possess the authority to contract on her own behalf that the shipmaster ultimately exercises, but as a matter of fact the owner is unable to exercise this authority because the shipmaster is unable to communicate with her. Using the classification scheme for incapacity set out in the previous chapter, we would say that the owner is *contextually* incapable of acting on her own behalf. While in each of these cases there is a different explanation of the beneficiary's inability to exercise the relevant power, it remains significant that where such an inability exists, and where important practical or legal interests are at stake, the law entrusts and authorizes the fiduciary to act on behalf of the beneficiary by empowering the fiduciary to subject the beneficiary to new obligations.

In the shipmaster case, the authority of the shipmaster to change the legal relations of the cargo owner depends on the shipmaster herself being subject to fiduciary obligations to act in good faith and with due regard for the cargo owner's best interests. In other words, the law's subjection of the shipmaster to fiduciary duties is at the same time power-conferring: because the shipmaster is subject to fiduciary duties when she is lawfully possessed of imperilled cargo, the law can and does confer agency powers on her. The subjection of the shipmaster to fiduciary duties arises from her lawful possession of the owner's property, and distinguishes her from strangers who are not empowered to contract on behalf of the owner, even if doing so would preserve the goods or their value.

The power-conferring aspect of subjection to fiduciary duty is a general feature of fiduciary relations. Judges commonly explain the fiduciary's power to change the legal position of the beneficiary by pointing to her duty of loyalty to her beneficiary.[41] Fiduciaries are empowered to subject their beneficiaries to new obligations precisely because all such exercises of authority *must* be made on behalf of the beneficiary, as if the beneficiary herself had exercised her own autonomy and had acquired the new obligations herself. It is important to underscore that the benefit accruing to the beneficiary from an exercise of fiduciary power is incidental to (and not constitutive of) the fiduciary's authority. The fiduciary's authority arises instead from the obligation under which her power must be exercised. The presence of the fiduciary obligation distinguishes the fiduciary's authority to change the legal position of her beneficiary from a benefactor's *de facto* power to confer an unsolicited benefit: the fiduciary alone is under an obligation to exercise entrusted power on behalf of the beneficiary, and so the fiduciary alone can change the beneficiary's legal position by subjecting her to a new obligation. Thus, a solicitor can compromise a suit on behalf of her client, but a stranger cannot, even if a failure to so compromise the suit would seriously set back the client's interests.

The power-conferring aspect of subjection to fiduciary duty is present in the state-subject fiduciary relationship. In this relationship, the state is under a fiduciary obligation to govern through the rule of law. The state's subjection to this duty empowers or authorizes the state to change the legal position of its subjects by announcing and enforcing law. The important

[41] See eg *HL Misener and Son Ltd v Misener* (1977) 77 DLR (3d) 428 (NSCA), p 440, Macdonald JA.

point brought out by agency of necessity is that the agent's fiduciary authority to change the normative position of the principal does not rely on the principal suffering from a child-like incapacity. All that is required, in the relevant circumstances, is an inability on the part of the principal to exercise the power the law has entrusted to the agent. Under these circumstances, the agent is authorized to change the legal relations of the principal *vis-à-vis* third-parties. From this it follows that the principal may owe those third-parties new legal obligations as a consequence of the agent's exercise of authority. The law does not view the principal as the victim of a forced sale, but rather as the beneficiary of a legitimate exercise of legal authority. The same is true of legal subjects in a rule-of-law abiding state while residing within it.

5.7 OPTING OUT

As indicated above, the state-subject relationship differs from private agency relations in that the state is a fiduciary of everyone subject to its jurisdiction, and so in this public relationship there are no 'third-parties' who are not also 'principals'. Yet another consequence, I argue now, is that individuals are not entitled to opt out of a rule-of-law abiding state.

Simmons claims that non-consenting individuals should be able to opt out of the state through a public declaration. He accepts that others have freestanding or natural moral rights against us to 'do our fair shares in contributing to acceptable levels of security and well-being for all', but insists that 'the rights of others can be respected by us individually' because 'I can do my duty without accepting a member's obligations'.[42] The actual threat posed by a resident dissident to members of the state, Simmons says, is much less than it would be in the state of nature, and less than the threat posed by evil fellow members and other sovereign states. Simmons' central claim is that a prohibition on opting out is unjustifiably oppressive because '[i]f my refusal of membership is public and if I respect the rights those members possess *qua* persons, any threat I represent will be relatively minor and easy to counter'.[43] Since we are willing and able to live with greater threats (eg the threats of other states and evil fellow members), it is arbitrary for the state to impose itself on individuals who respect the rights of others but do not consent to membership in the state.

Simmons, however, presupposes what he needs to show. It is not enough for him to show that it is empirically possible for a non-consenter to respect the rights of others, and that the good-willed individual in fact poses a relatively minor threat. These claims are irrelevant to the salient issue,

[42] Simmons, *supra* note 1, p 154. [43] Ibid, p 141.

which is whether the non-consenter is *entitled* to determine unilaterally whether she has respected the rights of others. Simmons commits himself to this proposition when he says that one can do one's duty without accepting a member's obligations, and elsewhere when he affirms 'the natural right of all persons to enforce morality (by coercion, if necessary)'.[44] Presumably, to be able to enforce morality one must be able to determine for oneself what morality requires, even if one takes initial pointers from others, the law, religion, and so on. Simmons grants that morality requires us to respect the rights of others. So from this acknowledgement and his commitment to a natural right to enforce morality we can fairly ascribe to him the view that the dissident is entitled to determine unilaterally whether she has respected the rights of others. If the resident dissident were not so entitled, who else could be? The obvious answer is the state, but Simmons' argument is intended to show that the state lacks authority on such matters.

The important issue for present purposes is this: if the dissident is entitled to determine unilaterally whether she has respected the rights of others, then as a conceptual matter she would still be in a state of nature with the state's members, even supposing that, as an empirical matter, she posed only a minor threat to them. On Simmons' assumptions, neither the non-consenting dissident nor a willing member of the state can rightfully compel the other to submit their disputes to an arbitrator. If the willing member could rightfully force adjudication on the unwilling (as she would be able to do with another willing member), then the unwilling would have a duty to obey the court's sentence because, by hypothesis, the imposition of adjudication would be *rightful* (ie required by principles of right or legality). Under conditions in which neither party can rightfully impose third-party adjudication on the other, and if the dispute cannot be resolved through negotiation or voluntary acceptance of arbitration, then the only means available to end the conflict is a unilateral use of force. As Hobbes tells us in the epigraph to this book, 'their controversy must either come to blows, or be undecided' (L v.iii, 23). This is the problem of unilateralism that legal institutions alone appear able to resolve.

It may seem that in some cases leaving the dispute undecided is not all that bad. If the plaintiff or claimant has no legitimate claim to press, then leaving the dispute undecided will uphold the rights of the disputants. Leaving all disputes undecided, however, would institutionalize an arbitrary bias in favour of the status quo. Parties can (and frequently do) innocently invade the rights of others. And as we shall see, even disputants who agree on general moral and legal principles may in good faith disagree on the

[44] Simmons, *supra* note 2, p 192.

specific rules of their application, rules which are necessary to make the principles determinate in particular cases. Following Hobbes, I will argue that only an impartial third-party can settle good faith disagreements justly.

But let us consider first the merits of Simmons' claim that an individual dissident is entitled to opt out because the threat she would pose would be relatively minor. (Below I will grant this claim for the sake of argument, and will suggest that even on this rosy assumption the case for opting-out has not been made.) Now, the actual threat that an individual might pose is an empirical matter that may be quite significant and change over time. Suppose the individual came to possess a weapon of mass destruction. It is difficult to see how, as a conceptual matter, her possession of such a weapon would deprive her of a right to opt out that she would otherwise enjoy. Would she regain the right if she surrendered the weapon, or exchanged it for a less dangerous weapon? Would the state be required to buy the weapon from her (why should she give up her property for nothing?) so that she could then opt out? Who would set the purchase price if the dissident and the state could not agree on terms? The state? The individual? Or a neutral third-party, a kind of supra-state? If the latter, why should the dissident (or the state) be compelled to submit their price dispute to a supra-state if that kind of submission is intrinsically wrongful? These considerations hint that the problem of unilateralism will not easily go away, and that the *de facto* inability of the dissident to threaten others is an inadequate basis from which to infer an entitlement to opt out.

The underlying problem with the argument based on the alleged *de minimis* threat of the dissident is that threat levels are entirely contingent matters, while what is needed, from Simmons' point of view, is a normative and conceptual argument that explains why the state is never entitled to announce and enforce law over the unwilling. Simmons' main argument against state authority is appropriately of this kind: the state is an institution, no institution is entitled to impose obligations on the unwilling, therefore the state is not entitled to impose obligations on the unwilling. My reply has been that the state is not just another institution, it is a public and fiduciary institution, and as a consequence it is entitled to impose obligations on non-consenting parties. Both Simmons' main argument and my reply are conceptual and normative in that they do not (and need not) depend on the actual and contingent threat posed by would-be resident dissidents. As the following argument will show more systematically, the issue of whether the state can in fact defend its members from dissidents is irrelevant to the normative question of whether potential dissidents are entitled to opt out.

Opting out is wrongful because it entails that private parties are entitled to set unilaterally the terms of their interactions with others; the resident dissident becomes the sole judge of her every cause. To see why this is wrongful *independently of any possible threat of wrongful harm*, let us assume that the dissident could not possibly threaten to harm others (perhaps she is infirm and incapable of rallying others to her cause). Even with threats taken entirely out of the equation, the dissident would not have authority to resolve disputes between herself and others because those others can make an equally valid claim to such authority. On the liberal assumption that individuals are moral equals, no individual, as a private party, can enforce morality by claiming dispute-resolution authority over another. As Hobbes put it, without reliance on even this modest liberal assumption, there is no 'right reason constituted by Nature', and so when individuals 'seek no more but that things should be determined by no other men's reason but their own, it is as intolerable in the society of men, as it is in play after trump is turned to use for trump on every occasion that suit whereof they have most in their hand' (L v.iii, 23). The idea of a resident dissident pushes inexorably towards a contest of wills, and away from the regime of secure and equal freedom that the rule-of-law-abiding state makes possible.

An objector might reply that opting out does not entail converting the dissident into a petty Leviathan if the dissident in fact does respect the rights of others, as Simmons insists she must. Once again, however, the problem is not whether as a matter of fact the dissident happens to respect the rights of others, but rather how we are to establish publicly and authoritatively that she has done so. Let us suppose for the sake of argument that the dissident and others within the state agree on a robust number of general moral and legal principles (do not injure others, respect property, perform one's contracts, and so on). We would still need public institutions to make these principles determinate and consistently applicable to particular fact situations. As a venerable principle of the common law insists, not only must justice be done, it must also be seen to be done.[45]

Consider the common law of contract in which ownership in the thing or subject matter of the contract passes only upon delivery. The principle that ownership passes only upon delivery tells us nothing about what constitutes delivery. We need some means to determine whether delivery has occurred as a matter of law. The rule adopted might focus on the moment the good has been shipped, when the buyer physically takes possession of it, or some other point in time. The principle regarding delivery directs our inquiry to a range of possible indicia, but the principle is too abstract to pick out the specific rule that will allow the principle to apply to a given set

[45] *Rex v Sussex Justices, Ex parte McCarthy* [1923] All ER 233; [1924] 1 KB 256.

of circumstances. Other principles of analogous indeterminacy abound in contract law, as well as property law, tort, unjust enrichment, fiduciary law, criminal law, family law, and public law generally.

There is good reason to suppose that leaving the determination of specific rules to individuals necessarily results in unilateralism. As Arthur Ripstein observes, even if we all agree (as private parties) on the general principles of right, we might yet fail to agree on the specific rules that are necessary to apply the principles to particular circumstances.[46] The fact that a variety of equally valid rules can be used to implement the same principle implies that we can fail to agree even if we all act in good faith. Because distinct implementing rules are equally valid, no party can gainsay the other in the event of a dispute. The only means left standing to end the dispute (though not to resolve it in any morally significant sense) is unilateralism, ie the submission of one party to the unilateral will of the other. The state resolves the problem of indeterminacy (and with it the problem of unilateralism) by setting out the specific rules that will be used to apply general principles to particular facts. The state can thereby guarantee a regime of equal freedom in the sense that the freedom of each is made subject to the same reciprocal limits that apply equally to all. As a consequence, the (rule-of-law-abiding) state's members enjoy a known and reliable framework of equal freedom from within which to plan their lives and interact with others, a theme to which we will return in Chapter IX.[47]

At the risk of some repetition, it is worth emphasizing that the argument against unilateralism applies even if we grant real-world conditions in which the good-willed dissident, like everyone else, is coercively subject to state law. Simmons argues, quite credibly, that under these conditions the dissident would not pose an especially dangerous threat given her peaceable nature and the law's deterrent and coercive force.[48] It may appear that insistence on a moral duty to obey the law under these conditions is unduly stingy. How can unilateralism be a genuine problem if there is no serious threat of the dissident acting unilaterally? But, once again, the *de minimis* factual threat posed by the dissident is beside the point. The problem of unilateralism is a normative and conceptual problem about who gets to set the terms under which people are entitled to interact with one another. That the state can so restrain the dissident is not a reason for thinking that she is entitled to set unilaterally the terms of her interactions with others. The law

[46] Arthur Ripstein, 'Authority and Coercion' (2004) 32(1) *Philosophy and Public Affairs* 2, p 28.

[47] For insightful discussion of how the law's universality (or generality) and necessity (or peremptory and coercive force) provide independence from the wills of others, see Nigel E Simmonds, *Law as a Moral Idea* (Oxford: Oxford University Press, 2007), esp pp 141–3.

[48] Simmons, *supra* note 2, pp 176–7.

must set those terms, and the law needs the state (or at least legal institutions) to be able to do so.

5.8 A PUBLIC AGENT OF NECESSITY

In Chapter I, we looked to Kant's analysis of parent-child relations to explain the moral basis of the fiduciary's obligation to her beneficiary, and in this chapter I have relied extensively on the Kantian axiom that no party may impose unilaterally the terms of interaction on another. Should we adopt Kant's theory of the state?

Kant was a social contractarian. He believed that the state derived its legitimacy from a contract that we each must be understood to make with each other to form a 'General Will'. Through our agreement and the General Will, Kant alleged, we jointly authorize the state to announce and enforce law in accordance with the doctrine of right that underlies private law.[49] Kant did not think that people actually contracted with one another to set up the state through referenda or any other such means. Rather, he claimed that we are under an obligation to agree to leave the state of nature to render our rights determinate and secure. Even granting some mutual recognition of provisional rights in the state of nature, 'when rights are *in dispute* (*ius controversum*), there would be no judge competent to render a verdict having rightful force'.[50] Thus, Kant says, 'each may impel the other by force to leave this state and enter into a rightful condition'.[51]

So, for Kant, the social contract is hypothetical, but not in the counterfactual sense that it is something to which we would all agree if we put our minds to it. Rather, the contract is hypothetical in the sense that it is purely normative and conceptual, a requirement of Kant's idea of right. As Ripstein puts it, the contractors must agree because 'they cannot object to being forced to accept those procedures [that will make right possible], because any objection would be nothing more than an assertion of the right to use force unilaterally'.[52]

Let us assume that Kant is correct: individuals cannot object to submitting the determination and adjudication of their rights to public legal institutions, and therefore individuals must agree—are morally required to

[49] Kant also believed that the social contract authorized the state to enforce criminal law, and to tax its citizens to alleviate poverty so that the poor would not be unduly subject to the will of others. Immanuel Kant, *The Metaphysics of Morals*, trans by Mary Gregor (New York: Cambridge University Press, 1991) (first published in 1797), pp 6:331–6:337 (pp 140–5); 6:326–6:327 (pp 136–7). For lucid discussion, see Arthur Ripstein, *Force and Freedom: Kant's Legal and Political Philosophy* (Cambridge, MA: Harvard University Press, 2009).

[50] Kant, *supra* note 49, p 6:312 (p 124) (emphasis in original).

[51] Ibid. [52] Ripstein, *supra* note 46, p 33.

agree—to some form of social contract that establishes legal order. Even taking Kant's assumptions onboard, a familiar objection to hypothetical consent accounts of the state applies with equal force here. The idea that we must or ought to consent to the state does not establish that we have consented, and so the state's authority does not flow from our actual consent. The better view is that the fiduciary principle authorizes state authority on our behalf in light of Kant's most basic premises: our lack of a right to use force unilaterally, our possession of a right to interact with others on terms of secure and equal freedom, and the state's ability to supply and guarantee those terms.

We do not need to subscribe to a social contract to recognize the force of the principle that no one is entitled to impose terms unilaterally on others, and therefore that no one is entitled to be judge and party to the same cause. This principle of impartiality stands on its own, as Hobbes made clear in *Leviathan* long before Kant. Once the principle of impartiality is in place, we can explain the need for the state and the wrongfulness of opting out. Nothing is added by supposing that we must consent to the state, since whether we must consent or not makes no difference to either the state's authority or our duty to obey the law.

Kant has an additional argument to support his reliance on a social contract and the General Will. Like Hobbes before him, Kant trades on the people's alleged authorship of the sovereign's actions to claim that the acts of the legislature are really the acts of the people, and thus the legislature can do the people no wrong[53]:

> The legislative authority can only belong to the united will of the people. For since all Right is to proceed from it, it *cannot* do anyone wrong by its law. Now, when someone makes arrangements about *another*, it is always possible for him to do the other wrong; but he can never do wrong in what he decides upon with regard to himself (for *volenti non fit iniuria*). Therefore, only the concurring and united will of all, insofar as each decides the same thing for all and all for each, and so only the general united will of the people, can be legislative.

Kant's conclusion—'only the general united will of the people, can be legislative'—does not follow from his premises. It does not follow from the possibility that the people can jointly authorize the state through a general will that this is the *only* way the state can come to enjoy their authorization. The law can authorize the state to act on their behalf as a fiduciary, as a public agent of necessity. When the state acts within the bounds of its fiduciary mandate, it necessarily acts exclusively for and on

[53] Kant, *supra* note 49, p 6:314 (p 125).

behalf of the people. This is what it means to act as a public fiduciary. And just as a person cannot do wrong to herself, the law is likewise incapable of authorizing an agent to wrong her principal. But there is reason to prefer the fiduciary account of the state to Kant's.

Like Kant's social contract, the necessity that gives rise to state agency and fiduciary authority is conceptual and normative rather than empirical: the necessity arises from the juridical incapacity of private parties to announce and enforce law in circumstances in which public institutions are able to do so. But unlike Kant's social contract, the basis of the state's authority—the state-subject fiduciary relationship—is actual rather than hypothetical. There is no need to pretend or insist that the people have consented. It is enough that the state possesses irresistible administrative power that individuals, as private parties, are not entitled to exercise, and that the fiduciary principle places the state and its institutions under an obligation to govern in accordance with the rule of law.

The fiduciary model of the state shares a number of features with two contemporary theories supportive of the duty to obey the law: Philip Soper's deference theory and Christopher Wellman's samaritan theory.[54] I will briefly compare and contrast them to the fiduciary theory. As we shall see, the fiduciary theory's distinctive qualities offer fresh resources with which to reply to Simmons' objections to the samaritan and deference theories.

Soper's theory is that we have a defeasible, general, and non-instrumental moral reason to defer to the normative judgments of people who are doing necessary (valuable) jobs in good faith. By deferring to the judgments of such people, we show them the respect we would wish for ourselves were we the ones doing those jobs, and we act consistently with our own values because we recognize the job's value and necessity. The application of this Kantian theory of respect to the state is straightforward: the state and its institutions do a necessary job when, in good faith, they impose legal norms claimed to be just on behalf of all. Therefore, so long as they do their job in good faith, we have a *prima facie* reason to show them respect by deferring to their normative judgments, even if we disagree with them on the merits.

Soper's theory and the fiduciary theory are both Kantian and non-instrumental, and both underscore that law must be imposed on behalf of all subject to limiting conditions (good faith and compliance with the rule of law, respectively).[55] The theories differ, however, in that only the fiduciary

[54] See Soper, *supra* note 21 and Wellman, *supra* note 3; Christopher Wellman, 'Samaritanism and the Duty to Obey the Law' in A John Simmons and Christopher Wellman (eds), *Is There a Duty to Obey the Law?* (New York: Cambridge University Press, 2005). See also Philip Soper, *A Theory of Law* (Cambridge: Harvard University Press, 1984).

[55] Soper uses good faith to get at the idea that legal institutions must do the best they can, but that if they err they are not culpable because this is the most we can ask of human institutions. He allows,

theory affirms that the state and its institutions are under an *obligation* to act on behalf of their people subject to the rule of law, and only the fiduciary theory claims that the state is under this obligation *because* the state and its people are in a morally significant relationship with one another. Furthermore, only the fiduciary view relies on this morally significant relationship and the state's ensuing obligation to explain the state's authority and the duty to obey. To see the difference this makes, consider Simmons' main objection to Soper's deference theory, and the reply made available by the distinctive features of the fiduciary theory.[56]

Simmons claims that the value or necessity of the state on which Soper relies goes to the state's overall *justification* (eg the benefits of security and coordination that it provides) rather than its *legitimacy* with respect to particular individuals when it announces and enforces law over them (as discussed at 5.3 above). Simmons reiterates his now-familiar claim that 'legitimating an arrangement that involves some claiming authority to control others involves showing that a special relationship of a morally weighty kind exists between those persons', and that the mere fact that 'an arrangement is a good thing plainly cannot give persons authority over simply whomever they might choose to select as subjects'.[57] Soper's deference theory is vulnerable to this objection because although it plausibly insists that the state is good or necessary, it does not explain how or in what way the (non-consensual) state-subject relationship is a 'special relationship of a morally weighty kind'. By contrast, the fiduciary theory addresses Simmons on his own terms by showing that the non-consensual state-subject relationship is a 'special relationship of a morally weighty kind' precisely because it is a fiduciary and public relationship regulated by a Kantian conception of secure and equal freedom.

Wellman's theory, on the other hand, seems to chart a middle ground between theories of obligation that rely on a special relationship and those that do not. Although we shall see that his theory does not assume a special moral relationship between state and subject (the state and subject could be strangers to one another), the state nonetheless occupies a special role or

however, that in cases of grave injustice (eg crimes against humanity), the good faith defence would fail because a purported legal authorization of acts such as crimes against humanity would have no practical consequences other than pure coercion (eg the purported legal authorization cannot prop up a 'just following orders' defence in a Nuremburg-like proceeding). Soper, *supra* note 21, pp 97–8.

[56] In addition to the criticism discussed in the text, Simmons argues that even if in some sense we owe public institutions and officials respect, it is far from clear that the respect we owe them is of a morally important kind capable of authorizing them to direct and coerce us against our will. Simmons, *supra* note 2, pp 145–7. Indeed, some theorists argue that we can (or should) show respect (or civility) to our public institutions in part *because* we are not obligated to do what they say but nonetheless belong to reasonably just societies. See eg Raz, *supra* note 10, ch 13 (respect); Green, *supra* note 5, ch 9 (civility).

[57] Simmons, *supra* note 2, pp 148–9.

position. For Wellman, the state is in the position of a samaritan uniquely capable of rescuing its subjects from the perils of the state of nature by providing for their mutual security. To perform its samaritan mission, the state must infringe the natural rights of its people by subjecting them to non-consensual coercion. The state is entitled to do this because the benefits of mutual security to (virtually) everyone are great, and the net cost to (virtually) everyone is relatively small (ie the benefits of security less the burden of state coercion).

The state, Wellman says, is akin to the samaritan who uses the property of another without permission to perform an easy rescue. Usually persons cannot use the property of others without permission. The presence of someone in need of rescue, however, gives the samaritan rescuer a liberty-right to use another's property without the owner's consent. The state enjoys a like liberty-right to coerce its subjects because state coercion is necessary to secure peace and stability. Wellman deploys two further premises to move from the state's liberty-right to coerce to the subject's duty to obey. First, he claims that persons can have samaritan duties and not just liberty-rights to rescue one another. Second, he argues that individuals have a general duty to obey the law because this duty is their 'fair share' of the communal 'samaritan chore' of securing political stability.[58] So a samaritan view of the state combines with a fairness principle to generate the duty to obey.

The most important point of intersection between Wellman's theory and the fiduciary theory is that both justify state coercion over any given individual on grounds of ensuring the security of *others*. Thus, both avoid the charge of paternalism that would follow from coercing a non-consenter for the sake of benefiting *her*. Both theories also claim that the state is entitled to use coercion that ordinarily persons are not entitled to use. Under Wellman's theory, coercion can be used only when necessary to perform a rescue, while under the fiduciary theory only public officials are entitled to use coercion. Finally, both theories can claim that the state has an obligation to establish legal order given its samaritan or fiduciary position, although Wellman speaks only of the samaritan 'task' or 'chore' as a 'communal responsibility' rather than the state's duty.[59]

[58] Wellman, *supra* note 55, p 749.

[59] Ibid. It is somewhat surprising that Wellman does not discuss the implications for his theory of the idea that the state is under an obligation to perform its samaritan duty. Of course, if the state really has only a liberty-right to coerce, then the fact that the state is under an obligation to secure legal order is irrelevant because we can explain the liberty-right without making reference to the obligation. Still, if the state does have an obligation to act as a samaritan on behalf of its citizens, then perhaps the state has more than a liberty-right. Perhaps the state has a moral claim-right to their allegiance that is explained by the samaritan principle's imposition on the state of a samaritan duty to use its coercive powers properly (eg consistently with the rule of law). I will not explore this possibility, but if it bears fruit it would bring the samaritan theory closer to the fiduciary theory.

The major difference between the samaritan theory and the fiduciary theory lies in the distinct moral theories which underpin them. The fiduciary theory relies exclusively on Kant's theory of right, while the samaritan theory relies on a consequentialist understanding of morality that trades in Mill's vocabulary of benefits and harms rather than in the Kantian language of rights and wrongs.[60] Under Kant's cold theory, there is no (private and enforceable) duty of easy rescue because any such duty would make the need or welfare of one party the sole basis of another's obligation, and would thereby place the purported duty-bearer under an obligation set unilaterally by the rescuee.[61] The Kantian denial of the duty to rescue is just an implication of the unswerving Kantian principle that *private* parties cannot set unilaterally the terms of their interactions with others; any such imposition would constitute subjection to the will of another. The (rule-of-law abiding) state is not so precluded because it subjects individuals to law rather than a private party's will. Plausibly, the state is entitled under its public safety mandate to conscript temporarily private parties into public duty through samaritan or like statutes that require individuals to perform easy rescues.

Wellman claims that an implication of his theory is that liberals must either qualify Mill's harm principle (the principle that people should enjoy liberty to do as they please so long as they do not harm others) to include a benefit-to-others principle attuned to private samaritan duties or give up on political obligation.[62] As a corollary, Wellman says, liberals must accept that political obligation cannot be explained without accepting that others have positive rights to be benefited. As the Kantian and fiduciary theory of the duty to obey shows, however, liberals do not need to commit themselves to a private benefit-to-others principle in order to explain the duty to obey. All liberals need to commit themselves to is a Kantian understanding of the fiduciary position of the state, a theory that entitles the state (but not private parties) to demand the performance of easy rescues.

The distinct moral underpinnings of the fiduciary theory and samaritanism permit us to reply on behalf of the former to Simmons' main objections to the latter. One of those objections begins by noting that the samaritan

[60] Wellman at one point claims that his argument shares with Kant the idea that 'autonomy in ourselves and others is the source of our duty to eliminate the injustice of the state of nature', Wellman, *supra* note 3, pp 751–2. I have acknowledged this similarity, but as the discussion in the text makes clear, his samaritan argument is deeply inconsistent with Kant's underlying moral theory because Kant's theory entails a rejection of private samaritan duties.

[61] For discussion, see Arthur Ripstein, 'Three Duties to Rescue: Moral, Civil, and Criminal' (2000) 19(6) Law & Phil 751.

[62] Wellman, *supra* note 3, pp 752–3.

duty more closely resembles a duty of charity than a duty of rescue.[63] Duties of rescue fall haphazardly on specific individuals who confront emergencies, while duties of charity address an impersonal, ongoing, and non-occasional problem. We can make sense of contributing a fair share to an ongoing collective moral task such as the alleviation of poverty. But it is far less clear, Simmons says, that duties of rescue can bind us to perform a fair share of them because we cannot anticipate the emergencies in which they arise. The trouble is that only a duty of rescue can resolve the 'particularity problem' by localizing the moral duty in a way that will explain why an individual owes a duty to provide security to the members of *this* state rather than to individuals in some other state who are in greater need of security. Moreover, if the samaritan duty is a duty of charity, it becomes far more difficult for Wellman to claim that state institutions are necessary to fulfil it. Private charities or personal efforts could surely satisfy it.

The fiduciary theory is immune to these attacks because the Kantian moral theory on which it rests eschews rather than relies on private duties of rescue. The fiduciary theory's response to the particularity problem, as we have seen, is to coopt Simmons' strategy of insisting on a special moral relationship between state and subject capable of legitimising state authority. The presence of this special (fiduciary) relationship localizes state authority and the duty to obey.

Simmons further objects to the samaritan theory on grounds similar to those canvassed at 5.7 above in the discussion of opting out: even if individuals were bound to contribute their fair share locally to the samaritan chore of providing security to others, it is not obvious that they must have a duty to obey the law *qua* law to contribute their fair share.[64] Let us assume real-world conditions in which all are subject to legal coercion. Let us also assume that the anarchist refrains from violence, deception, and so on, and lets others know her intentions in this regard. If she contributes locally but privately to the security of others such that she makes a *greater* contribution to security than is required by Wellman's samaritan duty, how can the mere refusal to admit a duty to obey constitute a failure to contribute her fair share to the security of all?

The samaritan theory is vulnerable to this criticism because it is a theory about benefits and harms which relies on the *actual* harms alleged to flow from subject's failure to contribute her fair share to the samaritan chore of providing security. If the anarchist can contribute her fair share through means other than obedience to the law *qua* law, then she has done her moral

[63] Simmons, *supra* note 2, pp 184–8. True to form, throughout his critique Simmons declines to take the easy path of saying that duties of charity are optional whereas duties of rescue are mandatory.

[64] Ibid, pp 187–8.

duty, and insistence on a duty to obey begins to look like stingy and dogmatic statism. The fiduciary theory is not susceptible to this critique because, as discussed, it conceives of and addresses the problem of unilateralism as a conceptual and normative problem about who is entitled to determine whether the rights of others (including their rights to security) have been respected. I have argued that the state, as a public agent of necessity, is so entitled, but private parties are not.

Simmons might reply that all of this begs the question by making the determination and security of rights necessarily institutional, where what the Kantian needs, he says, is 'an empirical claim that institutional enforcement is the only way to genuinely secure people's legitimate claims'.[65] Simmons' arguments against Wellman and others, I think, make it plain that no such empirical argument is likely to succeed. Instead, I have offered a principled argument against unilateralism based on the normative claim that no one is entitled to be judge and party to the same cause.

***

I will conclude with a gesture towards a topic worthy of further inquiry that I address only in passing in the next chapter, but which connects us to the forthcoming discussion of public law. The idea that the state is a public agent of necessity points congenially towards a particular ideal of government: democracy. Recall that one of the conditions of agency of necessity is that the agent must attempt to communicate with the principal to obtain her consent before embarking on a particular course of action. When communication is impossible and consent is unavailable, the agent is entitled to act in what she reasonably perceives to be her principal's best interests, subject to fiduciary constraints. In modern democratic societies, government seeks the consent of its people through periodic elections, and is liable to removal if its policies or conduct fall out of favour with the electorate. Between elections the government is entrusted to administer the state, but like the private agent of necessity, its public administration is subject to fiduciary constraints. Having explored some of the theoretical aspects of the idea of the state as fiduciary, we turn now to consider the extent to which public administration and the law that governs it can be understood to reflect the aspirations and structure of the fiduciary theory of the state.

[65] Ibid, p 177.

PART III

THE FIDUCIARY NATURE OF THE RULE OF LAW

VI

Judicial Ambivalence to Public Fiduciary Duties

6.1 INTRODUCTION

I argued in the Prologue that Hobbes' conception of public authority rests on principles of legality and the idea that the sovereign and the people are in an ongoing relationship with one another. The relationship is mediated by a presumption of trust rather than consent, and it is reciprocal in that if the sovereign violates the principles of legality, he subverts his authority and the people's correlative obligation to obey. In Chapter I, we saw that the fiduciary theory of the state has legal, relational, and Kantian elements. In Chapters II and III, we explored the Crown-Native fiduciary relationship, the existence of which demonstrates that it is possible for common law courts to view the state as a fiduciary of a diverse class of its subjects. The Crown-Native case, I claimed, is much like Dworkin's hard cases in that both bring to the surface what is always present in the ordinary case. In Chapter IV, we saw that fiduciary relationships may be thought to rest on a presumption of trust. They arise if one party holds irresistible administrative power over another, where administrative power is conceived of as other-regarding, purposive, and institutional in nature. I concluded that the state's sovereign powers to announce and enforce law are both irresistible and administrative, and so the state stands in a fiduciary relationship with its people. In Chapter V, I defended the fiduciary view against philosophical anarchism and its claim that non-consenting members of a state do not have a duty to obey the state's laws. It is time now to investigate the fiduciary nature of public administration, and implications of the fiduciary model for public law.

This chapter addresses concerns underlying the reluctance of some courts to view the administration as a fiduciary of the people. The point of this chapter and the next two is to show that the fiduciary theory helps us understand and justify the most important doctrines and practices constitutive of administrative law. In common law jurisdictions, these doctrines and practices are arguably the most salient and important features of the rule of law, for they control directly the everyday interactions between public authority and the people.

Perhaps the most obvious similarity between private fiduciary relationships and decision-making contexts of administrative law is that in both cases one party holds administrative power which is to be used exclusively for the sake of someone else. Just as the private fiduciary owes a duty of loyalty to the beneficiary, the public administrator possesses powers, as Sir William Wade says, 'solely in order that it may use them for the public good'.[1] But in the public realm it is not immediately clear who the analogue of the private beneficiary is supposed to be. If public authority must always be used for the public good, then the set of candidate public beneficiaries may include some or all of the public (including some *and* all of the public in a single case), and so the set ranges from the public at large down to the individual who confronts an administrative tribunal.

Sometimes the public interest and the interest of the individual are bound to conflict, such as when a board decides to dismiss a public employee whose work performance is considered substandard. From the outset, then, there appears to be a significant asymmetry between fiduciary duties at private law and the duties of public law. Private fiduciary duties typically require the entrusted party to act solely for the benefit of a discrete beneficiary. Public law, on the other hand, does not divide the world into beneficiaries and non-beneficiaries. Nonetheless, I argue now that public decision-makers can be faithful fiduciaries of both the individuals immediately subject to their powers and the public at large. Recall the suggestions from Chapter I that such an argument is possible because the *content* of fiduciary obligations is context-sensitive, and in public settings the content of the duty changes; the duty of loyalty is necessarily transformed into duties of fairness (the topic of Chapter VII) and reasonableness (the topic of Chapter VIII).

Many common law courts have shown considerable reluctance to characterize as fiduciary the relationship between front-line decision-makers and the individuals subject to them. Indeed, they have sometimes deemed what otherwise would be a trust in a private law context (and so a relationship which gives rise to fiduciary obligations) to be a 'political' rather than a legal trust, and therefore one that admits of no enforceable legal obligations. Moreover, where judges do explicitly consider the connection between fiduciary doctrine and public duty, they often do so subject to a limitation that helps to explain the relative absence of the fiduciary principle in public law: for a fiduciary obligation to be found, the claimant must show either a statutory entitlement or a pre-existent right to property that a public official has a duty to administer. If the individual has neither a statutory nor a

[1] HWR Wade and CF Forsyth, *Administrative Law*, 9th edn (Oxford: Oxford University Press, 2004), p 355.

common law entitlement to the interest at stake, as is often the case in employment and immigration cases, then she is unlikely to receive the benefit of a fiduciary obligation.

In this sense, a rights/privileges distinction operates so as to limit the application of public fiduciary duties. We saw in Chapter I that it was this same distinction that animated Cartwright J's legal void thesis in *Roncarelli v Duplessis*,[2] the thesis that administrators, within their province, exercise authority as a 'law unto themselves'.[3] Here I address the asymmetries noted above between the private and public law contexts, and argue that, in the public domain as much as in the private sphere, there is no reason to limit application of the fiduciary principle on the basis of a rights/privileges distinction. As discussed in Chapter IV, some fiduciary relationships give rise to 'pure' fiduciary duties that protect important practical interests, such as business opportunities, even though the beneficiary has no legal claim to those interests apart from the claim on the fiduciary. As in the cases of pure fiduciary duties, administrative decisions that affect important interests trigger controlling legal duties. The fiduciary nature of administration explains and justifies why this is so.

We shall see in the final sections of this chapter that a number of judges and scholars from various common law jurisdictions have recognized or explored the connection between fiduciary doctrine and public law. But we shall also see that for a number of historical reasons the mainstream of commonwealth public law has disregarded the implications that might be drawn from the fiduciary position of the state and its officers. This history explains public law's ongoing neglect of the fiduciary standing of public decision-makers. Yet as I will argue in this chapter, and show more systematically in Chapters VII and VIII, the explanation of this neglect falls well short of a persuasive justification.

6.2 POLITICAL TRUSTS

The fiduciary obligation is the fundamental duty owed by a trustee to her beneficiary. Since the trust remains the paradigmatic case in which fiduciary duties apply, it is worth taking a moment to consider the courts' view of the Crown as trustee. The Crown may be a trustee of another's property, and at times has been held liable for breach of trust.[4] A trust upon the Crown generally arises from a prerogative, statute, or treaty, but even a statutory

2 *Roncarelli v Duplessis* [1959] SCR 121. 3 Ibid, p 167.

4 See eg *Canada Central Railway Co v The Queen* (1873) 20 Gr 273; *Miller v The King* [1950] SCR 168; *Re Wentworth Insurance Co* (1968) 69 DLR (2d) 448; *aff'd* [1969] SCR 779 *per* Laskin JA (as he then was); *Town Investments Ltd v Department of the Environment* [1978] AC 359.

obligation framed in terms of holding an interest in trust for a particular party may fail to generate legal obligations. If the court considers the trust to be merely a 'political' rather than a 'true' trust, then no legal obligations arise. For this reason, a 'political' trust is not really a trust at all, for the putative beneficiary has no entitlement to the interests allegedly held in trust for her. The vacuity of the political trust has led Peter Hogg and Patrick Monahan, the authors of the leading Canadian text on Crown liability, to describe it as a 'nothing'.[5] The controlling jurisprudence supports their assessment.

In *Kinloch v Secretary of State for India* (1882)[6] and *Tito and Waddell (No 2)* (1977),[7] the courts held that despite the words 'in trust for' and 'on trust' within the instruments that authorized the Crown to hold war booty and royalties respectively for the benefit of others, the trusts were political and so did not create enforceable legal obligations. In *Tito*, Megarry V-C distinguished the Crown from a private party—one in which a true trust would have been found—on the basis of the government's public powers and obligations. He found that one explanation of the Crown holding property for the benefit of others was that 'without holding the property on a true trust, the Crown is nevertheless administering that property in the exercise of the Crown's governmental functions'.[8] Cases such as *Kinloch* and *Tito* lead Hogg and Monahan to conclude that for beneficiaries to avoid 'the catastrophe of the political trust', the statute 'will have to provide a fairly clear indication that enforceable private rights are contemplated, as opposed to merely public duties'.[9]

Furthermore, for a trust to be found the Crown must hold or administer property capable of forming the subject matter of a trust.[10] Some legal interests will not count as property for this purpose. In the years prior to *Guerin v The Queen*,[11] Aboriginal peoples argued that the Crown was a trustee of lands over which they had treaty rights to hunt and fish. The courts denied their claim on the grounds that the Aboriginal treaty right was a 'privilege' and therefore not property capable of forming the subject matter of a trust.[12] In *Guerin*, Dickson CJ found that the Crown was not the band's trustee but was nonetheless subject to a fiduciary obligation in virtue of its discretionary authority over surrendered lands and the band's legal interest in them. The majority thereby side-stepped the issue of whether an Aboriginal interest in land is property capable of forming the subject matter of a trust.

[5] PW Hogg and PJ Monahan, *Liability of the Crown*, 3rd edn (Toronto: Carswell, 2000), p 259.

[6] *Kinloch v Secretary of State for India* (1882) 7 AC 619 (*Kinloch*).

[7] *Tito and Waddell (No 2)* [1977] 3 All ER 129 (*Tito*).

[8] Ibid, p 216.

[9] Hogg and Monahan, *supra* note 5, p.259.

[10] *MA Hanna Co v The Provincial Bank of Canada* [1935] SCR 144, p 167.

[11] *Guerin v The Queen* [1982] 2 SCR 335 (*Guerin*). See Chapter II (2.2) for discussion.

[12] See eg *Pawis v R* [1980] 2 FC 18 (FCTD).

In sum, a party seeking to convince a court that the Crown is a trustee faces the dual challenge of satisfying the property requirement of a trust and showing that the trust in question is not merely political. These hurdles have led litigants, especially post-*Guerin*, to seek remedies on the basis of fiduciary duties alleged to arise independently of a formal trust. But, as we shall see, even in these cases the courts tend to recognize the obligation only in relation to property or some interest in which a pre-existent right can be identified, suggesting an unwillingness to see the mere relationship between the Crown and the complainant as a sufficient basis of a public fiduciary duty.

6.3 *AUTHORSON: GUERIN* EXTENDED

Authorson v Canada (Attorney General)[13] may be the most important non-Aboriginal case in Canadian law that deals explicitly with public fiduciary duties. In a unanimous decision, the Ontario Court of Appeal held that the Crown owed a fiduciary duty to Authorson in respect of pension and disability benefits it had administered on his behalf since World War II. Authorson brought a class action suit on behalf of roughly 1,000 veterans from World War I and later conflicts. Many of the veterans were unable to administer their statutory entitlements due to disabling injuries received while in service. The Court of Appeal had to determine whether the Crown was liable for interest on monies that it administered on Authorson's behalf but did not invest or otherwise place into interest-bearing accounts until 1990. The Crown did not contest that fiduciaries are responsible for investing monies under their administration. The main issue with respect to the Crown's potential liability was whether the Crown was in fact a fiduciary of Authorson when it managed his funds pre-1990.

Taking its cue from *Guerin*, the Court of Appeal looked to the specific features of the Crown's relationship with the veterans to see if they reflected the defining characteristics of a fiduciary relationship. Important in this regard was the Crown's statutory obligation to administer the funds for the veterans' benefit, and the Crown's broad discretionary authority to fulfil this mandate. The Court noted too that, due to his disability, Authorson could not manage the funds himself, and so he (like many other veterans) was especially vulnerable to the Crown's discretionary power over his

[13] *Authorson v Canada (Attorney General)* (2002) 58 OR (3d) 417 (Ont CA); *rev'd* 2003 SCC 39 (*Authorson*). Although the Supreme Court reversed, it did so on the narrow ground that the complainants could not rely on the Canadian Bill of Rights, SC 1960, c 44 to block the operation of an unambiguous statutory bar to recovery. The Court of Appeal had used the Canadian Bill of Rights to uphold Authorson's claim in the face of explicit legislation enacted in 1990 that purported to extinguish it. The Supreme Court summarily affirmed that the Crown owed a fiduciary duty, and that it breached its duty as alleged, but that any claims based on this breach were statute-barred.

interests. These features of the relationship brought it within the scope of the fiduciary principle.

Finally, the Court distinguished Authorson from the 'political trust' cases of *Kinloch* and *Tito*. The Court did so on the basis of Authorson's property interest in his pension and disability monies. It is neither necessary nor desirable, however, to rely on this distinction. Suppose the relevant statutes had ordered that the monies be held in trust for Authorson rather than distributed to him as his property, as was the position of the complainants in *Kinloch*. For reasons that follow, it would have been arbitrary to block Authorson's claim merely on the basis of the statutory characterization of monies intended to benefit Authorson alone.

Rejecting Authorson's claim would be arbitrary because the characterization of a beneficiary's interest as legal or proprietary is unrelated to the constitutive features of the fiduciary relationship (ie possession of administrative power over vulnerable interests). If the relationship bears these trust-like characteristics, it is enough if the beneficiary has a significant, practical interest in the subject matter of the obligation. As the discussion of pure fiduciary relationships in Chapter IV revealed, a beneficiary's interest in the subject matter of the obligation need not be a property interest. Indeed, the interest may underlie no legal consequences aside from the fiduciary obligation that constrains the fiduciary.

Still, the Court's stated reliance on Authorson's property interest cannot be dismissed out of hand. As noted already, the manner in which the Court uses this interest to distinguish Authorson's case from a political trust is reminiscent of the rights/privileges distinction that courts in the past have used to limit an individual's rights before administrative tribunals. That is, where there is neither a pre-existent right nor a statutory entitlement, there are no rights; there are only privileges. The political trust cases are similar in that, legally, the political trust is a 'nothing'. In both cases, public authority is left to operate in a legal void, with virtually unfettered discretion. Thus, the critical question *Authorson* leaves unresolved is whether an aggrieved party can escape the legal void and benefit from a fiduciary obligation if she is unable to show a pre-existent right to something the Crown has a duty to administer.

As we shall now see in *Harris v Canada*,[14] judges will sometimes require the hopeful beneficiary of a public fiduciary obligation to establish not just a pre-existent right, but also the further proposition that she is owed a private law-like duty of loyalty. We consider *Harris* in some detail because Dawson J's opinion is the most thorough and explicit judicial articulation of the

[14] *Harris v Canada* 2001 FCR 1408; [2002] 2 FC 484 (FCTD) (*Harris*).

orthodox view in Canada that the fiduciary principle has only limited application to public law.[15]

6.4 *HARRIS: GUERIN* RETRENCHED

In May 1996, the Auditor General of Canada reported serious concerns about the movement out of Canada of at least $2 billion of assets held in trusts belonging to a wealthy family. The movement of the funds followed a 1991 advance tax ruling in favour of the family. In October 1996, Harris—an individual unrelated to the family—brought an action as a public interest litigant to challenge the advance ruling. Harris sought a declaration that the Minister responsible was obligated to use all available powers under the Income Tax Act to collect any unpaid tax that was properly due as a result of the transactions referred to in the ruling. Harris alleged that in disposing of the 1991 request for a ruling, the Minister 'was acting in a fiduciary capacity, or acting in a capacity akin to a fiduciary' towards the class of taxpayers Harris represented (all taxpayers except those who benefited from the advance ruling). He further alleged that by granting the advance ruling, the Minister had breached a fiduciary or fiduciary-like duty through an improper exercise of discretionary authority.[16]

Dawson J dismissed all of Harris's claims at trial. She examined the particular features of the relationship between the class Harris represented and the Crown in light of the 'rough and ready' guide for identifying fiduciary relationships set out by Wilson J in *Frame v Smith*.[17] Recall that Wilson J's guide points to the ability of a candidate fiduciary to exercise discretionary power unilaterally over the legal or practical interests of a peculiarly vulnerable party (see

[15] A host of judgments support Dawson J's position: *Norfolk v Roberts* (1913) 28 OLR 593; 13 DLR 463 (App Div); *aff'd* 50 SCR 283; 23 DLR 547; *Swain v Law Society* (1982) 2 All ER 827; *Windsor Roman Catholic Separate School Board v Windsor (City)* (1988) 64 OR (2d) 241 (CA); leave to appeal to the SCC refused; *Callie v Canada* [1991] 2 FC 379 (FCTD); *Fairford First Nation v Canada (Attorney General)* [1999] 2 FC 48 (FCTD); *Chippewas of the Nawash First Nation v Canada (Minister of Indian and Northern Affairs) et al* [1999] 251 NR 220 (FCA); *Hogan v Newfoundland (Attorney General)* (2000) 183 DLR (4th) 225; leave to appeal to the SCC refused, [2000] SCCA No 191; *Squamish Indian Band v Canada* 2001 FCT 480; [2000] FCJ No 1568 (TD) (QL); *Pritchard v Ontario (Human Rights Commission)* 2004 SCC 31; [2004] 1 SCR 809 (*Pritchard*), para 25. But see *British Columbia v Canadian Forest Products Ltd* 2004 SCC 38; [2004] 2 SCR 74, para 81, where Binnie J, for the majority, contemplates that the Crown might owe the public a fiduciary duty to safeguard the environmental integrity of public lands.

[16] *Harris*, *supra* note 14, para 4. Prior to trial, the Crown sought to strike the statement of claim on the grounds that it disclosed no cause of action, and succeeded at first instance: *Harris v Canada* (1997) 98 DTC 6072 (FCTD). On appeal, however, the Federal Court of Appeal found that it was not 'plain and obvious' that the Crown owed no fiduciary obligation to the class of taxpayers Harris represented: *Harris v Canada* [2000] 4 FC 37; 187 DLR (4th) 419 (FCA); leave to appeal to SCC refused (without reasons); [2000] SCCA No 364 (QL).

[17] *Frame v Smith* [1987] 2 SCR 99.

Chapter IV). Dawson J recognized that the Minister had discretion to provide advance rulings that were favourable or unfavourable to the applicant. But she insisted that there was nothing within or outside of the Income Tax Act to suggest that the Minister was under a fiduciary obligation when he exercised the discretion conferred on him by statute.

The theme that unites Dawson J's judgment is that fiduciary law is and should be restricted to private law-like interactions in which there is a discrete beneficiary. Dawson J held that the sole source of the Minister's obligation is the Income Tax Act, that the Minister performed a public duty in providing the advance ruling, and that there were no indicia in either the statute or the relevant ministerial guidelines to suggest that the Minister had a duty in the nature of a private law fiduciary duty.

Dawson J, however, did not explain why the presence or exercise of the Minister's discretion should not count towards finding a common law obligation that might be characterized as a public fiduciary obligation. Whenever legislation empowers a public decision-maker to administer a statutory regime, it typically confers administrative and discretionary power capable of affecting the significant interests of others. In both public and private cases, the power is administrative in that it is other-regarding, purposive, and institutional. Moreover, since the public is vulnerable to officials' unilateral exercise of their powers, it appears that as a rule the authority conferred by legislation is consistent with Wilson J's guide to fiduciary relationships.

Dawson J was sensitive to the parallel, and countered with the following argument[18]:

> I am unable to conclude that it is Parliament's intent that in providing advance rulings the Minister must forego his public law duties and instead be placed in the untenable position of trying to reconcile potentially conflicting duties of loyalty owed to both a particular taxpayer requesting an advance ruling and the larger group of taxpayers who, implicit in the plaintiff's submission, would often be best served by a refusal to rule or by a negative ruling.

Dawson J's view, then, is that even if the Minister and Harris were in a relationship that appeared to conform to the fiduciary indicia set out in Wilson J's guide, there was no such relationship in these public law circumstances because, if there were, the Minister would face a hopeless conflict between the loyalty owed to the class Harris represents, on the one hand, and the taxpayer who requested the advance ruling, on the other. The only discretion-constraining principles appropriate to public law, Dawson J says, are the rule-of-law protections found in cases such as *Roncarelli*. Thus, in addition to the asymmetry between private fiduciary duties and the duties of public law,

[18] *Harris*, *supra* note 14, para 192.

Dawson J dismisses the need for fiduciary doctrine to regulate discretion in the public sphere, because administrative law principles, she thinks, are adequate to the task at hand and stand in need of no further justification.

I tackle these objections in turn. The first reply, immediately below, looks to a line of English case law on municipal powers that supports application of the fiduciary principle to public decision-making, despite the worry over conflicting duties of loyalty. The English cases, similar to *Authorson*, are trust-like cases in which the beneficiaries rely on pre-existent rights to anchor fiduciary obligations. But they nonetheless cast doubt on the orthodox view in Canada that public law duties and fiduciary obligations are, except in special circumstances, anathema to one another. In fact, the English jurisprudence suggests that public law duties—such as the duty of reasonableness—arise *because* the relationship between the decision-maker and the affected individual is fiduciary.

The second reply to the orthodox view begins with an inquiry into the content of the duty in cases where a fiduciary stands as such to distinct parties with separate interests. As foreshadowed in Chapter I, the content of the duty in these cases is not loyalty to a particular beneficiary at the expense of other beneficiaries, but rather fairness and reasonableness. Adherence to these principles, I claim, is consistent with—and demanded by—the overarching fiduciary obligation owed by public decision-makers to both the public at large and the individuals immediately affected by their decisions.

Finally, as discussed in Chapter I, administrative law principles do stand in need of justification because many judges believe that they undermine the separation of powers by turning judges into law-makers. We shall see in subsequent chapters that this is as true today as it was when Rand and Cartwright JJ squared off in *Roncarelli*. To anticipate, the fiduciary theory offers a persuasive reply to this concern. Judges who recognize common law duties arising from legal relationships do not violate the separation of powers. They are merely recognizing duties flowing from the fiduciary relationship that exists between the primary decision-maker and the individual.

6.5 ENGLISH LAW'S MARRIAGE OF ADMINISTRATIVE POWER TO FIDUCIARY DUTY

In *Roberts v Hopwood*,[19] a 3–2 majority of the House of Lords explicitly recognized the trustee-like position of a borough council *vis-à-vis* its ratepayers. The issue was the authority of a borough council to pay wages to its

[19] *Roberts v Hopwood* [1925] All ER 24 (*Roberts*). In *Harris*, Dawson J neglected to discuss *Roberts*, and the line of cases that follow it.

servants which were well in excess of the going rate. The district auditor found that certain payments made in excess of the going rate were in fact illegal gratuities, and disallowed them.

Lord Atkinson, writing with the majority, upheld the auditor's order. He held that the council 'stands somewhat in the position of trustees or managers of the property of others'.[20] The majority ultimately concluded that the council breached its trustee-like obligation to conduct administration 'in a fairly businesslike manner with reasonable care, skill and caution, and with a due and alert regard to the interest of those contributors who are not members of the body'.[21] Lord Atkinson emphasized that the council's duty was not statutory, nor in need of statutory support to be fully actionable: 'To make an act contrary to law it is not necessary that it should be prohibited by some legal enactment such as a statute or a by-law or the like'.[22]

Subsequent English cases have confirmed that local authorities stand in a fiduciary relationship to their ratepayers. Two prominent decisions are *Prescott v Birmingham Corp*[23] and *Bromley London Borough Council v Greater London Council*.[24] In *Prescott* the municipal corporation sought to provide the elderly with limited free access to public transportation, and intended to cover the corresponding shortfall in revenue from its general rate fund. Similarly, in *Bromley* the Greater London Council acted on an election promise and reduced public transportation fares by 25 per cent. The Council then directed London's 35 boroughs to raise taxes to recover the revenue. In both *Prescott* and *Bromley*, ratepayers challenged the municipalities' policy initiatives and won, largely on the basis of the fiduciary obligation established in *Roberts*.

Prescott and *Bromley* met with an academic roasting that warned of 'judicial lawlessness'[25] and a conservative judiciary determined to thwart progressive local democracy.[26] Yet it would be hasty to conclude that fiduciary doctrine is to blame. There is no reason to suppose that a public fiduciary with multiple constituencies must favour the status quo at the expense of policy reform. Fiscal policy changes that favour one group to the detriment of another are inevitable in democratic societies. So far as public policy decisions are concerned, perhaps the most that can be asked of fiduciary law is that it supply a transparent decision-making framework

[20] *Roberts*, *supra* note 19, p 33. [21] Ibid.

[22] Ibid, p 34. [23] *Prescott v Birmingham Corporation* [1954] 3 All ER 299 (*Prescott*).

[24] *Bromley London Borough Council v Greater London Council* [1983] 1 AC 768 (*Bromley*).

[25] JAG Griffith, 'Administrative Discretion and the Courts: The Better Part of Valour?' (1955) 18(2) Mod L Rev 159, p 163.

[26] Martin Loughlin, *Legality and Locality: The Role of Law in Central-Local Government* (Oxford: Clarendon Press, 1996), ch 4.

structured by legal principles such as fairness and reasonableness. Within these constraints, shielding one constituency's present wealth from democratically mandated redistribution places the partisan demands of private claims above public order, and betrays the public trust on which the state's democratic legitimacy depends.

Although the English judges in *Prescott* and *Bromley* disagree with Dawson J on the place of fiduciary doctrine in public law, they commit a similar mistake in their application of the fiduciary principle to a public setting. Dawson J wrongly assumes that the fiduciary principle has limited application to public law because, she thinks, it can generate only a private law duty of loyalty. The English judges acknowledge the fiduciary position of public authority, but wrongly suppose that the content of the ensuing obligation is loyalty to one group at the expense of another. All bring too much private law baggage to their analysis of the fiduciary character of public law. More interesting for present purposes, however, is the subsequent use English courts have made of *Roberts* and its progeny to access insights from mainstream *public* law for the purposes of determining the proper bounds of a *private* fiduciary's discretion. These courts assume the fiduciary character of public bodies, and then look to administrative law for guidance to the resolution of disputes involving private fiduciaries with multiple classes of beneficiaries.

Equitable Life Assurance Society v Hyman[27] was a class action concerning some 90,000 pension fund beneficiaries who received significantly varying payments. The issue was whether the directors could exercise their broad discretion to award the worse-off beneficiaries greater profit-sharing bonuses than the better-off policyholders. The better-off policyholders argued that the maturity policies did not state that one's choice of payment option would affect one's profit-sharing bonus.

Lord Woolf MR, writing with the majority of the Court of Appeal, found a fiduciary relationship between the Society's directors and its policyholders. The directors' powers had to be used 'to further purposes for which they [were] conferred', and had to be exercised 'fairly and justly'.[28] The difficulty lay in determining the content of these obligations. The challenge was especially pronounced because the directors had scarce resources to distribute, and had to act with due regard for the best interests of all classes of policyholders, and not just the worse-off.

To illuminate the nature and content of the directors' duty, Lord Woolf MR looked to the public realm. He noted that the fiduciary doctrine relied on in *Roberts*, *Prescott*, and *Bromley* is part of a 'well established

[27] *Equitable Life Assurance Society v Hyman* [2000] 2 All ER 331, CA (Eng); *aff'd* [2000] UKHL 39; [2002] 1 AC 408; [2000] 3 All ER 961, HL (Eng) (*Equitable Life*).

[28] Ibid, p 337.

tradition'.[29] But he went much further than *Roberts et al.* He generalized that 'Parliament confers wide discretionary powers on the government of the day', and that '[t]he recipients of the powers, whether national or local, are in very much the same position as they would be if they had fiduciary powers conferred upon them'.[30] His Lordship underscored that Parliament entrusts powers to delegated bodies solely for use on behalf of the public, and that the public in turn may be thought 'to place its trust in the public bodies to exercise their powers for the purposes for which they are conferred'.[31] That is, Parliament and its administrative delegates exercise public powers on the basis of public trust. Those constraints, Lord Woolf MR said, are found in the leading English decisions on judicial review, *Padfield v Minister of Agriculture and Food*[32] and *Associated Provincial Picture Houses Ltd v Wednesbury*,[33] which clarify the fiduciary and trust-like position of public bodies.[34]

Like *Roncarelli*, the English cases emphasize that an administrator's discretion is not absolute, and so it must be exercised in accordance with the object and purpose for which it is granted. What is novel in *Equitable Life* is that Lord Woolf MR takes this principle of the rule of law to flow from the fiduciary nature of public authority.

Applying the rule-of-law/fiduciary principle to *Equitable Life*, the majority held the Society liable because the directors exercised their powers to the detriment of some beneficiaries (the better-off policyholders) on the basis of their exercise of a right they enjoyed under the policy (ie the right to choose one's maturity option). Here too the similarity with *Roncarelli* is striking: there, Duplessis unlawfully exercised discretionary power in response to Roncarelli's exercise of an unchallengeable right (ie the right to post bail or surety for bail).

Equitable Life and *Roncarelli* reveal two rule-of-law principles which follow from Lord Woolf MR's fiduciary argument for limiting exercises of discretion to the purposes for which the relevant powers are conferred. The first is

[29] *Equitable Life Assurance Society v Hyman* [2000] 2 All ER 331, CA (Eng); *aff'd* [2000] UKHL 39; [2002] 1 AC 408; [2000] 3 All ER 961, HL (Eng) (*Equitable Life*), p 338.

[30] Ibid. [31] Ibid.

[32] *Padfield v Minister of Agriculture and Food* [1968] 1 All ER 694 (*Padfield*).

[33] *Associated Provincial Picture Houses Ltd v Wednesbury* [1947] 2 All ER 680 (*Wednesbury*).

[34] There has been some resistance to using public law to inform inquiry into the consequences of a trustee's breach of duty, mainly on the grounds that defective decisions in public law are void whereas in private law they are and ought to be, in the main, voidable rather than void. See Raymond Davern, 'Impeaching the Exercise of Trustees' Distributive Discretions: "Wrong Grounds" and Procedural Unfairness' in D Hayton (ed), *Extending the Boundaries of Trusts and Similar Ring-Fenced Funds* (London: Kluwer, 2002), p 437. The basic public/private parallel, however, remains unchallenged, and Davern recognizes that in cases where the private fiduciary fails to turn her mind at all to a power entrusted to her or commits a 'fraud on a power', the fiduciary's action is void rather than voidable.

a prohibition on using entrusted power in a manner that prejudices the beneficiary's exercise of a right the fiduciary is authorized to administer. Call these 'entrusted rights'. A fiduciary could hardly be said to be acting as such if he restricted his beneficiary's enjoyment of an entrusted right.

The second rule-of-law principle is related, but takes the beneficiary's entrusted rights as the subject of the principle rather than as its object: a fiduciary to multiple beneficiaries may not exercise discretion to the prejudice of a particular beneficiary *on the basis* of that beneficiary's enjoyment of an entrusted right. A fiduciary may sometimes have to exercise discretion in a manner that benefits some at the expense of others (as may occur in zero-sum funding settings, such as *Equitable Life*), but he cannot use a beneficiary's enjoyment of an entrusted right as the justification for these kinds of discriminations. Some other basis must be found, for the fiduciary would subvert the rationale of his office if he could use his power to infringe the very rights he is entrusted to safeguard.

These two rule-of-law principles are especially significant to the main argument offered here in defence of the fiduciary nature of public authority, and to the connection the fiduciary model reveals between public authority and legality. Viewing the principles under the light of the fiduciary model lets us see the sense in which their violation consists in a kind of arbitrariness that strains legality: an exercise of public power that infringes these principles subverts the rationale for which those powers are entrusted, and thus subverts the legal authority the law grants to public bodies on behalf of those subject to it.

In another private pension fund case, *Edge and Others v Pension Ombudsman and Another*,[35] Chadwick LJ also looked to the general features of public law relationships to inform his understanding of the duties of private trustees. *Edge* concerned a board of trustees' distribution of an actuarial surplus to three distinct classes of beneficiaries: employers, employees, and pensioners. The trustees divided the predicted surplus between the employers and the employees alone, allotting nothing to the pensioners.

Like Lord Woolf MR in *Equitable Life*, Chadwick LJ relied heavily on the principles governing discretion in public law, quoting at length several full paragraphs from the reasons of Lord Greene MR in *Wednesbury*. He concluded that[36]:

> [T]he so-called duty to act impartially [between different classes of fund beneficiaries]... is no more than the ordinary duty which the law imposes on a person who is entrusted with the exercise of a discretionary power: that

[35] *Edge and Others v Pension Ombudsman and Another* [1999] 4 All ER 546, CA (Eng) (*Edge*).

[36] Ibid, pp 567–8.

> he exercise the power for the purpose for which it is given, giving proper consideration to the matters which are relevant and excluding from consideration matters which are irrelevant.

Among the interesting features of *Edge* was that the fund's beneficiaries did not have a pre-existent or proprietary right to the actuarial surplus, for the surplus existed only as a mathematical prediction contingent on the trustees' policy decisions. In other words, the trustees owed their beneficiaries a pure fiduciary obligation arising exclusively from the trust-like nature of the relationship.

Also relevant is what Chadwick LJ does not say. At no point does he suggest that the trustees are not fiduciaries because they owe obligations to beneficiaries with separate and divergent interests, none of whom can point to a pre-existent right to the actuarial surplus. On the contrary, he holds that it is exactly the context of entrusted discretionary authority, multiple beneficiaries, and an absence of pre-existent rights that makes public law an apposite place to look for the content of fiduciary duties owed by similarly situated private trustees.[37]

6.6 CROSS-FERTILIZATION BETWEEN PUBLIC AND PRIVATE FIDUCIARY CONTEXTS

Chadwick LJ and Lord Woolf MR's jurisprudential inquiry is the mirror image of the inquiry of the Canadian judges in *Authorson* and *Harris*. The British judges begin with private legal relationships in which there is no question that the trustees in *Edge* and the directors in *Equitable Life* owe fiduciary duties. This threshold question is settled because the relationships are paradigmatically fiduciary in nature. The issue is determining the content of the fiduciary obligation given multiple beneficiaries.

In the Canadian cases, the primary issue is the threshold question that the British courts take for granted: whether or not the Crown and its subjects are in a fiduciary relationship. The Canadian courts in *Authorson* and *Harris* already had available to them the general *Roncarelli* constraints on discretion, but nonetheless considered whether the circumstances pointed to a common law fiduciary relationship. Given the British courts' view that the fiduciary nature of public administration discloses essentially *Wednesbury* or *Roncarelli*-type duties, one might think that, in practice, Dawson J has it right

[37] Canadian pension fund law recognizes the fiduciary position of fund administers who must contend with the multiple-beneficiary issues that arose in *Equitable Life* and *Edge*, but denies that fiduciary duties are owed in relation to actuarial surpluses, and has thus far neglected to explore public law for inspiration. See eg *Association provinciale des retraités d'Hydro-Québec v. Hydro-Québec* 2005 QCCA 304.

after all, and that little is gained by qualifying as 'fiduciary' the rule-of-law duties already recognized at public law.

Recognition of the fiduciary nature of administration, however, is valuable for several reasons. First, it permits the common law to carry out a fruitful, reciprocal cross-fertilization between private and public fiduciary relationships. *Equitable Life* and *Edge* are cases in which private law looks to public law to inform itself of the content of the relevant fiduciary duty. *Guerin* and *Authorson* are cases in which public law looks to private law to specify the kind of obligation that is due.

In *Authorson*, for example, it is conceivable that the lower courts could have reached the same substantive result in favour of the veterans (setting to one side the statutory bar to recovery) applying only the public law principle that a statutory scheme must be administered in accordance with its purpose. Because one purpose of the relevant statutes was the administration of the veterans' monies for their benefit, one could argue that failing to invest the funds constituted a straightforward breach of public duty. The difficulty is showing why this failure to exercise discretion attracts liability, and why this liability should be equivalent to what the veterans would have received had the Crown invested their monies in interest-bearing accounts.

The Crown might say that it did administer the monies in accordance with the stated statutory purpose of providing reasonable care for veterans. The Crown had already provided for the living expenses of most of the veterans because they lived in public hospitals. So giving interest to veterans whose living expenses the government had already paid would have resulted in a kind of double recovery, or even an unjustifiable windfall for distant relatives. The Crown argued at trial that it was duty-bound to hold and preserve the funds for the veterans' sole benefit, which it did, but that it was not duty-bound to invest the funds. The Crown's main argument was that the legislature had not imposed a statutory obligation of this kind, an obligation the legislature did impose in 1990 with the amended Department of Veteran Affairs Act.[38]

If the Crown is a common law fiduciary of the veterans, however, arguments that rely on an explicit statutory basis for the duty are of no effect because statutory silences enable rather than frustrate common law obligations. Moreover, because the duty breached is the fiduciary duty to invest monies, the *quantum* of damages is justified as being exactly the sum the veterans would have received had the Crown performed its fiduciary duty.

There are at least two ways to understand the Crown's fiduciary obligation in *Authorson*. One approach is Dawson J's, according to which the Crown

[38] Department of Veteran Affairs Act, SC 1990, c 43, s 2.

essentially acts as a private fiduciary subject to a private fiduciary obligation that applies exceptionally in light of the circumstances. On this view, the private fiduciary duty is superimposed on the Crown, and is distinct from public law duties which arise in virtue of the Crown's administration of the statutory regime.

Another, better approach looks to fiduciary doctrine to supplement—not supplant—the requirements of public law. On this approach, the fiduciary relationship between the Crown and the veterans in *Authorson* informs us of the legal context in which the statute has been enacted, one in which public law responds to a legitimate concern that veterans do not live impoverished. For the Crown to exercise its discretion in accordance with the purpose of the statutory scheme, it must comply with default fiduciary obligations that set legal standards within which the statute is presumed to operate.

Put slightly differently, the fiduciary principle supplies specific legal content—the duty to invest a beneficiary's monies—to the framework within which the statute's substantive purpose must be interpreted and implemented. The framework constitutes and reflects the authorization the administration enjoys to exercise statutory powers, while setting benchmarks for determining the Crown's fidelity to the rule of law. Fiduciary doctrine can plausibly spell out with greater specificity the Crown's general public law duty to administer statutory regimes in accordance with their purposes. Seeing the Crown's fiduciary responsibilities as Dawson J does, as merely 'in the nature of private law duties', fails to capture the constructive and constitutional role they can play in establishing the standards of the legal framework required by the rule of law.

More generally, the fundamental mistake of the Canadian orthodox view propounded in *Harris* is to assume that the fiduciary principle is indifferent to the circumstances of its application. Thus, the orthodox view supposes that the content of the fiduciary obligation is necessarily the private law duty of loyalty in which the fiduciary acts solely on behalf of a discrete beneficiary. As *Equitable Life* and *Edge* reveal, however, this understanding of fiduciary doctrine is hard pressed to take account of even private law contexts with multiple classes of beneficiaries. In these settings, the fiduciary must treat the beneficiaries of different classes fairly or impartially, and she must exercise her discretion reasonably, with due regard for the interests of each person subject to her power.[39]

[39] See, generally, PD Finn, *Fiduciary Obligations* (Sydney: Law Book Co, 1977), chs 12–14. By way of analogy, the Civil Code of Quebec, Art 1317, CCQ also tells us that in cases involving the administration of the property of another in which there are several beneficiaries, the administrator holds a legal power and 'is bound to act impartially in their regard'.

I offered in Chapter I a theoretical explanation of the fiduciary principle's sensitivity to context, arguing that, in public settings, fiduciary duty comprises fairness and reasonableness rather than a duty of loyalty to a particular beneficiary. The British cases discussed in this Chapter—from *Roberts* through *Edge*—demonstrate that the context-sensitive interpretation of the fiduciary principle is practicable and cognizable within the common law. They also suggest that the fundamental fiduciary obligation is not loyalty *per se*, but rather a duty to act exclusively in accordance with the other-regarding purposes for which fiduciary power is held or conferred. Loyalty, fairness, and reasonableness are the context-dependent contents of this fundamental duty.

Edge also confirms that a fiduciary relationship may exist where there are multiple classes of beneficiaries with no pre-existent entitlement to the subject matter of the obligation. *Edge* points to a tight analogy between, on the one hand, private law fiduciary cases with multiple beneficiaries, and, on the other, public law cases in which a decision-maker must act in the public interest while exercising power over a particular individual who lacks a pre-existing right to the interest at stake. The analogy is tight because in both cases the power held is administrative (ie it is other-regarding, purposive, and institutional), and in both there are multiple beneficiaries whose practical interests are vulnerable in the sense that none is entitled to exercise the fiduciary's entrusted power. In short, *Edge* presupposes that pure fiduciary duties are possible in public law, notwithstanding the reluctance of Canadian courts to recognize them.

6.7 THE EMERGENCE OF PUBLIC FIDUCIARY DUTIES

The connection of fiduciary doctrine to public law has attracted the attention of judges and legal scholars from numerous jurisdictions. Sir Anthony Mason, former Chief Justice of the High Court of Australia, has observed in his extra-judicial writing that modern administrative law 'from its earliest days has mirrored the way in which equity has regulated the exercise of fiduciary powers'.[40] Building on this idea, a majority of the High Court of Australia found that judicial review remedies, such as injunction and declaratory relief, originated in courts of equity, and that, as in equity, public interest litigants do not have to establish a proprietary interest in the subject matter of their litigation.[41]

[40] A Mason, 'The Place of Equity and Equitable Remedies in the Contemporary Common Law World' (1994) 110 LQR 238, p 247.

[41] *Bateman's Bay Local Aboriginal Land Council v The Aboriginal Community Benefit Fund Pty Ltd* [1998] HCA 49, paras 24–53, Gaudron, Gummow, and Kirby JJ.

Spigelman AC, Chief Justice of the High Court of New South Wales, draws the comparison between equity and public law in the following sharp terms[42]:

> In both cases something like what equity calls 'fraud on a power' is involved. In both public law and equity, powers granted for a particular purpose can only be exercised for that purpose and not to achieve some collateral purpose. Also, in both cases, powers must be exercised *bona fide* for the persons or objects for whom or which the power was conferred. Finally, in both cases powers must be exercised rationally, without reference to irrelevant considerations and within the bounds of reason.

Spigelman AC calls for the development of 'institutional law'.[43] Institutional law would be thematically unified through recognition of general fiduciary principles applicable to private and public institutions alike, such as corporations and administrative agencies.

In Israel, the Supreme Court has long held that public authority, even in its business dealings, is 'a trustee with regard to the public and as such is bound to treat equals in an equal manner'.[44] In *Peretz* a local council refused to rent a hall to an unpopular religious minority. The Supreme Court held that this decision was indefensible on the basis of freedom of contract because the council was a public trustee. As such, the relationship between the council and the petitioners was not that of contracting strangers, so the council could not exercise its public power to the detriment of a religious minority. Daphne Barek-Erez describes *Peretz* as 'fundamental' in Israeli public law because it lays down the principle that 'also in their business actions public authorities are bound to follow their public law duties'.[45] As we shall see in the next two chapters, the Supreme Court of Canada resists this principle in *Dunsmuir v New Brunswick*.[46]

An emerging and international scholarly literature is starting to grapple systematically with the idea of the state as fiduciary and its implications for public law. In the United Kingdom, Dawn Oliver has argued against a conceptual division between exercises of judicial supervision of discretionary decision-making in public and private spheres of law.[47] She suggests that review in each sphere is justifiable as a legal check on power over vital

[42] JJ Spigelman, 'Foundations of Administrative Law: Toward General Principles of Institutional Law' (1999) 58(1) *Australian Journal of Public Administration* 3, p 9.

[43] Ibid, p 3.

[44] *Israel Peretz and Others v The Chairman, Local Council and Inhabitants of Kfar Shmaryahu* [1962] HC 262/62, Selected Judgments of the Supreme Court of Israel 191, p 205, Sussman J (*Peretz*).

[45] Email correspondence with author of 12 April 2008.

[46] *Dunsmuir v New Brunswick* 2008 SCC 9; [2008] 1 SCR 190.

[47] Dawn Oliver, 'Review of (Non-Statutory) Discretions' in CF Forsyth (ed), *Judicial Review and the Constitution* (Oxford: Hart Publishing, 2000), p 307.

interests and that it operates on the basis of general principles common to both.[48] Matthew Conaglen pursues this argument by developing in depth the particular analogy that Oliver draws between the doctrines of fiduciary conflicts and judicial bias.[49] Conaglen points to similarities in the methodologies, underlying rationales, and remedial considerations that emerge from the jurisprudence constituting these doctrines. He takes these similarities as evidence that the analogy is present not only at a high level of abstraction, but also at a level deep enough to justify cautious and context-sensitive use of private law concepts in public law and vice versa.

In Canada, Roderick Macdonald has commented that the administrative decision-maker 'acts no differently than a trustee administering a trust indenture'.[50] Lorne Sossin has offered a compelling account of how the duty of reasonable decision-making in Canadian administrative law may be thought of as a public equitable obligation.[51]

Evan Criddle argues that a fiduciary model best explains many features of administrative law in the United States, including judicial deference to agency interpretations of ambiguous statutes.[52] Supportive American jurisprudence announces that 'a public office is considered a public trust',[53] and that '[public officers] stand in fiduciary relationship to the people whom they have been elected to serve'.[54]

Corporate law scholars are pointing to the increasingly public role played by large corporations and the idea of corporate social responsibility to propose a public dimension of directors' fiduciary duties to their corporations. Cynthia Williams and John Conley argue that with increased global sensitivity to human rights and the possibility of claims by non-citizens for extra-territorial breaches of international law under the US Alien Tort Claims Act,[55] directors' fiduciary duties include minimizing risks in these

48 Ibid.

49 Matthew Conaglen, 'Public-Private Intersection: Comparing Fiduciary Conflict Doctrine and Bias' (2008) PL 58.

50 Roderick Macdonald, 'On the Administration of Statutes' (1987) 12 Queen's LJ 488, 493.

51 L Sossin, 'Public Fiduciary Obligations, Political Trusts and the Evolving Duty of Reasonableness in Administrative Law' (2003) 66 Sask L Rev 129.

52 Evan J Criddle, 'Fiduciary Foundations of Administrative Law' (2006) 54 UCLA L Rev 117. See also Evan J Criddle, 'Fiduciary Administration: Rethinking Popular Representation in Agency Rulemaking' (2010) 88(3) Texas L Rev 441; Evan J Criddle, 'When Delegation Begets Domination: Due Process in the Administrative State' (forthcoming) Georgia L Rev. Professor Criddle and I have since collaborated on a number of projects extending the fiduciary model to explain various aspects of international law in a series of four papers, discussed briefly in Chapter IX.

53 *Bonner v District Court* (1949) 206 P 2d 166 (Sup Ct Mont), p 169.

54 *Driscoll v Burlington-Bristol Bridge Co* (1952) 86 A 2d 201 (Supreme Court of New Jersey), p 221, Vanderbilt CJ.

55 Alien Tort Claims Act, 28 USC §1350.

areas.[56] Others, including Spigelman AC, argue that various private bodies exercising public powers (powers which significantly affect the public) are and should be subject to judicial review because such private exercises of public power carry fiduciary (or institutional) duties owed to the public.[57]

The most developed scholarship that foreshadows the arguments of this book, however, is found in the writings of Justice Paul Finn. While still an academic, Finn became the most important contemporary pioneer of the related ideas of popular sovereignty, public trust, and the state as fiduciary.[58] Finn's enduring contribution is his resuscitation of the fiduciary state as an embodiment of popular sovereignty, which is the republican idea that public power comes from the people, and so public officials are the people's fiduciary agents.[59] The state and its officials, in other words, hold power in trust for the people and exercise their authority on the basis of that public trust.

How does the fiduciary view of the state condition the exercise of public power? Finn points to the 'community of purpose' shared by equity and administrative law, with potent consequences for the duty of procedural fairness, including a presumption in favour of the duty to give reasons.[60] More contentiously, he suggests that Parliament, as a donee of the people's sovereignty, cannot 'reconstitute the general scheme of government in a way that denies its fundamental character', nor impair arbitrarily fundamental rights.[61] Yet other implications of the fiduciary state include equal suffrage, an openness to direct and participatory democracy as alternatives or adjuncts to representative democracy, the development of codes of conduct applicable to public officials, open access to public information, and non-judicial but independent accountability mechanisms such as Auditors General and Ombudspersons.[62]

[56] Cynthia A Williams and John M Conley, 'Is there an Emerging Fiduciary Duty to Consider Human Rights?' (2005) 74(1) U Cin L Rev 75.

[57] Spigelman, *supra* note 42, pp 5–7. Spigelman cites cases in which courts have reviewed the decisions of private bodies as diverse as the Panel on Takeovers and Mergers in the United Kingdom and the New South Wales Trotting Club. See also Michael Taggart, 'The Province of Administrative Law Determined?' in M Taggart (ed), *The Province of Administrative Law* (Oxford: Hart Publishing, 1997), p 1.

[58] PD Finn, 'The Forgotten "Trust": The People and the State' in Malcom Cope (ed), *Equity: Issues and Trends* (Sydney: Federation Press, 1995), p 132 (*Forgotten Trust*); PD Finn, 'A Sovereign People, A Public Trust' in PD Finn (ed), *Essays on Law and Government, Vol 1: Principles and Values* (Sydney: Law Book Co, 1995) (*Sovereign People*); P. Finn, 'Public Trust and Public Accountability' (1994) 3 Griffith L Rev 224.

[59] Finn, *Forgotten Trust, supra* note 58, pp 132–3. A concise expression of this idea, cited by Finn, is found in the Pennsylvania Declaration of Rights (1776): '[A]ll power being . . . derived from the people: therefore all officers of government, whether legislative or executive, are their trustees and servants, and at all times accountable to them', ibid, p 131.

[60] Finn, *Sovereign People, supra* note 58, p 16; Finn, *Forgotten Trust, supra* note 58, p 141.

[61] Finn, *Sovereign People, supra* note 58, pp 20–1.

[62] Ibid, pp 23–32.

Parallel to these collective manifestations of popular sovereignty, Finn claims that the common law affirms the people's sovereignty at the individual level by regarding the individual as 'an object of worth, respect and civic entitlement in her or his own right'.[63] In other words, the common law, properly understood, regards the individual as a bearer of human rights, and thereby serves as a moral and legal framework for the fiduciary principle's authorization of public power on behalf of the people. Finn's conclusion is that 'particular values, some human, some democratic or social' are 'intrinsic' (though not immutable) to the legal order of the common law.[64]

Finn also shows that the fiduciary ideal expresses a principle of integrity underlying standards of conduct applicable to public officials. Like their private law counterparts, officials cannot let duty conflict with interest, nor can they misuse their position or opportunities arising from it. If they breach these obligations, they breach the public trust, and commit a public wrong, which explains why their liability is criminal as well as civil. Dishonest officials may be charged with offences such as extortion, corruption, bribery, and breach of trust.[65]

In the remaining chapters we will explore much of the ground broken by Finn, including the implications of the fiduciary model with respect to the duty of procedural fairness (Chapter VII) and the legal limits of legislative power (Chapter IX).

6.8 THE PAUCITY OF FIDUCIARY DOCTRINE IN PUBLIC LAW

Notwithstanding the jurisprudence and scholarship cited above, it remains the case that fiduciary doctrine is largely absent from the mainstream of public law. Leading commonwealth administrative law textbooks do not discuss the relationship of public law to fiduciary law, nor contain so much as a reference to 'fiduciary' in either their indices or their tables of contents.[66] The Supreme Court of Canada reaffirmed the orthodox view in 2004, finding that a Human Rights Commission 'neither has a trust relationship, nor owes a fiduciary duty to, the parties appearing before it'.[67] If the state and its officials really are the people's fiduciaries, why has this dimension of public authority not come to the fore in contemporary administrative law?

[63] Ibid, p 7. [64] Ibid, p 8.

[65] Ibid, pp 26–7; Finn, *Forgotten Trust*, *supra* note 58, pp 142–51. In Canada these offences are found under ss 119–28 of the Criminal Code, RSC 1985, c C-46.

[66] See eg Wade and Forsyth, *supra* note 1; Paul Craig, *Administrative Law*, 5th edn (London: Sweet & Maxwell, 2003); David Mullan et al, *Administrative Law: Cases, Texts and Materials*, 5th edn (Toronto: Emond Montgomery, 2003); David Mullan, *Administrative Law* (Toronto: Irwin Law, 2001).

[67] *Pritchard*, *supra* note 15, para 25.

Finn provides a valuable historical explanation which shows that the fiduciary principle's muted role is not due to some intrinsic defect that renders it inapplicable to public bodies.[68] Rather, its anaemia in public law is the result of adventitious political and doctrinal developments peculiar to the consolidation of both the Westminster system of government and Dicey's understanding of the British constitution.

Finn points out that through the 18th and early part of the 19th century, English judges viewed the position of public office holders through a fiduciary prism. Lord Mansfield characterized public offices in 1783 as offices of 'trust and confidence concerning the public'.[69] Taking as its point of departure the trusteeship of public office holders, a body of criminal, civil, and equitable law developed to supervise the use of public power. But by the latter half of the 19th century, this 'law of offices' had passed into disuse and obscurity.[70]

Finn attributes the demise to a series of factors. The enlargement of the electoral franchise in England after 1832 and the advent of cabinet government signalled a growing expectation that grievances with public authorities were to be settled through the political channels of Parliament or at the polls. During this same period, parliamentary sovereignty came into its own as a foundational constitutional principle, leading Dicey to reject outright the idea that Parliament was in any legal sense a trustee of the people. Maitland too claimed that the trust concept in this context was really just a political metaphor.[71] And finally, the remedy-driven prerogative writs of administrative law, such as *habeas corpus* and *certiorari*, rose to prominence in the 19th century, and would continue to dominate judicial review well into the mid-20th century.[72] Whereas the old 'law of offices' explicitly ascribed trusteeship to public office holders, the prerogative writs merely presupposed that government must abide by the rule of law, the second of Dicey's foundational constitutional principles. With its practical work being done by the prerogative writs, and its place in constitutional law eclipsed by other principles, the idea that public bodies were fiduciaries of the people became a 'casualty in legal thought'.[73]

[68] Finn, *Forgotten Trust*, *supra* note 58, pp 132–53; Finn, *Sovereign People*, *supra* note 58, pp 9–14.

[69] *R v Bembridge* (1783) 22 State Tr 1, pp 155–6.

[70] Finn, *Sovereign People*, *supra* note 58, p 11.

[71] FW Maitland, *Collected Papers*, vol 3 (Cambridge: Cambridge University Press, 1911), p 403.

[72] For discussion of the prerogative writs, see Wade and Forsyth, *supra* note 1, pp 591–630. *Habeas corpus* requires the Crown to justify an individual's detention. *Certiorari* seeks the quashing of an administrative decision for abuse of power.

[73] Finn, *Sovereign People*, *supra* note 58, p 11.

Additionally, the representation of the state and its offices as the Crown, with sole corporate and legal personality, runs counter to the historical conception of the state's disaggregated personality in the public law of the Westminster tradition.[74] Administrative law has typically viewed public authority as the occupier of various roles and functions rather than as a particular legal personality. The prerogative writs were called such because originally they could be brought by the Crown alone to ensure that public officials acted within their authority. By the end of the 16th century, ordinary subjects could begin proceedings in the Crown's name without seeking permission, but at least formally the remedies still relied on the legal prerogative of the Crown. Thus, the writs challenged the decisions of officials who were viewed as the holders of specific public offices rather than as representatives of the state. Arguably, this disaggregated conception of public authority has impeded inquiry into the consequences of viewing the state as a fiduciary, and liable for the defaults of its officials.

Following Hobbes, I have assumed that the state is an artificial person, but that, like a corporation, the state cannot act for itself. Its actions must be performed by public officials who represent the state by acting in its name. Because the state is a person, actions performed under the colour of public office are attributable to it. As a result, the state can be held vicariously liable for the actions of its representatives. It follows that both the state and its officials may be said to owe fiduciary duties to the people.

In Canada, the after-effects of the Westminster legacy are visible in the orthodox view of public fiduciary duties: fiduciary duties owed to First Nations are considered *sui generis*, while fiduciary duties owed to non-Aboriginals must be in the service of a pre-existent right, and they must assume the content of a private law duty of loyalty. I have tried to show already, in this chapter and in Chapter III, that the orthodox view underestimates the context-sensitivity of the fiduciary principle and its suitability to public law. The legal history recounted above explains the short shrift the fiduciary principle has received in today's common law of judicial review, but does nothing to justify it.

Developments in Canada's modern public law also help to explain, but not justify, the orthodox view. The Crown was not acknowledged as a fiduciary of First Nations until *Guerin* in 1985, so public fiduciary duties in Canada, while not in their infancy, are still a relatively recent phenomenon. Furthermore, in mainstream Canadian public law, the idea that a duty of procedural fairness might be owed without the prompt of statute did not surface until 1979, the same year in which the Supreme Court committed itself to a policy of deference towards expert administrative

[74] Janet McLean, 'The Crown in Contract and Administrative Law' (2004) 1 Oxford J Legal Stud 129.

decision-makers.[75] Not only are these developments fairly recent, they were led by progressive judges such as Laskin CJ who were sympathetic to the redistributive public law mission of the administrative state. Because fiduciary doctrine has its origins in private law, for progressive judges it would have seemed an odd place to look for inspiration and resources to develop public law. Private law, with its emphasis on freedom of contract and its celebration of property rights, permitted the anti-union and discriminatory legal order that public law was supposed to remedy.[76]

Again, these considerations explain but do not justify the present disregard of the fiduciary principle in public law. Should that principle prove capable of illuminating public law within a conceptual framework that explains and justifies central doctrines of administrative law, such as procedural fairness and curial deference, then the foregoing explanation of the principle's limited application will not justify its continued neglect. The next two chapters attempt to show that the fiduciary principle is so capable.

We conclude this chapter with a conceptual puzzle that must be faced by the fiduciary theory. It is puzzling to think that an individual issued with a deportation order (or dismissed from her job, or denied statutory benefits, and so on) could be said to benefit from a decision-maker fulfilling her fiduciary duty to the very person she has ordered deported. Yet this is exactly the implication of the argument which has at its centre the idea that the state's administrative bodies stand in fiduciary relationship with each person affected by the exercise of their legal powers. The deportee benefits to the extent that the decision-maker exercises her powers fairly and reasonably. As will soon become evident, procedurally fair and substantively reasonable exercises of public power do not guarantee a favourable outcome.[77] But where important interests are at stake, they generally guarantee the individual an opportunity to reply to the case against him, and they place the decision-maker under an obligation to justify her determination. In these respects and others, I will argue, the fiduciary constitution of public law lends the individual the protection of legal principles where otherwise an unfettered discretion may prevail.

[75] *Nicholson v Haldimand-Norfolk Regional Board of Commissioners of Police* [1979] 1 SCR 62; *Canadian Union of Public Employees Local 963 v New Brunswick Liquor Corp* [1979] 2 SCR 227.

[76] For discussion of the history of labour law in Canada, see Judy Fudge and Eric Tucker, *Labour Before the Law: The Regulation of Workers' Collective Action in Canada, 1900–1948* (Don Mills: Oxford University Press, 2001).

[77] As Finn notes in the private law context, 'finding a formula to achieve fairness can lead [the fiduciary] to decisions which bring little joy to some of his beneficiaries. A fair decision actually may occasion prejudice to them. Many an ill-advised beneficiary has appealed unsuccessfully to the courts disbelieving that an action which seems to affect his rights adversely can nonetheless still be held to have been taken in his interests', Finn, *supra* note 39, p 59.

VII

Procedural Fairness—A Pandora's Box of Legality

7.1 INTRODUCTION

The duty of procedural fairness in Canadian administrative law requires public decision-makers to provide a fair hearing to individuals subject to their authority. Frontline decision-makers must hear the other side and decide the matter impartially. The duty does not necessarily entail an oral hearing; sometimes written submissions are enough. But the individual must receive notice of the proceedings and have an opportunity to respond to the facts and arguments on which the decision-maker may ultimately rely. These incidents of procedural fairness are sometimes referred to as participatory rights or procedural safeguards. If the decision affects an important interest, the decision-maker may also owe the individual reasons for the decision.

Canadian judges agree that decisions must be made impartially, or without bias, but generally adopt one of three approaches towards participatory rights and reason-giving.[1] The first approach enforces the duty of fairness only if it can be anchored in positive law, such as statutory provisions or the terms of a contract. Under this approach, which I call the *positive law view*, only positive law is recognized as a potential source of legal rights and obligations. The second approach affirms that a duty of fairness may apply even if the statute is silent, because 'the justice of the common law will supply the omission of the legislature'.[2] This is the *legislative intent view*. The third approach, *common law constitutionalism*, also asserts that procedural fairness may be due if the statute is silent, but for a different reason. On this view, procedural fairness is intrinsic to and constitutive of public authority,

[1] For convenience, I will generally refer to procedural safeguards and reason-giving collectively as 'the duty of procedural fairness', 'the duty of fairness', 'procedural fairness', or simply 'fairness'. Historically the common law has kept these aspects of the duty separate, and we will see that in Canada a freestanding right to procedural safeguards was recognized as early as 1979, but that a similar right to reasons for the decision did not surface until 1999.

[2] *Cooper v Board of Works for Wandsworth District* (1863) 143 ER 414, p 420, CP (Eng), Byles J.

and thus procedural fairness can apply as a common law duty. I defend common law constitutionalism. I argue that a duty of procedural fairness is one of the rule-of-law obligations that flows from the fiduciary position of the administration *vis-à-vis* the people it is entrusted to serve.

Until 1979 and the landmark decision *Nicholson v Haldimand-Norfolk Regional Board of Commissioners of Police*,[3] the positive law approach dominated judicial review of procedure in Canada. *Nicholson* was an employment case that set the stage for the rise to prominence of the common law constitutionalist view of the duty of fairness. This approach became entrenched with respect to participatory rights in 1990 in another employment case, *Board of Education of the Indian Head School Division No 19 of Saskatchewan v Knight*.[4] It was later extended to cover reason-giving in 1999 in an immigration case, *Baker v Canada*.[5] But in 2008 a unanimous Supreme Court in *Dunsmuir v New Brunswick*[6] reversed its prior holding in *Knight*, finding that non-unionized public office holders were not owed procedural fairness. Such office holders, the Court said, are governed by contract law, which allows an employer to dismiss without cause and without a hearing by giving the employee notice or pay in lieu of notice. *Dunsmuir* exemplifies the positive law view. As we discuss the cases mentioned above, it is important to keep the following question in mind: why the reversal in *Dunsmuir*?

I suggest that *Dunsmuir* was possible, in part at least, because the arguments for common law constitutionalism from the cases that preceded it are unconvincing. Judicial advocates of common law constitutionalism attempt to derive the duty of fairness from principles familiar to public lawyers, such as an aversion to arbitrariness and the public's interest in seeing that public powers are put to proper use. But the most those arguments show is that fairness is in some sense an important value, and that it is capable of placing a bulwark between the individual and arbitrary state action. These intuitively appealing claims do not show that fairness is an important value in a legal rather than in a moral or political sense, nor do they establish that in any particular case a board or tribunal owes a legal duty of fairness to the individual before it. As noted in Chapter I, what is morally required is not, without more, legally required.

A moral principle can support a legal duty, however, if the principle operates within a legal relationship, such as we find in private law in the common law tradition. Yet judges sympathetic to common law constitutionalism have failed to situate fairness within a legal relationship capable of supporting a duty of

3 *Nicholson v Haldimand-Norfolk Regional Board of Commissioners of Police* [1979] 1 SCR 62 (*Nicholson*).

4 *Board of Education of the Indian Head School Division No 19 of Saskatchewan v Knight* [1990] 1 SCR 653 (*Knight*).

5 *Baker v Canada* [1999] 2 SCR 817 (*Baker*).

6 *Dunsmuir v New Brunswick* 2008 SCC 9; [2008] 1 SCR 190 (*Dunsmuir*).

fairness. The lack of such a relationship presents a gulf between fairness as a free-floating moral principle, on the one hand, and the imposition of a legal duty of fairness on particular officials in particular cases, on the other. It is this gulf that makes jurisprudence in favour of the common law view seem at times more aspirational than declaratory.

I hope to bridge the gulf by showing that a public fiduciary relationship exists between the state's administrative delegates and its subjects. This relationship arises as a matter of law from the circumstances that attend public administration. The power delegated to public agencies is quintessentially administrative power, as characterized in Chapter IV; it is always other-regarding, purposive, and institutional. And, the individual subject to public administrative power is vulnerable in the sense that she is not entitled to exercise public power and yet she is subject to it. These circumstances reveal that the administration's powers are fiduciary, and therefore they are constrained by fiduciary obligations. One of those obligations is the duty of procedural fairness. A practical implication of this theory is that *Dunsmuir* represents an unwarranted scaling-back of procedural fairness.

7.2 PROCEDURAL FAIRNESS AS A PUBLIC FIDUCIARY DUTY

Nicholson was a close decision, 5–4, with Laskin CJ writing for the majority, and Martland J writing a vigorous dissent. Nicholson was a probationary police constable dismissed after 15 months' service without the benefit of a hearing. A regulation made under the police board's enabling legislation provided that no officer could be disciplined except after a hearing, but that '[n]othing herein affects the authority of a board or council [. . .] to dispense with the services of any constable within eighteen months of his becoming a constable'.[7] Thus, within the probationary period, the statute appeared to give the board authority to dismiss without cause.

Martland J adopted the positive law view of procedural fairness, noting that the board was not called on by the statute to investigate Nicholson's conduct, and that the board's authority to dismiss was not limited to specific causes. A firm defender of Cartwright J's view from *Roncarelli* that administrators, within their province, are a 'law unto themselves' (see Chapter I), Martland J wrote: '[t]he only interest involved was that of the Board itself. Its decision was purely administrative. This being so, it was under no duty to explain to the appellant why his services were no longer required, or to give him an opportunity to be heard'.[8] For the minority writer, procedures could be

[7] *Nicholson*, *supra* note 3, p 318, citing the Police Act, RSO 1970, c 351, Regulation 680, s 27.

[8] *Nicholson*, *supra* note 3, p 335.

inferred from the statutory scheme only if the decision-maker's statutory powers could be classified as judicial or quasi-judicial rather than administrative. Because Martland J classified the board's power to dismiss as 'purely administrative', he concluded that Nicholson had no statutory entitlement (and so no entitlement at all) to be heard. In other words, Nicholson fell on the wrong side of a rights/privileges distinction because he had no statutory right to a hearing.

Laskin CJ rejected the idea that Nicholson could be dismissed without first being heard. The dominant theme of the Chief Justice's reasoning is that public, statutory powers must be exercised fairly. To this end, he questioned the old common law doctrine that permitted public employers to treat 'at pleasure' employees as servants bereft of any rights, saying that it had 'an anachronistic flavour' in light of pervasive collective agreements governing public and private employment.[9] Under the 'at pleasure' doctrine, public employees could be summarily dismissed without cause or notice, without pay in lieu of notice, and without a hearing.

More generally, Laskin CJ noted that the board had only statutory powers. Because the board's powers were based entirely in statute, 'any attempt to measure the issue in this case by resort to the common law position of a constable is inapt'.[10] In short, the board's statutory authorization affects the legal framework in which the issue is to be determined, displacing the 'at pleasure' common law regime of unfettered discretion with one of public law and fairness. As we shall see, the Court in *Dunsmuir* neglects these crucial findings, and pushes Canadian public employment law towards the anachronism Laskin CJ tried to banish.

The Chief Justice did not rule on whether Nicholson was entitled to reasons for the decision after the fact, but he did require the board to disclose its possible reasons prior to making its decision so that Nicholson might respond. The actual reasons were unclear from the record. Still, Laskin CJ considered whether Nicholson received the procedural fairness he was due, willy-nilly, through two prior exchanges with his superiors. A sergeant had told Nicholson that he had disobeyed a direct order by making a phone call to police headquarters to obtain an overtime slip. An inspector subsequently informed Nicholson that 'he had no future in the department'.[11] Laskin CJ held that neither the phone call nor telling Nicholson that 'he had no future' were reasons capable of justifying dismissal. Therefore, having failed to disclose adequate reasons to facilitate a fair hearing, the board breached its duty of fairness to him. As we shall see when we turn to *Knight* below, this is the critical juncture at which process

[9] *Nicholson*, *supra* note 3, pp 322–3.

[10] Ibid, p 320.

[11] Ibid, p 329.

touches substance, which David Dyzenhaus and I have referred to elsewhere as the justification requirement of procedural fairness.[12]

It is time now to consider a series of related arguments which aim to make the following points: the board is a public fiduciary; the fiduciary model of administration provides a coherent and illuminating framework for Laskin CJ's judgment; the duty of fairness is a public fiduciary duty; and the common law constitutionalist view of fairness flows inexorably from the fiduciary conception of administration. The arguments supporting these claims will help us to understand better the rule of law within public administration.

7.2.1 *The implicit constitutive argument*

As noted, Laskin CJ makes much of that fact that the board's powers are based in statute, and infers from this that the board cannot subject Nicholson to 'arbitrary removal'.[13] In arriving at this conclusion, the Chief Justice implicitly uses arguments which reveal sensitivity to the three constitutive features of fiduciary relationships found in *Frame v Smith*,[14] as developed in Chapter IV.

First, Laskin CJ recognizes that the statute grants the board broad discretionary power over Nicholson's employment. The discretion is at its widest in cases such as Nicholson's, where a constable is still in the probationary period. The power is administrative in the sense that it is other-regarding (the board cannot use its power to satisfy the private ends of its members), purposive (the power must be used solely for the sake of the statute's purpose, the supply and control of police services), and institutional (the power is held by a public institution).

Second, the board can exercise its discretionary power unilaterally. So long as the board acts in good faith, Laskin CJ said, its decision will not be reviewable elsewhere.

Third, Laskin CJ notes that Nicholson is vulnerable to the board's authority because he is subject to its unilateral power to dismiss, and because 'the consequences to the appellant are serious'.[15] Since Nicholson's employment is something in which he has a significant practical interest, it may form the subject matter of a fiduciary obligation. As the discussions of 'pure' private and public fiduciary duties in Chapters IV and VI revealed, a beneficiary need not have a pre-existent entitlement to an entrusted interest for that interest to underlie a fiduciary duty. If a fiduciary relationship exists, and the interest at stake is important, then the fiduciary relationship itself

[12] David Dyzenhaus and Evan Fox-Decent, 'Rethinking the Process/Substance Distinction: *Baker v Canada*' (2001) 51 Univeristy of Toronto LJ 193, p 196.

[13] *Nicholson, supra* note 3, p 321.

[14] *Frame v Smith* [1987] 2 SCR 99.

[15] *Nicholson, supra* note 3, p 328.

entails that the entrusted party must exercise her power in accordance with fiduciary constraints.

We can conclude from the foregoing that the argument in favour of the fiduciary status of public administration is a constitutive argument: the relationship of the administration to the affected individual is fiduciary because it possesses the constitutive characteristics of fiduciary relations discussed in Chapter IV. Public administration is fiduciary through and through. Two immediately visible consequences flow from the fiduciary model, and both weigh in favour of Laskin CJ's reasoning and common law constitutionalism's understanding of the duty of fairness.

One consequence is that the rights/privileges distinction on which Martland J relies is a red herring. It is a red herring because in fiduciary relationships the beneficiary need not have a pre-existent right to an important but vulnerable interest in order to benefit from a fiduciary duty. So the fiduciary model explains systematically, using a conceptual framework indigenous to law, the irrelevance of the rights/privileges distinction to procedural fairness.

The other implication is that the fiduciary model challenges the fundamental premise of the positive law approach, ie that in public law all legal rights and obligations, including the duty of fairness, must emanate from a positive law source. Many fiduciary relationships exist and generate legal duties independently of statute. If the relationship between the administration and the people is one such fiduciary relation, then the administration will owe public fiduciary obligations that do not depend on the requirements of positive law.

Of course, most public power flows from legislation, and so public fiduciary duties that constrain such power are not wholly statute-independent or free-standing; there must be some public power on which the fiduciary principle can seize if it is to operate at all. Public fiduciary duties, such as procedural fairness, will generally trace the origin of the power they constrain to a statute. But they remain common law duties twice over. First, they apply even if the words of the statute do not require them. Second, they arise from an overarching relationship that both transcends the particularities of specific statutory regimes and possesses the defining characteristics the common law uses to identify fiduciary relationships (ie administrative power, vulnerability, and significant entrusted interests).

7.2.2 The argument from public trust

A further aspect of the police board's authority in *Nicholson* reflects its fiduciary nature. The board holds and exercises public powers as a matter of public trust, which here refers to the entrusted authority which flows from the people to the legislature, and from the legislature through the

Police Act and the regulations made under it to the board.[16] The board's authority to implement the purposes of its statute, then, is literally entrusted to it by the legislature, on behalf of the people. It consists in a grant of legal power that is to serve exclusively the public interest.

The idea that public authority is entrusted authority is just a fleshing out of the republican vision of popular sovereignty discussed in Chapters IV and VI. Recall that the legislature gets its *political authority* to determine the substantive content of law from the democratically expressed will of the people. The legislature's *legal authority* to announce law applicable to everyone within its jurisdiction comes from the fiduciary principle, which authorizes the state to govern in accordance with the rule of law on behalf of the people. Political and legal authority crystallize in the legislature as *legislative authority.* Legislative authority, then, is the authority to announce law of determinate content and potentially universal application within the legislature's jurisdiction.

When the legislature exercises its authority and produces legislation that delegates public powers, it entrusts the administration to implement statutory regimes which necessarily exist exclusively for the public good. This remains true notwithstanding that some regimes are designed to benefit particular groups, and some powers can be exercised over certain individuals only (such as public employment powers *vis-à-vis* employees). Public law regimes necessarily exist exclusively for the public good because the legislature's authority to create them derives solely from the people, and therefore the legislature can exercise power legitimately (including the power to set up administrative regimes) only if it does so on behalf of the people. This understanding of public authority sheds light on the significance that Laskin CJ attributes to the fact that the board's powers are based in statute and that, as a consequence, they cannot be used arbitrarily.

7.2.3 The argument against arbitrariness

The fiduciary model lends a congenial framework to Laskin CJ's claim that statutory powers cannot be used arbitrarily, an historic preoccupation of the rule of law. The rule-of-law bulwark against arbitrariness has a positive and a negative dimension. The positive side is captured in the *Roncarelli* principle that public powers must be used exclusively for the purposes for which they are conferred. This aspect of the rule of law is positive in the sense that it

[16] 'Public trust' here does not refer to either a trust in the literal sense of a legal and property-based trust as discussed in the previous chapter, nor to the public trust doctrine according to which certain resources are preserved for public use. See eg *Illinois Central Railroad v Illinois* (1892) 146 US 387 (certain resources are preserved for public use and the government is required to maintain them for the public's reasonable use).

looks to legislation in order to limit administrative action to acts consistent with the statute's purposes. The positive dimension of the rule of law reflects the most fundamental fiduciary obligation: fiduciary power must be exercised exclusively for the sake of the purposes for which it is granted (see Chapters I and VI).

The negative dimension of the rule-of-law proscription against arbitrariness is based on the principle that even broad grants of discretion do not authorize decision-makers to use public power arbitrarily. The presumption is that all delegated power is to be pursued non-arbitrarily because the arbitrary use of power, by definition, does not concern itself with statutory purposes. This side of the rule of law is negative in that it does not depend on a particular legislative scheme to determine its content and meaning, but rather imposes a default condition on the exercise of public powers. This negative dimension of the rule of law is explained within the fiduciary model as a corollary of the fundamental fiduciary obligation to use entrusted power solely for the purposes for which it is conferred. The corollary is that such power cannot be used arbitrarily or for just any purpose.

Putting the positive and negative dimensions together, we have the following principle: public powers may be used only for the purposes for which they are conferred, and the purposive exercise of public power excludes arbitrary uses of power. Consider now the argument that can be made for procedural fairness in *Nicholson* once we see that a public fiduciary relationship exists between the board and the people, one of whom is Nicholson.

7.2.4 A fiduciary argument

Suppose Nicholson was caught taking what appeared to be a bribe, and so there was an allegation before the Board that, if true, would establish cause to dismiss. The board would have a duty to dismiss, since its primary fiduciary duty to the public is to ensure the presence of a well-functioning police force with honest and competent personnel. But the board's duty to the public is fully consistent with providing Nicholson with disclosure of the allegation and a chance to reply. Indeed, the board's duty to ensure a properly staffed police force supports rather than weakens the call for fair procedures, as those procedures help to make certain that the board does not dismiss in error an honest and competent officer. Laskin CJ stresses this point.[17] Because the content of the board's public fiduciary obligation to Nicholson is procedural fairness, the obligation is consistent with—and

[17] *Nicholson*, *supra* note 3, p 328.

supported by—the board's general duty to administer the statutory regime in accordance with its purpose.

As we saw in the previous chapter, when a fiduciary has a mandate that extends to multiple beneficiaries with divergent interests, its duty is to treat each principal's interests with fairness and reasonableness. As a fiduciary of both the public at large and the individual immediately subject to its decision-making authority, the board is duty-bound to treat each fairly or even-handedly. With respect to the public, this might include a duty to ensure that the police force under the board's supervision does not engage in discriminatory practices such as racial profiling. But of course Nicholson was not merely a member of the public *vis-à-vis* the board; he was also one of its employees.

More precisely, what distinguishes Nicholson from the public is his vulnerability to the board's powers to hire and dismiss its staff, and his interest in continued employment. These differences suggest that the board's fiduciary duty of fairness to Nicholson is thicker than its more general duty of fairness to the public. Fair treatment does not entail identical treatment. As Dworkin puts it in the context of liberal political theory, equality does not mean equal treatment, it means equal concern and respect.[18] Relevant differences between two persons or their circumstances can justify differential treatment on grounds of fairness.

Similarly, fair exercises of public and fiduciary powers do not necessarily treat everyone equally; they treat everyone in a way that acknowledges the standing of important interests vulnerable to public power. In cases such as *Nicholson*, this necessarily translates into a duty of procedural fairness that precludes arbitrary removal, since statutory power cannot be used arbitrarily. To deny Nicholson the opportunity to know and reply to the case against him, or to remove him arbitrarily, would deny altogether the legal significance of his vulnerable employment interest, and would therefore breach the board's fiduciary duty of fairness to him.

What if the board based its decision on a non-arbitrary policy that had nothing to do with Nicholson, but was in the public's interest? For instance, suppose the board wished to dismiss for budgetary reasons, and there was nothing Nicholson could say at a hearing (or through written submissions) to change the board's mind. Does the board owe Nicholson a duty of fairness under these conditions, when its performance of the duty could not possibly lead to a different outcome for Nicholson? The view of Canadian public law is that Nicholson would not be entitled to procedural fairness because the duty does not extend to policy-setting or legislative

[18] See eg Ronald Dworkin, *Sovereign Virtue: The Theory and Practice of Equality* (Cambridge: Harvard University Press, 2000), pp 1–3, 6–7.

decisions.[19] Under the fiduciary view, on the other hand, Nicholson would be owed the duty, but its content *in relation to him alone* would be thin: Nicholson would be entitled to know the reason for his dismissal (budget cuts), which is more than he received in the actual case. The board's general fiduciary duty of fairness to the public, however, supplies a compelling theoretical basis for public consultations prior to policy decisions, as well as an argument for granting Nicholson standing in such proceedings.

The board, as the people's agent, ought to listen to the people to the extent practicable when it sets policy. Recall from Chapter V that agents of necessity must make reasonable efforts to communicate with their principals before acting on their behalf. On matters of policy that affect the wider community, it would be inappropriate for the board to grant a hearing to just its employees. But usually the board will have to retain some gate-keeping discretion with respect to who is allowed participate at a public hearing. The fiduciary model points to the employees' special vulnerability to policy changes as a sufficient reason to grant them standing at a public hearing. A similar argument can be made for other stakeholders whose interest in the policy decision is greater than an ordinary member of the public. The fiduciary view of public administration, then, supports a common law duty to carry out feasible public consultations on policy matters, and regulates standing through attentiveness to vulnerability.

The question of whether the board would have a duty to provide a hearing even if it is highly unlikely that it could affect the outcome raises the issue of whether procedural fairness is intrinsically valuable (valuable in-and-of-itself) or merely instrumentally valuable (valuable solely in relation to its capacity to affect the outcome). The notion that a duty of fairness may be due even if it cannot affect the outcome may seem implausible. From the point of view of the individual, at least, the major point of the duty is to give her an opportunity to influence or change the mind of the decision-maker.[20] The question is whether this instrumental value is the *only* point of participation in a hearing, or whether, *in addition to* its instrumental value, participation has intrinsic value as well.

[19] *Attorney General of Canada v Inuit Tapirisat et al* [1980] 2 SCR 735; *Knight*, *supra* note 4. For extended critique of the doctrine and argument for a duty to conduct public consultations on policy matters, see Geneviève Cartier, 'Procedural Fairness in Legislative Functions: The End of Judicial Abstinence?' (2003) 53(3) UTLJ 217.

[20] For discussion, see Robert Leckey, *Contextual Subjects: Family, State and Relational Theory* (Toronto: University of Toronto Press, 2008), pp 200–2. Leckey offers a thick but (he claims) instrumental account of participatory rights based on the ability of the individual to influence constructively how facts and law will emerge within the decision-making context so as to bear on its outcome. My sense is that Leckey has really offered an account of the intrinsic value of participatory rights, since the participation he envisions appears rich and valuable even if it cannot affect the outcome. The subsequent text aims to explain how this is possible.

Let us suppose there exist some non-policy, discrete, decision-making contexts in which there is almost nothing the individual can say to alter the outcome. From the perspective of setting up an institutional framework of administrative decision-making, it would be difficult to specify in advance the kinds of cases that would fit into this category. And even if such specification were possible, presumably the individual ought to have an opportunity to challenge the inclusion of her case in the 'cannot-alter-the-outcome' category. From the standpoint of institutional design, it may be unjustifiable to adopt any policy other than one that in practice treats participation as intrinsically valuable, and therefore generally required, because to do otherwise risks subjecting the individual to an arbitrary determination.

On the fiduciary view of administration, the duty of procedural fairness is intrinsically valuable because it is a rule-of-law obligation that reflects the requirements of the right, or legality. In Chapter IX, I will argue that the right can be distinguished from the good in much the same way as we distinguish wrongs from harms, and that the state's breach of a rule-of-law obligation may be a wrong even if it occasions no harm. The administration commits a wrong, for example, if it carries out illegal wiretaps, but causes no harm or damage because it does not use the information collected to the detriment of the programme's victims. Violation of a rule-of-law obligation, I will argue, is a wrong because it constitutes a breach of a public fiduciary duty to the people or some portion of them. Fulfilment of rule-of-law obligations, on the other hand, is intrinsically valuable because such fulfilment necessarily respects the intrinsic moral demands of the right, even if this makes no difference in the sphere of the good. The duty of fairness is one such rule-of-law obligation. Compliance with it is intrinsically valuable in the sphere of the right, even if such compliance does not affect the final outcome in the sphere of the good.

Additionaly people often appear to value the opportunity to express themselves publicly even though it can do nothing to change the course of events. Many vote in elections, march, and demonstrate knowing that their actions are unlikely to change the status quo, but on the grounds that expressing one's political convictions in democratic processes is morally valuable. Likewise, many victims of atrocities tell their stories to truth and reconciliation commissions knowing full well that they will not be made whole and the perpetrators will not be brought to justice. More dramatically still, the condemned facing execution get to say a few last words. Why bother with this final mercy if the value of public expression is fully exhausted by the prospect of changing the outcome?

Consider, however, cases in which an individual's participation in an oral hearing cannot change the outcome because she does not speak the same language as the decision-maker, or because the decision-maker has already made a decision but nonetheless agrees to hear from the individual without letting her know that a decision has been made. These 'hearings' are really shams because they deny from the outset the possibility of influencing the final determination of the decision-maker. They mock and belittle the participant because they take the form of hearings but in substance are akin to show trials. They may appear to suggest that the value of participation in a hearing is entirely instrumental rather than partially non-instrumental.

Arguably, the sham cases show that the instrumental ground of participation (the possibility of influencing the decision-maker) is a necessary condition of a genuine hearing. But these cases do not imply that participation itself, *within a genuine hearing*, is not intrinsically valuable. They show that the instrumentalist norm must be respected for there to be a genuine hearing at all. Thus, the intrinsic value of participation within a hearing is conditional; it relies on respect for the instrumental justification of participation, since such respect is a necessary condition of a genuine hearing. There is no question that genuine hearings have instrumental value; the issue is whether participation within them is *also* intrinsically valuable. At the risk of repetition, the conditional and instrumental constraint ensures that participatory rights are exercised within a genuine hearing rather than a sham procedure. This constraint does not deny or negate the non-instrumental value of participation within a genuine hearing. The intrinsic value of appropriately constrained and instrumentally valuable participation is itself revealed by the many instances, some surveyed above, in which people value the ability to participate even if it is unlikely to alter the final outcome.

To sum up and situate the intrinsic value of participatory rights within the fiduciary interpretation of Laskin CJ's judgment in *Nicholson*: the board's public fiduciary relationship to the people establishes a common law framework of principle within which the board may hire and dismiss employees, but subject to requirements of procedural fairness that have intrinsic as well as instrumental value. Let us consider now the interaction between procedural fairness and substantive decision-making, and how this interaction has influenced the debate over procedural fairness.

7.3 THE JUSTIFICATION REQUIREMENT

The Supreme Court in *Knight* split 4–3, with L'Heureux-Dubé J and the majority adopting the common law constitutionalist view of fairness. Sopinka J and the minority assumed the positive law approach, albeit with the caveat that under some circumstances they would be prepared to infer procedural safeguards from the statutory scheme, tilting them toward the legislative intent view. The divided judgment was somewhat surprising because just four years earlier, in *Cardinal v Director of Kent Institution*,[21] the Court (through the decision of Le Dain J) appeared to rule in favour of the common law view, finding that 'there is, as a general common law principle, a duty of procedural fairness lying in every public authority making an administrative decision which is not of a legislative nature and which affects the rights, privileges and interests of an individual'.[22]

Knight merits close examination because it exposes both the tenacity of the positive law approach and the instability of the majority's rendering of common law constitutionalism in relation to procedural fairness, an instability that made *Dunsmuir* possible 18 years later. As we shall see, both the majority and the minority subscribe to a hallmark tenet of the positive law view: judges are not entitled to impose duties on decision-makers that denote substantive rights held by affected individuals, such as a right to security against arbitrary removal. The right against arbitrary removal is weaker than an entitlement to dismissal for cause, since the latter requires a show of cause whereas the former can include dismissal for reasons unrelated to work performance, such as a change in policy. L'Heureux-Dubé J's subscription to the positive law tenet drives her to defend a strong version of the process/substance distinction according to which judges will review procedure but defer on issues related to the substance of the decision (ie the outcome and the reasons given for it). I argue that the process/substance distinction cannot bear the weight the majority places on it. But to avoid reliance on the distinction requires a rejection of the positive law tenet and an affirmation that procedural fairness has substantive implications, including a substantive right to security against arbitrary removal. This affirmation calls for an argument capable of displacing the positive law tenet. The fiduciary model supplies the missing argument.

The issue in *Knight* was whether a board could dismiss without granting an 'at pleasure' office holder procedural safeguards. A board of education had terminated Knight's employment on three months' notice, pursuant to the terms of its contract with him, after he refused to accept a renewal of his contract that was for a shorter term than the original. The Court agreed that, as a matter of fact, Knight had been treated fairly, but split over whether the board owed him a duty of fairness. Nothing in the education statute or

[21] *Cardinal v Director of Kent Institution* [1986] 2 SCR 643 (*Cardinal*).

[22] Ibid, para 14. Le Dain J added that '[t]he right to a hearing must be regarded as an independent, unqualified right which finds its essential justification in the sense of procedural justice which any person affected by an administrative decision is entitled to have', ibid.

the contract indicated that the board was required to grant Knight a hearing or advise him of the reasons for its decision.

For L'Heureux-Dubé J, this lack of indications was not a bar to fairness because she understood the duty to arise from common law principles embedded in the rule of law, and not from the particular provisions of a statute or a contract. Fairness, she said, occupies a place in legal order that is on a par with the principles of fundamental justice entrenched in s 7 of the Canadian Charter of Rights and Freedoms.[23]

Much of her judgment focused on the relationship between the board and Knight, and the importance of his interest in employment. She adopted the classification scheme for public employees developed by Lord Reid in *Ridge v Baldwin*,[24] the House of Lords decision that set the duty-of-fairness train in motion. Under this scheme, public employment relationships fall into one of three categories: (i) master-servant; (ii) 'at pleasure' public office holders; and (iii) employees who can be dismissed only for cause. Lord Reid had found that a general duty of fairness was owed to employees falling into the third category.

L'Heureux-Dubé J conceded at the outset that Knight did not hold a position from which he could be dismissed only for cause. He was a non-unionized public servant under contract, the board's legislation deferred to the terms of the contract, and the contract provided that he could be dismissed without cause on three months' notice. Although Knight's contract with the board suggested a master-servant relationship, L'Heureux-Dubé J concluded that his position had a 'strong statutory flavour'.[25] Thus, Knight was a public office holder who held his office 'at pleasure', placing him in the second of Lord Reid's categories. However, the majority writer denied that procedural safeguards would turn Knight's office into one for which cause must be given for termination.

Her main argument for a common law duty of fairness stresses the importance of the decision to the individual, and arises from the understanding she shares with Laskin CJ regarding the legal significance of the board's statutory powers. She expressed this understanding as a principle of legitimacy[26]:

> The powers exercised by the appellant Board are delegated statutory powers which, as much as the statutory powers exercised directly by government,

[23] Canadian Charter of Rights and Freedoms, Part I of the Constitution Act, 1982, being Sch B to the Canada Act 1982 (UK), 1982, c 11, s 7 (Charter); *Knight*, *supra* note 4, p 683.

[24] *Ridge v Baldwin* [1963] 2 All ER 66 (*Ridge v Baldwin*).

[25] *Knight*, *supra* note 4, p 672.

[26] Ibid, p 675. In a similar vein, she says elsewhere that the duty of fairness 'stems from the fact that the employer is a public body whose powers are derived from statute, powers that must be exercised according to the rules of administrative law', ibid, p 688.

should be put only to legitimate use. As opposed to the [private law] employment cases dealing with 'pure master and servant' relationships, where no delegated statutory powers are involved, the public has an interest in the proper use of delegated power by administrative bodies.

From the principle of legitimacy L'Heureux-Dubé J inferred that 'the fact that an office holder could be dismissed for cause or at pleasure would not warrant a distinction with regard to the existence of a duty to act fairly, since in both cases statutory powers are exercised'.[27] The logical extension of her argument is that the duty of fairness would apply if the individual were not a public office holder but merely an employee in a contractual relationship to the public employer (Lord Reid's first category of 'master and servant'), since in this case too, upon dismissal, 'statutory powers are exercised'. Regarding the board's contractual right to dismiss on three months' notice, she found that the contract's silence with respect to a hearing in these circumstances 'does not amount to a clear implicit waiver of the application of the duty to act fairly'.[28]

Nonetheless, as indicated, she based her understanding of fairness on a strong reading of the process/substance distinction: once procedures were in place, 'mere displeasure is still justification enough to validly terminate the employment'.[29] Elsewhere she entertained the idea, at least for the sake of argument, that 'the employer can dismiss his employee for unreasonable or capricious reasons'.[30] Although she required the board to communicate 'the broad grounds revealing the general substance of the reason for dismissal',[31] if 'mere displeasure' or 'capricious reasons' were really enough, then the grounds for dismissal could amount to anything. At the limit, Knight would be subject to arbitrary removal.

But what L'Heureux-Dubé J must have known all along—and what the dissent feared—was that requiring fair procedures would open a Pandora's Box of legality. Once procedures are in place, both the content of the decision-making process and the substance of the decision are exposed to scrutiny. As Rand J showed in *Roncarelli*, even decisions where there is a wide discretion must be conducted in good faith, for proper purposes, with regard to all the relevant factors, and without regard to irrelevant considerations. It was this framework that allowed Laskin CJ in *Nicholson* to reject as reasons for dismissal Nicholson's allegedly disobedient phone call and an inspector telling him that 'he had no future'.

Sopinka J worried about this consequence of fairness, and accused the majority of adopting an approach that 'converts the exception into the rule'.[32] Procedural safeguards, for him, had to be anchored in the board's

27 Ibid, p 676.
28 Ibid, p 681.
29 Ibid, p 676.
30 Ibid, p 675.
31 Ibid, p 685.
32 Ibid, p 690.

legislation or the contract. He did allow that procedures could be imposed exceptionally, in the absence of an explicit positive law requirement, but only if some basis in the statutory framework or contract could be cited to support them. He concluded that in this case no such interpretation of the statute was possible because 'the employer can terminate without cause and without giving any reason. It would therefore be inconsistent with the above to require the employer to give a reason for terminating the employee's employment in order to comply with the dictates of procedural fairness'.[33] In other words, because procedural fairness implicitly requires the employer to give reasons for termination, the duty would convert an office held at pleasure into one for which dismissal requires cause or at least non-arbitrary reasons.

Sopinka J's dissent reveals the sense in which procedural fairness has substantive implications, and cracks open the Pandora's Box of legality that L'Heureux-Dubé J seemed anxious to keep closed. If procedural fairness requires the communication of reasons, either as part of a pre-hearing duty to disclose or after the decision has been made, then the board is compelled to justify its decision. For a reason to be a reason at all it cannot be an arbitrary expression of displeasure such as 'I don't like your haircut'. This sort of claim is not a reason because, unlike genuine reasons, it has no capacity to justify other claims, such as 'You are no longer entitled to work here'. Notwithstanding L'Heureux-Dubé J's assertion to the contrary, 'mere displeasure' is not enough. The reasons for a decision must live up to the anti-arbitrariness rationale for imposing the duty of fairness in the first place. A decision's reasons, therefore, must show that the dismissal is based on non-arbitrary grounds, and this denotes a freestanding substantive right to security against arbitrary removal.

If judges are not entitled to vindicate such rights, however, as both the majority and the minority in *Knight* appear to contend, then the common law constitutionalist view of fairness disintegrates. It does so because, as Sopinka J insists, the duty of fairness really does entail a substantive right to security against arbitrary removal. To rescue the common law view requires an explanation of how such a right can arise independently of positive law, and a further explanation of how judges can enforce this right without 'making law' and exceeding the judicial function. The fiduciary theory offers both.

I have argued already that the fiduciary view of administration explains the rule of law's proscription against arbitrary exercises of public power (7.2.2 and 7.2.3 above), and that procedural fairness, viewed as a public fiduciary duty, necessarily precludes arbitrary removal (7.2.4 above). It

[33] Ibid, p 688.

follows that public employees have a correlative and common law right to security against arbitrary removal.

Judges have authority to enforce this freestanding right because it arises from a public but common law fiduciary relationship. Judges who enforce such a right no more trench on the law-making authority of the legislature than judges who uphold rights arising from contract or tort in private law. Even if such adjudication is in some sense judicial law-making, it is not the kind of law-making that common law judges shy away from. Rather, it is adjudication that looks to the legally significant features of the context in which the parties confront one another, and then proceeds to enforce the relevant duties that arise from it. The fiduciary view invites judges to engage in this contextual inquiry.

7.4 CONTEXTUALISM, CONTENT, AND IMPORTANT INTERESTS

The move to contextual inquiry is well underway, and arguably it marks the most important methodological shift in judicial reasoning on the issue of procedural fairness in the history of Canadian public law.[34] Laskin CJ inaugurated the shift in *Nicholson* by doing away with the quasi-judicial/administrative distinction as a threshold test for procedural fairness, and by emphasizing the significance to public law of the legal context produced by the creation and exercise of statutory powers. The roots of contextualism deepened in *Knight* as L'Heureux-Dubé J expressly elevated the significance of statutory powers to a principle of legitimacy, and placed renewed emphasis on the importance of the decision to the individual. *Knight* essentially established that few administrative decisions over particular individuals would be exempt from procedural fairness because the only decisions plainly excluded were ones that were policy-setting in nature or objectively unimportant to the individual.[35] The major issue left unresolved was the content issue: which specific procedures must agencies adopt to satisfy the duty of fairness? In *Knight*, L'Heureux-Dubé J had found that the content of the duty was 'eminently variable'.[36]

[34] See eg Colleen Flood and Lorne Sossin, 'The Contextual Turn: Iacobucci's Legacy and the Standard of Review in Administrative Law' (2007) 57 UTLJ 581; Leckey, *supra* note 20, pp 176–83.

[35] But see Cartier, *supra* note 19, pp 252–3, citing David Mullan, 'Fairness: The New Natural Justice' (1975) 25 UTLJ 281. Cartier argues compellingly that the best reading of *Knight* is one that supports abandonment of inquiry at the threshold so that inquiry can focus on Mullan's 'real questions'—content questions—concerning the appropriate procedures to adopt given the consequences of the decision for the individual.

[36] *Knight*, *supra* note 4, p 682.

Contextualism re-emerged in *Baker* as the preferred method for determining the content of agency procedures on review. Baker was a Jamaican woman who overstayed in Canada on a visitor's visa for 11 years, during which time she had four Canadian-born children. She was ordered deported and applied to remain in Canada on the basis of humanitarian and compassionate considerations. The Minister had discretionary authority to grant such applications, but the delegated officer refused Baker's request.

For the Court, L'Heureux-Dubé J established a framework for determining the content of procedural fairness. The framework consists of five contextual factors that reviewing courts must weigh together.[37] The first concerns the nature of the decision, and brings the old quasi-judicial/administrative distinction to bear on the content inquiry: the more the decision can be said to be judicial or quasi-judicial, rather than administrative, the weightier the procedural safeguards must be. The second factor is the role and place of the decision within the statutory scheme. For example, if procedural safeguards are present elsewhere in the Act, and if the decision is final, then more stringent procedures will be due. The third factor is the importance, in practical terms, of the decision to the individual affected. The fourth is the individual's legitimate expectations arising from past practices or representations of public officials. The fifth factor calls for a measure of deference to the Minister or agency's choice of procedure.

Applying this framework to determine the content of Baker's participatory rights, L'Heureux-Dubé J found that she had a right to make written submissions, and to have those submissions fully considered. But she was not entitled to an oral hearing, and her children were denied independent standing on the grounds that their interests in the proceedings could be communicated to the Minister by Baker's counsel. The Court also found that Baker was entitled to reasons for the decision, and established a general common law principle in support of reason-giving: if the decision touches an interest of practical importance to the individual, then she must receive reasons.

A common denominator that runs through the contextual approach to review of procedure, from *Nicholson* through *Baker*, in both threshold and content inquiries, is the practical importance to the individual of the decision. The prominence of practical interests raises a thorny question we have glimpsed already: how does a practical interest in one's employment or immigration status, interests to which one has no pre-existing right, give rise

[37] *Baker*, *supra* note 5, paras 21–7. Iacobucci and Cory JJ dissented in part, rejecting the majority's reliance on international law as a source of legality capable of placing constraints on the Minister's discretionary power, ibid, pp 78–81. I discuss the substantive aspects of *Baker* in the next chapter.

to a legal obligation to provide procedural safeguards and reasons for the decision?

One answer is an argument L'Heureux-Dubé J offers in *Knight*: procedural fairness is an unwritten principle of fundamental justice that inheres in the basic tenets of our legal system. As such, the duty of fairness is an immanent and constitutive part of the common law constitution Canada inherited from the United Kingdom, an unwritten constitution of fundamental values and principles sometimes referred to as an 'implied Bill of Rights'.[38] However, even on the assumption (not shared by all) that fairness does inhere in the basic tenets of our legal system, there are at least two weaknesses to this argument, one of which leads to the dissenting judgments in *Nicholson* and *Knight*, while the other leads to *Dunsmuir*.

The first weakness is that Martland and Sopinka JJ can point to their own unwritten constitutional principle to offset the force of fairness: the separation of powers.[39] The positive law view flows directly from the separation of powers, according to which the legislature alone has authority to create legal rights and obligations. The grip of the separation of powers on the judiciary explains how the dissent in *Knight* was possible after Laskin CJ's majority judgment in *Nicholson*, and after subsequent confirmation of the common law constitutionalist view in *Cardinal*. The separation of powers also explains L'Heureux-Dubé J's insistence in *Knight* that public employees do not have a freestanding right to security against arbitrary removal. As we saw, it was this concession to the positive law view that drove her to adopt a strong and implausible version of the process/substance distinction.

The second weakness of the 'inheres in the basic tenets' argument arises from the fact that the common law contains values and doctrines other than fairness, such as individual autonomy and contract law. We shall see now

[38] *Reference re Alberta Statutes* [1938] SCR 100; *Saumur v The City of Quebec* [1953] 2 SCR 299; *Switzman v Elbling* [1957] SCR 285; *Reference re Remuneration of Judges of the Provincial Court of Prince Edward Island* [1997] 3 SCR 3; *Reference re Secession of Quebec* [1998] 2 SCR 217. For commentary on Canada's common law or unwritten constitution, see David Dyzenhaus, 'The Deep Structure of *Roncarelli v Duplessis*' (2004) 53 UNBLJ 111; Mary Liston, 'Governments in Miniature: The Rule of Law in the Administrative State' in Lorne Mitchell Sossin and Colleen M Flood (eds), *Administrative Law in Context* (Toronto: Emond Montgomery Publications, 2008); Mark Walters, 'The Common Law Constitution in Canada: Return of Lex Non Scripta as Fundamental Law' (2001) 51 UTLJ 91; Mark Walters, '"Common Public Law in the Age of Legislation": David Mullan and the Unwritten Constitution' in G Huscroft and M Taggart (eds), *Inside and Outside Canadian Administrative Law: Essays in Honour of David Mullan* (Toronto: University of Toronto Press, 2006).

[39] See eg *Cooper v (Canada Human Rights Commission)* (1996) 3 SCR 854; *Canada (House of Commons) v Vaid* [2005] 1 SCR 667. For argument that the separation of powers cannot do the work judges such as Martland and Sopinka JJ ask of it, see David Dyzenhaus, 'Constituting the Rule of Law: Fundamental Values in Administrative Law' (2002) 27 Queen's LJ 445. Dyzenhaus argues that the separation of powers must serve the fundamental values of legal order (eg fairness) because these values are constitutive of legal order. The present argument tries to supply a framework capable of explaining why fairness is (partially) constitutive of legal order, and how it can support legal duties.

that these were the aspects of the common law on which the Court chose to focus in *Dunsmuir*, with devastating consequences for procedural fairness.

7.5 THE *DUNSMUIR* REVERSAL

Dunsmuir was hired in February 2002 as Legal Officer for the Fredericton Court Services Branch of the New Brunswick Department of Justice. Within three weeks he was appointed by Order-in-Council to offices of Clerk and Administrator within the Court Services Branch. He was disciplined three times during the course of his 30-month tenure, and apparently there were complaints outstanding from other staff prior to his dismissal. The Regional Director and the Assistant Deputy Minister ultimately decided to terminate him not for cause but with four months' pay in lieu of notice, pursuant to s 20 of the Civil Service Act.[40] Section 20 stipulates that '[s]ubject to the provisions of this Act or any other Act, termination . . . shall be governed by the ordinary rules of contract'. Dunsmuir did not receive a hearing. He received notification of his dismissal on the day he had been scheduled to meet with the Regional Director and the Assistant Deputy Minister for a performance review.

Dunsmuir was entitled to grieve his dismissal under s 100.1 of the Public Service Labour Relations Act.[41] He did so on substantive and procedural grounds. The PSLRA adjudicator held that as both a civil service employee and an 'at pleasure' public office holder, he occupied a 'hybrid' position that straddled the first two categories of Lord Reid's classification scheme. The adjudicator concluded that *Knight* entitled Dunsmuir to procedural fairness, and that the province had breached its duty to him. The Supreme Court of Canada disagreed.

The majority reasons were delivered by Bastarache and LeBel JJ, with Binnie and Deschamps JJ (for herself, Charron and Rothstein JJ) writing separate concurring opinions that affirmed the majority's view of fairness. The Court held that *Knight* relied crucially on the distinction between contractual employees and public office holders, with procedural fairness applying to the latter but not the former. Bastarache and LeBel JJ held that it was time to abandon the distinction because it is hard to apply in practice and 'does not correspond with the justifications for imposing public law procedural fairness requirements'.[42] There is a sense in which this is true.

[40] Civil Service Act, SNB 1984, c C-5.1 (Civil Service Act).

[41] Public Service Labour Relations Act, RSNB 1973, c P-25 (PSLRA).

[42] *Dunsmuir*, *supra* note 6, para 112. The majority writers cited Lord Wilberforce in *Malloch v Aberdeen Corp* [1971] 2 All ER 1278, HL (Eng) (*Malloch*) as well as Wade and Forsyth to support their attack on the contractual-employee/public-office-holder distinction. But the passages they cite from these authorities

We have seen already that the arguments given by Laskin CJ and L'Heureux-Dubé J suggest that contractual employees as well as office holders are owed a duty of fairness.

The Court in *Dunsmuir* saw the matter differently. It found that '[w]here a public employee is employed under a contract of employment, regardless of his or her status as a public office holder, the applicable law governing his or her dismissal is the law of contract, not general principles arising out of public law'.[43] The Court criticized the adjudicator for having adopted 'a reasoning process that was fundamentally inconsistent with the employment contract'.[44] Bastarache and LeBel JJ held at various junctures that the relationship between Dunsmuir and the Department of Justice was contractual,[45] and that 'the existence of a contract of employment, not the public employee's status as an office holder, is the crucial consideration'.[46] The Court found that contract law adequately protects most non-unionized public employees against arbitrary exercises of delegated powers because it enables them to bargain for procedural fairness, and because, if the contract is silent, dismissal must be for cause or with notice, or pay in lieu of notice.

As David Mullan points out, however, *Dunsmuir*'s setting back of common law labour rights may go well beyond a reversal of *Knight*.[47] If an employee under contract has a statutory right to be dismissed only for cause, and there are no statutory procedural safeguards in place, it is not apparent from *Dunsmuir* that the employee would have a right to be heard. The same would be true if the employee had a contractual right to dismissal only for cause, but no explicit contractual right to be heard prior to termination. The issues of whether an employer has cause, on the one hand, and whether the employee has a right to participate in the decision-making process that determines cause, on the other, are conceptually distinct. Participation rights do not flow by necessary implication from a right to be dismissed only for cause. To infer a duty of fairness, one must import the premise from *Nicholson* that statutory powers can be used only fairly, and that fairness requires hearing from the individual prior to termination. *Dunsmuir* calls for the abandonment of this critical premise in favour of contract law. If *Dunsmuir* thereby ousts common law procedural safeguards in cases where

are taken badly out of context, and misleadingly quoted, for the authorities questioned the distinction with a view to *extending*, not limiting, the reach of procedural fairness. *Dunsmuir, supra* note 6, paras 92–3, citing Sir William Wade and Christopher Forsyth (eds), *Administrative Law*, 8th edn (New York: Oxford University Press, 2000), pp 532–3; *Malloch, supra* note 42, p 1294.

[43] *Dunsmuir, supra* note 6, para 81. [44] Ibid, para 74.

[45] Ibid, paras 80, 84, 117. [46] Ibid, para 102.

[47] David Mullan, '*Dunsmuir v New Brunswick*, Standards of Review and Procedural Fairness for Public Servants: Let's Try Again!' (2008) 21 Can J Admin L & Prac 117, pp 144–5.

dismissal is possible only for cause, the Court has in effect repudiated *Ridge v Baldwin*.

The depth and temper of the Court's commitment to the contractualization of public employment law is revealed by a single fact that went unmentioned: Dunsmuir was not, in fact, protected by a written contract of employment.[48] Dunsmuir had accepted an offer of employment that resulted from a competition under the Civil Service Act.[49] So there was an oral contract that arose from this offer and acceptance, as there would be underlying the origin of many employment relationships, public or private.[50]

The Court's conclusion that Dunsmuir's fundamental relationship to the Department of Justice was contractual rested on two premises: (i) s 20 of the Civil Service Act, which provided for termination under the rules of contract; and (ii) the similarity between the Crown's position as an employer and private employers.

The Court did not make much out of s 20, saying that the provision simply 'made clear' the contractual terms of Dunsmuir's employment.[51] Arguably, Bastarache and LeBel JJ gave s 20 merely a supporting role because they did not want to limit the scope of their judgment to cases in which provisions such as s 20 happen to be in play. Had they made s 20 the centrepiece of their decision, the law from *Knight* would have remained unaffected, since its common law duty of fairness was always subject to derogation by explicit legislation.

The major argument in *Dunsmuir* against the duty of fairness is that, as an employer, the Crown's relationship to a non-unionized employee under contract is essentially the same as the relationship of a private employer to non-unionized employees. The Court relied heavily on its prior decision in *Wells v Newfoundland*.[52] In that case, a senior public servant was held to be entitled to sue for breach of contract when he lost his job as a consequence of a legislated restructuring of the public service. The Court in *Dunsmuir* cited *dicta* from *Wells* acknowledging that public employment 'has all the

[48] *New Brunswick (Board of Management) v Dunsmuir* 2005 NBQB 270; [2005] NBJ No 327, para 43.

[49] Ibid, para 3.

[50] Curiously, the Court distinguished Dunsmuir's case from *Nicholson* on the grounds that Nicholson did not enjoy contractual rights (*Dunsmuir, supra* note 6, para 101), and yet Nicholson too was initially hired under an oral contract (*Nicholson, supra* note 3, pp 311, 314). Furthermore, the statute in *Nicholson* that appeared to grant the board authority to dismiss without cause did not purport to restrict any rights that may have arisen from Nicholson's oral contract. The Court in *Dunsmuir, supra* note 6, para 86, interprets Laskin CJ's judgment to have relied on a finding that Nicholson fell into Lord Reid's third category. In fact, Laskin CJ said only that Nicholson's case fits 'more closely' into the third rather than the second category of an office held 'at pleasure', which he thought was an anachronism, *Nicholson, supra* note 3, p 322. *Dunsmuir* thus appears to overturn *Nicholson* as much as it overturns *Knight*, notwithstanding the majority's efforts to distinguish the two earlier judgments.

[51] *Dunsmuir, supra* note 6, para 74.

[52] *Wells v Newfoundland* [1999] 3 SCR 199 (*Wells*).

hallmarks of contract', and that as an employer the Crown is engaging in commercial relations 'much as an ordinary citizen would'.[53] Bastarache and LeBel JJ inferred that '[i]f the Crown is acting as any other private actor would in hiring its employees, then it follows that the dismissal of its employees should be viewed in the same way'.[54]

The Court's use of *Wells* is misleading. The Court in *Wells* reaffirmed that, generally speaking, an office holder could be dismissed only in accordance with procedural fairness. On the particular facts of the case the doctrine did not apply because the complainant had lost his job as a result of legislation rather than an administrative decision. The duty of fairness does not apply to legislation, which is presumed to be an act of a democratically legitimate and accountable power. In other words, the contract in *Wells* no way displaced the duty of fairness from *Nicholson* and *Knight* that applied to administrative decisions. Both of these cases were affirmed in *Wells*. But the substantive issue remains: Is the Crown as an employer the same as 'just any other private actor', and should it be viewed as such when it exercises statutory powers to dismiss?

There is reason to think not. The descriptive incidents of public employment differ from employment in the private sector in telling ways, some of which *Dunsmuir* brings to light. There is an air of unreality to the suggestion that people in Dunsmuir's position negotiate the terms of their employment with the Crown. In practice, they will usually enter competitions, as Dunsmuir did, and the terms of their employment will be set in advance. The choice for most prospective public employees is to take it or leave it. Although the Crown must offer competitive terms to attract and retain its workforce, for those who seek public service *because* it is public service, the Crown possesses a monopoly on employment at the federal and provincial levels. This monopoly denotes a stark inequality of bargaining power between public employers and people who seek a career in public service. Few if any private actors can lay claim to such a monopoly over their respective industry.

Also, the civil service is public service in a way that working for a private corporation is not. One of the symbolic markers of this difference is the requirement to swear an oath that comes with many public positions. Dunsmuir and Nicholson, for example, had to swear oaths of office.[55] Oath-taking has a slightly quaint ring in modern ears. And yet the affirming of an oath reflects the fact that public employees assume a measure of the

[53] *Dunsmuir, supra* note 6, para 103, citing *Wells, supra* note 52, para 22.

[54] *Dunsmuir, supra* note 6, para 103.

[55] Civil Service Act, *supra* note 40, s 22; *Nicholson, supra* note 3, p 321.

public trust, and that their position is something more than the commercial outcome of two rationally self-interested parties reaching mutually agreeable terms. It would strike us as odd if a private employer required its rank-and-file employees to swear an oath of allegiance, since the commercial ends of others do not usually warrant separate and self-disregarding avowals of loyalty. Asking an employee to swear an oath to a private employer smacks of gratuitous subjection to the will of another. Dunsmuir's oath of public office, however, does not denote subjection to the will of another, since public offices have no self-regarding will or interest. The only interest of a public office is the public interest, one in which the employee figures simultaneously as agent and co-beneficiary. Thus, a pledge to serve the public is also, necessarily and concomitantly, a pledge to serve a collective good to which the employee has an equal claim as a member of the community. Such oaths express solidarity rather than subjection.

In short, the Crown as employer is different from private actors in that it has a monopoly on career positions in public service, one of the distinctive features of which is institutionalized solidarity with the wider community, a feature that makes public service an attractive calling for many. In practice, dismissed employees such as Dunsmuir will be hard pressed to find other work in the civil service in the near future, since prospective public employers, understandably, will wish to see the dismissed employee's prior work record and references. Bearing these considerations in mind, consider the assertion of Bastarache and LeBel JJ that dismissal from the civil service with 'reasonable notice' is a 'good faith exercise of the contractual rights of the employer', and 'cannot be qualified as arbitrary'.[56]

Elsewhere the Court defends this claim with an argument taken from private employment law: an 'employer's right to terminate the employment relationship with due notice is simply the counterpart to the employee's right to quit with due notice'.[57] A critical assumption underlying both sides of this alleged *quid pro quo* is that with due notice the employer can find a substitute employee, and the employee can find another similar job. The market is presumed to offer a ready supply of new employees to the employer, and relevantly similar new jobs to the employee. Even in the private sphere this assumption is tenuous, and neglects the main animating theme of labour law, which is inequality of bargaining power between employer and employee.

In *Slaight Communications v Davidson*,[58] Dickson CJ for the majority adopted the following characterization of the employment relationship[59]:

[56] *Dunsmuir*, *supra* note 6, para 104.

[57] Ibid, para 105.

[58] *Slaight Communications v Davidson* [1989] 1 SCR 1038 (*Slaight*).

[59] Ibid, pp 1051–2, citing P Davies and M Freedland, *Kahn-Freund's Labour and the Law*, 3rd edn (London: Stevens & Sons, 1983), p 18.

> [T]he relation between an employer and an isolated employee or worker is typically a relation between a bearer of power and one who is not a bearer of power. In its inception it is an act of submission, in its operation it is a condition of subordination.... The main object of labour law has always been, and we venture to say will always be, to be a countervailing force to counteract the inequality of bargaining power which is inherent and must be inherent in the employment relationship.

The majority judgments from *Nicholson* and *Knight* presuppose this understanding of labour law, which is why Laskin CJ refers to collective agreements and the broad protection they provide against arbitrary dismissal. In *Dunsmuir*, on the other hand, inequality of bargaining power is never mentioned.

This inequality casts doubt on the notion that the purported due-notice *quid pro quo* in private employment relations is genuine. In public employment the inequality on termination is grimmer still, given the Crown's monopoly on public employment positions and the difficulty a dismissed employee will face acquiring another job in public service. The acute vulnerability of dismissed public employees suggests that the ordinary justification underlying the due-notice *quid pro quo* (a justification that depends on the availability of similar work) is incapable of justifying dismissal in the public sphere with mere notice or pay in lieu.

There is, however, a deeper, conceptual problem with Bastarache and LeBel JJ's claim that dismissal with notice 'cannot be qualified as arbitrary': the majority of writers confuse the conditions of dismissal with the grounds for dismissal. On their view, if the province had decided to terminate Dunsmuir on the flip of a coin, his dismissal would not have been arbitrary so long as he was given notice or pay in lieu. This is why the real inequity of the case was never discussed in the Court's decision. The real inequity was that Dunsmuir was actually dismissed as a result of concerns related to his work performance, as was evident from the record, but his superiors were able to pretend otherwise because they did not wish to disclose their reasons or give Dunsmuir a chance to reply. In the termination letter, the Deputy Minister said simply that Dunsmuir's 'particular skill set' did not meet the needs of his employer.[60] In other words, the province had in fact dismissed Dunsmuir for what it took to be cause and pretended otherwise. Its pretence was allowed to stand because, having provided pay in lieu of notice, neither its actual nor purported reasons were subject to scrutiny, even once publicly available.[61]

[60] *Dunsmuir, supra* note 6, para 7.

[61] The Court noted that special or '*Wallace*' damages can flow from unfair dealing or bad faith upon dismissal, and upheld the labour adjudicator's alternative remedy (not based on *Wallace* damages) of increasing Dunsmuir's notice period from four to eight months. *Dunsmuir, supra* note 6, para 110, citing *Wallace v United Grain Growers Ltd* [1997] 3 SCR 701. The Court did not find that Dunsmuir was entitled to *Wallace* damages, nor that the province had acted in bad faith.

In a nutshell, whereas *Nicholson* and *Knight* affirmed a duty of fairness that implied a substantive right to security from arbitrary removal, *Dunsmuir* excises the duty and the substantive protection against arbitrariness that came with it. *Dunsmuir*, in other words, closes the Pandora's Box of legality that troubled Sopinka J in *Knight*.

If there is a glimmer of hope within *Dunsmuir* that the common law constitutionalist view of fairness may one day be revived in cases of public employment, it lies in the starting point of Bastarache and LeBel JJ. They held that inquiry must begin with a contextual determination of 'the nature of the employment relationship with the public authority'.[62] Although the Court's conclusion was that the relationship in *Dunsmuir* was strictly contractual, we have seen in the discussion of agency in Chapter V that some contractual relationships are also fiduciary relationships. The presence of one kind of relationship does not necessarily preclude the other. While the Court did not consider this possibility, its findings do not undermine the basic premises of the fiduciary model for which I have argued above. The discretionary power of the public employer remains quintessentially administrative in nature, and the employee's important interest in continued employment remains vulnerable to the employer's unilateral exercise of its statutory power. These premises are reinforced by the Crown's monopoly over entry into public service, the dismissed office holder's heightened vulnerability to exclusion from her chosen career path, and the distinctive public service dimension of public employment that distinguishes the Crown from private actors as an employer.

There is no inconsistency between contractual public employment and the fiduciary view of public administration. As a public fiduciary, the employer's attitude towards the employee cannot be one of indifference. Some solicitude is owed to the employee's interest in keeping her job. But as we have seen, dismissal with mere notice can be on any ground, however arbitrary or capricious. To give the employee the solicitude she is due, there must be *some* non-arbitrary ground for the employee's dismissal (it need not be cause, but must be more than mere displeasure), the ground must be communicated to the employee, and she must have an opportunity to reply. This follows from viewing procedural fairness as a public fiduciary duty, one that takes seriously the legal significance of the employee's vulnerable interest in a career of public service. Because the Court in *Dunsmuir* failed to apprehend the fiduciary dimensions of public administration, it failed to give legal credit to this interest, and allowed contract and arbitrary removal to fill the void.

[62] *Dunsmuir*, *supra* note 6, para 113.

Although Canadian jurisprudence on procedural fairness has yet to embrace the normative vocabulary of public fiduciary duties, the shift to contextualism has helped pave the way for it to do so. The method of contextualism and the normativity of the fiduciary principle both regard practical interests as a basis for public legal obligation. In a sense, the fiduciary model just makes explicit the latent promise of contextualism.

I have argued that a fiduciary view of administration strengthens Laskin CJ and L'Heureux-Dubé J's arguments in favour of fairness by explaining the importance they attribute to statutory powers and vulnerable interests. The fiduciary model explains public authority in terms of a relationship of public trust that exists between the legislature and its delegates, the beneficiaries of which are the people. Because the overarching fiduciary relationship between decision-makers and individuals is legal in nature, so too is the duty of procedural fairness that flows from it. Furthermore, the fiduciary position of the administration explains *why* procedural fairness inheres in the basic tenets of our legal system: fairness is a constitutive aspect of our legal system because public administration is subject to the fiduciary principle, and this principle bars public authority from exercising its powers arbitrarily. The fiduciary model thus vindicates the common law constitutionalist view of fairness, showing that fairness is an intrinsic and constitutive aspect of public authority.

We have also seen that procedural fairness has substantive implications in that the rationale for imposing the duty ultimately requires decision-makers to exercise their powers justifiably, using procedures that expose the grounds of their decisions to public and judicial scrutiny. In the next chapter we will explore these substantive implications as we consider the implications of the fiduciary model in relation to the merits of agency determinations and judicial review.

VIII

Administrative Law as Solicitude—Reasonable Decision-Making

8.1 INTRODUCTION

Administrative law is shot through with a number of deep-seated tensions that bedevil attempts to justify, simultaneously, judicial review of agency determinations and the legitimacy of the administrative state. In the previous chapter we saw an example of one such tension in the controversy over whether administrative decision-makers owe a duty of procedural fairness without the prompt of statute. More specifically, we saw that the common law constitutionalist approach to the duty of fairness stood in tension with a formal understanding of the separation of powers according to which the legislature alone is entitled to create legal rights and obligations. The fiduciary theory seeks to resolve this tension by showing that the duty of fairness arises from a fiduciary relationship that exists between the decision-maker and the individual. Under this theory, reviewing judges do not create and impose the duty of fairness as a judicial fiat, placing stress on the separation of powers, but rather recognize the duty as a feature of an underlying legal relationship.

There is, however, a deeper tension in play. It perhaps explains Michael Taggart's provocative observation, citing de Smith, that 'there are many lawyers who disparage public law... as "a diet of soft vagueness, conducing to intellectual flabbiness and other regrettable forms of degeneration"'.[1] The deeper tension, also discussed in the previous chapter, concerns important interests in which the individual has no pre-existing right to a favourable decision, such as Nicholson's interest in continued employment as a police constable. Recall that in *Nicholson v Haldimand-Norfolk Regional Board of Commissioners of Police*[2] Martland J held that '[t]he only interest involved

[1] Michael Taggart, 'The Tub of Public Law' in David Dyzenhaus (ed), *The Unity of Public Law* (Oxford: Hart Publishing, 2004), p 455, citing SA de Smith, *The Lawyers and the Constitution* (London: G Bell & Sons Ltd, 1960), p 8 (published Inaugural Lecture at the University of London, London School of Economics, 10 May 1960).

[2] *Nicholson v Haldimand-Norfolk Regional Board of Commissioners of Police* [1979] 1 SCR 62 (*Nicholson*).

was that of the Board itself'.[3] It is at least unclear how practical interests, critical to the individual but lacking in explicit legal protection, can trigger an obligation to interpret and exercise statutory powers in a way that takes them seriously. Administrative decisions that touch unprotected interests are subject to judicial review, but the idea that practical interests deserve legal standing is far from entrenched.

Consider, for example, the so-called nominate grounds for judicial review of discretion. We saw in *Roncarelli v Duplessis*[4] that these grounds include improper purposes, irrelevant considerations, and bad faith. Yet they are all specifiable in terms of respecting the limits of statutory powers (a kind of review known to public lawyers as *ultra vires* review), and independently of the individual over whom the power is exercised. And as we shall soon see, when Canadian courts review an agency's interpretation of its enabling statute's provisions under the present 'standard of review' analysis (formerly the 'pragmatic and functional' approach), they look to contextual factors to determine the intensity of review, but none of these factors explicitly refers to the individual's interest in the decision. Judicial review then proceeds to determine whether the agency's interpretation of its statute is 'correct' or 'reasonable', without necessarily pausing to consider the impact of the interpretation on the individual.

At the same time, however, cases such as *Baker v Canada*[5] insist that exercises of statutory powers must take account of fundamental values, and in *Baker* this meant taking seriously the best interests of Baker's children. So the deeper tension that permeates modern administrative law arises from the apparent conceptual gap separating interpretation of legislation (including interpretations of grants of discretion) from recognition of the legal significance of practical interests. Statutory interpretation, without more, does not seem to require or presuppose solicitude towards the interests of the people subject to statutory authority, making demands for solicitude appear to some as 'a diet of soft vagueness'.

One of the arguments of this chapter is that agencies and reviewing courts alike can close the apparent gap by interpreting statutes in light of fundamental values sometimes said to reside within the common law, such as equality and a concern for children's best interests. This is the idea of common law constitutionalism discussed in the previous chapter. Agencies and judges are under an obligation to interpret statutes in light of fundamental values, I claim, because they stand in a fiduciary relation to the people over whom administrative and judicial power is exercised. This

[3] Ibid, p 335. [4] *Roncarelli v Duplessis* [1959] SCR 121 (*Roncarelli*).

[5] *Baker v Canada* [1999] 2 SCR 817 (*Baker*).

argument begins with the premise, developed in Chapters I and VI, that the fiduciary principle requires agencies and judges to exercise their decision-making powers reasonably. Reasonable exercises of these powers, I argue, must give significant weight to important, practical interests.

Doubts may arise with respect to whether a particular interest in a given set of circumstances is of sufficient importance to deserve much weight. Certainly some interests (even constitutionally protected interests) may count for relatively little in some contexts. Consider, for example, a company's interest in freedom of expression with respect to an unjustly dismissed employee *vis-à-vis* the employee's interest in acquiring a new job without the burden of overcoming prejudicial comments from the company.[6] Fundamental values, I will suggest, inform inquiry into reasonableness by pointing to practical interests of sufficient importance to guide statutory interpretation. The fiduciary principle requires decision-makers and judges to take account of fundamental values because those values signal the kinds of interests that must be taken seriously as officials interpret statutes in compliance with their duty of reasonable decision-making. Fundamental values, in other words, put flesh on the bones of the fiduciary conception of administration by supplying it with an objective moral vocabulary capable of distinguishing important from unimportant interests in concrete cases. And conversely, the fiduciary model helps explain the place of fundamental values in administrative law by celebrating their attentiveness to important, practical interests.

The combination of the fiduciary model and fundamental values, I argue, casts administrative law in its best light, as a project of unabashed solicitude towards both the public at large and the individual immediately subject to administrative power. Under this conception, the public law duty of reasonable decision-making is best thought of as a public fiduciary duty of solicitude. The duty requires decision-makers and judges to exercise public power with due regard for the interests of the people subject to it. As a rule, this will translate into a duty to give significant weight to the important interests of individuals immediately subject to public power. The fiduciary model thus supplies a conceptual framework to the idea of public law that underlies cases such as *Baker*, an idea that properly orients administrative law towards solicitude. Put another way, the fiduciary theory points to solicitude as a governing principle of statutory interpretation within a common law constitutionalist understanding of public law.

[6] *Slaight Communications v Davidson* [1989] 1 SCR 1038 (*Slaight*) (a company's constitutional right to freedom of expression may be justifiably infringed to protect the future job prospects of an unjustly dismissed employee).

Yet another tension that permeates administrative law concerns the legitimacy of judicial review. Some on the left of the political spectrum call for its near abandonment, pointing to a history of labour law decisions that favour employers at the expense of employees. I canvass their arguments below. The legitimacy crisis is made worse by the fact that most labour boards are protected by statutory privative clauses which expressly declare the board's decision to be final and not subject to judicial review.

The fiduciary model makes a number of valuable contributions to the legitimacy debate. Its understanding of administrative law as solicitude resists the equation of administrative law to judicial review. On this understanding, the legitimacy of administrative law lies in its capacity to acknowledge the legal significance of vulnerable interests subject to public power, an acknowledgement that can (and must) come from agencies as well as from judges. Moreover, we shall see that the fiduciary theory offers a fresh and principled basis for restricting judicial review in some administrative contexts, such as labour law regimes, but supports more searching review in other settings, such as immigration.

Finally, I will argue that the duty of solicitude arising from the fiduciary model requires agencies and courts to give reasons if their decisions set back important interests, and that these reasons generally must have a certain form and substance. The substance is informed by fundamental values and important interests. The preferred form is proportionality; the reasons should show that the objective of a policy is compelling, and that the means used to attain it impair minimally important interests. First, however, we need to address the critic's question: Given judicial hostility to labour boards and other agencies, why not give up on judicial review altogether, or replace it with a specialized statutory appellate body from which no judicial review is possible?

8.2 THE LEGITIMACY OF THE ADMINISTRATIVE STATE

Canada's five major banks are the most profitable businesses in Canada and the workplaces of roughly 250,000 Canadians. All are non-unionized.[7] Attempts to bring collective bargaining to Canada's financial institutions have been impeded by Supreme Court of Canada decisions such as *National Bank of Canada v Retail Clerk's Union*,[8] a judgment that reveals the danger of judicial review as much as *Roncarelli* speaks to its promise.

[7] There are no unions in any of the five major banks of Canada, which typically post quarterly profits of over $1 billion. The top six banks, which include the National Bank of Canada, enjoyed a combined annual profit in 2007 of more than $19.5 billion. See the website of the Canadian Bankers Association, online: <http://cba.ca/>.

[8] *National Bank of Canada v Retail Clerk's Union* [1984] 1 SCR 269 (*National Bank*).

On Friday 27 June 1980, the Retail Clerk's Union was certified as bargaining agent for the employees of the National Bank of Canada's Maguire Street branch in Quebec City. The following Monday, 30 June, the bank announced its intention to close the branch, and did so in September of that year, selling off the premises shortly thereafter. Two of the unionized employees of the Maguire Street branch were declared surplus upon its closure and lost their jobs.

In detailed and careful reasons running over 40 pages, the Canada Labour Relations Board concluded, and the bank eventually admitted, that contrary to various sections of the Canada Labour Code[9] it had closed the Maguire Street branch and sold its premises to eliminate the union.[10] The Board found that the bank adopted the 'most odious method possible to deny its employees the right to bargain', and did so to deliver a chilling message: 'If you exercise this fundamental right [to bargain collectively] . . . we will give you no quarter'.[11]

The Board had broad remedial powers under the Code 'to remedy or counteract any consequences' of unfair labour practices.[12] Bearing in mind the chilling effect of the Maguire Street closure, the Board ordered the bank to put $144,000 into a trust fund that was to be administered jointly by the bank and the union to further the objectives of the Code (freedom of association and the right to collective bargaining). Another order, following established labour board practice, required the bank to send a letter to all of its employees reporting that it had been found in violation of the Code, and that its management personnel 'have the responsibility of respecting the choice of those employees who opt for free collective bargaining'.[13] The letter also said that the bank intended to contribute $144,000 to the trust fund 'as a concrete manifestation of [its] commitment to this principle'.[14]

A unanimous Supreme Court of Canada set aside both orders. Chouinard J held that the trust fund was intended to promote the unionization of all the bank's employees, and therefore the fund was 'not something intended to remedy or counteract the consequences harmful to realization of [the Code's] objectives that may result from closure of the Maguire Street branch'.[15] The order to send the letter was quashed because it referred to the trust fund, now set aside.

Beetz J offered additional reasons for a majority of the Court. He found that both orders were punitive rather than remedial. He characterized the letter as 'totalitarian and as such alien to the tradition of free nations like Canada'.[16] He

[9] Canada Labour Code, RSC 1970, c L 1 (Code), ss 184(1)(a) and 184(3)(a).

[10] *Retail Clerks' International Union, complainant, and National Bank of Canada, respondent* [1982] 2 Can LRBR 3, p 42 di 352; CLRB Decision No 335 (*National Bank (CLRB)*).

[11] Ibid, p 38. [12] Code, *supra* note 9, s 189.

[13] *National Bank (CLRB)*, *supra* note 10, p 41. [14] Ibid.

[15] *National Bank*, *supra* note 8, para 66. [16] Ibid, para 82.

objected to the letter on the grounds that it infringed the bank's common law right to freedom of expression because, he thought, it could be interpreted as the bank's own approval of the right to bargain collectively. Beetz J deployed the common law method of reading down a broad discretionary power using what David Dyzenhaus, Murray Hunt, and Michael Taggart refer to as 'the old set of pre-democratic, property-based values'.[17] Neither Chouinard nor Beetz JJ engaged with the Board's concern to counteract the chilling effect of the Maguire Street closure, nor attempted to explain why the freedom of expression of an artificial person (the bank) was more important than substantive equality, the value underlying collective bargaining and the statutory grant of remedial discretion to the Board.

Decisions such as *National Bank* have led labour lawyers and scholars such as Harry Arthurs to call for the 'virtual abandonment' of judicial review.[18] The abolitionists have several arguments that are important to have in sight, since they point to a justificatory threshold that any limited defence of judicial review must overcome.

- Judges' commitment to 'pre-democratic, property-based values' hinders the administrative state's promotion of values such as substantive equality.
- The norms of bipolar adjudication (backward-looking rectification, bias towards the status quo, technical evidentiary and procedural requirements) are ill-suited to public administration, which is forward-looking, sensitive to multiple constituencies, and guided by the ongoing delivery of a programme that seeks to change the status quo.
- Judicial review is expensive, privileging the well-off to the detriment of the disadvantaged.
- Review is time-consuming: the point of an agency's decision—such as creating conditions favourable to collective bargaining—may be lost by the time review has run its course.
- Judicial review usurps the democratic will of the legislature because the legislature has entrusted administration of a particular field or industry to an agency rather than the courts, a usurpation that is especially pronounced when the enabling legislation contains a privative clause.

[17] D Dyzenhaus, M Hunt, and M Taggart, 'The Principle of Legality in Administrative Law: Internationalisation as Constitutionalisation' (2001) 1(1) OUCLJ 5, p 7. I do not mean to suggest that freedom of expression is 'pre-democratic', but the weight given to the freedom of expression of an artificial person (the bank) in this case is roughly analogous to the weight common law judges used to accord freedom of contract for the sake of upholding discriminatory practices.

[18] Harry Arthurs, 'Protection Against Judicial Review' (1983) 43 R du B 277, p 284. Arthurs would make an exception for constitutional questions, with the caveat that jurisdictional issues concerning the scope of an agency's power do not fall into this excepted category. See also Harry Arthurs, 'Rethinking Administrative Law: A Slightly Dicey Business' (1979) 17 Osgoode Hall LJ 1.

- Boards have specialized expertise that courts lack regarding both factual determinations and the interpretation of their enabling statute.
- And finally, abuse of power is best controlled not by judicial review but by in-house measures, such as enhanced public participation and transparency, staff training, policy guidelines and manuals, codes of ethics and best practices, access to information, and internal statutory appeal mechanisms.[19]

The fiduciary view of administration, I will suggest, provides a further argument for judicial restraint towards labour boards and decision-makers in like contexts, one that reveals deference as an implication of both the rule of law, properly understood, and the legitimacy of the administrative state. It may be jarring to imagine that the rule of law can require judicial deference to agency determinations. For AV Dicey the judiciary was the lone guardian of the rule of law, and as we shall see, many judges today still operate in his shadow.[20] On the fiduciary conception, however, where administrative law is guided by solicitude, the driving concern is not to determine who has the last word as between the courts or the administration on the basis of a rigid separation of powers. Rather, the inquiry into deference asks the following question: Who is best situated to interpret statutory purposes and fundamental values protective of vulnerable interests in this decision-making context, the judiciary or the legislature's delegates? A corollary of this approach, I argue below, is that decisions such as *National Bank* are as much a threat to the rule of law as administrative arbitrariness, for both deny the legal significance of important interests. But before setting out this argument we need to have in view the legal landscape it will traverse, a landscape in which deference emerges as a response to interventionist judicial review of agency jurisdiction.

8.3 FROM JURISDICTIONAL REVIEW TO DEFERENCE?

The landmark case in which the Supreme Court of Canada asserted a commitment to deference is *Canadian Union of Public Employees Local 963 v New Brunswick Liquor Corp.*[21] The issue in *CUPE* concerned the authority of the Public Service Labour Relations Board of New Brunswick to interpret an ambiguous provision of its constitutive statute, the Public Service Relations

[19] Roderick Macdonald, 'The Acoustics of Accountability—Toward Well-Tempered Tribunals' in András Sajó (ed), *Judicial Integrity* (Netherlands: Koninklijke Brill, 2004), p 141. See also Simon Halliday, 'The Influence of Judicial Review on Bureaucratic Decision-Making' (2000) PL 110 (empirical evidence suggests that exposure to judicial review is neutral or even harmful to agency compliance with the norms of administrative law).

[20] David Dyzenhaus, 'Dicey's Shadow' (1993) 43 UTLJ 127.

[21] *Canadian Union of Public Employees Local 963 v New Brunswick Liquor Corp* [1979] 2 SCR 227 (*CUPE*).

Labour Act.[22] The union alleged that, during the midst of a lawful strike, the employer illegally replaced union personnel with management staff. The PSLRA prohibited management from replacing striking workers with 'employees', but management argued that their staff were not employees within the meaning of the Act because management personnel were explicitly excluded from the Act's definition of 'employee'. A plain and literal reading of the statute appeared to support management's interpretation of the PSLRA.

The Board disagreed. It found that the Act prohibited the union from mounting picket lines, and as a *quid pro quo* barred management from using replacement workers. For the *quid pro quo* to be effective, the Board determined that the prohibition on replacement workers had to include management personnel. Dickson J (as he then was) upheld the Board's interpretation, overturning the Court of Appeal.

Dickson J noted that the PSLRA contained a privative clause which stipulated that the Board's rulings were 'final and shall not be questioned or reviewed in any court'.[23] These clauses in the past had done little to deter judges anxious to read down the employee-friendly provisions of labour legislation. This reading-down exercise typically began with the uncontroversial point that legislative grants of power are always limited to particular statutory purposes. When this truism is combined with the Diceyan idea that courts have a monopoly on the interpretation of law, the foundation is set for judges to conclude that the legislature could never have intended to oust courts from policing the limits of a board's jurisdiction, even in the face of an explicit privative clause.[24] If the courts were ousted from their supervisory role, then boards could determine conclusively the extent of their own jurisdiction, and for judges the only institution with that power is the judiciary.[25]

Judges prior to *CUPE* sometimes paid lip service to the idea that their role was to control jurisdictional bounds, but that within those bounds an agency 'may err in fact or in law'.[26] Frequently, however, it seemed that any error of law could result in a judge finding that an agency had overstepped its

[22] Public Service Labour Relations Act, RSNB 1973, c P-25, s 19 (PSLRA).

[23] Section 101(1) of the PSRLA, ibid cited in *CUPE*, *supra* note 21, para 14.

[24] See eg *Jarvis v Associated Medical Services Inc* [1964] SCR 497 (*Jarvis*), Cartwright J, p 502: 'I cannot take the [privative clause] to mean that if the Board purports to make an order which, on the true construction of the Act, it has no jurisdiction to make the person affected thereby is left without a remedy'.

[25] This line of reasoning led to *Crevier v Attorney General of Quebec* [1981] 2 SCR 220 (*Crevier*), a judgment in which the Court held that s 96 of the Constitution Act 1867—the section granting appointment power of superior court judges to the federal Crown—supplies a constitutional basis to jurisdictional review of provincial boards, rendering privative clauses of no effect in relation to this species of review. But as cases such as *Jarvis* indicate, *Crevier* was really just window-dressing for an argument to which judges were already deeply committed.

[26] *Jarvis*, *supra* note 24, p 502.

jurisdictional limits. Cartwright J said as much in *Jarvis*, citing a prior labour case for the 'governing principle' that 'jurisdiction cannot be obtained nor can it be declined as a result of a misinterpretation of the law. . . notwithstanding the existence in the Act of a *no certiorari* [privative] clause'.[27]

To make matters worse, the distinction between 'mere errors of law' and jurisdictional errors is arguably unsustainable in principle.[28] A decision that relies on a 'mere' error in the interpretation of the relevant statute is necessarily a decision taken without that statute's authority, and thus beyond the decision-maker's jurisdiction. This argument is reinforced by the apparent view of many judges that statutory terms admit of one 'true construction', and that judges have special access to it.[29] But the argument does not depend on this attitude. Ambiguous or open-textured statutory terms present the possibility of more than one reasonable and permissible interpretation, but a decision based on a construction of the statute that lies outside the set of (judicially) permissible interpretations would remain an error of law, and therefore would be a decision taken without statutory authority, and so without jurisdiction.

Moreover, for judges such as Cartwright J who think that administrative tribunals operate, within their jurisdiction, as 'laws unto themselves',[30] it follows that all questions of law *must* be questions of jurisdiction, since jurisdictional questions related to the limits of a tribunal's authority are the only kinds of questions to which law applies. And, if the only legal standard to which a board is subject is one defined as a limit (because within the limits

[27] Ibid citing *In re Ontario Labour Relations Board, Toronto Newspaper Guild, Local 87 v Globe Printing Co* [1953] 2 SCR 18, p 41, Fauteux J. The leading case in the UK that tends to the same conclusion is *Anisminic Ltd v Foreign Compensation Commission* [1969] 2 AC 147 (*Anisminic*). This decision entrenched the 'wrong questions' doctrine: agencies act outside their jurisdiction if they ask themselves questions not remitted to them by Parliament. The 'wrong questions' doctrine was subsequently deployed in *Metropolitan Life Insurance Co v International Union of Operating Engineers* [1970] SCR 425 (*Metropolitan Life*), the case described as the 'high water mark' of hostile judicial intervention in Canadian labour law: Janisch Evans, David Mullan, and Richard Risk, *Administrative Law: Cases, Text, and Materials*, 3rd edn (Toronto: Emond Montgomery, 1989), p 565, later cited by Wilson J in *National Corn Growers Association v Canada (Import Tribunal)* [1990] 2 SCR 1324, p 1335.

[28] Roderick Macdonald catalogues 28 'errors' that courts claim to detect on review, all of which could fit within the wide scope of, roughly, a decision taken without lawful authority. Roderick Macdonald, 'Absence of Jurisdiction: A Perspective' (1983) 43(2) R du B 307, pp 311–12.

[29] See eg *Jarvis*, *supra* note 24, p 502.

[30] The idea that administrators exercise authority as 'laws unto themselves' is one that applies in the first instance to exercises of discretion rather than to interpretations of law. However, as L'Heureux-Dubé J points out in *Baker*, 'there is no easy distinction to be made between interpretation and the exercise of discretion; interpreting legal rules involves considerable discretion to clarify, fill in legislative gaps, and make choices among various options'. *Baker*, *supra* note 5, para 54. This was just the kind of authority exercised by the Board in *CUPE*. The point is simply that if tribunals really operate as 'laws unto themselves' within jurisdictional limits, then questions of law (including questions of interpretation) must be questions of jurisdiction, since it is only in questions of jurisdiction that law is to be found.

there is just a legal void), then review of a question of law is necessarily review of jurisdiction. Therefore, on this view, the standard of review for all questions of law is the same searching standard as it is for questions of jurisdiction—correctness. On the correctness standard, the board's interpretation of the legislation and its resulting decision must coincide with the reviewing court's view of the matter, even if the court admits that there is more than one reasonable interpretation of the statutory provisions in play. In short, for the Cartwright J camp, questions of law collapse into questions of jurisdiction which are reviewable only on a standard of correctness, leaving no room for deference to agency determinations of issues of law.

To think, as Dickson J did in *CUPE*, that a board may make an 'error of law' and not exceed its jurisdiction shatters this paradigm, for supposing that an 'error of law' is at all possible *within* the limits of a board's jurisdiction implies that some law exists within those limits, that the board is not a law unto itself. This affirmation of the interpretive authority of agencies carries with it an affirmation of the legitimacy of the administrative state, and explains why *CUPE* remains an exalted judgment.

Speaking to the effect of the privative clause in relation to the ambiguous statutory provision in *CUPE*, Dickson J articulates a justification for deference premised explicitly on the Board's expertise and accumulated jurisprudence in the field of collective bargaining.[31] In other words, Dickson J justifies deference not on the basis of a separation-of-powers-driven submission to the legislature's privative clause, but for substantive reasons (expertise and the Board's own accumulated jurisprudence) that should lead reviewing courts to respect the decisions of labour boards whether or not a privative clause is in place.

The *CUPE* Court, however, could not bring itself to abandon altogether the framework that jurisdiction supplies as a basis for review. Although Dickson J cautioned that courts 'should not be alert to brand as jurisdictional, and therefore subject to broader curial review, that which may be doubtfully so',[32] he also confirmed the place of jurisdictional review, saying that 'jurisdiction is typically to be determined at the outset of the inquiry'.[33] Moreover, he described the deferential standard of patent unreasonableness using the 'wrong questions' language previously deployed to test the limits of jurisdiction in interventionist cases such as *Anisminic* and *Metropolitan Life*.[34]

[31] *CUPE*, *supra* note 21, paras 14–15.

[32] Ibid, para 10.

[33] Ibid, para 9. This is sometimes referred to as the 'preliminary' or 'collateral' questions doctrine, one that separates review into two stages: preliminary review of jurisdictional issues, and subsequent review of everything else. In *CUPE* the New Brunswick Court of Appeal had used this doctrine en route to setting aside the Board's decision.

[34] Ibid, para 16: 'Did the Board here so misinterpret the provisions of the Act as to embark on an inquiry or answer a question not remitted to it?'

The Court's approach to substantive review since *CUPE* bears the hallmarks of a problem *CUPE* left unresolved: how do courts determine whether an agency's interpretation of law merits deference as opposed to jurisdictional review, notwithstanding Dickson J's call for restraint? In *Union des employés de service, Local 298 v Bibeault*,[35] Beetz J, writing for the Court, held that courts must adopt a 'pragmatic and functional' approach to determine whether the relevant statutory provisions were jurisdiction-conferring and therefore subject to review on a standard of correctness.[36] If the provisions were not jurisdiction-conferring, then review would take place on the patent unreasonableness standard. The contextual factors included 'not only the wording of the enactment conferring jurisdiction on the administrative tribunal, but the purpose of the statute creating the tribunal, the reason for its existence, the area of expertise of its members and the nature of the problem before the tribunal.'[37] The presence of a privative clause was relevant too, since it helped to answer what Beetz J took to be the underlying question of the pragmatic and functional inquiry, ie 'Did the legislator intend the question to be within the jurisdiction conferred on the tribunal?'[38] This question, however, is always asked against the separation-of-powers assumption that the legislature would never intend agencies to be the final arbiters of their own jurisdiction.

In 1997 the Court in *Canada (Director of Investigation and Research) v Southam Inc*[39] introduced an intermediate standard of review, reasonableness *simpliciter*, according to which a decision would have to 'stand up to a somewhat probing examination', but courts should be prepared to defer if 'any reasons support it'.[40] Writing for the Court, Iacobucci J questioned the correctness of the tribunal's decision but nonetheless deferred in light of the comprehensive reasons given. Iacobucci J subsequently emphasized, in *Law Society of New Brunswick v Ryan*,[41] that '[u]nlike a review for correctness, there will often be no single right answer to the questions that are under review against the standard of reasonableness', and that '[e]ven if there could be, notionally, a single best answer, it is not the court's role to seek this out when deciding if the decision was unreasonable'.[42] A decision will be unreasonable, Iacobucci J said, 'only if there is no line of analysis within the given reasons that could reasonably lead the tribunal from the evidence before it to the conclusion at which it arrived'.[43]

[35] *Union des employés de service, Local 298 v Bibeault* [1988] 2 SCR 104 (*Bibeault*).

[36] Ibid, paras 114, 122. [37] Ibid, para 122. [38] Ibid, para 119.

[39] *Canada (Director of Investigation and Research) v Southam Inc* [1997] 1 SCR 748 (*Southam*).

[40] Ibid, para 56. [41] *Law Society of New Brunswick v Ryan* 2003 SCC 20; [2003] 1 SCR 247 (*Ryan*).

[42] Ibid, para 51. [43] Ibid, para 55.

The zenith of the submersion of jurisdictional review within the pragmatic and functional approach was reached in *Pushpanathan v Canada (Minister of Citizenship and Immigration)*.[44] Bastarache J, for the majority, held that 'a question which "goes to jurisdiction" is simply descriptive of a provision for which the proper standard of review is correctness, based upon the outcome of the pragmatic and functional analysis'.[45] The pragmatic and functional analysis was to be applied by weighing together four contextual factors taken largely from *Bibeault*, except that now the approach was to be applied without regard to whether the statutory provision in question was jurisdiction-conferring. And as indicated, the approach now had three standards—correctness, reasonableness *simpliciter*, and patent unreasonableness—rather than just two (correctness for jurisdictional issues and patent unreasonableness for non-jurisdictional questions). The four contextual factors were: the presence or absence of a privative clause or statutory right of appeal, the agency's expertise relative to the court's, the purpose of the statute and the particular provision at the root of the controversy, and the nature of the question before the court (law, mixed fact and law, or fact).[46] A year later the Court in *Baker* extended the pragmatic and functional approach to review of discretion, applying in that case the standard of reasonableness *simpliciter*.[47] The courts had traditionally taken a very 'hands off' approach to discretion, viewing it as Cartwright J did, as a legal void.

In subsequent years doubts began to surface about the tenability of the distinction between the reasonableness *simpliciter* and patent unreasonableness standards of review. The latter standard was said to require deference unless the decision was 'clearly irrational'.[48] David Mullan objected that 'to maintain a position that only the "clearly irrational" will cross the threshold of patent unreasonableness while irrationality *simpliciter* will not is to make a nonsense of the law'.[49] LeBel echoed this concern in two concurring judgments,[50] and

[44] *Pushpanathan v Canada (Minister of Citizenship and Immigration)* [1998] 1 SCR 982.

[45] Ibid, para 28.

[46] The four-factor, three-standard approach was reaffirmed in *Ryan*, *supra* note 41 and *Dr Q v College of Physicians and Surgeons of British Columbia*, 2003 SCC 19; [2003] 1 SCR 226.

[47] *Baker*, *supra* note 5, paras 51–62.

[48] *Canada (Attorney General) v Public Service Alliance of Canada* [1993] 1 SCR 941, 963, Cory J for the majority.

[49] David Mullan, 'Recent Developments in Standard of Review', *Taking the Bar to Court: A Practical Guide for Administrative Law Practitioners* (Canadian Bar Association, 2000), p 24.

[50] *Toronto (City) v CUPE, Local 79* 2003 SCC 63; [2003] 3 SCR 77, paras 60–135; *Chamberlain v Surrey School District No 36* 2002 SCC 86; [2002] 4 SCR 710, paras 190–205 (*Chamberlain*). Another important concern was the malleability of the pragmatic and functional approach, and a growing sense that judicial determinations of the appropriate standard of review were being driven by the judge's view of the merits. Judges who approved the decision tended to find that the appropriate standard of review was one of the reasonableness standards, while those opposed on the merits often held that correctness was the

in 2008 the Court in *Dunsmuir v New Brunswick*[51] collapsed the two reasonableness standards into one. While the contextual factors of the pragmatic and functional approach remain more or less in place under the renamed 'standard of review' analysis, we shall see that in *Dunsmuir* the Court's application of the reasonableness standard was far from deferential. Moreover, the Court affirmed its readiness to review so-called 'true questions of jurisdiction' on a standard of correctness, characterizing these questions with language reminiscent of jurisdictional review from pre-*CUPE* cases such as *Jarvis* and *Metropolitan Life*: 'true jurisdiction questions arise where the tribunal must explicitly determine whether its statutory grant of power gives it the authority to decide a particular matter'.[52] With some of the tensions and contours of substantive judicial review in view, let us consider now how deference to agencies such as labour boards supports rather than threatens the rule of law under the fiduciary conception of public law.

8.4 DEFERENCE AS A POSTULATE OF THE RULE OF LAW

Arthurs supplies the first premise in the argument that claims deference as a postulate of the rule of law[53]:

> There is no reason to believe that a judge who reads a particular statute once in his life, perhaps in a worst-case circumstance, can read it with greater fidelity to legislative purpose than an administrator who is sworn to uphold that purpose, who strives to do so daily, and is well-aware of the effect upon the purpose of the various interpretations.

Although Arthurs' claim can be read as one evincing a contest between administrators and judges over the question of who is best placed to determine the legislative intent behind a statutes terms and purpose, it need not be read so narrowly. The more controversial claim I wish to attribute to Arthurs, or at least defend myself below, is the following: expert administrators such as labour boards are better placed to interpret and administer their statutes in a way that conforms to the *statutory values* underlying the legislation's purpose, such as substantive equality. More contentiously still, I will further suggest that some expert administrators are better placed than judges to take account of *common law values*, such as freedom of expression and equality.

appropriate standard of review. See eg *Canada (Attorney General) v Mossop* [1993] 1 SCR 554; *Council of Canadians with Disabilities v VIA Rail Canada Inc* 2007 SCC 15; [2007] 1 SCR 650.

[51] *Dunsmuir v New Brunswick* 2008 SCC 9; [2008] 1 SCR 190 (*Dunsmuir*).

[52] Ibid, para 59.

[53] Arthurs, 'Protection Against Judicial Review,' *supra* note 18, p 289.

The second premise of the argument that features deference as an element of the rule of law trades on the convergence of the fiduciary principle and the rule of law discussed in prior chapters (I, VI, VII). We have seen that the fiduciary principle and the rule of law converge on an overarching purposive obligation: both require delegated powers to be exercised exclusively for the purposes for which they are conferred, so arbitrary exercises of power are excluded. Ordinarily, legislative purposes are value-laden. Where this is the case, exercising power in accordance with statutory purposes requires an inquiry into the statutory values they are intended to promote. Moreover, the fiduciary theory insists that statutes be read in light of common law values. The usual reason given for this assumption is that the legislature is presumed to enact law cognizant of the entire context in which the statute operates, which includes common law values that guide interpretation.[54] Under the fiduciary model, however, this presumption follows not from an implicit intent attributed to the legislature, but from the protection common law values lend to important interests vulnerable to public and fiduciary power. The overarching purposive obligation, then, is a principle of legality that mandates inquiry into both the values underlying the statute and the values of the common law. We explore the structure of this inquiry further below. The point here is that the fiduciary model requires boards and courts alike to engage in the inquiry because it is constitutive of the overarching purposive obligation—the principle of legality—that regulates the exercise of public power.

Bringing the two premises of the argument together, when boards and courts are called on to interpret legislation, both must comply with the principle of legality embodied in the overarching purposive obligation. Sometimes, however, for the reasons Arthurs gives and for reasons developed below, expert boards may be better placed than judges to appreciate the statutory and common law values that regulate the exercise of statutory power. In these circumstances, deference follows from the fiduciary view of the rule of law because deference ensures that the legality of administrative action is decided by the institution best situated to assess the statutory and common law values that govern questions of legality arising from statutory interpretation. Therefore, if courts fail to defer when it is appropriate for them to do so, they place a strain on the rule of law.

At a higher level of abstraction still, the argument for deference can be seen to flow from the fundamental fiduciary relationship of the people to

[54] See eg Ruth Sullivan and EA Driedger, *Sullivan and Driedger on the Construction of Statutes*, 4th edn (Markham, Ont: Butterworths, 2002), pp 154–5. As we shall see at 8.6 below, the presumption is variously referred to as the 'clear statement principle' or 'the principle of legality', according to which only express words will authorize an infringement of common law rights.

the state. The state's basic fiduciary obligation to the people is to govern in accordance with the rule of law. On the assumption (defended next chapter) that the state can comply or not with the rule of law to varying degrees, and that the state's basic rule-of-law duty is a *prima facie* obligation to achieve the rule of law to the extent practicable, then the state is duty-bound to rely on the judgment of those institutions best able to guarantee the rule of law. Regarding the administration of statutes, in some cases the state's fiduciary duty to govern in accordance with the rule of law will require the state to rely on specialized boards rather than generalist courts, since in those cases boards are better placed to meet the requirements of the principle of legality discussed above. Once again, deference follows from the fiduciary conception of public authority.

Of course, the meaning of deference is hotly contested, and many would question the assumption that agencies are sometimes better placed than courts to determine and weigh common law values, while others may question the very inclusion of such values in the interpretive process. I argue now that, with respect to labour boards and similarly constituted tribunals, there are distinctive democratic and republican arguments in favour of restricting judicial review, and neither have anything to do with submission to the will of the legislature. These arguments will help illuminate some of the conditions (there may be others) under which agencies are better placed than courts to interpret statutory purposes and common law values.

A labour board is composed of, and answerable to, the people it represents. The typical board will have a member from management, another from the union, and an impartial chair. There is a real sense in which the public trust on which the board acts comes from the bottom up, from the people the board is authorized to serve, as well as from the top down, from the enabling legislation. Because the members of the board have a direct relationship with employers and employees, their interpretation of the statutory terms of their authorization is readily susceptible to the scrutiny of the people they represent and on whose behalf they conduct administration. Labour law regimes, in other words, let participatory democracy enrich representative democracy, and are, as Paul Weiler puts it, 'intrinsically valuable as an experience in self-government'.[55]

To varying degrees, the same holds true of many other public bodies, such as school boards[56] and the disciplinary committees of law societies.[57] As Robert Leckey points out, although the decision-maker's democratic

[55] P Weiler, *Reconcilable Differences* (Toronto: Carswell, 1980), p 33.

[56] *Chamberlain*, *supra* note 50.

[57] *Ryan*, *supra* note 41.

qualities do not figure explicitly among the contextual factors of the standard of review analysis, in both school board and law society cases, reviewing courts have held that such qualities call for heightened deference.[58]

The republican argument in favour of judicial restraint is perhaps more specific to labour law regimes and collective bargaining, and trades on the ideal of non-domination discussed in previous chapters. Weiler claims that 'good collective bargaining tries to subject the employment relationship and the work environment to the "rule of law"', and that this protection from abuse of managerial power is 'the primary value of collective bargaining'.[59] That is, the evil that collectively bargained labour law regimes try to displace is domination, or as Phillip Pettit puts it, 'the grievance expressed . . . by the employee who dare not raise a complaint against an employer, and who is vulnerable to any of a range of abuses, some petty, some serious, that the employer may choose to perpetrate'.[60] Perhaps the most salient rule-of-law features of a unionized workplace are the employee's right to be dismissed only for cause, and the opportunity to grieve termination and lesser disciplinary measures. These features undermine domination by restraining the employer's capacity to exercise power arbitrarily.

Although the rule of law is usually used to describe constraints on the exercise of public power, in the next chapter I argue that its deepest justification lies in the recourse it provides against subjection to all arbitrary exercises of power, public and private. This justification reflects the republican ideal of non-domination. Judgments such as *National Bank* and *Dunsmuir* suggest that courts are not alive to this more expansive understanding of the rule of law, and so they miss the importance of its operation in labour settings. Labour boards, on the other hand, view the introduction of the rule of law into employment relations as 'the primary value of collective bargaining'. Thus, for this reason too, a commitment to the rule of law implies a commitment to judicial deference to labour boards. Let us consider now the shape this deference might take.

8.5 THE CONTENT OF DEFERENCE

As noted, at one end of the deference spectrum is Arthurs' calls for the 'virtual abandonment' of non-constitutional judicial review. At the other end of the spectrum is the pre-*CUPE* position of the Courts under which jurisdictional review is used to test the legality of agency determinations on a standard of

58 Robert Leckey, *Contextual Subjects: Family, State and Relational Theory* (Toronto: University of Toronto Press, 2008), pp 188–90.

59 Weiler, *supra* note 55, p 31.

60 Philip Pettit, *Republicanism: A Theory of Freedom and Government* (Oxford: Clarendon Press, 1997), p 5.

correctness. Between these poles lie two other well-established views. The first is the *Dunsmuir* Court's present standard of review analysis. The Court claims that its standard of review analysis respects the message of deference from *CUPE*, and, as we have seen, uses contextual factors to determine whether review should be conducted on a standard of correctness or reasonableness.[61] The second is David Dyzenhaus' idea of 'deference as respect', which requires of the courts 'not submission but a respectful attention to the reasons offered or which could be offered in support of a decision'.[62]

Dyzenhaus emphasizes that the point of deference as respect is to focus review on the reasons for decision rather than the outcome. The underlying ideas are that the administrative state is a legitimate part of legal order, that democratic legal order aspires to embody a legal culture of public justification, and so the reasons offered by administrative agencies must be taken seriously. Taking reasons seriously means deferring to them if they provide a rational basis for decision, and making best efforts to supplement rather than reject them if they are found to be deficient. Thus, deference as respect generally requires agencies to offer reasons, and in principle permits review of every kind of substantive agency decision. But, as Dyzenhaus has since clarified, deference as respect precludes review on a standard of correctness because under that standard only the outcome is subject to review; the actual or possible reasons for the decision are swept aside.[63] According to Dyzenhaus, the only question on review is the reasonableness of the reasons offered or which could be offered for the decision. The reasonableness standard should apply, he claims, even if a particular decision implicates jurisdictional, constitutional, human rights, or common law issues over which the courts have traditionally claimed an interpretive monopoly.[64]

[61] In his concurring judgment in *Dunsmuir*, Binnie J notes that the new consolidated reasonableness standard is now a 'big tent' that will have to accommodate many contextual variables: *Dunsmuir, supra* note 51, para 144. David Mullan suggests that the Court's attempt to simplify the standard of review analysis may really just push back complex contextual analysis to a subsequent stage if reasonableness is found to be the governing standard, since it appears that reasonableness now may involve varying degrees of deference: David Mullan, '*Dunsmuir v New Brunswick*, Standards of Review and Procedural Fairness: Let's Try Again!' (2008) 21 Can J Admin L & Prac 117, pp 134–5. Lorne Sossin and Colleen Flood also suggest that the courts should calibrate deference along a spectrum in order to take account of the variability of decision-making contexts, as well as the importance to the individual of the decision: Colleen Flood and Lorne Sossin, 'The Contextual Turn: Iacobucci's Legacy and the Standard of Review in Administrative Law' (2007) 57 UTLJ 581.

[62] David Dyzenhaus, 'The Politics of Deference: Judicial Review and Democracy' in M Taggart (ed), *The Province of Administrative Law* (Oxford: Hart Publishing, 1997), p 286 (quoted with approval in *Dunsmuir, supra* note 51, para 48; *Baker, supra* note 5, para 65; *Ryan, supra* note 41, para 49).

[63] D Dyzenhaus, 'David Mullan's Theory of the Rule of (Common) Law' in G Huscroft and M Taggart (eds), *Inside and Outside Canadian Administrative Law: Essays in Honour of David Mullan* (Toronto: University of Toronto Press, 2006), pp 462, 465.

[64] Ibid, p 475.

In *Dunsmuir*, Bastarache and LeBel JJ claimed that their 'standard of review analysis' borrows from Dyzenhaus' theory of deference as respect. Yet they also held that 'the standard of correctness must be maintained in respect of jurisdictional and some other questions of law', and that '[w]hen applying the correctness standard, a reviewing court will not show deference to the decision maker's reasoning process; it will rather undertake its own analysis of the question'.[65] In other words, despite the lip service paid to deference as respect, the Court's standard of review analysis differs markedly from Dyzenhaus' understanding of deference.

The fiduciary view of deference combines elements of Arthurs' position with Dyzenhaus' account of deference as respect. In the case of agencies such as labour boards, where the decision-makers both represent the constituency subject to their authority and are better placed to implement the rule of law in private order, the argument against judicial review is especially compelling. Labour boards have local democratic credentials, and they are better placed to weigh the importance of the rule of law in the workplace against contending common law values. The board in *National Bank* was well aware that the remedy it ordered infringed the bank's freedom of expression, but explained at length that this measure was necessary to give the union half a chance to bring collective bargaining and the rule of law to an institution where the employer was willing to use illegal means to block unionization. Courts should not undermine the rule of law by second-guessing such judgments, and the surest way for them to resist the temptation in these cases is by declining altogether the invitation to review.

In a now-heralded dissent in *Cooper v Canada (Human Rights Commission)*,[66] McLachlin J (as she then was) held that '[t]he Charter is not some holy grail which only judicial initiates of the superior courts may touch. The Charter belongs to the people'.[67] Her finding that the Canadian Charter of Rights and Freedoms[68] 'belongs to the people' became the *cri de cœur* in *Martin*, the judgment that amplified agency jurisdiction to apply the Charter to constitutive statutes. The rule of law also belongs to the people, but in labour relations the courts have frustrated rather than enabled the people's attempts to bring the rule of law to their everyday lives.

Even in labour board and like cases, however, some scope for review, even jurisdictional review on a standard of reasonableness, is consistent with the

[65] *Dunsmuir, supra* note 51, para 50.

[66] *Cooper v (Canada Human Rights Commission)* (1996) 3 SCR 854.

[67] Ibid, para 70, cited with approval in *Nova Scotia (Workers' Compensation Board) v Martin* [2003] 2 SCR 504, para 29 (*Martin*).

[68] Canadian Charter of Rights and Freedoms, Part I of the Constitution Act 1982, being Sch B to the Canada Act 1982 (UK), 1982, c 11 (Charter).

fiduciary view of deference. The problematic kind of jurisdictional review generally involves review of a board's interpretation of its enabling statute or closely related statutes. But not all questions of jurisdiction (and judicial review more broadly) are of this kind. Review of constitutional issues by the courts may be warranted not solely on the basis of the court's expertise in relation to such issues, but on grounds of equality before the law: the people have an interest in being subject to uniform constitutional standards, and the courts are best placed to ensure these standards. This does not mean that constitutional review must be conducted on a standard of correctness. The better standard is reasonableness, for the reasons Dyzenhaus gives. But once a tribunal has determined that a statutory provision violates the *Charter*, and this determination survives reasonableness review, a subsequent reviewing court would be justified in quashing as unreasonable an agency determination that gave effect to the provision that had previously been held to infringe the Charter. Similarly, there are cases in which it is not obvious which administrative agency really has jurisdiction over a matter, or whether a board rather than the courts has first-instance jurisdiction, and here too the courts are arguably best placed to resolve the dispute.[69]

Given the deep entrenchment of the standard of review analysis and jurisdictional review in Canadian administrative law, it is doubtful that the preceding argument for severe judicial restraint in labour and like cases will find much traction among the judiciary. Moreover, scores of administrative decision-makers (eg immigration officials, licensing bodies, social assistance decision-makers) lack the bottom-up democratic and republican credentials of labour boards. These decision-making contexts tend to pit a front-line decision-maker against the individual rather than instate a tribunal *vis-à-vis* separate parties to a dispute. In these cases, judicial review ought to take place on the basis of deference as respect (as Dyzenhaus understands it), since offering and taking reasons seriously contributes to a democratic and republican culture of public justification. Public justification promotes non-domination and thereby serves the people by making decision-makers and judges accountable to public legal standards. Although I will argue that the Court in *Dunsmuir* fails to satisfy the demands of deference as respect, its continued lip service to the idea suggests openness to its implications, at

[69] See eg *St Anne Nackawic Pulp & Paper Co Ltd v Canadian Paper Workers Union, Local 219* [1986] 1 SCR 704 (jurisdiction to assess damages resulting from an illegal strike rests with the statutory arbitral procedures, not the courts); *Saskatchewan Human Rights Commission v Cadillac Fairview Corp Ltd* (1999) 173 DLR (4th) 609 (Sask CA); *rev'g* (1998) 168 Sask R 290 (QB) (human rights board of inquiry, not collective bargaining grievance procedure, has jurisdiction to hear certain complaints of discrimination and harassment). But see Macdonald *supra* note 28: even apparently paradigmatic cases of jurisdictional review (eg review of a decision-maker who takes jurisdiction on the basis of a repealed or void statute) involve a messy consideration of the merits.

least under the standard of reasonableness. It is time now to consider these implications in light of the fiduciary view of administration.

8.6 FUNDAMENTAL VALUES

Deference as respect requires courts and agencies alike to justify their determinations. The fiduciary view of public authority offers fresh insight to the appropriate form and substance of these justifications. In this section we consider some of their substantive features, as well as the relationship between fundamental values and the fiduciary theory of administrative law. We begin with the landmark *Baker* decision that brought fundamental values to the surface of judicial review in Canada.

Recall that in *Baker* the issue was the legality of a discretionary decision made by an immigration officer charged with determining whether there were humanitarian and compassionate grounds to grant relief from a deportation order to an overstayer with Canadian-born children. Writing for the Court, L'Heureux-Dubé J set out a number of ground-breaking propositions. She held that where important interests are at stake, thicker procedural safeguards are required, and the decision-maker must provide reasons (see Chapter VII). Furthermore, as noted already, she brought review of discretion within the pragmatic and functional approach that previously had been reserved for review of agency interpretations of enabling statutes. Finally, she held that although discretionary decisions continue to merit deference, they must be made consistent with 'the boundaries imposed in the statute, the principles of the rule of law, the principles of administrative law, the fundamental values of Canadian society, and the principles of the Charter'.[70] In sum, L'Heureux-Dubé J demanded reasons that demonstrate conformity with legal standards, and thus she brought Canadian administrative law on discretion out of the legal void cast by Dicey's shadow.

In the case before her, she found that the notes of a junior immigration officer were the reasons for the decision, but they were so riddled with stereotypes and prejudice that they gave rise to a reasonable apprehension of bias. She could have disposed of the case on this ground alone, but instead proceeded to review the decision on a standard of reasonableness. Her judgment is guided by the idea that discretion must be exercised in a manner that respects the values underlying the grant of discretion as well as the fundamental values of Canadian society.[71] She found that one such

[70] *Baker, supra* note 5, para 56.

[71] See Geneviève Cartier, 'The *Baker* Effect: A New Interface Between the Canadian Charter of Rights and Freedoms and Administrative Law—The Case of Discretion' in David Dyzenhaus (ed), *The Unity of Public Law* (Oxford: Hart Publishing, 2004), p 61.

fundamental value is a concern for children's best interests, and that for the decision-maker to respect the humanitarian and compassionate values underlying the grant of discretion, he had to do more than simply indicate that he had taken those interests into account as one of many relevant (or even mandatory relevant) factors. The decision-maker 'should consider children's best interests as an important factor, *give them substantial weight*, and be alert, alive and sensitive to them'.[72] She gleaned evidence for the significance of children's best interests from a wide variety of legal sources, including the object of the legislation, ministerial guidelines, and international law (most notably, the Convention on the Rights of the Child).[73]

The lesson that emerges from *Baker* is that decision-makers must interpret and apply their statutory powers in a manner that is solicitous of important interests, and that they are entitled to consider non-statutory sources of law—such as guidelines and international law—as evidence of fundamental values protective of vulnerable interests. As we shall see now, under the fiduciary theory this evidentiary understanding of international law shields L'Heureux-Dubé J's judgment against the charge raised in the partial dissent of Iacobucci and Cory JJ. The dissenters objected that reliance on the Convention undermines the separation of powers. They worried that by invoking the Convention to interpret the scope of the discretionary power, Baker would be able to bring the Convention in through the 'backdoor', and thereby effectively confer on the executive illegitimate law-making powers.[74]

On the fiduciary view, however, the decision-maker's obligation to be 'alert, alive, and sensitive' to the best interests of Baker's children does not arise from the Convention or its ratification. It arises from the fiduciary relationship between the decision-maker and the individual. Yet the Convention remains relevant because it provides compelling evidence of a relevant fundamental value, ie a concern for children's best interests. This fundamental value signals the presence of an important interest capable of forming the subject matter of a fiduciary obligation (see Chapter IV). The obligation is the decision-maker's duty to be 'alert, alive, and sensitive' to the best interests of Baker's children.

[72] *Baker*, *supra* note 6, para 75 (emphasis added).

[73] Ibid, paras 69–74. At the heart of the appeal in *Baker* was the question of whether the decision-maker had to treat the best interests of Baker's children as a 'primary consideration', as per Art 3 of the Convention on the Rights of the Child, 20 November 1989, 1577 UNTS 3 (entered into force 2 September 1990) (Convention). The courts at all levels held that the Convention was ratified but unimplemented in domestic law, and therefore of no direct effect. Armand de Mestral and I challenge this assumption in Armand De Mestral and Evan Fox-Decent, 'Implementation and Reception: The Congeniality of Canada's Legal Order to International Law' in Oonagh E Fitzgerald and Elisabeth Eid (eds), *The Globalized Rule of Law: Relationships between International and Domestic Law* (Toronto: Irwin Law, 2006), p 31.

[74] *Baker*, *supra* note 5, para 78.

The contribution of the fiduciary theory is brought out by the inability of fundamental values, by themselves, to explain or justify how a legal obligation may be owed by a particular decision-maker to a particular individual. Fundamental values express merely abstract normative principles, and abstract principles alone cannot establish obligations, let alone legal obligations. For example, it does not follow from the principle that I should generally keep my promises that I owe someone in particular a duty to keep a promise. I would actually have to make a promise, and thereby place myself in a promissory relationship with the promisee, to be subject to a promissory duty. This is reflected in the private law doctrine of privity of contract: one must be a party to a contract to owe a contractual obligation. Similarly, it does not follow from the principle that children's best interests are of fundamental concern that any action is required of particular decision-makers in the absence of an actual relationship with particular children. The idea of a fiduciary relationship between the decision-maker and the affected children in *Baker* thus explains how an abstract concern for children's welfare can become a legal norm that requires the decision-maker to be 'alert, alive, and sensitive' to the best interests of Baker's children.

Put simply, the fiduciary model lets us explain how fundamental values can underlie and inform legal norms that regulate the interpretation and exercise of statutory powers. In *Baker* the space between the value and the norm is not especially apparent, since L'Heureux-Dubé J frequently expressed the value of children's best interests in conjunction with an imperative, insisting that immigration officials must take those interests seriously. But an earlier dissenting judgment of hers in *Mossop* lets us see plainly the space between values and norms that the fiduciary model helps to bridge.

Mossop turned on an issue of statutory interpretation. The majority of the Court held that 'family status', a prohibited ground of discrimination under the Canadian Human Rights Act, could not be interpreted to protect the partner of a same sex-couple from discriminatory treatment. Mossop, a federal government employee, had been denied bereavement leave on the grounds that such leave was available to common law spouses only, and the governing collective agreement defined 'common law spouse' as persons of the opposite sex. Sheila Wildeman points out that the concurring majority judgments of Lamer CJ and La Forest J adopted a 'positivist approach to statutory interpretation' which relied on an originalist view of legislative intent.[75] For the majority writers, the legislature did not intend to extend protection to same-sex couples because sexual orientation had been left out

[75] Sheila Wildeman, 'A Fine Romance? The Modern Standards of Review in Theory and Practice' in C Flood and L Sossin (eds), *Administrative Law in Context* (Toronto: Emond Montgomery, 2008), p 239.

of the prohibited grounds of the Act, and because the 'usual and ordinary sense' of 'family' in Canada, La Forest J said, is the 'traditional family'.[76]

L'Heureux-Dubé J, however, insisted that the point of human rights statutes is to ensure equality, and that there are statute-independent 'fundamental principles' that must be at the forefront of the interpretation of human rights codes.[77] In other words, she subscribes to a common law constitution that contains fundamental values expressive of human rights, such as equality, and she believes these values are to guide statutory interpretation. Interpretations of contested terms that promote such values are to be preferred, while explicit language will be required if the statute is to be interpreted in a manner that restricts or infringes them. This principle of statutory interpretation is the obverse formulation of the clear statement principle according to which judges will read down a general statutory provision relied upon by public authorities to infringe rights or important interests.[78]

With the clear statement principle and its obverse formulation from *Mossop* in place, it may appear that the work the fiduciary theory intends to do has already been done. Yet cases such as *Mossop* demonstrate that many judges are reluctant to depart from their favoured interpretation of the original intent of the legislature, and others still are reluctant to move beyond their understanding of the 'usual and ordinary' meaning of statutory words. Now, it would be naïve to think that any theory of common law constitutionalism might convert a committed originalist, but the fiduciary idea both strengthens L'Heureux-Dubé J's argument and exposes the majority's error.

As public fiduciaries, tribunals and judges are legally required to endeavour to interpret statutes in a manner solicitous of the well-being of the people subject to them. As discussed in Chapters I and VI, fiduciaries must exercise their entrusted powers in what they reasonably regard as the best interests of their beneficiaries. This requirement is especially demanding when there are no significant competing interests, as was the case in *Mossop*.

Statutes regulate the relationship between the administration and the people subject to its powers. Recall that in the Aboriginal context literal interpretations

[76] *Mossop, supra* note 50, pp 580–2 (Lamer CJ, Sopinka, and Iacobucci JJ concurring); pp 585–6 (La Forest J, Iacobucci J concurring).

[77] Ibid, p 585.

[78] The clear statement principle is sometimes referred to as 'the principle of legality'. A much-cited example of the principle is found in the judgment of Lord Hoffman in *R v Secretary for the Home Department, Ex parte Simms* [2000] 2 AC 115, HL (Eng), p 131: 'The principle of legality means that Parliament must squarely confront what it is doing and accept the political cost. Fundamental rights cannot be overridden by general or ambiguous words. This is because there is too great a risk that the full implications of their unqualified meaning may have passed unnoticed in the democratic process. In the absence of express language or necessary implication to the contrary, the courts therefore presume that even the most general words were intended to be subject to the basic rights of the individual'.

of treaties are to be avoided, ambiguities are to be resolved in favour of the Aboriginal party, and it is an error of law to disregard these and other like principles (see Chapter II). If the administration and the judiciary stand in a fiduciary relationship to non-Aboriginals as well as Aboriginals, as I contend, then they are under an obligation to interpret positive law in a large and liberal fashion solicitous of important interests, such as the interest in equality protected under human rights legislation. Thus, in the context of statutory interpretation as well as discretion, the fiduciary model explains how fundamental values such as equality can inform legal norms supportive of them.

L'Heureux-Dubé J's judgments in *Baker* and *Mossop*, of course, do not mention or otherwise rely explicitly on the fiduciary theory defended here. But they can be read to presuppose such a theory, and once they are so read, the emptiness of concerns regarding the separation of powers and legislative intent becomes apparent.

It bears emphasizing that taking account of fundamental values and important interests does not guarantee the individual a favourable outcome. There may be countervailing considerations, or the circumstances may be such that an ordinarily relevant fundamental value is not relevant (suppose Baker were a recidivist criminal or her children were estranged). Solicitude to the vulnerable interests of an affected individual does not entail indifference to the public interest. The relationship between the state and the affected individual does not always map neatly onto a distinction between the strong and the weak: sometimes the public may be the vulnerable party *vis-à-vis* concentrations of private power, such as the power held by financial institutions, manufacturers, and other large corporations. For this reason, some governmental agencies, such as regulators, stand in a quasi-adversarial relationship to the entities they regulate. Leckey argues convincingly that in these cases and others the desirable relationship between the administration and the people is one that maintains a 'respectful distance'.[79] But even from a respectful distance, decision-makers can still be asked to justify their decisions in light of both fundamental values and the views and interests of the affected party. We consider now the structure or form appropriate to such a justification under the fiduciary theory.

8.7 PUBLIC JUSTIFICATION

The most familiar justificatory framework in Canadian public law is the proportionality test developed in *R v Oakes*[80] (the '*Oakes* test') to review the

[79] Leckey, *supra* note 58, p 236. See generally, ibid, pp 220–40.

[80] *R v Oakes* [1986] 1 SCR 103 (*Oakes*).

constitutional validity of legislation under s 1 of the Charter. Section 1 guarantees the rights and freedoms set out in the Charter 'subject only to such reasonable limits prescribed by law as can be demonstrably justified in a free and democratic society'.[81] The *Oakes* test asks first whether the impugned legislation pursues a pressing and substantial objective, and, assuming that it does, proceeds to the issue of whether the means employed to achieve the objective are proportional to the end sought. Under this branch of the test, courts will review whether the means are rationally connected to the objective, whether they minimally impair the infringed right, and whether on balance the benefit flowing from the legislation outweighs the harm caused by the rights infringement. Majorities of the Supreme Court have since declared that this is the analytical framework to be used to review administrative decisions that clearly infringe Charter rights.[82] In the leading case on this issue, Dickson CJ held that the Charter framework was preferable because review under administrative law principles 'rests to a large extent on unarticulated and undeveloped values and lacks the same degree of structure and sophistication of analysis'.[83]

Interestingly, the *Oakes* test resembles an approach developed elsewhere. It is virtually identical to the proportionality aspect of the analytical framework the Court later developed in *R v Sparrow*[84] to review the legality of legislation and administrative action that infringes Aboriginal rights protected under s 35 of the Constitution Act 1982.[85] In *Sparrow*, the Court derived the proportionality test from the fiduciary position of the Crown without reference to *Oakes*, and acknowledged that 'the justificatory standard to be met may place a heavy burden on the Crown'.[86] In other words, because the Crown is in a fiduciary relationship with Aboriginal peoples, the Crown must satisfy an *Oakes*-like proportionality test if its actions impair their rights. So, implicit in the fiduciary position of the Crown is an obligation to justify the exercise of public power within the analytical framework supplied by the principle of proportionality.

[81] Charter, *supra* note 68, s 1.

[82] *Slaight, supra* note 6; *Multani v Commission scolaire Marguerite-Bourgeoys* [2006] 1 SCR 256.

[83] *Slaight, supra* note 6, para 11.

[84] *R v Sparrow* [1990] 1 SCR 1075 (*Sparrow*). See Chapter II (2.2). The test in *Sparrow* also requires the Crown to consult and accommodate Aboriginal peoples, and to give their constitutional rights (eg the right to fish for food) priority over non-Aboriginal statutory and common law rights.

[85] Constitution Act 1982, being Sch B to the Canada Act 1982 (UK), 1982, c 11, s 35(1) (Constitution Act 1982).

[86] *Sparrow, supra* note 84, para 81. The Charter encompasses ss 1–33 of the Constitution Act 1982, and thus s 1 does not apply to s 35. For argument that the Court went too far by permitting *Oakes*-type justifications of infringements of s 35 rights, see the dissent of McLachlin J (as she then was) in *R v Van der Peet* [1996] 2 SCR 507, paras 308–21.

Now, common law courts historically have not used proportionality to review administrative action.[87] The absence of proportionality may account for Dickson CJ's claim in *Slaight* that administrative law lacks the 'structure and sophistication' of review under the *Charter*. Nonetheless, many Canadian jurists have noted that the values underlying the *Charter* and administrative law are the same, and that their respective methodologies have grown closer over time.[88] Geneviève Cartier fruitfully suggests that '*Baker* proposes a methodology and an understanding of the rule of law that lay down the foundations for the development of a relationship that is likely to ensure cross-fertilisation between the Charter and administrative law'.[89]

The fiduciary theory points to just such a possible site of cross-fertilization. If proportionality flows from the fiduciary position of the Crown in the First Nations case, then there is reason to think that the same justificatory structure (or significant aspects of it) should apply when decision-makers, as public fiduciaries, justify administrative action capable of adversely affecting important interests. Naturally, the extent of the justification required would vary with context, bearing in mind the cost and burden of providing detailed reasons, and the relative importance of the interest at stake. And no doubt there are polycentric decision-making contexts and others where proportionality will not be appropriate.[90] But the spread of proportionality through administrative decision-making, even if it necessarily took an abbreviated form in many cases, would help to bring fundamental values such as equality to the surface, and would let the affected individual know that her views and interests had been seriously considered.

[87] But see Paul Craig, 'Unreasonableness and Proportionality in UK Law' in Evelyn Ellis (ed), *The Principle of Proportionality in the Laws of Europe* (Oxford: Hart Publishing, 1999). Craig suggests that proportionality had been a quiet but steady part of UK reasonableness review prior to the UK Human Rights Act (1998) which brought the European Convention on Human Rights into UK municipal law, and with it the proportionality doctrine. See also *Dunsmuir, supra* note 51, para 151, Binnie J, observing that '[i]n some cases, the court will have to recognize that the decision maker was required to strike a proper balance (or achieve proportionality) between the adverse impact of a decision on the rights and interests of the applicant or others directly affected weighed against the public purpose which is sought to be advanced'. To the extent that proportionality already implicitly governs administrative law, in Canada and elsewhere, the argument in the text can be read as an argument in favour of making the commitment to proportionality more explicit.

[88] See eg Cartier, *supra* note 71; John M Evans, 'The Principles of Fundamental Justice: The Constitution and the Common Law' (1991) 29 Osgoode Hall LJ 51, 92: 'The Charter has undermined the artificial barriers that have for too long separated administrative and constitutional law, and revealed the concerns and methodology that they share as components of our public law'. Evan Fox-Decent, 'The Charter and Administrative Law: Cross-Fertilization in Public Law' in C Flood and L Sossin (eds), *Administrative Law in Context* (Toronto: Emond Montgomery, 2008).

[89] Cartier, *supra* note 71, p 63.

[90] See Tom Hickman, *Public Law after the UK Human Rights Act* (Oxford: Hart Publishing, 2010), ch 6, pp 183–4.

Crucially, under proportionality review, important interests establish the justificatory threshold that decision-makers must cross to exercise powers or interpret open-textured statutory provisions in a manner that impairs those interests. The fiduciary model explains the centrality of important interests to public justification because those very interests are the subject matter of the public and solicitous fiduciary obligation of reasonable decision-making.

8.8 FUNDAMENTAL VALUES AND DEFERENCE AS RESPECT CUT DOWN

The focus on *Baker* and fundamental values up to this point may give the impression that Canadian judges no longer call on a formal separation-of-powers doctrine at the expense of important interests. In fact they continue to do so. In this final section we consider two unanimous judgments delivered since *Baker* that evince backsliding towards, on the one hand, the legal void conception of discretion, and on the other, interventionist review that fails to take seriously *CUPE*'s message of deference. The two decisions are *Suresh v Canada (Minister of Citizenship and Immigration)*[91] and *Dunsmuir*. As with the discussion of *Dunsmuir* in the previous chapter, these cases reveal the continued pull of the separation of powers, and how fundamental values and important interests may be lost in the absence of an underlying theory that explains why judges are under an obligation to take them seriously.

Suresh involved a Tamil refugee claimant with alleged ties to a terrorist organization. He faced deportation and a serious risk of torture upon his return. Under the relevant immigration legislation, the Minister had discretionary authority to declare Suresh to be a danger to the security of Canada and order him deported, even if Suresh's life and freedom were threatened by the return. On review, a unanimous Court (including L'Heureux-Dubé J) determined that the standard of review applicable to the Minister's decision to declare Suresh a danger was not the standard of reasonableness *simpliciter*, as it had been in *Baker*, but rather the most deferential standard, patent unreasonableness. Whereas L'Heureux-Dubé J in *Baker* had pointed to the purposes of the statute, ministerial guidelines and international law to buttress her claim that children's best interests must be taken very seriously in the deportation context, the Court in *Suresh* explicitly rejected the idea that reviewing courts should inquire into the weight or significance of the relevant factors that go into a discretionary decision.[92] Thus, the Court left it for the Minister alone to

[91] 2002 SCC 1; [2002] 1 SCR 3 (*Suresh*).

[92] Ibid, para 37: '*Baker* does not authorize courts reviewing decisions on the discretionary end of the spectrum to engage in a new weighing process, but draws on an established line of cases concerning the

weigh, almost as a law unto himself, the significance of Suresh's interest in security from torture against the alleged danger he posed to Canada.

The Court ultimately allowed the appeal on grounds of procedural fairness. And, prior to its discussion of procedural fairness, the Court held that generally (but not necessarily always) s 7 of the Charter would preclude deporting a person to torture. The Court did not specify the exceptional circumstances in which deportation to torture might be allowable under s 7. In non-exceptional cases a decision to deport will turn on whether the Minister can establish that there is no serious risk of torture. The Court insisted that in such cases the Minister must provide responsive written reasons that 'articulate and rationally sustain' a finding that there are no substantial grounds to believe that torture will occur.[93] But the plea for responsive reasons came only after the Court established that it would review the actual decision to deport on a standard of patent unreasonableness.The Court justified this renewed commitment to the law-unto-themselves view of discretion on familiar separation-of-power grounds, effacing the idea that important interests subject to public power have legal significance.[94] Similarly absent was any reference to the non-statutory constraints on discretion that played such a prominent role in *Baker*, such as the rule of law, the principles of administrative law, and fundamental values. This is not surprising, because without a theory to underscore the significance of vulnerable practical interests, fundamental values and rule-of-law constraints that serve those interests have no sure footing.[95]

failure of ministerial delegates to consider and weigh implied limitations and/or patently relevant factors'.

[93] Ibid, para 126. [94] Ibid, para 38.

[95] *Canada (Citizenship and Immigration) v Khosa* 2009 SCC 12; [2009] 1 SCR 339 (*Khosa*) continues the retreat from *Baker* signalled by *Suresh*. In *Khosa*, Binnie J, for the majority (Fish J dissenting), upheld a decision of the Immigration Appeal Board (IAB) that rejected an application for discretionary relief from a deportation order on humanitarian and compassionate grounds. Khosa, a permanent resident who immigrated to Canada at age 14, had been convicted of criminal negligence causing death following a car accident for which he was responsible. He was 18 when the accident occurred. In a 2–1 decision, four years after the accident, the IAB refused to grant him relief. Khosa had an immaculate criminal and driving record before and after the accident, as well as supportive documents from employers, his parole officer, and the criminal sentencing judge. The IAB majority refused relief because Khosa would not admit that the accident arose from street racing. Four years later, Binne J reversed the Federal Court of Appeal, deferring to the IAB on grounds that courts are not entitled to reweigh relevant factors. He declined to consider whether statutory purposes, fundamental values, or international law were relevant to the legality of the IAB's decision, notwithstanding that the Act in question stipulates that it must be 'construed and applied in a manner that... complies with international human rights instruments to which Canada is a signatory', Immigration and Refugee Protection Act, SC 2001, c 27, s 3. In particular, Binnie J failed to discuss whether refusing relief was lawful in these circumstances given Canada's ratification of the International Covenant on Civil and Political Rights, Art 23 of which protects the right to family life.

In the previous chapter we saw that the lack of such a theory explains the Court's removal of procedural fairness from employment law in *Dunsmuir*. The Court's review of the merits in that case is also instructive for what it tells us about the direction substantive review may take when conducted without regard to fundamental values and important interests. Recall that in *Dunsmuir* a New Brunswick civil servant was dismissed with pay in lieu of notice, and without a hearing. Dunsmuir grieved his termination before an adjudicator appointed under the PSLRA, which stipulates that '[w]here an adjudicator determines that an employee has been discharged or disciplined for cause . . . the adjudicator may substitute such other penalty for the discharge or the discipline as to the adjudicator seems just and reasonable in all the circumstances'.[96] Dunsmuir alleged that he had in reality been dismissed for cause and was entitled to grieve his dismissal and seek reinstatement. As a preliminary matter, the government challenged the authority of the adjudicator to assess the reasons behind Dunsmuir's termination, insisting that it did not have to show cause because Dunsmuir was dismissed with pay in lieu of notice rather than for cause. The adjudicator ruled against the government, finding that s 97(2.1) of the PSLRA empowered him to consider the reasons for dismissal. He held that the province could not avoid an inquiry into cause by simply stating that cause was not alleged.

The Court determined that the standard of review was reasonableness, and that the adjudicator's decision was unreasonable and had to be set aside. Bastarache and LeBel JJ, for the majority, found that contract law governed termination, per s 20 of the Civil Service Act,[97] and that under contract law employers do not have to show cause if they choose to dismiss with notice or pay in lieu. In essence, they objected to the adjudicator's interpretation of the PSLRA because, they claimed, it 'treated the appellant, a non-unionized employee, as a unionized employee', and thus created 'a requirement that the employer show cause before dismissal'.[98]

As David Mullan rightly observes, however, Bastarache and LeBel JJ mischaracterize and overstate the adjudicator's interpretation of his powers.[99] The adjudicator's ruling, Mullan says, may be read as asserting that non-unionized employees dismissed for cause, whether alleged or actual, are entitled to grieve and seek reinstatement if the purported cause does not justify dismissal. Thus, the employer cannot immunize from grievance proceedings a dismissal that in reality was for cause by simply

[96] PSLRA, *supra* note 22, s 97(2.1).

[97] Civil Service Act, SNB 1984, c C-5.1, s 20: 'Subject to the provisions of this Act or any other Act, termination of the employment of a deputy head or an employee shall be governed by the ordinary rules of contract'.

[98] *Dunsmuir, supra* note 51, para 75.

[99] Mullan, *supra* note 61, pp 137–40.

declaring that the dismissal was not for cause. The employer would still be entitled to dismiss with notice or pay in lieu (an option not available under most collective agreements), but with the qualification that the dismissal may be grieved to determine whether the dismissal was in reality for cause. Certainly on its face s 97(2.1) is open to this interpretation, beginning as it does with the words '[w]here an adjudicator determines that an employee has been discharged or disciplined for cause . . .'. Furthermore, under s 20 of the Civil Service Act, the contract regime is '[s]ubject to the provisions of this Act *or any other Act*',[100] thus enabling s 97(2.1) to operate as the adjudicator claimed.

Although the Court in *Dunsmuir* explicitly reaffirmed its commitment to *CUPE*'s message of deference, the standard of review under *CUPE* (and later under the pragmatic and functional approach) would have been patent unreasonableness. While the Court insisted that its jettisoning of this most deferential standard is not an invitation for more searching review, Mullan's analysis of *Dunsmuir* shows that it is a stretch to characterize the adjudicator's interpretation of the statute as unreasonable. It would have required a further distortion of language to call it patently unreasonable. The Court relieved itself of this burden by eliminating patent unreasonableness as a standard of review, all on the back of the very statutory scheme that produced *CUPE*. Notwithstanding the theoretical difficulties in distinguishing reasonableness from patent unreasonableness, *Dunsmuir* warns that the loss of patent unreasonableness may lead to greater judicial intervention in labour law.

Recall too that the Court reaffirmed its commitment to deference as respect. We have seen, however, that Dyzenhaus' theory requires more than just respectful attention to the reasons offered for the decision. Reviewing courts are also supposed to attend to the reasons that *could* be offered for the decision, such as the reasons Mullan adduces in support of the adjudicator's preliminary ruling. Moreover, Bastarache and LeBel JJ held that '[i]n judicial review, reasonableness is concerned mostly with the existence of justification, transparency and intelligibility within the decision-making process', and that so far as review of the outcome is concerned, the issue is 'whether the decision falls within a range of possible, acceptable outcomes which are defensible in respect of the facts and law'.[101] The puzzle is explaining why the Court concluded that the adjudicator's preliminary ruling, one that is arguably 'defensible in respect of the facts and law', fell outside the range of possible outcomes.

[100] Civil Service Act, s 20 (emphasis added).

[101] *Dunsmuir*, *supra* note 51, para 47.

Dunsmuir is good grist for the mill of left-leaning scholars who may read the case as further evidence of judicial hostility to labour law. One will search the case in vain to find any reference to the underlying purpose of the PSLRA and labour law generally—remedying inequality of bargaining power between employers and employees. The remedial purpose of labour law draws on a fundamental value, substantive equality, which is also absent from the Court's interpretation of the PSLRA. One might think that the Court is implicitly relying on another fundamental value—autonomy—and that this value explains the Court's celebration of contract in *Dunsmuir*, as well as its unwillingness to defer. However, where labour legislation is in play, substantive equality arguably takes precedence over contractual freedom, since the very point of the legislation is to limit or modify contractual freedom to protect vulnerable employees.

The argument in favour of privileging equality can be understood in a number of ways. It can be understood as a formal requirement that decision-makers and judges must respect simply because the legislature has commanded them to do so through its enactment of equality-driven labour legislation. The argument can also be understood substantively, as deriving from the rationale for enacting labour law in the first place, ie the protection of vulnerable and important employment interests otherwise subject to employer domination. Many, but as *Dunsmuir* reveals, judges who view public employment as an exclusively contractual relationship are unlikely to be moved by either the formal or substantive arguments.

The fiduciary theory contributes a legal argument in favour of substantive equality that may fare better than the others (assuming, perhaps implausibly, that the commitment to contract is not incorrigibly ideological) because it operates on the same plane as claims about the exclusively contractual nature of public employment. The fiduciary and contractual ideas both ask after the nature of the legal relationship between the parties. Recall that Bastarache and LeBel JJ begin their analysis of procedural fairness with the proposition that '[w]hat matters is the nature of the employment relationship between the public employee and the public employer'.[102]

I argued in the previous chapter that employees in public service are especially vulnerable to public power, and that as a consequence they are owed a public fiduciary duty of procedural fairness prior to dismissal. Implicit in the duty of fairness, I said, is a right to security against arbitrary removal. Public authorities, as fiduciaries, must treat their employees' interest in continued employment with a measure of solicitude, and solicitude precludes arbitrary dismissal. By the same token, the employment interest

[102] Ibid, para 81.

merits solicitude when decision-makers and judges interpret statutory provisions that bear upon it. So interpretations that protect employees against arbitrary dismissal are to be preferred, first, because public fiduciaries owe solicitude to the people subject to their power, and second, because such interpretations conform with the common law right to security against arbitrary removal implicit in the duty of fairness. All of this flows from a proper understanding of the fiduciary character of 'the nature of the employment relationship between the public employee and the public employer'. Thus the legal significance of substantive equality and important interests is revealed as a deep normative commitment intrinsic to labour law.

8.9 CONCLUSION

I have advanced two main arguments to flesh out some of the implications of the fiduciary conception of public law. First, I claimed that agencies with 'bottom-up' democratic credentials and a republican, rule-of-law-installing mandate, such as labour boards, deserve to have a privileged say over interpretations of their constitutive statutes. In these contexts, near total deference surfaces as a postulate of the rule of law because deference helps the rule of law to enter and promote non-domination in labour relations.

Assuming, however, that this message is unlikely to be heeded, that judicial review is warranted in other contexts, and that agencies and courts alike are under an obligation to justify their determinations, I argued, secondly, that the fiduciary theory provides valuable guidance to the appropriate form and substance of public justification. Building on lessons taken from First Nations jurisprudence, I argued that the principle of proportionality should be expressly incorporated into Canadian administrative law. I also argued that the fiduciary theory strengthens the call from *Baker* to take fundamental values seriously, and that it explains other rule-of-law constraints on discretion as justification-guiding principles that respond to the legal significance of important interests subject to public power. Similarly, I suggested that the fiduciary model places courts and agencies under an obligation to interpret statutes with sensitivity to fundamental values, such as equality, because these values reflect important interests to which the appropriate attitude of public authority is solicitude. Put slightly differently, solicitude is the thread that unites the values of the common law constitution within a legal order governed by the fiduciary principle.

In the concluding chapter we address contentious issues of immemorial standing in legal philosophy. Is there a necessary connection between law and morality? And if so, does the concept of law, as embodied in the rule of law, place limits on the substantive content of otherwise valid legislation? On the fiduciary understanding of legal authority, the answer to both questions is 'yes'.

IX

The Rule of Law and Human Rights

9.1 INTRODUCTION

In the previous two chapters, I argued that the administration and its various decision-makers stand in a fiduciary relationship with the people over whom they exercise delegated power. As a consequence of this relationship, public officials are legally required to exercise their powers fairly and reasonably: they must abide by the duties of procedural fairness and reasonable decision-making. But to say that officials must exercise their delegated powers fairly and reasonably tells us nothing about the permissible content or goals of their authorizing legislation. The principal aim of this chapter is to show that legislatures as well as administrative bodies stand in a fiduciary relationship with their people. As a consequence, they cannot empower officials to engage in gross violations of human rights, and lesser infringements will require justification. Put another way, the fiduciary relationship between the state and the people places substantive constraints on legislative power, constraints which are best understood as constitutive elements of the rule of law.

This is, of course, a highly controversial interpretation of the rule of law. A broad range of scholars contend that the rule of law is indifferent to human rights. As Joseph Raz puts it, the rule of law 'is not to be confused with democracy, justice, equality (before the law or otherwise), human rights of any kind, or respect for persons, or for the dignity of man'.[1] Raz underscores the point a few pages later: '[t]he law may, for example, institute slavery without violating the rule of law'.[2] Let us call the view that the rule of law is compatible with slavery and other violations of human rights the 'no-rights thesis'.

One might be tempted to think that the no-rights thesis is limited to positivists such as Raz who view law and the rule of law in strictly

[1] Joseph Raz, 'The Rule of Law and Its Virtue', *The Authority of Law: Essays on Law and Morality* (Oxford: Clarendon Press, 1979), p 211.

[2] Ibid.

instrumental terms, and lacking any necessary connection to morality. Yet some of Raz's critics support the no-rights thesis as well. Colleen Murphy argues against Raz, claiming that the rule of law has non-instrumental moral value,[3] but she nonetheless thinks that respecting human rights is not part of the ideal. She adopts the no-rights thesis because she accepts Raz's premise that the primary function of law is to guide behaviour, a function that the rule of law helps the law to perform. She then infers that '[r]especting rights is not a precondition for guiding behaviour'.[4] Law, on this view, can guide the behaviour of slaves and their masters just as well as it can guide the behaviour of fully free and autonomous legal persons.

Law can guide conduct because human beings have cognitive and volitional capacities which permit them to interpret, comprehend, and follow rules. However, merely noting a connection between the rule of law and human agency does not show, without more, that the rule of law constrains the ends to which law can be put. As Daniel Brudney observes[5]:

> [E]ven if laws are designed for and directed at human beings insofar as human beings possess certain cognitive and volitional capacities, that would still pose no bar, for instance, to slave laws. For there is no conceptual link (no obvious one, anyway) between the possession of the relevant capacities and being a source of 'strong' moral claims—that is, a source of moral claims sufficient to preclude such things as being enslaved.

Although the conceptual link may not be obvious, I will argue that the fiduciary relationship between lawgiver and legal subject allows us to see it.

The no-rights thesis reflects an additional theme that runs through the literature, the idea that the rule of law goes to the manner in which laws are formulated and enforced rather than to the substantive content of particular laws. On this understanding, a baldly discriminatory statute would not violate the rule of law on account of its discriminatory substance, whereas any statute may infringe the rule of law if it authorizes retroactive sanctions,

[3] Colleen Murphy, 'Lon Fuller and the Moral Value of the Rule of Law' (2005) 24 Law & Phil 239. For a similar conditional argument which denies a necessary or conceptual connection between the rule of law and morality, but recognizes that the rule of law may have some substantive moral consequences within societies sufficiently attuned to liberal values (such as western liberal democracies), see Daniel Brudney, 'Two Links of Law and Morality' (1993) 103 *Ethics* 280.

[4] Murphy, *supra* note 3, p 262. There is widespread support for the idea that the purpose of the rule of law is to help the law guide human conduct. For Raz, '[t]his is the basic intuition from which the doctrine of the rule of law derives: the law must be capable of guiding the behaviour of its subject'. Raz, *supra* note 1, p 214. See also Andrei Marmor, 'The Rule of Law and Its Limits' (2004) 24 Law & Phil 1, p 5; Margaret Jane Radin, 'Reconsidering the Rule of Law' (1989) 69 BUL Rev 781, p 785. The idea is also present in Fuller's formulation of lawgiving as 'the enterprise of subjecting human conduct to the governance of rules', Lon L Fuller, *The Morality of Law*, revised edn (New Haven: Yale University Press, 1969), p 96.

[5] Brudney, *supra* note 3, p 285.

or if its provisions are not made public, or if it is excessively vague. In this sense, the rule of law is widely taken to be formal rather than substantive in nature.[6] The basic idea that compels allegiance to formal rather than substantive constraints is that to go beyond the formal is to confuse the rule of law with the rule of *good* law. We should not give credit to the rule of law—nor cloak political arguments with rule of law apparel—when liberal political values such as liberty and equality are the values doing the heavy lifting.[7] Thus, in addition to the notion that the principal function of law is to guide conduct and that this purpose can be fulfilled without reference to law's substantive morality, the no-rights thesis seems to follow from a form/substance distinction which is driven by a concern for analytic clarity.

As we shall see, the arguments in support of the no-rights thesis are unconvincing. They would be persuasive only in the absence of a substantive account of the rule of law capable of showing that the rule of law, properly understood, involves a commitment to human rights, including freedom from slavery. I defend such an account below. While some overlap with liberal political morality is inevitable, the conception of the rule of law under consideration trades on moral precepts intrinsic to law, and so does not collapse the ideal into an undifferentiated affirmation of liberal political morality.

The inspiration for this conception comes from two related ideas taken from Lon L Fuller. The first is his 'internal morality of law', a set of formal constraints and desiderata that apply to legislation and administration, and which safeguard the subject from certain forms of domination and abuse. The best justification for the internal morality, I argue, is based on a Kantian conception of human agency that, in the relevant circumstances, has substantive implications for human rights.

The second idea concerns the relevant circumstances to which I have just referred. These circumstances are all those in which lawgivers and legal subjects interact with one another. These include a legislature passing legislation, a judge deciding a case, or a police officer directing traffic. But the interaction flows in the other direction as well. In democratic states the people influence law through public institutions such as town hall meetings,

[6] See Paul Craig, 'Formal and Substantive Conceptions of the Rule or Law' (1997) PL 467. For some contemporary defences of substantive conceptions of the rule of law, or at least conceptions which seek to draw substantive implications from the rule of law's formal requirements, see TRS Allan, *Constitutional Justice: A Liberal Theory of the Rule of Law* (Oxford: Oxford University Press, 2003); David Dyzenhaus, 'Hobbes and the Legitimacy of Law' (2001) 20 Law & Phil 461; John Finnis, *Natural Law and Natural Rights* (Oxford: Oxford University Press, 1980); Jennifer Nadler, 'Hart, Fuller and the Connection between Law and Justice' (2007) 27 Law & Phil 1; Kristen Rundle, 'The Impossibility of an Exterminatory Legality: Law and the Holocaust' (2009) 59 UTLJ 65; Nigel E Simmonds, *Law as a Moral Idea* (Oxford: Oxford University Press, 2007).

[7] Roughly, this is Craig's main argument: Craig, *supra* note 6.

public hearings, petitions, marches, the media, and elections. The people also make a valuable contribution to the fabric of legal order by simply living in a world in which they must interpret legal norms and, in light of their interpretations, govern their interactions with others and the state.[8] These interactional dimensions of legal order, Fuller claims, reveal that lawgivers and legal subjects stand in a relationship of reciprocity to one another.

This relationship of reciprocity, I claim, has an important fiduciary dimension we have already explored in some detail: the state is a fiduciary of its people. The fiduciary nature of the relationship places lawgivers under a legal as well as a moral obligation to respect the agency of the people subject to their powers. The content of the obligation is to govern in accordance with the rule of law. And the rule of law, properly understood, involves a commitment to human rights.

Part of the forthcoming argument is interpretive in that it seeks to provide the best interpretation of what Fuller took to be the theoretical underpinnings of the internal morality of law. Fuller was at times profoundly ambivalent. His most famous illustration of the internal morality is the story of a bumbling monarch, Rex. Rex, as both legislator and judge, failed to make law that his subjects could obey by failing to adhere to the principles of the internal morality.[9] Because Fuller cast Rex's failure mainly in terms of an inability to establish rules capable of obedience, he was easy prey for positivists such as Hart and Raz. They would later claim that the internal morality is not really a morality at all, but merely a description of the requirements of efficacy that any system of rules must meet to function as a system of rules capable of guiding conduct.[10] Put slightly differently, the positivist claim is that although the principles of the internal morality may succeed in specifying certain minimal conditions that must to some degree be satisfied for a set of rules to count as a legal system, there is no reason to think that satisfying these minimal conditions entails that the rules have morally acceptable content.

Be that as it may, I argue that subscription to the internal morality, as a conceptual matter, entails that there is necessarily something morally good about the kind of order—legal order—that the internal morality makes possible. This anti-positivist argument flows from the justification of the internal

[8] For insightful discussion of the significance of these interactional aspects of legal order, see Roderick Macdonald, *Lessons of Everyday Law* (Montreal: Published for the Law Commission of Canada and the School of Policy Studies, Queen's University by McGill-Queen's University Press, 2002); Roderick Macdonald, 'Here, There and Everywhere . . . Theorizing Legal Pluralism; Theorizing Jacques Vanderlinden' in N Kasirer (ed), *Mélanges Jacques Vanderlinden* (Montreal: Yvon Blais, 2006).

[9] Fuller, *supra* note 4, pp 33–8.

[10] HLA Hart, 'Review of the Morality of Law' (1965) 78 Harv L Rev 1281, pp 1285–6, as reproduced in HLA Hart, *Essays in Jurisprudence and Philosophy* (Oxford: Oxford University Press, 1983), p 350.

morality noted above. This justification is agency-based: it conceives of individuals as sources of legal and moral claims in virtue of their agency and the legal relationships in which they find themselves. Given the reciprocal and fiduciary relationship that exists between lawgiver and legal subject, a set of conclusions follows: a commitment to the internal morality entails respect for human agency; respect for human agency entails respect for human dignity; and respect for human dignity entails respect for human rights.

9.2 THE INTERNAL MORALITY AND THE FIDUCIARY INTERPRETATION OF RECIPROCITY

Most writers take Fuller's eight canons of the internal morality of law to comprise the content of the rule of law, or at least a significant component of it.[11] The first principle is the most elemental: lawgivers should strive to use general rules rather than *ad hoc* or particularized commands. To subject human conduct to the governance of rules, some rules must exist. These rules, generally speaking, are to be made public, clear, prospective, relatively constant over time, possible to obey, and consistent with one another. Lastly, there should be congruence between declared rules and their application by public officials.

The principles of Fuller's internal morality are intended to reflect the requirements of legality rather than substantive demands of a particular political programme. The internal morality does not tell us whether law makers should either permit or prohibit activities over which there is little consensus, such as euthanasia, abortion, prayer in school, and so on. Nevertheless, the internal morality does have substantive implications in that it sets limits and establishes a framework within which legislation must operate, a structure that is alleged to give law a measure of moral authority by enabling it to function as law properly understood as such, rather than merely as a set of rules backed by force.

Fuller doubted, however, the contribution his theory could make to underpinning public legal duties, and considered the internal morality to be more a morality of aspiration than one of duty. As a perfectionist morality of aspiration, the internal morality seeks to identify the conditions necessary for legal order to enable persons 'to find the good life in a life shared with others'.[12] Fuller worried that reducing the internal morality to one of legal duties would

[11] See eg Allan, *supra* note 6, chs 1–3; Craig, *supra* note 6; David Dyzenhaus, 'Fuller's Novelty' in W Witteveen and W van der Burg (eds), *Rediscovering Fuller: Essays on Implicit Law and Institutional Design* (Amsterdam: Amsterdam University Press, 1999), p 78; Marmor, *supra* note 4; Murphy, *supra* note 3; Nadler, *supra* note 6; Raz, *supra* note 1; Rundle, *supra* note 6; Simmonds, *supra* note 6; Jeremy Waldron, 'Why Law—Efficacy, Freedom, or Fidelity?' (1994) 13 Law & Phil 259.

[12] Fuller, *supra* note 4, p 13.

diminish rather than enhance its effect, since legal duties enforce minimal standards that tend to be the forbearances of negative duties (do not kill, do not steal, and so on), whereas a morality of aspiration invites the pursuit of excellence and affirmative duties: make the law clear, coherent, prospective, and so forth. Fuller concluded that the 'inner morality of law is condemned to remain largely a morality of aspiration and not of duty. Its primary appeal must be to a sense of trusteeship and to the pride of the craftsman'.[13]

But Fuller doubted his theory's potential as a basis for public legal obligation because he did not have at his disposal (or simply overlooked) the idea of a fiduciary relationship in which to situate the reciprocal interaction between lawgiver and subject. Because the fiduciary relationship is legal in nature, it can supply the necessary conceptual structure that Fuller lacked to transform the otherwise free-floating, and non-binding, principles of the internal morality into concrete legal obligations which the state owes to its subjects. The principles of the internal morality contribute content to the rule of law, but it is not until they are situated within a legal relationship that they have the potential to give rise to legal obligations.

In Chapter IV we saw that fiduciary relationships arise if one party (the fiduciary) has discretionary power of an administrative nature over the important interests of another (the beneficiary), and the beneficiary is unable, either as a matter of fact or as a matter of law, to exercise the entrusted power. We also saw that the state, through its legislative, judicial and administrative institutions, assumes discretionary power of an administrative nature over the people affected by its power, and that its subjects, as private parties, are not entitled to exercise public powers. It follows that the state's possession of sovereign powers gives rise to a fiduciary obligation. Plausibly, the minimal content of the state's obligation is to govern in accordance with the rule of law, which for present purposes I equate with Fuller's internal morality of law.

Seeing that rule-of-law obligations have a legal character helps us to understand the sense in which the state would subvert the basis of its legal authority—its authority to announce and enforce law—if it were to violate the rule of law. As discussed in Chapter V, the state, as a fiduciary of its people, acts with legal authority if, and only if, it respects the fiduciary obligations of the rule of law that both constrain and constitute its legal authority. The fiduciary and rule-of-law obligations constitute the state's legal authority in the sense that they ensure that legal powers are used for only the other-regarding purposes for which they are held. Compliance with

[13] Ibid, p 43.

these obligations permits us to distinguish exercises of legal authority from exercises of mere power.

The fiduciary and legal nature of the state-subject relationship also explains why states do not owe rule-of-law obligations to persons unaffected by their powers ('non-subjects'). Although non-subjects are just as much human agents and bearers of human rights as the state's own subjects, the state is not in a fiduciary relationship with non-subjects, and therefore states do not owe them the rule-of-law duties they owe the people over whom they hold or exercise legal power. States may owe moral duties to non-subjects, but states do not owe them legal obligations that flow from the rule of law.[14]

Returning now to Fuller's understanding of the consequences of the internal morality of law, he thought that if a rule failed completely to live up to any one of the conditions of the internal morality, then it would fail to have moral authority, as well as practical capacity, to command the subject's obedience. In that sense, the rule would fail to be law properly so-called[15]:

> Certainly there can be no rational ground for asserting that a man can have a moral obligation to obey a legal rule that does not exist, or is kept secret from him, or that comes into existence only after he had acted, or was unintelligible, or was contradicted by another rule of the same system, or commanded the impossible, or changed every minute.

It follows that the moral authority of a legal system would be cast in doubt if its legislation and administration—or significant parts of it—systematically violated one or more of the eight principles. There would be 'a compromise of principle, an impairment of the integrity of the law'.[16] The use of secret rules and secret police to persecute political dissidents, for example, would put in question the legitimacy of a regime disposed to such tactics.

Conversely, a legal system that does conform to the eight principles may impose legal obligations which could have moral force and which therefore could be binding; the rules could be laws. But as Kenneth Winston has pointed out, even jointly the principles do not comprise a set of sufficient

[14] To clarify, 'subjects' refers to a wider class of persons than 'citizens'. I am using 'subjects' to refer to anyone affected by an exercise of state power, including non-citizens outside the state's territorial jurisdiction. The exercise of state power over an agent triggers the state's fiduciary and rule-of-law obligations, and so these obligations arise irrespective of whether the affected agent is a citizen or not. For example, detainees in Guantanamo Bay may not be American citizens, but they are subjects of the US administration, in the sense used here, and so they are protected by the rule of law *vis-à-vis* the United States. Working out the details of the extra-territorial scope of the fiduciary theory is well beyond the remit of this book, but plausibly would proceed on the assumption that international institutions must authorize foreign intervention, and that intervention would be subject to fiduciary limits. There is an obvious analogy between international law *vis-à-vis* independent states and the arbitrator *vis-à-vis* individuals in the state of nature: in both cases, the parties to a dispute cannot set the terms of its resolution.

[15] Fuller, *supra* note 4, p 39.

[16] Ibid, p 203.

conditions that guarantee the morally obligatory nature of a legal rule, for there may be countervailing substantive considerations of equal or greater weight.[17] The most that could be plausibly claimed in this regard, as discussed in Chapter V, is that a state's compliance with the rule of law gives rise to a defeasible obligation to obey the law that can be defeated if a particular law or legal regime is especially wicked. Nonetheless, the general canons of the internal morality embody a morality of role which Fuller thought applied to law-makers and administrators. That is, the internal morality guides lawgivers as they strive to fulfil their legislative, adjudicative, or administrative role within legal order. Violation of this morality undermines the legal obligation that may otherwise attach to a rule or system of rules.

Fuller claims that when lawgivers abide by the principles of the internal morality,[18]

> there is a kind of reciprocity between government and the citizen with respect to the observance of rules. Government says to the citizen in effect, 'These are the rules we expect you to follow. If you follow them, you have our assurance that they are the rules that will be applied to your conduct'.

Reciprocity is important, Fuller says, because 'maintaining a legal system in existence depends on the discharge of interlocking responsibilities—of government toward the citizen and of the citizen toward government', and so 'the citizen's voluntary cooperation must be matched by a corresponding cooperative effort on the part of the government'.[19] But Fuller does not think that the government's responsibility to the legal subject is one that can be analogized to contract.[20] Instead, he says that the state's obligations reflect interlocking but often unarticulated expectations, such as our expectation that electoral officials will count the votes we cast in favour of the candidates we indicate on the relevant ballots.[21] As Fuller points out, our underlying expectation arises from our sense that the very purpose of having electoral officials would be frustrated if they did not faithfully exercise the powers entrusted to them for the purpose for which those powers are conferred.

Now, it is possible to imagine a slave-holding society that complied with the principles of the internal morality, and in which the slaves were treated as

[17] See his Introduction in Kenneth I Winston, *The Principles of Social Order: Selected Essays of Lon L. Fuller* (Durham, NC: Duke University Press, 1981), pp 35–6.

[18] Fuller, *supra* note 4, pp 39–40.

[19] Ibid, p 216.

[20] Fuller writes: '[A]ny attempt to conceive of a legal system as resting on a contract between lawgiver and subject not only stirs inconvenient historical associations, but has a certain incongruity about it, especially when we recall that in a democratic society the same citizen may be both lawgiver and legal subject', ibid, p 217.

[21] Ibid.

fully capable of understanding the rules they had to obey to avoid punishment. In such societies it would make good sense to say that slaves and non-slaves interacted on the basis of certain interlocking (and perhaps unarticulated) expectations.[22] It is not the mere presence of such expectations, however, that is significant. What is significant is that these expectations point to a moral basis other than consent on which to ground the state's legal authority to announce and enforce law.

This idea is consistent with the structure of modern fiduciary doctrine. Fiduciary law is premised on the idea that the purpose of any relationship in which one party is entrusted and empowered to act on behalf of another would be frustrated if the authorized party could act without due regard for the other's interests and the purposes for which fiduciary power is authorized. At the core of Fuller's conception of the state-subject legal relationship, then, is an idea of reciprocity in which the participants relate to one another on a moral basis other than consent. Indeed, explicit consent cannot be the basis of the state's obligation to abide by the internal morality because some members of the state may not consent, or may reject the state's authority outright.

The relevant moral basis, as explained in Chapter IV, is trust, though not in the sense that subjects actually trust the state to comply with the rule of law. Whether they do so or not is irrelevant to the state's rule-of-law obligations because, as in all fiduciary relationships, the obligations remain regardless of whether the beneficiary has actually entrusted the fiduciary to act on her behalf. We saw in Chapter IV that the fiduciary principle covers fact situations in which the beneficiary's consent to particular exercises of the fiduciary's power is unattainable (either right from the beginning, as in the parent-child case, or subsequent to one party assuming a fiduciary position, as in the officer-corporation case). Recall that the resulting position of the fiduciary is trust-like in at least two senses. First, trust-like obligations, such as the fiduciary duty of loyalty, attach to fiduciary power because the law will not permit one party to set unilaterally the terms of its interaction with another. Where consent is unavailable, the law, via the fiduciary principle, supplies the terms through the imposition of fiduciary obligations. The fiduciary principle's capacity to impose obligations of trust on the fiduciary reveals the sense in which trust is to fiduciary relations what consent is to contractual relations: both supply a non-instrumental and

[22] Brudney deploys this example to argue that unarticulated and interlocking expectations alone cannot establish that the relationship between lawgiver and legal subject is intrinsically morally desirable: Brudney, *supra* note 3, p 284. The argument in the text below attempts to rehabilitate Fuller's argument in light of this objection.

moral basis to legal obligations appropriate to the kind of relationship they each control.

The second sense in which the position of the fiduciary can be shown to be trust-like turns on our ability to use trust to explain the fiduciary's authority to act on the beneficiary's behalf, notwithstanding that in many cases the law rather than the beneficiary entrusts the fiduciary to exercise power on behalf of the beneficiary. The beneficiary's trust may be thought of as an unarticulated and legitimate expectation that the fiduciary's powers will be exercised on her behalf and for her ends, rather than, say, for the sake of the fiduciary's ends. Thus, a breach of trust would frustrate the beneficiary's expectation, just as frustrating the expectation would constitute a breach of trust. Arguably, this is the sense in which Fuller relies on unarticulated and interlocking expectations in his discussion of electoral officials: such officials act on the basis of a public trust which embodies our expectation that they will count faithfully the votes cast. We expect that public powers will be used exclusively for proper purposes, and we consider it a betrayal of the public trust if such powers are not so used.

Fuller at times describes the lawgiver as an authorized fiduciary of the people over whom she claims legal authority. In the context of a discussion on 'making arrangements' for the freedom of the individual, he characterizes the institutional role of public authorities as one that is 'animated by a sense of trusteeship'.[23] To that end, Fuller calls on the lawgiver to accept and respect 'the fiduciary restraints' of public office.[24]

We can see now that the idea of the state as fiduciary helps to illuminate reciprocity as a characterization of a relationship based on mutual duties of loyalty. As fiduciary, the state owes a duty of loyalty to those subject to its power. The content of the state's duty is to comply with the rule of law. The people, in turn, owe loyalty to the state in that they each have a defeasible obligation to obey the law. This is a significant sense in which the state-subject relationship is at once reciprocal and fiduciary, despite the fact that the state alone owes public fiduciary obligations to its people.

As important as a presumption of trust is as a moral vehicle to help explain the legal authority of the state to announce and enforce law, trust does not reveal the characteristics that legislation and administration must have in order to comply with the rule of law. Trust is simply a moral concept that mediates relations between parties. The principles of Fuller's internal morality are necessary to specify the rule-of-law-embodying characteristics of legislation and administration, and explaining these principles in turn

[23] Lon L Fuller, 'Freedom as a Problem of Allocating Choice' (1968) 112 *Proceedings of the American Philosophical Society* 101, pp 103–4.

[24] Ibid.

requires an additional moral argument beyond trust. Part of the point of the next section is to show that the internal morality really is internal to law, and that it has intrinsic moral content. Within the larger scheme, the aim is to identify further moral precepts, still intrinsic to law, which justify and explain Fuller's eight canons within the context of the state-subject fiduciary relationship. Freedom and dignity are two such moral precepts. Once we have them in view, we will be able to see how they restrict the scope of the no-rights thesis without reducing the rule of law to simply the rule of good law.

9.3 FULLER'S APPRECIATION OF FREEDOM AND DIGNITY

A commitment to the internal morality of law, Fuller says, entails a commitment to the view that the law regards persons as free, self-determining and responsible agents, and that they possess dignity in virtue of their autonomy[25]:

> To embark on the enterprise of subjecting human conduct to the governance of rules involves of necessity a commitment to the view that man is, or can become, a responsible agent, capable of understanding and following rules, and answerable for his defaults.
>
> Every departure from the principles of the law's internal morality is an affront to man's dignity as a responsible agent. . . . To judge his actions by unpublished or retrospective laws is no longer an affront, for there is nothing left to affront—indeed, even the verb 'to judge' becomes incongruous in this context; we no longer judge a man, we act upon him.

Fuller observes that the idea of the person as free and responsible is also entrenched within the concepts of fault and intent that permeate tort and contract law. In cases of tort, inquiry directs itself to whether the defendant was at fault when something she did led to the plaintiff's injury. If she is found to have acted negligently, and her negligence caused damage to the plaintiff, the defendant may be held responsible for her wrong-doing. In contract the first issue a court must decide is whether each party intended to enter into a mutually binding legal relationship with the other. If so, then the

[25] Fuller, *supra* note 4, pp 162–3. For other arguments that Fuller took freedom to be the bedrock concern of law, see Nadler, *supra* note 6; Rundle, *supra* note 6; Simmonds, *supra* note 6; KI Winston, 'Legislators and Liberty' (1994) 13 Law & Phil 389. For the idea that Fuller took agency to underwrite self-directed social interaction as well as reciprocity between implicit and explicit law, see Gerald Postema, 'Implicit Law' in W Witteveen and W van der Burg (eds), *Rediscovering Fuller: Essays on Implicit Law and Institutional Design* (Amsterdam: Amsterdam University Press, 1999), p 361. For the connection between agency and public administration construed as a nexus of implicit and explicit law, see Roderick Macdonald, 'Legislation and Governance' in W Witteveen and W van der Burg (eds), *Rediscovering Fuller: Essays on Implicit Law and Institutional Design* (Amsterdam: Amsterdam University Press, 1999), pp 278 and 302–3 in particular.

parties may be held liable to one another if either breaches the terms of their agreement. In difficult contract cases, where the written document is silent, inquiry is directed to what the parties would have intended had they considered the contingency that is not explicitly covered by the terms of the contract.

To underscore the centrality of human agency to private law, Fuller points out that our intuitions on legal justice slip loose from their moorings when an outside event frustrates the performance of a contract[26]:

> We can no longer ask: Who was to blame? What did they intend? Since our usual standards of justice fail us, we are at a loss to know what justice requires. If we were to lose throughout the law the view of man as a responsible center of action, all legal problems would become like those I have just suggested [ie problems where we are at a loss to know what justice requires].

For Fuller, then, both the coherence and moral authority of law depend on a view of the person as a free and responsible 'center of action'. The coherence of law depends on this conception of the person because without it 'we are at a loss to know what justice requires'. And the law's moral authority to punish crimes or rectify civil wrongs relies on the idea that a reasonable person could have done other than what the wrongdoer did, and so criminal guilt and civil liability each attach to the commission of a wrong that a reasonable person could have avoided.

One might think that throughout the passages cited above Fuller is slipping illegitimately between, on the one hand, cognitive and volitional capacities that permit people to choose between lawful and unlawful conduct, and, on the other, the idea that such capacities imply that human beings possess a certain dignity that can ground strong moral claims. But this charge of illegitimacy misses the point. For lawyers such as Fuller, this slippage is almost invisible because it is exactly the cognitive and volitional capacities underlying agency that ground the lawyer's understanding of 'what justice requires'. To say that agency can determine what justice requires is to say that there is something about agency capable of justifying legal (and moral) judgments in particular cases. Where a legal relationship exists, such as a tort, contract, or fiduciary relationship, agency can serve (and normally does so explicitly) as the basis of the wrongdoer's liability. It follows that if a legal relationship is present, agency can serve as the foundation for the aggrieved party's legal (and moral) claims.

When Fuller refers to a person's dignity as a responsible agent, then, he is best understood as referring to the justice-determining attributes of agency

[26] Fuller, *supra* note 4, p 167.

(and not just its purely descriptive cognitive and volitional dimensions) in virtue of which the agent may make claims against others and be held accountable for her defaults. In other words, Fuller subscribes to Kant's distinction between persons and things according to which persons alone have dignity—are ends in themselves—on account of their agency. But his subscription to the Kantian principle is not based on an *a priori* argument or a deontological assumption concerning the intrinsic value of agency. Rather, it flows from teasing out the consequences of elementary presuppositions found in the basic tenets and practices of legal institutions.

Fuller emphasizes the importance to law of agency and dignity not because he has a special love of private order (Fuller never takes the libertarian position that taxes constitute enslavement of the talented), but because he thinks that respect for agency is what distinguishes law from other forms of rules which guide human conduct, such as managerial direction. As the name suggests, managerial direction refers to a form of rules which structures relations between a superior and a subordinate, such as one finds typically in employer-employee relations. Rather than setting baselines for relations of non-domination between equals, managerial direction usually goes much further than law in defining the ends to be pursued (ends the subordinate may not share) as well as the specific means of achieving them. For this reason, Fuller concludes that managerial direction (the conception of legal rules he accuses Hart of adopting) involves a 'one-way projection of authority',[27] a projection of power which undermines the individual's autonomy by subjecting her to the arbitrary will of another.

For Fuller, the subject's self-determined participation in legal order reflects a liberal and republican conception of autonomy. The conception is liberal in the sense that individuals living under it are to be afforded an equal opportunity to choose, pursue, and revise their own conceptions of the good. Fuller thinks, however, that for freedom to be meaningful at all (both practically and morally) requires 'a congenial environment of rules and decisions'.[28] This environment is structured by the principles of the internal morality, and an indispensable aspect of it is 'the opportunity to participate in decision-making processes'.[29] Fuller thus subscribes to the republican ideal of freedom as non-domination discussed in previous chapters, for it is not freedom from interference in itself that guides his lawgiver (rules and decisions necessarily interfere with a person's actions), but rather freedom from the ongoing threat of arbitrary interference made possible by a 'one

[27] Ibid, p 204.

[28] Lon L Fuller, 'Freedom—A Suggested Analysis' (1955) 68 Harv L Rev 1305, 1314.

[29] Fuller, *supra* note 23, p 103.

way projection of authority'. The subject's participation in decision-making processes is to be encouraged because it contributes to a reciprocal conception of authority, shielding the individual from domination and securing her (republican) autonomy.

Pulling the various strands together, Fuller takes the narrower, legal conception of freedom implicated by concepts such as fault and intent (ie agency) and develops it into an internal morality capable of guiding lawgivers committed to a 'congenial environment' of legal order. This environment is 'essential to freedom'[30] in a wider, republican sense because it lets persons live out their own conceptions of the good life without the threat of arbitrary power hanging over them. Put another way, freedom as non-domination depends on a legal order structured by the principles of the internal morality, and those specific principles, I argue now, are themselves best justified and explained by a commitment to agency and dignity.[31]

Agency, as a mere cognitive and volitional capacity, entails the possibility of purposive action. One purpose legal subjects may give themselves is to act in accordance with the law. But in order to adopt lawfulness as one's purpose, the individual must have at least a general acquaintance with what the law is. Otherwise, her conformity with it is left to chance. This is why Fuller says that if an individual is found to have violated a secret rule (a rule made in secret that a reasonable person could not know existed), the person is not judged in any meaningful sense, but is simply acted upon. The subject is treated not as someone capable of purposive action for which she may be held responsible, but as a thing to which the idea of legal responsibility for intentional or negligent wrong-doing does not apply.

We can now trace the major steps of the argument implicit in Fuller from agency through to the rule-of-law requirement of publicity. The conceptual point of the argument is to show the sense in which the principle of publicity may be derived from agency, and thus agency may be seen to comprise the intrinsic moral content of the principle of publicity. The idea that legal subjects are free implies that they can engage in purposive action. The capacity to engage in purposive action implies that persons can obey or disobey the law. But the subject's ability to obey or disobey—the basis of legal responsibility—depends on her being able to know what the law is. A necessary (though not always sufficient) condition of her knowledge of the law is that the law be made public and knowable to her. A failure to make the law public is an affront to her dignity as a free and self-determining person because it denies her the ability to give herself the law as one of her

[30] Fuller, *supra* note 28, p 1314.

[31] Unless otherwise indicated, for convenience I will refer to agency and freedom interchangeably.

purposes. Thus, implicit in the law's recognition and affirmation of its subjects' freedom is the requirement that its rules be made public.

The principles of non-retroactivity, clarity, consistency, possibility of performance, and constancy over time all share the agency-based rationale that underlies the requirement of publicity: to respect the person as an autonomous and self-determining being, the law must impose only those obligations which an individual can adopt within the purposes that guide her actions. If she cannot align her actions with the law because of some defect in its formulation or character, subjecting her to it would fail to respect her agency. The person would not be treated as an end in herself, as a person whose agency permits her to make legal (and moral) claims against others with whom she is in a legal relationship.

A retroactive law, for example, fails to respect a person's agency because we cannot go back in time to make our actions conform to the law. Similarly, a law that is unclear or constantly changing fails to live up to law's internal morality because its vagueness, ambiguity, or evanescent nature subverts our ability to apprehend and obey it. Likewise, an inconsistent rule cannot guide action because a contradiction can give no guidance. But perhaps the most direct example of how a defective rule may infringe on agency is an enactment that is impossible to obey, since it denies from the start the idea that law must respect a person's capacity for purposive self-determination.

Fuller's two other principles—generality, and congruence between declared rule and official action—are not so transparently connected to freedom and dignity. It is not obvious, for example, that agency is compromised on account of whether or not a law is sufficiently general. However, Fuller's requirement of generality is not the requirement of impartiality which informs the principle of equality before the law, but is rather the elementary idea that the law must take the form of rules so that legal issues are not decided on an *ad hoc* basis. Were it not for rules, individuals would be at a loss to know the content of their legal obligations. The publicity requirement and the other principles which constrain the form of rules all depend in the first instance on the very existence of rules to which those principles may apply. This is why Fuller presents generality as the first and most elemental of the internal morality's principles.

A similar justification can be given for the last principle, congruence between official action and declared rule. If officials do not exercise the powers entrusted to them in a manner that is faithful to the rules they are charged with administering, then the entire enterprise of legal order is in jeopardy, regardless of how well publicized and clear the rules happen to be. If a person conscientiously obeys the declared rules only to be convicted by a judge who has taken a bribe, the conviction would make a mockery of the subject's obedience of the law. In this sense, the integrity of legal order is intimately connected to the faithfulness with which public authority fulfils its adjudicative, legislative, and administrative mandates.

To sum up: each of the principles of the internal morality of law can be justified and explained as prerequisites to the legal subject's exercise of agency within legal order. If a lawgiver infringes on the principles of the internal morality, she infringes on the dignity inherent to the person conceived of as a free and self-determining agent susceptible to legal justice. But what is critical to the argument is not a simple preoccupation with the ideas of self-determining freedom and dignity, it is the manner in which the principles of the internal morality follow from, and are therefore implicit in, these related moral ideas. It is this inferential and constitutive relationship between these moral concepts, on the one hand, and the principles of the internal morality, on the other, which shows that the intrinsic moral content of the internal morality is freedom and dignity, and thus that the principles of the internal morality have intrinsic moral value.

In the next section I defend this agency-based constitutive account of the internal morality against Raz's positivist interpretation, after which we turn to the kind of moral difference a regime's subscription to the internal morality necessarily makes, and then to how a commitment to the rule of law yields a commitment to human rights.

9.4 RAZ AND SLAVERY

Raz recognizes that for law to be capable of guiding effectively the behaviour of its subjects, the law must have features similar to Fuller's internal morality.[32] Raz thinks, however, that these principles speak solely to the *efficiency* with which law may operate. He counts efficiency as a virtue, but as a virtue with no moral implications. He attributes only an instrumental role to law[33]:

> It is a tool in the hands of men differing from many others in being versatile and capable of being used for a large variety of proper purposes . . . Like other instruments, the law has a specific virtue which is morally neutral in being neutral to the end to which the instrument is put. It is the virtue of efficiency; the virtue of the instrument as the instrument.

Thus, for Raz, 'conformity to the rule of law is one among many moral virtues which the law should possess',[34] but such conformity in itself tells us nothing about the moral status of the regime in question, since the regime

[32] Raz, *supra* note 1, pp 214–19. Raz says that the list is not exhaustive, and that it may change with context.

[33] Ibid, p 226. [34] Ibid, p 225.

may use the law to pursue wicked ends. While Raz thinks that claims made on behalf of the rule of law tend to be overblown in that they confuse the rule of law with substantive political theory, he is happy to admit that 'observance of the rule of law is necessary if the law is to respect human dignity', and that '[r]especting human dignity entails treating humans as persons capable of planning and plotting their future'.[35] Hence, the rule of law is necessary but not sufficient for the law to respect autonomy as well as dignity. Because the law has no inherent normative content, gross violations of autonomy and dignity are consistent with adherence to the rule of law, since the primary legal rules themselves may condone or even promote those violations, as Raz alleges in the case of slavery.

Raz argues that the rule of law is essentially a negative value in that it does not cause good but rather prevents evil, and the evil it prevents is only the evil made possible by law itself. While the rule of law may curb arbitrary abuses of power, those ills are ills that would not be possible but for the presence of law. So, Raz claims, the law deserves no moral credit for the evils it prevents.[36]

As Andrei Marmor points out, however, this evaluation of the rule of law is conducted through the lens of a theory of moral agency and virtue, rather than in terms of simply whether or not a state devoid of violations of the rule of law is to that extent good.[37] Marmor invites us to consider a world similar to ours, except that the people who inhabit this other world cannot possibly kill each other. While they would deserve no moral credit, the fact that they cannot kill each other is still a good thing. Similarly, even if the rule of law can claim no moral credit for eliminating certain abuses of public power, the absence of such abuses is morally valuable.

Moreover, while *some* rules must be posted and announced for there to be an effective system of rules capable of guiding people's actions, there is no reason to think that *all* (or even most) rules must be made public for an effective system of rules to operate. It follows that efficacy alone cannot explain the idea that all or most rules ought to be made public, since (other things being equal) they ought to be made public even if there is a cost in terms of efficacy. Raz cannot explain why this is so because for him the demands of the rule of law are simply the demands of efficacy.

Only a moral concern can explain the general and defeasible requirement that all rules must conform to all the relevant principles of the internal morality. Fuller acknowledges that a concern for efficacy and control by managerial direction could account for at least partial recognition of five of his eight principles: publicity, consistency, clarity, constancy, and possibility

[35] Ibid, p 221. [36] Ibid, p 224. [37] Marmor, *supra* note 4, p 40.

of performance. For any system of rules to function, there must be some fidelity to these principles. But generality, prospectivity, and congruence of official action with declared rules are different.

A manager who is the source of authority just because he is the manager may do away with the generality of commanding through rules at his convenience. Rules may help him to control those he governs, but he may use or discard rules depending on what will best assist him in achieving his goals. By the same token, there may be circumstances in which he finds it useful to use retroactive rules to set examples. Nor does efficacy compel the manager to apply the declared rules as they are declared, or to follow them himself, except as it suits his purposes. In these cases, efficacy explains *violations* of the internal morality, so efficacy cannot serve as a general explanation of fidelity to the internal morality. The problem is that efficacy places no constraint of principle on such exercises of power. In the result, the positivist concern for efficacy converts the internal morality into an unstable *modus vivendi*. Only a moral construction of the internal morality's principles can justify adherence to them in the face of political opposition or administrative inconvenience.

More important still, the ethos driving the rule of law runs deeper than the constraints it places on the wielders of public power. Law, and law alone, supplies a publicly accessible recourse against naked power. Certainly the powerful will often take advantage of law to the extent they can. Yet history is littered with countless instances in which the powerful resist law because law provides a forum in which public reason can operate as a check against concentrated and otherwise unaccountable power. The history of labour reform, for example, reveals a steady resistance on the part of employers to submit to labour laws that facilitate unionization and which replace dismissal at the employer's discretion with dismissal for cause. The willingness of the vulnerable to submit to law, on the other hand, is a phenomenon which holds true of such a wide range of nations, classes, ethnicities, communities, workers, groups, religions, individuals, and so on, that virtually the only thread that could be said to unite them is their vulnerability to public or private power which is held in check, if at all, by law alone.[38] This is why the powerful tend to shun law and, conversely, the weak and vulnerable tend to seek law's protection. It is not surprising that Hobbes begins his substantive justification of legal order with essentially this insight, the idea

[38] William Golding's classic, *Lord of the Flies*, is a powerful reminder of both the resistance to law by the strong and the value of law to the weak. In Golding's novel about a group of boys trapped on an island, no one treasures the order-instilling conch more than the asthmatic and near-sighted Piggy, and no one despises it more than the athletic and savage Jack, W Golding, *Lord of the Flies* (New York: Penguin Putnam Inc, 1962) (first published in 1954).

that in the state of nature every person is equal in the sense that all are ultimately vulnerable to the untrammelled power of others (L xiii.1, 74). The rule of law supplies the principles and institutional structure that permits legal order to protect the vulnerable from certain forms of arbitrary power that could otherwise fill the void, and so the justification of the rule of law runs deeper than merely protection from the abuse of power that law makes possible.

Put slightly differently, the rule of law establishes conditions under which secure and equal freedom is possible because under the rule of law we are subject to general rules and principles rather than the will or power of others. As Nigel Simmonds argues, subjection to law rather than the power of others ensures our freedom in the sense that law establishes domains in which we can interact with others independently (ie for our own ends, and secure from the power of others).[39] That the principles of the rule of law can jointly supply the conditions for secure and equal freedom should come as no surprise, for we have seen already that a commitment to agency justifies a commitment to each principle. Now, strictly speaking, it does not follow from the fact that agency justifies each principle that the set of principles itself is justifiable, as a set, in terms of agency. Nonetheless, if, as I have argued, an absence of the rule of law entails vulnerability to the power of others, and if this vulnerability entails a lack of secure and equal freedom, then the set of principles constitutive of the rule of law is also justifiable in terms of a commitment to agency and its exercise under conditions of secure and equal freedom.

Raz could reply that systematic violations of the rule of law which violate autonomy and dignity just show that the legal order in question is not a legitimate legal order. For Raz it is still in every sense a legal order, just one that violates our political ideals of autonomy and dignity. But this retort fails to address the point of the agency-based argument of the preceding section that the principles of the internal morality are implicit in and therefore partially constituted by ideals of agency and dignity, ideals which themselves presuppose nothing more than the agency implicit in legal personality. To the extent that the internal morality specifies the terms and requirements of legality, it follows that legality is, to this extent, constituted by ideals of agency and dignity. This constitutive argument suggests that violation of the rule of law places a strain on legality—and not merely on political morality—because such a violation infringes the moral precepts which constitute legality's normative dimension.

[39] Simmonds, *supra* note 6, pp 141–3, 182–9. See also Phillip Pettit, *Republicanism: A Theory of Freedom and Government* (New York: Oxford University Press, 1997), pp 174–7.

Consider now Raz's claim that the rule of law is consistent with slavery in light of the agency-based rationale of the internal morality, and in light of the overarching reciprocal and fiduciary relationship between lawgiver and subject. Because slavery entails a gross violation of human rights, it embodies an institutionalized practice we can use to test the no-rights thesis. One might agree that the rule of law secures a measure of freedom from the power of others, and that its principles can be justified on grounds of agency, and yet doubt that the rule of law necessarily requires a regime of secure and *equal* freedom. The argument immediately below addresses this concern.

Raz's view of slavery and the rule of law stands, I argue, only if one assumes that law and legal order do not contain implicit moral assumptions concerning the people subject to them and the kind of relationship that ties lawgiver to legal subject. Legal subjects may possess rights whereas slaves generally do not because slave-owning societies do not count slaves as persons and legal subjects. In a sense, slavery is an extreme form of what Fuller takes to be wrong with Hart's view of law, that positivism reduces law to a one-way projection of authority in which the role and importance of the subject in a reciprocal relationship with the state is all but obliterated.

In the case of slavery, so far as the slaves are concerned, the obliteration is total. The fiduciary idea brings the reason for the completeness of the obliteration into focus, and explains the tension between slavery and the rule of law. The state as fiduciary is authorized by the fiduciary principle to secure legal order exclusively for the benefit of each free and self-determining being subject to it. Free and self-determining beings are agents. Legal persons, on the other hand, are agents who public authority recognizes as having the capacity to acquire legal rights. Agents may or may not be persons, depending on the attitude of public authority towards them.

On the fiduciary view of the rule of law, the fiduciary principle authorizes state power exclusively for the purpose of securing legal order on behalf of each agent who is subject to such power. At a minimum, establishing legal order on behalf of every agent implies that each must have the possibility of acquiring rights which can enshrine and protect their respective interests. Otherwise, such interests would be entirely vulnerable to the power and caprice of others. In other words, each agent must be treated and regarded as a person, and this because each agent is equally free and self-determining, and so each agent is an equally valid subject of the fiduciary authorization of public authority. As a principle of legality, the fiduciary principle has no capacity to discriminate arbitrarily between agents who, in virtue of the state-subject fiduciary relationship, enjoy equal status *vis-à-vis* the state as co-beneficiaries of the rule of law.

Because slaves are denied the capacity to possess legal rights, a state that enforces slavery cannot claim to have secured legal order for the purpose of guaranteeing rights on behalf of each agent. It follows that if a state supports slavery, it does so in contravention of the rule of law, for it breaches its most basic fiduciary obligation to ensure that each agent subject to its powers is equally regarded as a person capable of possessing legal rights. Contrary to Raz's understanding of the no-rights thesis, then, slavery violates the rule of law as well as human rights. And, once we see the rule of law as an implication of the state's position as fiduciary, it becomes apparent that the rule of law does more than secure a measure of our freedom by insulating us from the power of others. The rule of law necessarily regards each of us as its equal co-beneficiaries, and therefore provides for our secure and *equal* freedom. As a consequence, the rule of law protects us against all forms of arbitrary discrimination, and not just slavery. In this way, the rule of law embodies the republican ideal of non-domination.

I have argued that the rule of law's commitment to agency entails a commitment to human dignity. Does the commitment to dignity, combined with the inability of the law to discriminate arbitrarily between agents, entail that all human beings necessarily possess equal dignity? Not quite: there may be grounds beyond the sphere of legality which justify the denial of equal dignity (though I doubt such grounds exist). The point to underline here, however, is that the law's inability to discriminate arbitrarily between agents implies that the rule of law must regard every agent as an equal co-beneficiary of the rule of law, and so the rule of law must regard every agent as possessing equal dignity, whether or not, as a matter of fact, every agent does so possess it.

It is worth reiterating that while agency is a vital component of the big picture, the simple fact of human agency does not entail that agents are sources of strong moral claims which preclude their enslavement. Rather, it is the fiduciary relationship between agents and the state that supplies the necessary conceptual link between human agency in the abstract and the concrete rule-of-law proscription against slavery and other forms of domination. States do not owe these rule-of-law obligations to every agent in the world at large. They owe them exclusively to the people under their power.

A critic might object that the preceding rule-of-law argument against slavery trades illicitly on slavery's deeply repugnant nature. Soon we will see that the argument against slavery can be extended to apply to unjustifiable violations of human rights. But first we need to address a further objection to the agency-based constitutive account of the internal morality I have attributed to Fuller, since this account, along with the lawgiver-subject fiduciary relationship, establishes the framework that makes the incorporation of human rights within legality possible. The objection is that the internal morality has no moral content because morally wicked regimes can adopt it as their means of governance. Addressing this objection will let us see some of the concrete moral benefits that necessarily flow from adherence to the internal morality.

9.5 THE MORAL DIFFERENCE THE INTERNAL MORALITY NECESSARILY MAKES

While improbable in our world today, it is conceptually possible for a wicked regime to subscribe faithfully to the internal morality, and it is in part this conceptual possibility that leads Raz and others to adopt the no-rights thesis and claim that the rule of law has only instrumental value. Arguably, Hart and Raz take the possibility of such a regime to demonstrate the positivist separation thesis that there is no necessary connection between law and morality.[40] Nonetheless, the fact that it is conceptually possible for such a regime to exist does not entail that its adherence to the internal morality makes no difference to our moral evaluation of it. To sustain the positivist view, in conceptual terms, would require showing that it is impossible for the internal morality to make a moral difference in wicked regimes. To sustain the anti-positivist view, in conceptual terms, would require showing that, even in wicked regimes, the internal morality necessarily makes some moral difference.[41] I discharge this burden now, and then return to the no-rights thesis.

The internal morality makes a moral difference that is limited, relative, and non-absolutist. It is limited in that it reflects the normativity intrinsic to legality rather than the all-things-considered virtue of a comprehensive theory of justice. It is relative in that it is based on a comparison between legal order structured by the principles of the internal morality and a regime unconstrained by those principles. It is non-absolutist in that it supposes that moral differences are discernible even in contexts of unrelenting oppression. I will unpack these three characteristics in turn. As we shall see, it is in the normativity intrinsic to legality that we find the principal moral resources to support the anti-positivist conceptual argument; the other characteristics (relativity and non-absoluteness) qualify further the nature of the moral difference legality makes.

[40] Hart may not have made quite this strong a claim. He admits that treating like cases alike inheres in the concept of justice, and that this principle is implicit in the idea of a legal system consisting in general rules, HLA Hart, 'Positivism and the Separation of Law and Morals' (1958) 71 Harv L Rev 593, as reproduced in Hart, *supra* note 10, p 81. But in his debate with Fuller (eg Hart, *supra* note 10), it is clear that he takes the possibility of wicked regimes complying with the internal morality to support the separation thesis.

[41] For the bold claim that legality made a positive moral difference to Jews living under Nazi rule, see Rundle *supra* note 6.

The normativity intrinsic to Fuller's view of legality is rooted in a Kantian conception of human agency and rights. This conception is intelligible independently of consequentialist considerations that typically attend full-blown theories of justice, such as distributive considerations of welfare and resource holdings. One way of putting the distinction between the norms of legality and justice writ large is in terms of the difference between wrongs and harms.[42] Legality tracks wrongs, which sometimes but not always involve harms.[43] Consider the following 'harmless' invasion of privacy. Suppose I am visiting a friend and ask to borrow his computer to check my email. He tells me to help myself, and leaves the room. When I go to his computer his email program is running, but it is minimized so that its contents are not visible. If I open and read his email, I am committing a wrong even if the email I read is meaningless spam, and even if he never becomes aware of my invasion of his privacy. In other words, I commit a wrong even if I do no harm, where harm is understood in the conventional sense of making someone worse-off. There is a plain moral difference between this scenario and one in which I respect my friend's right to privacy and resist the temptation to invade it.

The same kind of argument can be made with respect to the internal morality of law: even if violations of the internal morality occasion no harm, such violations would still constitute wrongs because they would constitute breaches of the state's overarching fiduciary duty to govern in accordance with the rule of law. For example, suppose the executive engages in an *ad hoc* secret surveillance programme and gathers emails from unsuspecting individuals. The executive would be in breach of the internal morality's principles concerning (at least) generality and publicity. But suppose the administration refrains from using the information it collects for nefarious purposes so that no one suffers material injury as a result. The executive would still wrong the people whose privacy it invades. We need to consider now, however, whether our moral evaluation of the state's surveillance programme would differ if the government complied with some or all of the internal morality.

Suppose the government makes public its intent to conduct surveillance on large segments of its population, and secures legislative authority to

[42] Another common way of explicating the distinction is in terms of the right and the good. As will become clear, I rely explicitly on this distinction. I begin with wrongs and harms because the wrong/harm distinction illustrates at a glance something important about the distinction between the right and the good, ie that infringements of the right are intelligible independently of infringements of the good.

[43] Conversely, some harms do not constitute wrongs, or at least do not constitute wrongs of a legal and actionable nature. For example, competitive activity in the market typically makes the competitors worse-off than they would be if any one or a group of them had a monopoly, but such harms are not wrongful. Indeed, they are encouraged.

do so. At the very least, individuals would be put on notice that their private communications were subject to the programme. Moreover, the programme would become susceptible to debate and scrutiny. These are morally significant differences even if the space for public debate is highly constrained and even if it appears that no amount of public criticism will deter an administration bent on wickedness. I will spell out in further detail below some of the moral benefits of transparency. For now I wish to make the conceptual point that notice and transparency are morally significant as a matter of right, independently of any contribution they may happen to make to democracy and the good, because they reflect the value of the executive's compliance with (rather than violation of) its fiduciary duty to respect the rule of law. The state's fulfilment of its rule-of-law obligations *qua* legal obligations necessarily entails a moral difference intelligible in terms of the right. From the standpoint of the right, subscription to the internal morality necessarily makes a moral difference relative to the state of affairs that would obtain in its absence.

As already noted, there may be circumstances where competing moral considerations outweigh the rule of law, and in such circumstances the rule of law ought to yield. But this merely suggests that, unsurprisingly, the rule of law's prescriptions are not trumps in a normatively heteronymous universe. That the rule of law must sometimes yield to other moral considerations is evidence for rather than against its moral character because exceptional circumstances reveal that moral arguments must be given to justify deviations from the rule of law.

Consider now a truly wicked plutocracy in which public power has been captured by a self-serving elite committed to its own enrichment at the expense of the people. Suppose also that the rulers are committed to ruling in accordance with the internal morality. They draft clear, public, and prospective legislation that permits them to acquire the lion's share of the state's wealth through ruthless exploitation of the people. Suppose further that if the relevant laws were not clear, public, and prospective, the elite would not be able to oppress the majority to the extent it can now. In other words, let us assume that the success of the oppressive regime depends to some degree on the subjugation that governance through the internal morality makes possible. There is, then, in this case, something of a causal relationship between abiding by the internal morality and fomenting substantive injustice. The causal relationship is not (nor could be) explained entirely by adherence to the internal morality—the elite's oppressive policies carry the burden of the blame—but let us assume that their wickedness is made worse by subscription to the internal morality. In such a world, can we say that the internal morality makes a positive moral difference?

The difference is discernible for reasons already canvassed, and relies on the idea that the rule of law operates in the sphere of legality or the right rather than the good. By hypothesis, the elite's oppression of the majority constitutes grave injustice, but it is an injustice of a political nature that infringes ideals of political equality and distributive justice. Although we have assumed for the sake of argument that such injustice is made possible in part because the plutocrats subscribe to the internal morality, this causal relationship (such as it is) does not negate the fact that the elite is nonetheless complying with its fiduciary obligation to rule in accordance with the internal morality. Even if on balance the people would be better off if their rulers governed them in violation of the internal morality, they would be better off in the sphere of the good rather than in the sphere of the right. And the idea that the internal morality figures at all in the balance indicates that it carries some moral weight.

The present case is really just an extreme case in which countervailing moral considerations outweigh the rule of law, perhaps to the extent that the best course of action is to jettison the rule of law and legal order altogether until more just rulers can be installed. But neither the competing moral considerations nor the elite's appropriation of the internal morality demonstrate that the rule of law is bereft of moral content. For the argument I am pressing to work, all we need to presuppose is a non-absolutist and variegated understanding of our moral universe in which we can discern moral differences in terms of the right as well as in terms of the good, regardless of how badly things are going in the domain of the good.

In the wicked regime sketched above I assumed a causal relationship between the rule of law and substantive injustice. Such a relationship is conceptually possible and has to be faced by any anti-positivist argument aiming to show that the rule of law, as a conceptual matter, has intrinsic moral content and therefore necessarily makes a moral difference to those who live under it. But such causal relationships, if any, are contingent matters. Thus, from a conceptual point of view, it is fair to compare the elite-driven regime under evaluation with one that is similar to it in all respects except that there is no causal relationship between the internal morality and substantive injustice; indeed, violations of the internal morality are commonplace. The elite in this other regime sometimes follows the internal morality, but when it is in their interest they violate it. For instance, they use paramilitary forces, illegal interrogation techniques, and clandestine jails to persecute dissidents. Let us assume that the strictly rule-of-law-abiding plutocracy uses similar tactics, but does so openly and with explicit legislative warrant.

The moral difference between the two worlds manifests itself in several important ways, the first two of which we have glimpsed already. The first is that the victims of oppression in the strictly rule-of-law-abiding regime will have a better sense of which sorts of activities may lead to their persecution. They will have a measure of notice and, if they choose to dissent, will be better able to take precautions and defend themselves. They will know where they stand. The second is that the oppressive measures in the rule-of-law-abiding regime will be more visible. While under present circumstances public scrutiny of wicked laws may not translate into policy reform, circumstances are contingent and may change over time. Exposing wickedness is a precondition to overcoming it, and the rule of law makes a significant contribution in this regard.

Furthermore, unmasking wickedness is morally valuable in the here and now, especially under conditions of apparently relentless oppression, for reasons that are independent of the benefits to be gleaned from a future state in which oppression no longer prevails. Transparency is important under conditions of oppression because it lets those who tolerate oppression know the moral cost of their acquiescence, as well as the cost they would face should they choose to resist. Similarly, transparency permits dissenters to marshal moral arguments and elicit the support of others. The value of transparency as a precondition of overcoming wickedness, then, is not located solely in the virtue of a future and better state that may or may not come into being. Transparency's value is also found in the manner in which it lets us, as members of a political community, determine the point at which we will no longer acquiesce oppression. The success or failure of reform efforts will always be an empirical matter. Because reform is possible, there is no *a priori* reason not to hope for reform. It follows that the basis for future reform that transparency supplies is also, in part, the basis of our hope today. This is a noteworthy moral consequence of the rule of law, and one that arguably gains in significance in rough proportion to the degree of wickedness a regime exhibits: the more wicked the regime, the more important transparency and the possibility of hope becomes.

Another moral difference brought about by subscription to the rule of law in wicked regimes concerns the means such regimes may use to terrorize their people. Most forms of state terrorism, as a conceptual matter, could be conducted with express and prospective legislative authority. But some cannot. One such form is the 'disappearing' of political opponents, a hideous violation of human rights and common tactic in much of Latin America in the latter half of the last century. Part of the point of such disappearances is to eliminate opposition, usually through their torture and murder, and this could, in principle, be achieved through draconian laws. Another goal of disappearances, however, is to instil fear in the general population and thereby repress dissent. Without knowledge of the actions for which one could become the victim of a disappearance, even low-level and non-violent opposition requires a much greater commitment to reform than would otherwise be the case.

Furthermore, for those close to the victim, the effects of a disappearance are worse than the effects of a straightforward murder. In the case of a disappearance—where the state denies all wrongdoing and the body is never found—the grief of the victim's family and friends is unending. They are cruelly tortured by the desperate but hopeless prospect of their loved one's return, and by the state's denial of responsibility. The transparency guaranteed by the rule of law precludes the special terror of disappearances because the evil they inflict depends vitally on the shroud of secrecy under which they are carried out.

While it is conceivable that a wicked state could publicly adopt a 'Disappearances Act' under which the administration could order individuals disappeared arbitrarily, even this would be an improvement over disappearances in their present form. Such an Act would have to delegate authority to a particular branch of the administration for the purposes of implementing the programme, and so the families of the victims would have some idea of who was responsible. Such families would also be better equipped to grieve and find closure. Moreover, by owning up to its wrongdoing, the state would provide fertile ground for strong moral opposition. This opposition could be supported by judges who understood their role as guardians of the rule of law as involving a commitment to human rights. On review, the executive would be forced to be explicit about its willingness to violate the rule of law and human rights.

These cursory remarks, together with those concerning notice and transparency, have attempted to provide a brief illustration of some of the concrete ways in which adherence to the internal morality of law can make a moral difference. I have argued that this difference is conceptual and necessary because it is intelligible in terms of the right, in terms of the state performing its overarching fiduciary duty to respect the rule of law. Transparency, notice, and independent judicial review of delegated authority are some of the consequences of the state complying with the rule of law.

If the reciprocal and fiduciary relationship between state and subject generally requires the state to adhere to the internal morality as a matter of law, as I contend, then the internal morality supplies a reservoir of principle from which the subject can make claims against the state as a matter of right. Because such claims can be made as a matter of right, they put pressure on the no-rights thesis, though admittedly the pressure flows from the substantive implications of the internal morality rather than from the specification of a realm of substantive policy that the internal morality might be said to proscribe. Such a realm, I argue now, includes policies that entail unjustifiable violations of human rights.

9.6 FROM THE RULE OF LAW TO HUMAN RIGHTS

For Fuller, as we have seen, the law's chief purpose is to enable people to interact with one another within the limits of the congenial environment established by a lawful regime of secure and equal freedom, a republican environment which enables each to choose and pursue her own conception of the good independently of the power of others. Of course, it is not the person's actual conception of the good, nor her actual possession of rights and obligations that underlies agency and dignity. Those are entirely contingent matters. Instead, it is the capacity of the person to choose and pursue her own conception of the good that reflects her status before the law as a free and self-determining being worthy of respect.

Put another way, a person's status before the law does not lie in the particularities of what she does or the rights she has, but rather in something about the kind of being she is. For Fuller, I have argued, that something is free and self-determining, which is why legal rules and their administration must conform to the principles of an internal morality that ensure respect for the free and self-determining nature of persons. But once we see that the best justification of the internal morality's principles involves a commitment to a view of the person as free and self-determining, as capable of making legal claims and being held accountable in virtue of her agency, and therefore as an end worthy of respect in her own right, we have committed ourselves to exactly the concept—human dignity—that commands respect for human rights. In this sense, because a commitment to the principles of the internal morality entails a commitment to agency, it also implies a commitment to human dignity and human rights.

A similar argument can be made from the macro-level perspective of the rule of law considered as a unified and moral ideal, as the combined set of principles which constitute the internal morality. I argued above that the fundamental justification underpinning the rule of law is its capacity to liberate us from the untrammelled power of others by subjecting us to law, a subjection that provides security and independence to the exercise of our agency. Human rights serve the same end by supplying mid-range principles which, like Fuller's internal morality, mediate the relationship between abstract ideals of agency and dignity, on the one hand, and the many conditions under which governance through law is possible, on the other.

Human rights, like the rule of law, protect us from domination by ensuring that we do not live under subjection to arbitrary power held by the state or third-parties. Some human rights, for instance, demarcate spheres of conduct in which we may interact autonomously with others, such as freedom of expression, religion, conscience, thought, and association. In this way, human rights contribute to the republican ideal of non-domination. Human rights also protect us from abuse by ensuring that we are treated as ends always and never as mere means. In other words, they reflect the Kantian principle of non-instrumentalization. Various human rights, for example, guarantee our bodily integrity, such as rights to life and security of the person. In this respect, human rights clearly have substantive implications that go beyond the formal prescriptions of the internal morality. Yet the rule of law's commitment to the security and independence of our agency is justifiable on the very same basis: by securing us from the power of others, the rule of law implicitly affirms our equal dignity by requiring that we not be treated as mere means to their ends (non-instrumentalization), nor subject to arbitrary power (non-domination). Thus, the rule of law affirms human dignity, and this affirmation, within the structure supplied by the lawgiver-subject fiduciary relationship, entails a commitment to human rights and a rejection of the no-rights thesis.

In a series of papers on international law,[44] Evan Criddle and I argue that human rights are best conceived in relational and legal terms as norms arising from the state-subject fiduciary relationship. On this relational account, human rights are not timeless and absolute moral rights that individuals possess merely because they are human. Rather, human rights represent the normative consequences of a state's assumption of sovereign powers, and are thus constitutive of sovereignty's normative dimension. More specifically, we claim that the fiduciary principle authorizes states to exercise power on behalf of their people, but subject to norms flowing from the Kantian principle of non-instrumentalization and the republican principle of non-domination. Human rights flesh out the contents of these norms. A state that fails to satisfy its fiduciary duty to respect human rights subverts its claim to govern and represent its people as a sovereign actor.

In this chapter I have argued that the fiduciary theory of human rights can be seen as an unfolding of Fuller's conception of the rule of law. Human rights, therefore, do not stand outside legality; they are a constitutive aspect of it.

9.7 IS THE RULE OF LAW NOW JUST THE RULE OF GOOD LAW?

One might think that the agency-based account of the internal morality, when conjoined with the fiduciary account of reciprocity and the state, succeeds in

[44] Evan J Criddle and Evan Fox-Decent, 'A Fiduciary Theory of Jus Cogens' (2009) 34 Yale J Int'l L 331–87; Evan Fox-Decent and Evan J Criddle, 'The Fiduciary Constitution of Human Rights' (2009) 15(4) *Legal Theory* 301–66; Evan J Criddle and Evan Fox-Decent, 'Human Rights, Emergencies and the Rule of Law' (forthcoming 2012) 34 Hum Rts Q; Evan Fox-Decent and Evan J Criddle, 'Interest Balancing v Fiduciary Duty: Two Models for National Security Law' (forthcoming) 12 German Law Journal.

undermining the no-rights thesis only at the expense of reducing the rule of law to the rule of good law. If all of morality can be based on the Kantian requirement that people must be treated as ends and never as mere means, then, on the view defended here, is not all of morality swept up into law?

Kant himself, however, distinguished the doctrine of right, which controls legality, from the doctrine of virtue, which controls ethics. Put succinctly, the point of the right is to establish and guarantee a regime in which individuals are subject to the same reciprocal limits on their freedom when they interact with others. The point of Kantian ethics is to specify a principle, the categorical imperative, that can instruct individuals on how to act in accordance with a good will. While in both cases the idea that people must be treated as ends plays a role, only the doctrine of right establishes claim-rights and correlative obligations that can be enforced coercively by the state.[45] Indeed, for Kant, the coercive enforceability of such obligations is the hallmark of their juridical status. So, if you ask me what I had for dinner yesterday and I lie to you, my lie is a wrong under the doctrine of virtue, but not under the doctrine of right. My lie is irrelevant to the doctrine of right because you have no right to call on the state to coerce me to tell you the truth, or to extract a remedy from me as a consequence of my lie. The world abounds with moral obligations that are legally unenforceable (eg duties of civility, magnanimity, collegiality, and so on). Kant's distinction between the doctrines of right and virtue suggests that a commitment to human dignity as a precept of legality does not entail subsuming all of morality into law.

Moreover, respect for human rights (especially civil and political rights) is consistent with a wide range of substantive economic and social policies, as well as a variety of means to implement them. A commitment to human rights does not in itself entail a commitment to social democratic rather than libertarian modes of government. Other arguments would have to be adduced using other principles, and these arguments would then have to address the likely effects of distinct economic policies. For example, the idea of equal dignity implicit in the rule of law does not entail a right to an equal distribution of resources. A more robust and substantive conception of equality (as well as its priority) would have to be defended against both the libertarian concern for individual property rights and the utilitarian imperative to maximize aggregate welfare.

In practice, scores of states have ratified numerous human rights conventions. Some are social democratic, while others are right-leaning democracies. In many, poverty is deeply entrenched. The widespread commitment to human rights, in states of distinct political stripe and socio-economic

[45] For discussion of the intimate relationship between authority and coercion in Kant, see Arthur Ripstein, 'Authority and Coercion' (2004) 32(1) Philosophy and Public Affairs 2.

development, speaks to the level of generality at which human rights principles operate. Indeed, a common complaint against human rights is that they are too general and universal in aspiration to be culturally relevant. These considerations all suggest that human rights principles leave ample scope for policy-making and locally appropriate good law.

Economic, social, and cultural human rights ('economic rights') may appear to complicate matters because respect for them may require wealth redistributions from the wealthy to the disadvantaged. Respect for civil and political rights, by contrast, requires wealth transfers for the sake of establishing public institutions for the benefit of all. To bring economic rights under the rule of law's aegis, much more would have to be said than I can say here.[46] If, however, economic rights really are human rights that reflect the demands of human dignity, then some commitment to them follows from a commitment to the rule of law.

A sceptic might object that although it may be possible to justify the rule of law on the basis of human agency and dignity, we can still distinguish a formal conception of the rule of law based exclusively on the internal morality from the more substantive conception defended above: the formal conception is justified on the grounds that its violation frustrates agency by subverting the legal subject's ability to be guided by law, whereas the substantive conception is not so justified because slaves, for example, retain sufficient agency to be guided by slave laws. The objection proceeds too quickly, however, because the claim I am advancing is not that agency alone, in the abstract, justifies a substantive conception of the rule of law. Agency participates in the justification of a substantive conception of the rule of law only once it is properly situated and accommodated within the state-subject fiduciary relationship. While slave laws can guide slaves, states that enforce slavery do so in violation of their overarching fiduciary obligation to treat every subject as an equal co-beneficiary of the rule of law. The obligation arises from the fiduciary principle's sensitivity to agency in contexts in which the agent is vulnerable to the fiduciary's exercise of irresistible discretionary power, such as the state's power to announce and enforce law. To conclude: a commitment to agency entails more than a commitment to possible exercises of agency; it also entails a commitment to treat the agent as a

46 A dignity-based argument for economic rights that does not reduce the rule of law to merely the rule of good law could proceed along the following lines: economic rights do not guarantee more than the minimal preconditions necessary for the reasonable enjoyment of civil and political rights under conditions of non-domination, ie conditions in which one is not at the mercy of another private party's charity. These considerations suggest that a principled commitment to economic rights may be thought to follow from a commitment to one of the moral underpinnings of the rule of law (non-domination), and that the real debate will focus on the difficult political questions concerning the best mix of public and private means to ensure respect for economic rights in the long run.

person in the context of legal relationships, including the state-subject fiduciary relationship.

To be sure, there is some overlap between liberal political morality and the agency-based conception of the rule of law: arbitrary violations of human rights offend both. Such an overlap is to be expected because both liberalism and the rule of law, on my construal, give pride of place to agency. This sharing of conceptual resources does not gut the rule of law of analytical clarity and purchase. Rather, it helps us see that the rule of law entails a commitment to human rights that politics requires a special justification to disturb.

Bibliography

Adams, GB (1926), *Council and Courts in Anglo-Norman England* (London and New Haven: Yale University Press)

Allan, Trevor (2003), *Constitutional Justice a Liberal Theory of the Rule of Law* (Oxford: Oxford University Press)

Anscombe, GEM, 'On the Source of the Authority of the State' in Joseph Raz (ed), *Authority* (New York: New York University Press, 1990), p 142

Arneson, RJ (1989) 'Liberal Egalitarianism and World Resource Distribution: Two Views' 23(3) *Journal of Value Inquiry* 171

Arthurs, Harry (1979), 'Rethinking Administrative Law: A Slightly Dicey Business' 17 Osgoode Hall LJ 1.

——(1983), 'Protection Against Judicial Review' 43 R du B 277

Avini, Avisheh (1996), 'The Origins of the Modern English Trust Revisited' 70 Tul L Rev 1139

Baier, Annette (1986), 'Trust and Antitrust' 96(2) *Ethics* 231

Bailey, Joanne (2002), 'Favoured or Oppressed? Married Women, Property and "Coverture" in England, 1600–1800' 17(3) *Continuity & Change* 351

Barnes, The Right Honourable Lord Woolf of (1994), 'Droit Public-English Style' PL 57

Behrendt, Larissa, 'Lacking Good Faith: Australia, Fiduciary Duties and the Lonely Place of Indigenous Rights' in Law Commission of Canada (ed), *In Whom We Trust: A Forum on Fiduciary Relationships* (Toronto: Irwin Law, 2002)

Bentham, Jeremy and Bowring, John (1843), *The Works of Jeremy Bentham* (Edinburgh: Tait)

Beran, Harry (1977), 'In Defense of the Consent Theory of Political Obligation and Authority' 87 *Ethics* 260

——(1987), *The Consent Theory of Political Obligation* (New York: Croom Helm)

Birks, Peter (ed) (1997,) *Privacy and Loyalty* (Oxford: Clarendon Press)

——(2000), 'The Content of the Fiduciary Obligation' 1 Isr LR 3

Bogert, George G and Bogert, George T (1973) *Law of Trusts*, 5th edn (St Paul, Minn: West Pub Co).

Borrows, John, 'Wampum at Niagara: The Royal Proclamation, Canadian Legal History and Self-Government' in Michael Asch (ed), *Aboriginal and Treaty Rights in Canada: Essays on Law, Equity, and Respect for Difference* (Vancouver: UBC Press, 1997)

——(2002), *Recovering Canada: The Resurgence of Indigenous Law* (Toronto: University of Toronto Press)

Bromwich, David (ed) (2000), *On Empire, Liberty, and Reform: Speeches and Letters* (New Haven: Yale University Press)

Brudner, Alan (1995), *The Unity of the Common Law* (Berkeley: University of California Press)

Brudney, Daniel (1993), 'Two Links of Law and Morality' 103 *Ethics* 280

Cartier, Geneviève (2003), 'Procedural Fairness in Legislative Functions: The End of Judicial Abstinence? 53(3) UTLJ 217

——'The *Baker* Effect: A New Interface Between the Canadian Charter of Rights and Freedoms and Administrative Law—The Case of Discretion' in David Dyzenhaus (ed), *The Unity of Public Law* (Oxford: Hart Publishing, 2004), p 61

Christie, G (2000), 'Justifying Principles of Treaty Interpretation' 26 Queen's LJ 143

Cicero, Marcus Tullius (1967), *On Moral Obligation: A New Translation of Cicero's De officiis*, trans by John Higginbotham (Berkeley: University of California Press)

Cohen, G, 'Self-Ownership, World-Ownership, and Equality' in Frank S Lucash and Judith N Shklar (eds), *Justice and Equality Here and Now* (Ithaca: Cornell University Press, 1986)

Conaglen, Matthew (2008), 'Public-Private Intersection: Comparing Fiduciary Conflict Doctrine and Bias' PL 58

Craig, Paul (1997), 'Formal and Substantive Conceptions of the Rule or Law' PL 467

——'Unreasonableness and Proportionality in UK Law' in Evelyn Ellis (ed), *The Principle of Proportionality in the Laws of Europe* (Oxford: Hart Publishing, 1999)

——(2003), *Administrative Law*, 5th edn (London: Sweet & Maxwell)

Criddle, Evan J (2006), 'Fiduciary Foundations of Administrative Law' 54 UCLA L Rev 117

——and Fox-Decent, Evan (2009), 'A Fiduciary Theory of Jus Cogens' 34 Yale J Int'l L 331–87

————(2009) 'Deriving Peremptory Norms from Sovereignty' 103 Am Soc'y Int'l L Proc 71–4

————(forthcoming, 2012) 'Human Rights, Emergencies and the Rule of Law' 34 Hum Rts Q.

Curley, Edwin (ed) (1994), *Leviathan with Selected Variants from the Latin Edition of 1668* (Indianapolis: Hackett Publishing)

Davern, Raymond, 'Impeaching the Exercise of Trustees' Distributive Discretions: "Wrong Grounds" and Procedural Unfairness' in D Hayton (ed), *Extending the Boundaries of Trusts and Similar Ring-Fenced Funds* (London: Kluwer, 2002)

Davies, P and Freedland, M (1983), *Kahn-Freund's Labour and the Law*, 3rd edn (London: Stevens & Sons)

De Mestral, Armand and Fox-Decent, Evan, 'Implementation and Reception: The Congeniality of Canada's Legal Order to International Law' in Oonagh E Fitzgerald and Elisabeth Eid (eds), *The Globalized Rule of Law: Relationships between International and Domestic Law* (Toronto: Irwin Law, 2006), p 31

de Smith, SA (1960), *The Lawyers and the Constitution* (London: G Bell and Sons Ltd)

Dicey, Albert Venn and Wade, ECS (1959), *Introduction to the Study of the Law of the Constitution*, 10th edn (London: Macmillan)

Dodderidge, Sir John, *The English Lawyer. Describing A Method for the Managing of the Lawes of this Land* (London: Printed by the Assignes of I More, 1631)

Dworkin, Ronald (1977), *Taking Rights Seriously* (Cambridge, MA: Harvard University Press)

——(1986), *Law's Empire* (Cambridge: Harvard University Press)

——(2000), *Sovereign Virtue: The Theory and Practice of Equality* (Cambridge: Harvard University Press)

Dyzenhaus, David (1993), 'Dicey's Shadow' 43 UTLJ 127

——'The Politics of Deference: Judicial Review and Democracy' in M Taggart (ed), *The Province of Administrative Law* (Oxford: Hart Publishing, 1997), p 279

——'Fuller's Novelty' in W Witteveen and W van der Burg (eds), *Rediscovering Fuller: Essays on Implicit Law and Institutional Design* (Amsterdam: Amsterdam University Press, 1999)

——(2001), 'Hobbes and the Legitimacy of Law' 20 Law & Phil 461

——and Fox-Decent, Evan (2001), 'Rethinking the Process/Substance Distinction: Baker v. Canada' 51 University of Toronto LJ 193

——D, Hunt, M, and Taggart, M (2001), 'The Principle of Legality in Administrative Law: Internationalisation as Constitutionalisation' 1(1) OUCLJ 5

——(2002), 'Constituting the Rule of Law: Fundamental Values in Administrative Law' 27 Queen's LJ 445

——(2004), 'The Deep Structure of Roncarelli v. Duplessis' 53 UNBLJ 111

——(2006), *The Constitution of Law: Legality in a Time of Emergency* (Cambridge: Cambridge University Press)

——'David Mullan's Theory of the Rule of (Common) Law' in G Huscroft and M Taggart (eds), *Inside and Outside Canadian Administrative Law: Essays in Honour of David Mullan* (Toronto: University of Toronto Press, 2006, p 448

Edmunson, William A (2004), 'State of the Art: The Duty to Obey the Law' 10 *Legal Theory* 215

Elliot, Steven (1999), 'Fiduciary Liability for Client Mortgage Fraud' 13 Trust Law Int'l 74

Epstein, RA (1990), 'No New Property' 56 Brook L Rev 747

Evans, Janisch, Mullan, and Risk (1989), *Administrative Law: Cases, Text, and Materials*, 3rd edn (Toronto: Emond Montgomery)

Evans, John M (1991), 'The Principles of Fundamental Justice: The Constitution and the Common Law' 29 Osgoode Hall LJ 51

Finn, PD (1977), *Fiduciary Obligations* (Sydney: Law Book Co)

——(1994), 'Public Trust and Public Accountability' 3 Griffith LR 224

——'The Forgotten "Trust": The People and the State' in Malcom Cope (ed), *Equity: Issues and Trends* (Sydney: Federation Press, 1995), p 131

——'A Sovereign People, a Public Trust' in PD Finn (ed), *Essays on Law and Government, Vol 1: Principles and Values* (Sydney: Law Book Co, 1995)

Finnis, John (1980), *Natural Law and Natural Rights* (Oxford: Oxford University Press)

Flood, Colleen and Sossin, Lorne (2007), 'The Contextual Turn: Iacobucci's Legacy and the Standard of Review in Administrative Law' 57 UTLJ 581

Fox-Decent, Evan, 'The Charter and Administrative Law: Cross-Fertilization in Public Law' in C Flood and L Sossin (eds), *Administrative Law in Context* (Toronto: Emond Montgomery, 2008)

——and Criddle, Evan J (2009), 'The Fiduciary Constitution of Human Rights' 15(4) Legal Theory 301–66

————(forthcoming) 'Interest Balancing v Fiduciary Duty: Two Models for National Security Law' 12 *German Law Journal*

Frankel, Tamara, 'Fiduciary Law: The Judicial Process and the Duty of Care', *The 1993 Isaac Pitblado Lectures: Fiduciary Duties/Conflicts of Interest* (Winnipeg: Law Society of Manitoba, 1993), pp 143–62

——(2008), *Fiduciary Law: Analysis, Definitions, Relationships, Duties, Remedies over History and Cultures* (Anchorage, AK: Fathom Pub Co).

Fridman, GHL (1996), *The Law of Agency*, 7th edn (Toronto: Butterworths)

Fudge, Judy and Tucker, Eric (2001), *Labour before the Law: The Regulation of Workers' Collective Action in Canada, 1900–1948* (Don Mills: Oxford University Press)

Fuller, Lon L (1955), 'Freedom—A Suggested Analysis' 68 Harv L Rev 1305

——(1968), 'Freedom as a Problem of Allocating Choice' 112 *Proceedings of the American Philosophical Society* 101.

——(1969), *The Morality of Law*, revised edn (New Haven: Yale University Press)

Gaskin, JCA (ed) (1994), *Human Nature and De Corpore Politico* (Oxford: Oxford University Press)

Glenn, Garrard and Redden, Kenneth (1945), 'Equity: A Visit to the Founding Fathers' 31(4) Va L Rev 753

Golding, W (1962), *Lord of the Flies* (New York: Penguin Putnam Inc)

Green, Leslie (1988), *The Authority of the State* (Oxford: Oxford University Press)

——'Who believes in Political Obligation?' in John T Sanders and Jan Narveson (eds), *For and Against the State* (Lanham, MD: Rowman and Littlefield, 1996)

Greenawalt, Kent (1989), *Conflicts of Law and Morality* (New York: Oxford University Press)

Griffith, JAG (1955), 'Administrative Discretion and the Courts: The Better Part of Valour?' 18(2) Mod L Rev 159

Halliday, Simon (2000), 'The Influence of Judicial Review on Bureaucratic Decision-Making' PL 110

Hampton, Jean (1988), *Hobbes and the Social Contract Tradition* (Cambridge: Cambridge University Press)

Hardin, Russell (1993), 'The Street-Level Epistemology of Trust' 21 *Politics and Society* 505

Harsanyi, John (1953), 'Cardinal Utility in Welfare Economics and in the Theory of Risk-taking' 61(5) *Journal of Political Economy* 434

Hart, HLA (1958), 'Positivism and the Separation of Law and Morals' 71 Harv L Rev 593

——(1965), 'Review of The Morality of Law' 78 Harv L Rev 1281

——(1983), *Essays in Jurisprudence and Philosophy* (Oxford: Oxford University Press)

Haskett, Timothy S (1996), 'The Medieval English Court of Chancery' 14(2) LHR 245

Hayek, Friedrich A von (1962), *The Road to Serfdom* (Chicago: University of Chicago Press)

Henderson, James Youngblood (1994), 'Empowering Treaty Federalism' 58 Sask L Rev 241

Hickman, Tom (2010), *Public Law after the UK Human Rights Act* (Oxford: Hart Publishing)

Higginbotham, John (trans), Cicero, *On Moral Obligation* (Berkeley: University of California Press, 1967) (first published in 44 BC)

Hobbes, Thomas, *Leviathan with Selected Variants from the Latin Edition of 1668*, ed Edwin Curley (Indianapolis: Hackett Publishing, 1994)

——*On the Citizen*, trans Richard Tuck and Michael Silverthorne (Cambridge; New York: Cambridge University Press, 1998) (first published in 1641)

——(1969), *The Elements of Law, Natural and Politic*, 2d edn, Ferdinand Tönnies (ed) (London: F Cass)

Hogg, PW and Monahan, PJ (2000), *Liability of the Crown*, 3rd edn (Toronto: Carswell)

Holton, Richard (1994), 'Deciding to Trust, Coming to Believe' 72(1) *Australasian Journal of Philosophy* 63

Hume, David, 'Of the Original Contract', *Social Contract* (London: Oxford University Press, 1987)

Kant, Immanuel (1991), *The Metaphysics of Morals*, trans Mary Gregor (New York: Cambridge University Press)

Klausner, Michael (1995), 'Corporations, Corporate Law, and Networks of Contracts' 81(3) Va L Rev 757

Klimchuk, Dennis (2012), 'Hobbes on Equity' in D Dyzenhaus and T Poole (eds), *Hobbes and the Law* (Cambridge: Cambridge University Press, forthcoming)

Klinck, DR (2006), 'Doing "Complete Justice": Equity in the Ontario Court of Chancery' 32 Queen's LJ 45

Klosko, George (1992), *The Principle of Fairness and Political Obligations* (Lanham, Maryland: Rowman & Littlefield)

Kramer, Matthew, 'Moral and Legal Obligation' in William A Edmundson and Martin P Goldberg (eds), *Blackwell Guide to the Philosophy of Law and Legal Theory* (Malden, USA: Blackwell Publishing, 2004)

Kymlicka, Will (1989), *Liberalism, Community, and Culture* (Oxford: Clarendon Press)

Ladenson, R, 'In Defense of a Hobbesian Conception of Law' in Joseph Raz (ed), *Authority* (New York: New York University Press, 1990)

Leckey, Robert (2008), *Contextual Subjects: Family, State and Relational Theory* (Toronto: University of Toronto Press)

Liston, Mary, 'Governments in Miniature: The Rule of Law in the Administrative State' in Lorne Mitchell Sossin and Colleen M Flood (eds), *Administrative Law in Context* (Toronto: Emond Montgomery Publications, 2008)

Locke, John, 'Second Treatise on Civil Government' in Ernest Barker and Gerard Hopkins (eds), *Social Contract; Essays by Locke, Hume and Rousseau* (London: Oxford University Press, 1948) (first published in 1690)

Loughlin, Martin (1996), *Legality and Locality: The Role of Law in Central-Local Government* (Oxford: Clarendon Press)

Macdonald, Roderick (1983), 'Absence of Jurisdiction: A Perspective' 43(2) R du B 307

——(1987), 'On the Administration of Statutes' 12 Queen's LJ 488

——'Legislation and Governance' in W Witteveen and W van der Burg (eds), *Rediscovering Fuller: Essays on Implicit Law and Institutional Design* (Amsterdam: Amsterdam University Press, 1999), p 278

——(2002), *Lessons of Everyday Law* (Montreal: published for the Law Commission of Canada and the School of Policy Studies, Queen's University by McGill-Queen's University Press)

——'The Acoustics of Accountability—Toward Well-Tempered Tribunals' in András, Sajó (ed), *Judicial Integrity* (Netherlands: Koninklijke Brill, 2004), p 141

——'Here, There and Everywhere . . . Theorizing Legal Pluralism; Theorizing Jacques Vanderlinden' in N Kasirer (ed), *Mélanges Jacques Vanderlinden* (Montreal: Yvon Blais, 2006)

Macklem, Patrick (2001), *Indigenous Difference and the Constitution of Canada* (Toronto: University of Toronto Press)

——(2007), 'What is International Human Rights Law? Three Applications of a Distributive Account' 52 McGill LJ 575

Main, Thomas O and Haskett, Timothy (2003), 'Traditional Equity and Contemporary Procedure' 78 Wash L Rev 429

Maitland, FW (1911), *Collected Papers*, vol 3 (Cambridge: Cambridge University Press)

Markesinis, BS and Munday, RJC (1986), *An Outline of the Law of Agency*, 2nd edn (London: Butterworths)

Markham, Jerry W (1992), 'Fiduciary Duties Under the Commodity Exchange Act' 68 Notre Dame L Rev 199

Marmor, Andrei (2004), 'The Rule of Law and its Limits' 24 Law & Phil 1

Mason, A (1994), 'The Place of Equity and Equitable Remedies in the Contemporary Common Law World' 110 LQR 238

McGhee, John and Snell, Edmund Henry Turner (2000), *Snell's Equity*, 30th edn (London: Sweet & Maxwell)

McLean, Janet (2004), 'The Crown in Contract and Administrative Law' 1 Oxford J Legal Stud 129

Mullan, David (1975), 'Fairness: The New Natural Justice' 25 UTLJ 281

——'Recent Developments in Standard of Review', *Taking the Bar to Court: A Practical Guide for Administrative Law Practitioners* (Canadian Bar Association, 2000)

——(2001), *Administrative Law* (Toronto: Irwin Law)

——(2003), 'Judging the Judgment of Judges: *CUPE v Ontario (Minister of Labour)*' 10 Canadian Labour and Employment LJ 431

——(2008), '*Dunsmuir v New Brunswick*, Standards of Review and Procedural Fairness for Public Servants: Let's Try Again!' 21 Can J Admin L & Prac 117

——*et al* (2003), *Administrative Law: Cases, Texts and Materials*, 5th edn (Toronto: Emond Montgomery)

Murphy, Mark (1995), 'Was Hobbes a Legal Positivist?' 105 *Ethics* 846

Murphy, Colleen (2005), 'Lon Fuller and the Moral Value of the Rule of Law' 24 Law & Phil 239

Nadler, Jennifer (2007), 'Hart, Fuller and the Connection between Law and Justice' 27 Law & Phil 1

Nozick, Robert (1974), *Anarchy, State, and Utopia* (New York: Basic Books)

Oakeshott, Michael (1991), *Rationalism in Politics and Other Essays*, new and expanded edn (Indianapolis: Liberty Press)

——(1991), *Rationalism in Politics and Other Essays*, new and expanded edn (Indianapolis: LibertyPress)

Oliver, Dawn, 'Review of (Non-Statutory) Discretions' in CF Forsyth (ed), *Judicial Review and the Constitution* (Oxford: Hart Publishing, 2000), p 307

Parfit, Derek (1984), *Reasons and Persons* (Oxford: Oxford University Press)

Pettit, Philip (1997), *Republicanism: A Theory of Freedom and Government* (Oxford: Clarendon Press)

Plucknett, TFT and Barton, JL (eds) (1974), *St. German's Doctor and Student*, vol 91 (London: Selden Society)

Pollock, Frederick and William Maitland, Frederic (1968), *The History of English Law Before the Time of Edward I*, 2nd edn (London: Cambridge University Press).

Postema, Gerald, 'Implicit Law' in W Witteveen and W van der Burg (eds), *Rediscovering Fuller: Essays on Implicit Law and Institutional Design* (Amsterdam: Amsterdam University Press, 1999), p 361

Purdy, Jedediah and Fielding, Kimberly (2007), 'Sovereigns, Trustees, Guardians: Private-Law Concepts and the Limits of Legitimate State Power' 70 Law & Contemp Probs 165

Purich, Donald J (1986), *Our Land: Native Rights in Canada* (Toronto: J Lorimer)

Radin, Margaret Jane (1989), 'Reconsidering the Rule of Law' 69 BUL Rev 781

Rawls, John (1971), *A Theory of Justice* (Cambridge, Mass: Belknap Press of Harvard University Press)

Raz, Joseph (1979), *The Authority of Law: Essays on Law and Morality* (Oxford: Clarendon Press)

——(1979), *The Authority of Law* (Oxford: Oxford University Press)

——'The Rule of Law and Its Virtue', *The Authority of Law: Essays on Law and Morality* (Oxford: Clarendon Press, 1979)

——(1986), *The Morality of Freedom* (Oxford: Oxford University Press)

——(1994), *Ethics in the Public Domain* (Oxford: Clarendon Press)

Reynolds, James I (2005), *A Breach of Duty: Fiduciary Obligations and Aboriginal Peoples* (Saskatoon: Purich Publishing)

Reynolds, FMB (2006), *Bowstead and Reynolds on Agency*, 18th edn (London: Sweet & Maxwell)

Ripstein, Arthur (2000), 'Three Duties to Rescue: Moral, Civil, and Criminal' 19(6) Law & Phil 751

——(2002), 'Three Duties to Rescue' 19 Law & Phil 751

——(2004), 'Authority and Coercion' 32(1) Philosophy and Public Affairs 2

——(2009), *Force and Freedom: Kant's Legal and Political Philosophy* (Cambridge, MA: Harvard University Press)

Rotman, Leonard Ian (1996), *Parallel Paths: Fiduciary Doctrine and the Crown-Native Relationship in Canada* (Toronto: University of Toronto Press)

——(1997), 'Taking Aim at the Canons of Treaty Interpretation in Canadian Aboriginal Rights Jurisprudence' 46 UNBLJ 11

Rundle, Kristen (2009), 'The Impossibility of an Exterminatory Legality: Law and the Holocaust' 59 UTLJ 65

Scott, Austin W (1949), 'The Fiduciary Principle' 37(4) Cal L Rev 539

Scott, Elizabeth S and Scott, Robert E (1995), 'Parents as Fiduciaries' 81 Va L Rev 2401

Sealy, LS (1962), 'Fiduciary Relationships' 20(1) Cambridge LJ 69

Seavey, WA (1920), 'The Rationale of Agency' 29 Yale LJ 859

Shaver, Robert (1999), *Rational Egoism: A Selective and Critical History* (Cambridge; New York: Cambridge University Press)

Simmonds, Nigel E (2007), *Law as a Moral Idea* (Oxford: Oxford University Press)

Simmons, A John (1979), *Moral Principles and Political Obligations* (Princeton, NJ: Princeton University Press)

——(2001), *Justification and Legitimacy* (New York: Cambridge University Press)

——'The Duty to Obey and Our Natural Moral Duties' in A John Simmons and Christopher Wellman (eds), *Is There a Duty to Obey the Law?* (New York: Cambridge University Press, 2005)

Skinner, Quentin (2002), *Visions of Politics* (New York: Cambridge University Press)

——(2002), 'The Proper Signification of Liberty', *Visions of Politics: Hobbes and Civil Science* (Cambridge: Cambridge University Press), p 209

Slattery, Brian (1987), 'Understanding Aboriginal Rights' 66 Can Bar Rev 727

Smith, Lionel, 'Constructive Fiduciaries?' in Peter Birks (ed), *Privacy and Loyalty* (Oxford: Clarendon Press, 1997)

——'The Motive, Not the Deed' in Joshua Getzler and Edward Hector Burn (eds), *Rationalizing Property, Equity, and Trusts: Essays in Honour of Edward Burn* (London: LexisNexis UK, 2003), p 53

Soper, Philip (1984), *A Theory of Law* (Cambridge: Harvard University Press)

——(1989), 'Legal Theory and the Claims of Authority' 18 *Philosophy and Public Affairs* 209

——(2002), *The Ethics of Deference: Learning from Law's Morals* (Cambridge: Cambridge University Press)

Sossin, L (2003), 'Public Fiduciary Obligations, Political Trusts and the Evolving Duty of Reasonableness in Administrative Law' 66 Sask L Rev 129

Spigelman, JJ (1999), 'Foundations of Administrative Law: Toward General Principles of Institutional Law' 58(1) *Australian Journal of Public Administration* 3

Stark, Cynthia (2000), 'Hypothetical Consent and Justification' 97(6) *Journal of Philosophy* 313

Stone, Richard (1996), *Law of Agency* (London: Cavendish Publishing)

Sullivan, Ruth and Driedger, EA (2002), *Sullivan and Driedger on the Construction of Statutes*, 4th edn (Markham, Ont: Butterworths)

Szto, M (2004), 'Limited Liability Company Morality: Fiduciary Duties in Historical Context' 23 Quinnipiac L Rev 61

Taggart, Michael, 'The Province of Administrative Law Determined?' in M Taggart (ed), *The Province of Administrative Law* (Oxford: Hart Publishing, 1997)

——'The Tub of Public Law' in David Dyzenhaus (ed), *The Unity of Public Law* (Oxford: Hart Publishing, 2004)

Thorburn, Malcom (2008), 'Justifications, Powers and Authority' 117 Yale LJ 1080

Tully, James, 'A Just Relationship between Aboriginal Peoples and Canadians' in Curtis Cook and Juan David Lindau (eds), *Aboriginal Rights and Self-government: The Canadian and Mexican Experience in North American Perspective* (Montreal: McGill-Queen's University Press, 2000), p 39

Vinter, Ernest (1955), *A Treatise on the History and Law of Fiduciary Relationship and Resulting Trusts, Together with a Selection of Selected Cases*, 3d edn (Cambridge: Heffer)

Wade, Sir William and Forsyth, Christopher (eds) (2000), *Administrative Law*, 8th edn (New York: Oxford University Press)

————(2004), *Administrative Law*, 9th edn (Oxford: Oxford University Press)

Waldron, Jeremy (1993), 'Special Ties and Natural Duties' 22 *Philosophy and Public Affairs* 3

——(1994), 'Why Law—Efficacy, Freedom, or Fidelity?' 13 Law & Phil 259

Walters, Mark (2001), 'The Common Law Constitution in Canada: Return of Lex Non Scripta as Fundamental Law' 51 UTLJ 91

——'"Common Public Law in the Age of Legislation": David Mullan and the Unwritten Constitution' in G Huscroft, and M Taggart (eds), *Inside and Outside Canadian Administrative Law: Essays in Honour of David Mullan* (Toronto: University of Toronto Press, 2006)

——(2006), 'The Morality of Aboriginal Law' 31 Queen's LJ 470

Weiler, P (1980), *Reconcilable Differences* (Toronto: Carswell)

Weinrib, Ernest Joseph (1995), *The Idea of Private Law* (Cambridge: Harvard University Press)

——'The Juridical Classification of Obligations' in Peter Birks (ed), *The Classification of Obligations* (Oxford: Clarendon Press, 1997)

Wellman, Christopher (2001), 'Toward a Liberal Theory of Political Obligation' 111 *Ethics* 735

——'Samaritanism and the Duty to Obey the Law' in Christopher Wellman and A John Simmons (eds), *Is There a Duty to Obey the Law?* (New York: Cambridge University Press, 2005)

Wildeman, Sheila, 'A Fine Romance? The Modern Standards of Review in Theory and Practice' in C Flood and L Sossin (eds), *Administrative Law in Context* (Toronto: Emond Montgomery, 2008), p 239

Williams, Cynthia A and Conley, John M (2005), 'Is there an Emerging Fiduciary Duty to Consider Human Rights?' 74(1) U Cin L Rev 75

Winston, Kenneth I (1981), *The Principles of Social Order: Selected Essays of Lon L. Fuller* (Durham, NC: Duke University Press)

——(1994), 'Legislators and Liberty' 13 Law & Phil 389

Index

References are to page numbers and footnotes indicated by 'n' eg 106n

The manufacturer's authorised representative in the EU for product safety is Oxford University Press España S.A. of El Parque Empresarial San Fernando de Henares, Avenida de Castilla, 2 - 28830 Madrid (www.oup.es/en or product.safety@oup.com). OUP España S.A. also acts as importer into Spain of products made by the manufacturer.
Printed and bound by CPI Group (UK) Ltd, Croydon, CR0 4YY
14/09/2026
02216308-0011